Praise for *Global Innovation Management*:

'A must-read for all who want a clear and authoritative guide to the challenges of managing innovation. Westland has produced one of those rare books that crosses a wide array of fields, from general management to marketing, strategy, operations research, information systems, and engineering. An original and compelling contribution.' – **John Leslie King**, *Professor and Vice Provost, University of Michigan*

'This book comprehensively describes the end-to-end process of innovation, from coming up with an initial idea, to managing activities within the firm, to understanding consumer and financial markets, to the societal factors of innovation. The book is a useful text for undergraduate and postgraduate students of innovation and is well supported by case studies, with discussion questions, sourced from companies based around the globe. I particularly liked the series of practical Innovation Workouts to help the reader to understand and build a toolkit of methods and techniques which can be used to assess the potential of an innovation at various stages across the product and service development process.' – **Dr Fiona Lettice**, *Senior Lecturer, Norwich Business School, University of East Anglia*

'Christopher Westland has produced a detailed and practical examination of the complex subject of managing innovation in a global context. Through the use of detailed, multi-national case studies and examples and well-structured explanatory text, the author examines all the critical aspects of innovation: from design and branding through the financial aspects of innovation to managing risk and IP issues in collaborative innovation activities. This book will be a valuable resource for both practitioners and researchers looking to better understand the complexities of strategic innovation management in our increasingly global business contexts.' – **Ross Chapman**, *Professor of Business Systems and Director of the Centre for Industry and Innovation Studies, College of Business, University of Western Sydney, Australia*

GLOBAL INNOVATION MANAGEMENT

Also by J. Christopher Westland

Global Electronic Commerce

Valuing Technology

Financial Dynamics

GLOBAL INNOVATION MANAGEMENT

A STRATEGIC APPROACH

J. Christopher Westland

University of Illinois at Chicago

First published 2008 by
PALGRAVE MACMILLAN
Houndmills, Basingstoke, Hampshire RG21 6XS and
175 Fifth Avenue, New York, N.Y. 10010
Companies and representatives throughout the world

PALGRAVE MACMILLAN is the global academic imprint of the Palgrave
Macmillan division of St. Martin's Press, LLC and of Palgrave Macmillan Ltd.
Macmillan® is a registered trademark in the United States, United Kingdom
and other countries. Palgrave is a registered trademark in the European
Union and other countries.

ISBN-13: 978- 0-230-52491-0
ISBN-10: 0-230-52491-5

This book is printed on paper suitable for recycling and made from fully
managed and sustained forest sources. Logging, pulping and manufacturing
processes are expected to conform to the environmental regulations of the
country of origin.

A catalogue record for this book is available from the British Library.

A catalog record for this book is available from the Library of Congress.

10   9   8   7   6   5   4   3   2   1
17   16   15   14   13   12   11   10   09   08

Printed and bound in China

To Randa, Sumar, Dina and Brendon

BRIEF CONTENTS

CONTENTS

FIGURES

TABLES

BOXES

PREFACE

TO THE STUDENT

Innovation pays. In a world increasingly ruled by the twin dictates of globalization and commoditization, innovation is one of the few ways in which a modern business can differentiate itself in the market. By one measure[1] innovators realized a median profit margin growth of 3.4 per cent a year between 1995 and 2007, compared with 0.4 per cent for the median Standard & Poor's Global 1200 company. That's a huge achievement, thanks in large part to innovation. And the group's median annual stock return of 14.3 per cent was a full three points better than the S&P 1200 median over the decade.

To realize the payoff, though, aspiring innovators must prepare to compete not just in one market, but in many. There is competition for ideas, for financing, for retailing of products and delivery of service (the two are increasingly hard to distinguish), and access to communities and networks.

Too often, inventors trust that if you build it, consumers will come, and someone else will do the legwork. Marketing will emphasize the importance of positioning, advertising and proper channels, and let the engineers sweat over the details; lawyers will worry about who owns the parts of an innovation; technologists stress good engineering inside; designers may not care what is inside a product, but want it to look and feel good; customers may not care about either, and instead may want the status, community access, or complementary products that come with it (consider: do you buy an iPod for the electronics or for the music?). Then there are whole new worlds involving innovations in services (tax preparation, customer relationship management and so forth) and for access to communities (social networks like Craigslist, or virtual worlds like Second Life and World of Warcraft) which don't fit within any traditional notion of 'product innovation'. Like the three blind men and the elephant (one who feels the trunk, one the tail, and one a foot), each of the specialist groups in a firm – marketing, accounting, R&D, production – will perceive innovation from a perspective that is constrained by their own limited experience. And for this reason alone, each will get it wrong.

It is my objective in this book to provide the student with a critical overview of all of the major disciplines that need to be addressed in the pursuit of profitable innovation. This book will not make you a master of any one of these referents; rather, I hope you will become a quick(er) study when the time comes to commercialize your own ideas, to size up the competition, to understand the technology and its complements, and to take on the many other tasks required for a holistic understanding of innovation in the contemporary world.

The process of innovation must, by definition, challenge convention. Illustrator Robert Fawcett observed that 'good taste is often the enemy of creativity' – the process of innovation is best when approached in a manner that is edgy, irreverent and most of all fun. Without these, we seldom have the energy or the stubbornness to challenge the status quo, and to endure the trials of delivering an entirely new idea to customers. If I can convey these values through topics and case studies that step outside the somewhat stodgy tradition of business texts, I will feel gratified. And if I can keep your interest as a student of innovation – a topic that is arguably the most complex and comprehensive topic now taught in business schools, but also the most exciting – I will be personally satisfied with my efforts in developing this text.

Objective of this book

This text presents the tools and methods for successful innovation, starting with the problems faced by anyone who thinks they might have a better idea for a service, product or community, and who wants to transform that idea into a profitable business. Successful innovators eschew the artificial borders of traditional corporate stovepipes – such as strategy, marketing, R&D, finance, operations. Instead they draw opportunistically from whichever discipline is needed to solve a particular problem facing the innovator at a specific point in the development lifecycle. This text follows the precedents set by successful innovators. Innovation is seen not just in terms of ongoing management processes. Superior innovators will devise holistic organizational philosophies that result in fundamentally different ways to structure their businesses. Innovators develop different lines of communication with their customers, vendors and employees; they have different ways of seeing a market, and even business in general. The task of this text is to detail how the fundamental shifts in business demanded by innovation can be managed successfully.

Just as importantly, I spend time answering the question, 'Why bother?' It is not uncommon to encounter objections to the myriad difficulties entailed in high-tech and high-innovation businesses with suggestions that the firm would be better served by 'sticking to its knitting' so to speak, and only engaging in traditional, well-understood businesses. Unfortunately, globalization and the rise of internet business have moved many such 'traditional' industries to places where labour costs are low, environmental standards lax, and factory scales are huge. It has commoditized them, making it difficult for new entrants or small operations to compete even if they wanted to. The greatest profits today are to be made in areas with high technological and business risk. The gains from innovation are substantially higher than for traditional commoditized businesses, but so are the risks of failure. Active and intelligent management of innovation is no longer an option – it has become an imperative of successful business!

Content and pedagogy

This book is a product of two classes that I have taught at several universities over the past five years. It addresses a question that I have encountered for at least a decade now – 'If you think you have invented a winning invention, how can you bring your invention out of the laboratory and turn it into a commercially successful product?'

Innovation is a combination of invention and commercialization. There are many books on the market that address innovation, the largest number being devoted to the first half of this combination – how to be inventive. Topics include systems for helping people to be more creative, or better manage laboratories or idea generation. Clearly these activities must predicate any commercial successes in the market. They are necessary but not sufficient. The second half of the combination has received less attention, though there are several good books on commercialization of innovations; but the study it has received has been incomplete.

Existing books in the market that address innovation tend to fall into three categories:

▶ behavioural texts on how to be more creative
▶ management books that focus on industrial design and R&D
▶ industrial organization books that study the sources and influence of innovation.

This book is intended to fill a slightly different niche – at once pragmatic, yet supported by field research and theory. It concerns the process of being a successful innovator. It is part history, part theory, and part practical guide to the myriad tasks involved in innovating for a living. I hope it will find an audience with inventors, not just in labs but in market channels and in service industries, who want to turn their ideas into profitable and sustainable businesses.

Many of the tasks in innovation parallel the concerns of entrepreneurs, but with substantially less historical information about how to structure business models, and substantially more uncertainty about products and customers. The main body of this text is concerned with the variations from traditional management that are required to manage innovations successfully.

I have avoided the overuse of the term 'technology' throughout this book. Many of the most significant innovations – automobiles, televisions, music players, airplanes, refrigerators and so forth – found commercial success only long after all of the detailed technological components were well understood and developed. The technology is often out there in the lab, waiting for the right 'formula' to make it attractive to a wider consumer base. This book assumes that the raw technological components are already with us, just waiting to be plucked from the laboratory, or to be searched on Google Patent Search, or called up over lunch with the engineering staff. Alternatively perhaps you have already identified your patent technology (maybe you have been hovering over it in your lab for the past two years) and you now want to figure out what to do next. Or you might be a salesperson, or product designer, or doing any one of a number of other jobs in a firm that require you to help seek out the next big thing. At this stage, the question that arises is how to manage all of the parts of the successful – with the emphasis on successful – design, development, introduction, sale and promotion of an innovation. In my system, technology is just one of the many components that have to be grafted into the overall innovation in order to achieve success.

This book is designed to be used as a textbook in a one or two-semester class on innovation, within a course on engineering, business or another science. There are 13 chapters, which fit with a 14-week semester. I teach my own courses in two seven-week sessions. The second semester tends to focus overwhelmingly on financial analysis, as both investment bankers and corporate management are quite interested in this aspect of innovation.

The text is divided into four sections of three chapters each:

▶ **Opportunities:** Chapters 1, 2 and 3 are concerned with identifying potential innovations. To come up with good innovations, firms need a lot of innovations. The approach is Darwinian – as many variations on ideas as possible should be generated in order to have a few that can pass production and market tests to become successful.

▶ **Operations:** Chapters 4, 5, 6 and 7 are concerned with the activities inside the firm that support innovation.

▶ **Markets:** Chapters 8, 9, 10 and 11 are concerned with external markets, and the sort of activities a firm must engage in to successfully adapt their strategy to the markets in which they compete.

▶ **Society:** Chapters 12 and 13 address social factors in innovation, where the final chapter surveys the evidence for continual innovation being essential to successful business.

Because of the breadth of topics covered in this text, each chapter is intended to present the main ideas, components, and their use and relevance to the innovation process. At the end of each chapter, I provide references for further reading that fills in the details that are needed for a practical implementation. You need to get the 'big picture' first, then go back and start filling in details. This is especially true since the details are likely to be different for every invention, every market and every project.

FOR INSTRUCTORS

I have used this material now for several different undergraduate and postgraduate classes, and have helped some of my colleagues in presenting the material as well. This has given me insight into the topics that are likely to be of greatest interest to students. Fundamental questions that should motivate a successful class are:

▶ How best can firms transform their R&D into successful new services, products and communities?

▶ How can firms institutionalize knowledge and creativity to invigorate their services, product lines and customer relationships?

▶ What do successful innovators look like?

▶ How can established firms overcome organizational inefficiencies brought on by rigid departmental structure, 'not invented here' wastage, and unprofitable research?

To answer these questions, the text provides numerous short case studies, and one comprehensive case study at the end of each chapter. The text webpages provide links to these companies, and to other sites that expand on the perspectives and methods presented in the text.

The following ancillaries are available to the instructor:

▶ an Instructor's Manual providing the answers to all end-of-chapter and chapter case study questions

- the Test Bank
- PowerPoint® presentations
- instructor resources on the website
- innovation business calculator (IBC) based on the framework presented in Chapter 11.

Web products
Log on to http://www.palgrave.com/business/westland to access learning resources. These include:

For students:
- study materials designed to help you improve your results
- self-test multiple choice questions, organized by chapter
- hotlinks to internet sites to further your understanding of the material.

For instructors:
- lecture notes and PowerPoint slides
- all figures and tables from the book in PowerPoint slides
- teaching case studies
- answers to chapter questions
- answers to the questions on the chapter case study
- multiple choice and short answer questions, organized by chapter for use in assessments.

The website allows me to continually update material, as well as provide supplemental presentation slides and exercises for in-class use. It also provides a server platform for software programs which support the text. Server-based software provides greater latitude than would a CD of software for three reasons. First, it is much easier to program a user interface as a web page than as a standalone shell (and there is also the opportunity to quickly correct the interface in the case of programming errors). Second, I can compute user input with powerful software on the server (such as MatLab), something that it would be infeasible and expensive to implement in standalone support programs. Finally, there are fewer copyright problems in placing material on a web page because sources can be linked to a broad range of sources that can be tapped to help solve a problem, complete a plan or update your current knowledge. Where intellectual property issues do crop up, they can be resolved quickly. I believe the combination of a printed textbook – which is portable, easy to read, annotatable and easy to search – in combination with a supplementary web page – which can include updates, classroom materials and software – offers the best of both worlds.

ACKNOWLEDGEMENTS

This project has evolved over several years, with the help and encouragement of many of my colleagues around the world. I am especially indebted to the many practitioners and academics who have advanced our knowledge of the business of innovation, both in their personal example, and in laying out theory and analyzing trends and practice.

It has been my pleasure to work with my editor Martin Drewe, who provided me with many new insights and valuable suggestions while seeing this text to its completion. The task of writing has been eased by the support and discourse from many people who either directly or inadvertently took part in my project: my family, my students, my colleagues and the reviewers employed by Palgrave Macmillan. And lastly, thanks to the team at Palgrave Macmillan for their continued support and tireless work in the realization of this text.

Permission from the authors and/or publishers to reproduce the following material is gratefully acknowledged:

On pp. 4, 12 and 17: material on Greer & Associates from Thomas L. Friedman, *The World Is Flat: A brief history of the twenty-first century*, published by Picador, 2007.

On pp. 68–9: material on Viagra from pp. 95–6 of Greg Critzer, *Generation Rx: How prescription drugs are altering American lives, minds, and bodies*, published by Houghton Mifflin, 2005.

On pp. 116-18: material on Paxil from pp. 62–7 of Greg Critzer, *Generation Rx: How prescription drugs are altering American lives, minds, and bodies*, published by Houghton Mifflin, 2005.

On p. 173, material on 'the father of Sudoku' from David McNeill, 'Numbers man', *South China Morning Post*, Saturday 12 May 2007, p.C1.

On pp. 239 and 240, material on Asia's diploma mills from Laurence Brahm, 'Cheating, Chinese style', *South China Morning Post*, 21 February 2006, p. A14

On pp. 310-12, interview with Gary Burton from M. Schrage, 'The Gary Burton Trio: lessons on business from a jazz legend', published in *Fast Company*, issue 6, page 110, December 1996.

NOTE

1   'Creativity pays', *Business Week*, 24 April 2006, reporting a study done for *Business Week* by the Boston Consulting Group using data from Standard & Poor's Compustat® database.

GUIDED TOUR

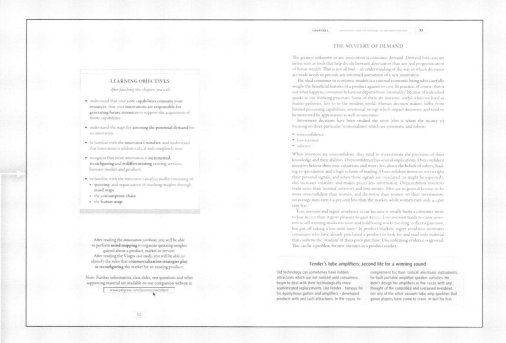

Learning objectives identify the key concepts covered in the chapter, and the key knowledge and skills that students will obtain by reading it. Separate objectives are provided for the innovation workout and case study in the chapter.

You can find further information, PowerPoint slides, revision questions and other support material on the **companion website**: www.palgrave.com/business/westland

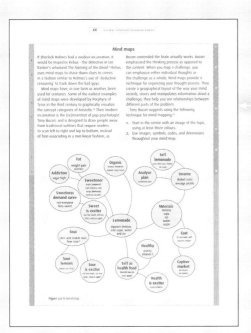

Innovation workouts in each chapter introduce techniques that can be used to hone your innovation skills, and give examples on how to use them.

Each chapter includes a full **case study**, drawing on a real-life business example to show how the material in the chapter is applied in the real world.

Case study questions for review are provided at the end of each case study, to encourage students to explore the issues raised and link the theory to the real-world examples.

Chapter questions for review are more general than the case-study questions. They are designed to develop students' knowledge and skills, and develop a wider sense of how innovation techniques can be used in a variety of contexts.

Key points are summarized at the end of each chapter, to aid with revision and review of the material.

Notes at the end of each chapter provide full reference information. (This is also provided in the bibliography at the end of the book.)

Recommended **further reading** on the issues covered is provided in a separate section starting on page 341.

As well as full and brief contents lists, you can locate subjects covered in the **index**.

INNOVATION, GLOBALIZATION AND COMMODITIZATION

LEARNING OBJECTIVES

After finishing this chapter, you will

- ▸ understand why **innovation is no longer optional**, but a necessary activity in every competitive business

- ▸ understand the difference between **innovation**, **invention**, **creativity** and **commercialization**

- ▸ understand the forces of **globalization** and **commoditization**, and identify their causes

- ▸ be able to identify **opportunities for innovation** in industries undergoing consolidation and commoditization

- ▸ understand that only innovations that ultimately will be **profitable** are of interest to firms

- ▸ be familiar with the **development and role of topics** in subsequent chapters of the text.

After reading the *innovation workout*, you will be able to perform **assumption reversals** to gain a new and innovative perspective on a product, market or service.

After reading the Apple (iPod+iTunes) *case study,* you will be able to identify the roles of **profitability**, **innovation, invention, creativity** and **commercialization** in the success of the iPod.

Note: Further information, class slides, test questions and other supporting material are available on our companion website at

www.palgrave.com/business/westland

INNOVATION

Innovation – both the word and its practice – has grown to be pervasive throughout industry, with the business press devoting cover stories and page after page of prose to the latest innovations destined to change our lives and enrich their inventors. In speech after speech, CEOs invoke the mantra of innovation to justify their strategy. New courses in marketing, strategy, finance and other functional areas in business schools have emerged that are devoted to explaining the role of innovation.

Innovation. It's not new, it's just not optional anymore

Many concepts for managing innovation today would have been familiar to Thomas Edison 150 years ago. Alfred DuPont Chandler wrote extensively and insightfully on the role of innovation in sustaining competitive advantage in his 1962 book *Strategy and Structure*,[1] which examines industrial giants of the day like General Motors and Sears. Innovation and its management have had central roles in many industries since the Industrial Revolution.

What makes the 21st century different is the pervasiveness and necessity for innovation. Neither nations nor businesses can expect to succeed – in software, shipping, steel or whatever – without continually innovating to stay ahead of competitors. As the Red Queen said to Alice in *Through the Looking Glass*, any country in which you don't have to run as fast as you can to stay in one place is now 'a slow sort of country'.

In Thomas Edison's day, there were many paths to wealth and power, and innovation could safely be ignored in their pursuit. The CEO no longer has the luxury of being able to ignore innovation. In the 21st century, innovation is coded into the DNA of every successful firm and nation. Those who fail to innovate are the endangered species, the evolutionary dead-ends in a global industrial ecosystem.[2]

Innovation has become the industrial religion of the 21st century. Firms describe innovation as key to increasing sustainable profits and market share. Governments invest billions to attain or maintain supremacy in innovation, or alternately reach for it when trying to explain why their people aren't competing. Around the world, the vernacular of innovation drives the pace of economics, politics, culture and health. Politicians, managers and the public maintain that competitive advantage is now predicated on successful innovation.

You might well ask 'Why?' *Because of rapid globalization and commoditization in goods and services.* These forces are the consequences of several decades of steady advances in logistics and information technology. They have advanced to a point now that makes it difficult for firms to sustain competitive advantage without constantly innovating.[3]

Innovations yield far better returns than traditional business ventures. Rates of return on successful innovations average over 50 per cent, compared with an average for traditional businesses in the range of 15 per cent. Improved profits come with elevated risk – business and technological – which confronts investors and managers with new challenges. Even when an innovation is successful, it may be difficult to figure out exactly why.

This has piqued the curiosity of investors and the financial press like never before. Despite their high risk, high return profile, investments in innovation have pushed the US asset base today to contain around 40 per cent of intellectual assets (patents, copyrights and the like). A bit more than 15 per cent of US gross domestic product (GDP) derives from the production of tangible goods; the rest is generated by ideas and service. Innovation is no longer optional.

The world is flat (Greer & Associates, part I)

Twenty-five years ago Jill and Ken Greer started Greer & Associates, their Minneapolis, Minnesota based photography firm specializing in developing commercials for television and doing commercial photography for retail catalogues. They built up a nice business in Minneapolis, with more than 40 graphic artists and web designers, and their own studio, with a local and national clientèle. But over the past several years Ken saw their competition change dramatically:

Today the dynamic is totally different. Our competition is not only those firms we always used to compete against. Now we have to deal with giant firms, who have the capability to handle small, medium and large jobs, and also with the solo practitioners working out of their home offices who, by making use of today's technology and software, can theoretically do the same thing that a person sitting in our office can do. What's the difference in output, from our clients' point of view, between the giant company who hires a kid designer and puts him in front

of a computer, and our company that hires a kid designer and puts him in front of a computer, and the kid designer with a computer in his own basement? The technology and software are so empowering that it makes us all look the same. In the last month we have lost three jobs to freelance solo practitioners who used to work for good companies and have experience and then just went out on their own. Our clients all said the same thing to us: 'Your firm was really qualified. John was very qualified. John was cheaper.' We used to feel bad losing to another firm, but now we are losing to another person!

Every part of the photographic process has now gone digital, virtual, mobile and personal. Digital cameras for professional photographers achieved a whole new technical level that made them equal to, if not superior to, traditional film cameras. And raw photos can be made instantly available anywhere in the world – notably in the places with the lowest labour costs – through the internet.[4]

Some industries, for example banking and insurance, are built entirely around managing information, or (even less tangible) the risk surrounding that information. Global competition and rapid advances in information technology, which have affected logistics, production, automation and the substitution of intangible for tangible assets, have shoved information to business's centre stage.[5] In turn, rapid growth, reduced cost, and the improved efficiency that information technology has lent to logistics, have translated into an unprecedented degree of globalization in production and sales. If there are economies of scale to be had in the production of any given product, then all of the world's production can easily migrate to wherever production costs are lowest. These shifts have brought about the rapid rise of the Chinese and Indian economies (among others) over the past decade.

Outsourcing

Europe, Japan, Korea and the United States have experienced steadily rising labour costs over the past decades. This has made more attractive – despite the additional investment required – the alternatives of automation and overseas outsourcing of labour-intensive jobs. The largest destination for industrial outsourcing since 1990 has been the People's Republic of China. China has two attractions. First, there is inexpensive labour, even though now labour costs are only 10 per cent of the total value added in export merchandise from China, and second is the massive scale of production facilities, where individual factory capacity may constitute 20–50 per cent of total world demand. Currently, trade between China, India, the United States and Europe accounts for 65 per cent of the more than 250 million containers moved around the world each year.[6] The utilization of China's industrial capacity is enormously complex, and creates many new jobs for innovators. Foreign capital accounts for 20 per cent of China's GDP, and two-thirds of China's exports are generated directly or indirectly by foreign-owned enterprises.[7] In essence this process creates jobs for design, financing, shipping logistics and marketing and retail logistics in Europe, the United States and Japan – and these countries also keep the profit from products. It creates huge numbers of jobs for China, which essentially produces goods to order on a cost-plus basis. Both sides have benefited. China has gained from the employment of its vast populace, helping to maintain social stability, and boosting the emergence of an educated middle and professional class. Multinational firms have been able to control their labour costs, and have gained scale by sharing factory costs – especially in electronics – with other manufacturers, creating or keeping markets for many new and innovative products. Figure 1.1 tracks the steady rise in the use of China's capacity for outsourcing the production of goods designed and marketed elsewhere.

Despite the West's simplistic views of China, it has more diversity than Europe. China has twice as many people as Europe, and the income difference between the richest and poorest provinces is three times as great in China as it is between countries in the Euro zone. Furthermore, China's huge trade surplus (see Figure 1.2) is largely a consequence of its

one-child policy implemented in 1979. But this creates a demographic savings bubble, which will eventually peak at US$10 trillion and last until 2025, after which China will experience deficits. In the 20 years it has before deficits become the norm, China has to create 300 million jobs (more than the entire population of the United States) to maintain social stability.

At the same time, the Chinese might be asking themselves, 'Can you ever be too popular?' Figure 1.2 tracks the annual trade surplus that China accumulates (the excess of its exports over imports). Most of this surplus arises in trade with the United States, and it

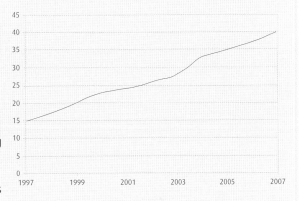

Figure 1.1 Percent of total Chinese exports originating from foreign-owned enterprises, 12-month average

Source: CEIC data

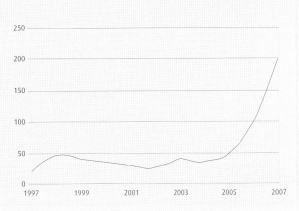

Figure 1.2 China's trade balance (US$ bn annually)

Source: CEIC data

leads to calls in the United States for China's currency to be revalued upwards to try to limit the quantity of goods exported. But in fact, as Figure 1.1 suggests, a lowering of the quantity traded (because prices are higher) is likely to hurt the profits of US multinationals, and may indeed reduce even further the number of industrial jobs, as a result of lowered profits and lower demand for more expensive goods.

US multinationals have learned two lessons from the industry restructuring that resulted from outsourcing to China:

▸ **Outsourcing increases the wealth of the outsourcing country by making possible the** production of goods – that is, turning innovations into real products – that otherwise would never be designed, financed, shipped, marketed and retailed. If this did not happen, the creative and service jobs generated would evaporate instead of (or possibly even alongside) industrial jobs.

▸ **Outsourcing helps corporations restructure their business models for a time when automation will ultimately be able to substitute for all human labour.** This transition has already taken place in disk drives, surface mount electronics and quartz watch movements. It is only a matter of time until physical production tasks can take place entirely by machine.

Returns on innovation make the activity worthwhile, and attract firms to invest billions in becoming more innovative. But with so much urban mythology, ambiguity and outright misinformation concerning what exactly 'innovation' is, it can be hard for firms to know just what they need to do to make themselves more innovative.[8]

Rapid advances in industrial innovation have created a market for all types of innovators. Technology is now so important to industry that governments compete to attract innovators. Corporations pay premiums, and shop the world for employees that can provide them with an innovative edge. The label of innovative entrepreneur is routinely used to flatter industrial magnates. Thanks to our business press, high-tech entrepreneurs are usually seen as being the most successful practitioners of innovation. But it is not really clear that any group has stopped to understand exactly how they go about doing this thing called 'innovation'. Advances in technology, materials, prices, taxes, demographics, regulation and so forth have in the past been a source of new value. In the past few decades, businesses have learned a great deal about the effective and efficient management of these advances in pursuit of wealth and competitive advantage. The goal of this book is to document the tools and techniques they have developed, and show you how to put them to work in your own area.

WHAT IS INNOVATION?

An innovation is a product or service with a bundle of features that is – as a whole – new in the market, or that is commercialized in some new way that opens up new uses and consumer groups for it. Beyond this very general definition, you will find that different professions perceive innovation in vastly different ways, and each profession tends to define innovation in terms of the parts with which its members are familiar. This explains the wide array of definitions for innovation put forward over the years. The focus of this book is *the business of innovation*. It narrows the context in which to define and study innovation to that of creating a profitable service or product, one that customers will buy.

Table 1.1: *The World's 20 most innovative companies (from a 2005 poll of 940 senior executives in 68 countries by Boston Consulting Group)*

Company	Chosen by % polled	Reasons for choosing
Apple	24.84	Delivers great consumer experiences with outstanding design: steady flow of new ideas that redefine old categories.
3M	11.77	Strong internal culture of creativity with formal incentives to innovate. Results in a high sucess rate in turning ideas into profitable products.
Microsoft	8.53	Strong management pushes continuous improvement of products, expansion into new markets and rapid strategy changes when necessary.
GE	8.53	Management practices that are ahead of the competition, along with strong training, are allowing CEO Jeffrey Immelt to reinvent GE's business mode and culture to promote innovation.
Sony	5.94	Understands the importance of media convergence; creates new user-friendly electronic products with great design.
Dell	5.62	Superior business-process model built on ruthless cost-cutting and innovative in supply-chain management.
IBM	5.29	Wants to use its powerful IT base to solve customers' problems and even run their businesses.
Google	5.18	Steady stream of new tools and services provide simple solutions to complex problems. Dominates online search and is growing fast in advertising.
P&G	4.21	Continuous product innovation based on understanding of changing consumer lifestyles. In a switch, now seeks outside partners for new expertise, ideas and even products.
Nokia	4.11	Sharp design, changes models rapidly, and adds features effortlessly, based on a close reading of customer desires.
Virgin	4.00	Reframed air travel as a lifestyle brand and extended the brand into retail stores, cell phone service and other products.
Samsung	3.89	Catches the pulse of the consumer; good design, understands emotion, moved from commodity producer to brand leader.
Wal-Mart	3.24	Uses supply-chain and logistics superiority to move into new markets and product areas. Data mining tracks customer preferences on a daily basis, contributing to fast growth despite its size.
Toyota	3.02	Quality and manufacturing efficiency are constantly upgraded. Strategic use of advanced technology yields big market advantages, in areas such as hybrid cars.
eBay	2.92	Forged a new retail business model based on customer power, cheap prices and community.
Intel	2.70	Dynamic business model with the ability to disrupt itself to meet competition in areas such as wireless computing.
Amazon	2.70	Overturned retail distribution with internet technology and a focus on the consumer experience.
Ideo	2.15	Top consultant on the process of innovation, uses design principles to guide companies through strategy changes that focus on consumer experience.
Starbucks	2.05	Reframed the coffee business as a lifestyle brand by watching customers; created a strong consumer affinity to the brand and uses that affinity to sell new products such as music.
BMW	1.73	Combines sleek design, advanced technology, and web-based marketing to increase brand leadership and move into extensions such as the revived Mini-Cooper and Rolls-Royce.

As a first step in providing a business definition of innovation, let's name some innovative companies, and try to identify just what makes them 'innovative'. Fortunately, this has already been done for us. Table 1.1 shows the results of a 2005 poll of 940 senior executives in 68 countries, carried out by Boston Consulting Group and published in *Business Week*, identifying the companies that executives feel to be the innovation leaders. A cursory look at the companies, and why they were perceived to be innovative, reveals that it is not simply creativity that makes a company innovative. Rather it is the ability to spot innovations and profitably commercialize them, in addition to a well-focused internal competence in design and creativity, that makes these companies innovation leaders.

Two things set apart organizations with a good record of innovation. One is that they foster individuals who are internally driven, whether they are motivated by money, power and fame, or simply curiosity and the need for personal achievement. The second is that they do not leave innovation to chance: they pursue it systematically. They actively search for change, the fount of innovation, and carefully evaluate its profit potential.[9]

Michael Porter observed that innovation is 'a new way of doing things (termed *invention* by some authors) that is *commercialized*. The process of innovation cannot be separated from a firm's strategic and competitive context.'[10] Porter's definition as a succinct formula will be adopted throughout this book:

$$\text{Innovation} = \text{Invention} + \text{Commercialization}$$

Inventions can be new products or services, but they can also be new ways of improving a product sufficiently for market entry; creation of a better product or process performing tasks; bundling services, or handling internal operations to provide a product cost advantage.[11] Innovation is often domain-specific, and because of this I shall spend very little time discussing how inventions come about. This reflects the reality of innovation. Many new ideas come not from the laboratory, but from marketing or from customers; most fail or languish in laboratory notebooks, never being commercialized; sometimes commercialization works only on the second, third or nth try.[12]

But when scientists, strategists and salespeople get together they become a formidable engine of profitability. I look at how to cost-effectively keep a steady flow of inventions coming out of the firm; what to do with the inventions you have; how to assess the financial value of an invention; what steps are necessary to commercialize an invention; how to choose and influence the competitive terrain in which you introduce the invention; and how to efficiently manage risk through adaptive execution and a continually evolving 'emergent' strategy.

THE TWIN CHALLENGES OF GLOBALIZATION AND COMMODITIZATION

In 1950, the United States produced 53 per cent of gross world product; by 2005 this had declined to 18 per cent, though the US GDP increased in absolute terms. The rise of new industrial powers like India, China, Russia and Brazil has provided new venues for traditional industries. Europe and the United States have responded by coming up with new ideas – by innovation. Rather than being hollowed out, developed economies have transformed, with varying success, into innovation societies. Now the emphasis is on developing the tools and management techniques needed to make the most of that. These developed economies enjoy traditions in software, electronics, cinema and television, music, and numerous other information industries that have given them a head start over the rest of the world in understanding what management of ideas – innovation with a profit motive – is all about.[13]

At the start of the Industrial Revolution, factories were located next to power sources such as rivers that could turn water wheels, and employees were expected to come to the factory when the machines were operating. Computers have changed all that by opening up production of nearly everything to the entire world. Purely informational services like software programming, engineering design, data entry and call answering can be distributed around the globe by the internet and international telephone cables. Physical goods are transferred globally by a logistics network of ships, airplanes and warehouses, all managed by increasingly sophisticated computer systems. Taken together, physical and informational distribution systems consume close to 20 per cent of gross world product; the value generated by globalization is substantially greater.

Commercializing innovations

The laser is about a half-century old – a young invention that has found widespread application in measurement, chemistry, navigation, surgery, cutting of materials and fibre optic communication for telephones. Yet lawyers at Bell Labs, where the laser was invented, were unwilling even to apply for a patent on the invention because it had no relevance to the telephone industry.

John Atanasoff built the world's first electronic-digital computer at Iowa State University in 1939. Over the first two decades of its existence, the concept evolved into an unreliable mess of thousands of vacuum tubes, miles of wires and associated hardware, and only crude concepts of programmed software to which no profit-minded firm would be willing to trust its accounting. IBM's

Thomas Watson Jr. was interested in commercializing the computer only when he felt it had evolved sufficiently to be more efficient, reliable and cost-effective than IBM's unit-record machines. He successfully commercialized IBM's version of the computer by bundling hardware, software and support in its System/360 series of upward-compatible machines designed to span the full circle (hence the name '360') from commercial data processing to scientific applications. At the time (c. 1964) its commercialization represented the largest investment in history, at a cost of US$5 billion, five new plants and 60,000 new employees. It was a 'bet the farm' investment that paid off. Clearly IBM's commercialization demanded substantial improvement on the invention in its own right.

No matter what you produce, or what service you provide, there are likely to be individuals or firms somewhere in the world that can and will do the work for less. This is the pressure that globalization generates to commoditize products and services. Commodities are differentiated primarily on price, and commodity markets will migrate to the cheapest producers. When an organization is not the cheapest producer, its only option is to differentiate its products, and that usually requires innovation. Developed economies, by definition, are seldom the low-cost producer (although they can attain this status with innovative production and logistics), and as a consequence, innovation is no longer optional. Thinking like an innovator is a prerequisite for business success.

THINKING LIKE AN INNOVATOR

Innovators enjoy a strong tradition of entrepreneurship whether they are firms or people. Innovators view the competitive landscape differently from the rest of us. With increasingly competitive, commoditized and globalized markets, the entrepreneurial perspective is now as relevant to large bureaucracies as it is to high-tech start-ups. The entrepreneurial perspective diverges from tradition in three important ways[14]

▶ Successful innovators are **action-oriented**. This book provides ideas, action strategies and innovation 'workouts' that walk through an invention's life-cycle, from fundamental R&D to successful commercialization and finally the search for an 'encore'.[15]

Waves of innovation

The economist Joseph Schumpeter observed that a healthy economy was not one in equilibrium, but one that was constantly being 'disrupted' by technological innovation. Others had noticed 'long waves' of economic activity before him, notably the Russian economist Nikolai Kondratieff, who drew attention to them in 1925. He used data on prices, wages and interest rates as well as industrial production and consumption, drawn from France, Britain and the United States. In Schumpeter's view, each of these long business cycles was unique, driven by entirely different clusters of industries. A long upswing in a cycle started when a new set of innovations came into general use, as happened with water power, textiles and iron in the late 18th century; steam, rail and steel in the mid-19th century; and electricity, chemicals and the internal combustion engine at the turn of the 20th century. In turn, each upswing stimulated investment and an expansion of the economy. These long booms waned as the technologies matured and returns to investors declined.

By the time Schumpeter died in 1950, the third cycle of his 'successive industrial revolutions' had already run its course. The fourth, powered by oil, electronics, aviation and mass production, is now in decline. And a fifth industrial revolution, based on the knowledge-intensive industries of semiconductors, fibre optics, genomics and software, powered the expansion of the global economy at the end of the 20th century.

The sixth industrial revolution is the revolution of the innovation economy. The tangible drivers of previous industrial revolutions have become commoditized into platforms onto which can be installed innumerable permutations of ideas and innovations. It is the ideas – data, designs, news, processes, software, pictures and so forth – that will power the global innovation economy of the 21st century.[16]

▶ Innovators need to be able to act quickly, and make decisions in a continually evolving competitive and technological landscape. Simple heuristics are more valuable that involved, complex and sluggish strategizing. When you are moving fast – as fast as you can to stay in one place – complexity creates confusion and delay. Innovation and technology management requires you to simplify complexity. Simplification is the secret to decisive leadership: co-workers, assistants and collaborators can act with self-confidence, and furthermore can feed back the information to keep the development of the innovation on track to be a success. The ideas presented here are standard items in the toolkits of successful innovators, as will be documented in the many mini case studies that accompany the text.[17]

▶ Successful innovators are continually learning – learning about the competition, learning about their products and technology, learning about themselves. By its very nature, innovation defies the use of checklists and rote exercises. Innovators think out of the box; they break the mould, defy convention and look at the world in new, exciting and profitable ways. Learning to innovate demands personal and intellectual growth. As you move through the chapters of this book, you will encounter increasingly challenging tools to help you learn to be a successful innovator. The goal is to *make innovation a habit*. Habitual innovators see every product, service or operation as a challenge for improvement. They make careers out of commercializing their ideas – starting a business, selling ideas within their own firms, and stimulating their friends and co-workers to take action on their ideas. Habitual innovators make careers by forging opportunities out of uncertainty.[18]

This text distills the ideas and action strategies of habitual innovators. It will show you how they think, how they behave and exactly what they do to achieve their goals. Innovators capitalize on the uncertainty of their competitors, create simplicity out of disorder and complexity, and know the difference between a risk and a calculated risk. They see windows of opportunity, recognizing that it is more expensive to be slow than to be wrong. They understand that making a mistake is not only unavoidable, but it is also the right thing to do. Mistakes offer an affordable opportunity to learn, provided you consciously minimize your exposure while taking action. Whether your aspirations are to be a manager, entrepreneur, artist or bureaucrat, you can learn a great deal from the stories and case studies of habitual innovators presented here. Throughout the text you will learn how to apply the insights of habitual innovators to your domain, whether it is your own firm or a major corporation.

MAKING INNOVATIONS PROFITABLE

The first challenge faced by firms wanting to be innovative is how to ensure that their innovations are profitable. If innovations are not profitable in a relatively short time, the firm is likely to run out of funds to pay for more innovation.

Only after a firm has solved the puzzle of making innovation pay for itself does it have the luxury of unfettered creativity or playing at the 'casinos of technology'. There is no greater source of corporate angst today than that generated by uncertainties about the ultimate profitability of inventions coming out of R&D. Innovative industries confront a high failure rate. Successful innovators need to manage both assets and people to ensure that the profits from successful products outweigh the costs of failure. They do this by taking small steps with tightly controlled expenditure in the early stages of R&D, scanning the environment for innovations that already exist in university labs or other firms, constructing 'emergent' strategy on the fly as they learn more about their customers, markets, competitors and technology along the way, and taking calculated risks.

Innovation in services (Greer & Associates, part II)

Ken Greer recounts:

> We bought a digital camera, it was incredibly liberating at first. All of the thrill and excitement of photography were there – except that the film was free. Because it was digital, we didn't have to buy film and we didn't have to go to the lab to have it processed and wait to get it back. If we were on location and shooting something, we could see if we got the shot right away.

For a year or so there was this new sense of empowerment, freedom, creativity and control. But then Ken and his team discovered that this new liberating technology could also be enslaving.

> We discovered that not only did we now have the responsibility of shooting the picture and defining the desired artistic expression, we had to get involved in the technology of the photograph. We had to become the lab. We woke up one morning and said, 'We are the lab' ... in addition to being the photographer, we had to become the processing lab and the color separator.

Once the technology made that possible, Greer's customers demanded it. Because Greer *could* control the image further down the supply chain, they said he *should* control it, he *must* control it. Then they also said that because it was all digital now, and all under his control, it should be included among the services his team provided as the photographic creators of the image. Greer says:

> The clients said, 'We will not pay you extra for it.' We used to go to an outside service to touch up the pictures – to remove red-eye or blemishes – but now we have to be the retouchers ourselves also. They expect red-eye to be removed by us, digitally, even before they see it. Now we had to learn to be good at all these other things. It is not what we signed up for, but the competitive marketplace and the technology forced us into it.

Source: adapted from Friedman, *The World is Flat*, pp. 341–5.

The objective of these activities is to encourage expenditures on inventions that will ultimately turn into profitable innovations. Internally, this means gaining access to people, labs and capital; externally, it means convincing venture capitalists to invest. Most innovators, though, find that one of their greatest challenges is finding the money they need to generate new ideas and turn them into products that customers will buy.

From the investors' standpoint, financing an innovation is no different than any other financial investment: it needs to be assessed on the basis of return, risk and maturity schedule. Where innovations differ is in their high-risk, high-return profiles. Investments in traditional industries with long time-series of performance histories, and widely understood business models, have over the past decade averaged around a 15 per cent return. Successful innovations, in contrast, average in excess of 50 per cent return on investment. But this higher return comes at a cost; innovations (by definition) lack a history of operations and customer acceptance. That translates into significantly elevated risk to the investor, since financial analysis of the innovation is not straightforward using traditional tools.

Innovations that involve new technologies or untested markets make investors especially nervous. Such concern is understandable. Investors may lack an understanding of the technology they are investing in, as well as the industry and markets that might buy it. If there is no history of business success in a particular product, or if business models are poorly articulated, the traditional tools for computing return will give them little insight into what to expect for an innovative product.[19] This bodes poorly for the innovator. In attempt to offset higher risk, investors may demand usurious returns from their investments in a start-up, sometimes at short maturity. They may demand active participation in management, and impose covenants that give them the power to completely take over management and operations should certain targets fail to be met by the entrepreneur. The only recourse for the innovator is to provide the better information on risks, returns and cash flows that will be required. I show you in later chapters exactly how to provide this information.

ABOUT THIS BOOK

The theme of this text is 'Building the profitable innovation company'. This is not a book about creativity, nor does it promise to bring you in touch with your inner Picasso (although I do discuss the characteristics of creative people in Chapter 12). Rather, this is a book about the *business of innovation*. For creative individuals and firms, I show you how to move through the creative process, to identify inventions with commercial potential, and how and when to bring an innovation to market.

In order to maintain focus, present the most useful knowledge in a one or two-semester time period, and to be an effective instructional tool, the text carefully prioritizes innovation topics into 'necessary', 'foundation' and 'optional' topics, with 90 per cent of the material concentrated on knowledge you need to know, or the foundations underlying that knowledge. To that end, the text sets the following five educational goals:

▶ to describe those tasks that must be systematically and continuously performed for a firm to sustain or boost its rate of innovation
▶ to provide a set of tools, metrics and concepts – a language of innovation – that will allow managers, scientists, salespeople and investors to communicate relevant information with each other
▶ to survey the activities that can create an innovative firm either from an existing firm, or as an entrepreneurial venture
▶ to describe who exactly are the innovative people that a firm needs in order to stay competitive
▶ to describe where and how to employ and manage these innovators.

Innovation is a risky business largely because it is difficult to winnow successful from failed innovations in advance of investment. It is difficult, but it is also clear that most firms and individuals can do better. Successful innovators may benefit from substantially higher returns than traditional businesses, but they suffer from substantially higher rates of failure. In most technology industries, for example, the failure rate exceeds 95 per cent. Of high-tech businesses that live by their innovations, pharmaceuticals is the most successful, with a 7.5 per cent success rate on new products, largely because marketing is usually included in product development at an early stage.

Innovation is too often confused with creativity. Creativity does indeed play an important role in being innovative, but innovation includes such extra-creative topics as management, strategy, technology valuation, competences and business alliances. Successful innovation firms such as 3M and Apple are experts at implementing their ideas, and they do so by getting the business basics right.

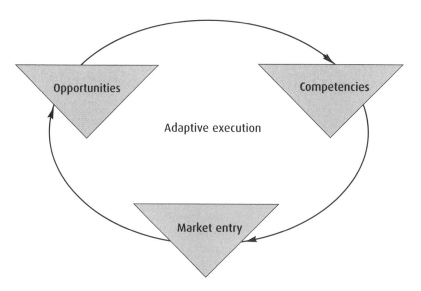

Figure 1.3 Adaptive execution and the innovation cycle

Neither is innovation solely the domain of so-called 'technology' companies. Globalization, commoditization and greater access to the fruits of technology – digital electronics, global networks and databases – affect everyone. This forces most businesses to come to grips with the single most important problem facing technology companies – the need to continually innovate to differentiate themselves in the marketplace. The difference between technology companies and traditional businesses like real estate is that technology companies have always known that they needed to be innovative. The importance of innovation is only beginning to dawn on professionals in other fields.

The methods presented in this book are directed towards managing innovation's inherent risk through two proven techniques. The first is the idea of 'staging' the development of an innovation, and seeking scale economies at each stage. The second is the idea of 'adaptive execution', which minimizes a firm's own investment in resources at each stage of development. I embed both ideas in a larger framework where innovation is executed in a continuous process which keeps creating, evolving and redifferentiating the firm's portfolio of products and ideas along the cycle shown in Figure 1.3. Most chapters conclude with a summary of key points to help students put chapter principles into practice. In this dynamic framework, inventions are identified; those that are consistent with firm competences and strategy are commercialized; commercialization attempts to control competition and minimize risk through adaptive execution, with emergent strategy which responds to competitor offerings and strategy. The text includes a case study at the end of each chapter, which applies the chapter concepts, and introduces concepts for later chapters. Supporting each section in the chapter are mini case examples which provide a comprehensive picture of how firms innovate successfully.

Topics are presented in four sets, three of which are sequential in the book, while the fourth set run throughout the book. The first set surveys the current competitive environment, and explains what an innovation is, why innovation is important and the challenges that need to be addressed in innovating. Chapter 2 defines innovation in a commercial context, while Chapter 3 lays out the tasks that are required to define what innovations are suitable for a particular firm at a particular point in the evolution of the underlying technology and markets. Chapter 3 frames the unique challenges that the process of innovation creates for the manager. It looks at the demand-based assessment of potential products, with the goal of constructing a portfolio of 'opportunities' – the idea being that any particular opportunity could be commercialized once resource availability and market readiness allow for it. Chapter 4 discusses the development of convincing, and ultimately successful, business models based on systematic analysis of the firm's capabilities, and the opportunities available in the competitive market, given specific assumptions of profit from component activities.

The second set of topics focuses on the operations required to develop and introduce new products and services – the 'inventions' that may ultimately become profitable 'innovations' for the firm. Chapter 5 focuses on how firms can assess their own capabilities and competences so that they can assure themselves of being able to deliver products and services that the market will pay for. Chapter 6 looks at the unique challenges that innovation presents in the relatively less tangible business environments of services. Services are now the primary source of wealth in developed economies. Fortunately, the concepts required for successful service innovation build upon what we have studied in product innovation. Chapter 7 surveys strategies for protecting innovations from theft by competitors. Although traditional intellectual property laws concerning patents, copyrights and trademarks receive the largest amount of discussion, in practice successful innovators often rely on secrecy combined with complex proactive strategies.

The third set of topics concern unique aspects of managing the markets for innovations. Chapter 8 describes the components of a successful entrance strategy. Because innovations have much higher risks of failure than traditional products and services, but potentially much higher profits on success, appropriate entrance strategies need to be adaptive – managing risk in real time – for the firm to realize profits consistently. Chapters 9 and 10 look at economic effects that tend to be unique to, or emphasized in technology products – network effects, exponential performance accelerations, and dramatic reductions in costs from labour and geographical distance.

Innovations must compete in both consumer and financial markets to get the up-front capital required to sustain the project until it starts earning customer revenues. Chapter 11 surveys the financial analysis required if an innovation is to receive venture funding. Because, by their very nature, there is no history of the commercialization of an innovation, the methods for financial analysis need to differ from those used in traditional investment analysis. The catastrophic losses associated with the dot-com meltdown were both large and unexpected primarily because investors ignored these differences when assessing the innovations that were enabled by new telecommunications technologies in the 1990s.

The final set of topics 'brackets' the other book topics, and recurs throughout the book. These topics are intended to present the larger context in which the business of innovation operates. Chapter 1 sets up the motivating problem that underlies other material in the text: how can you take an invention (a new product, process

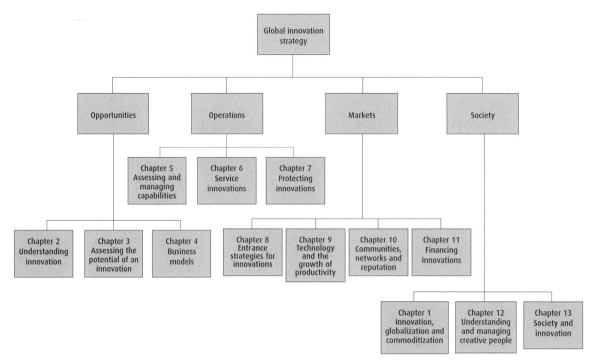

Figure 1.4 Sequence of topics in the book

or service) and make it commercially successful? Chapters 2 to 11 then proceed to lay out the components of a successful innovation strategy. Chapter 12 looks at the primary input factor required by all innovation businesses – that of the creative mind. The chapter provides managerial tips from one of the most successful innovators so far in the 21st century – Google – to guide other firms in making the transition to the innovation economy. Not just anyone can be creative, and different sorts of creativity are required for different tasks in the business of innovation. The chapter also analyses the ways in which truly creative individuals differ from the rest of us, providing tips for what a manager needs to do to get the most out of creative employees.

Finally, Chapter 13 shows how the world's economy is restructuring itself around a society of innovators. The new royalty in this world – measured in terms of power and wealth – are the creative classes. In the United States, for example, roughly 40 per cent of the US asset base, and over 80 per cent of GDP now derives from intellectual property. Industrial and service workers are the new underclass. For both good and bad, these new class divisions are reshaping the business environments that will employ our graduates.

Living with commoditization (Greer & Associates, part III)

Every aspect of photography has been commoditized. Film production went digital, so the marketplace and the technology forced photographers to become their own film editors, graphics studio, sound production facility and everything else, including producers of their own DVDs. Each of those functions used to be sourced out to separate companies. But then the whole supply chain shrank into one box that sat on someone's desktop. The same thing happened in the graphics part of the business: Greer & Associates became their own typesetters, illustrators and sometimes even printers, because they owned digital colour printers. Ken Greer says:

> Things were supposed to get easier. Now I feel like I'm going to McDonald's, but instead of getting fast food, I'm being asked to bus my own table and wash the dishes too. If we put our foot down and say you have to pay for each of these services, there is someone right behind us saying, 'I will do it all.' So the services required go up significantly and the fees you can charge stay the same or go down.

Greer responded to the commoditization threat to his company by locating his company's real core competencies. He says:

> What we sell now is strategic insight, creative instinct, and artistic flair. We sell inspired, creative solutions, we sell personality. Our core competence and focus is now on all those things that cannot be digitized. We have hired more thinkers and outsourced more technology pieces. In the old days many companies 'hid behind technology'. You could be very good, but you didn't have to be the world's best. There was a horizon out there and no one could see beyond that horizon. Three years ago it was inconceivable that Greer & Associates would lose a contract to a company in England, and now we have. Everyone can see what everyone else is doing now, and everyone has the same tools, so you have to be the very best, the most innovative thinker.[20]

The role of the innovation workout

Management is as much a matter of style as of substance. Creativity generates style from substance; innovation (invention + commercialization) is all about substance, and style is not necessary for success. Innovators are likely to lack the pragmatism, political sense and style of a good manager because they are more interested in their product-systems than in corporate and market politics. Great innovators, such as Thomas Edison, Henry Ford and John Warnock, have made their companies successful by surrounding themselves with good administrators to complement their strengths.

How do people in corporations generate ideas? There are countless ways. The market for innovation tools and consulting has expanded rapidly over the past few years, and at least some of this growth is demand-driven. Much of this meshes with the well-integrated sense of work-as-fun of Silicon Valley entrepreneurs. They might however be considered too frivolous for the buttoned-down corporate crowd. And that is the point. Much of the value added by business is now being generated by companies like Electronic Arts, Pixar, Apple and Google, which are comfortable with out-of-the-box innovation; with businesses predicated on idea generation. More conservative companies rightly see their survival as tied to their ability to generate and compete on ideas. There is a lot of pressure to be creative in more conservative industries, and this is forming the market for the 'innovation workouts' which are provided by consultancies.

The way to come up with good ideas is to generate lots of them. The way to generate lots of ideas is to use tools-heuristics such as our Assumption Reversal workout, which forces you to look at a particular business challenge from all sides. Our innate bias is to see any business challenge in terms of the successful businesses we have encountered. There's even a name for this: the 'X is good' syndrome. In this situation, a solution 'X' is considered good because it is the only thing people have ever seen. The innovation workouts are tools for getting those who haven't tried it before to think 'out of the box'.

Are managers actually drawing pictures and cutting up slides as we have instructed in some of our innovation workouts? Not always. As with most things today, many of the innovation workout techniques have been computerized. You can find write-ups by searching the World Wide Web (WWW). The intent and concepts of these computer tools are basically the same as our innovation workouts: they are tools-heuristics which:

- force you to look at a particular business challenge from all sides
- make sure that you have considered all processes and attributes that are relevant to the product-system
- free your mind from existing biases, prejudices and incorrigibility.

No matter what business you are in today, staying competitive these days means getting innovative. With the innovation workouts presented in this text, you will make innovative thinking a habit, making mistakes publicly and analysing them in front of peers, and showing patience as an innovation evolves and improves. And you will have a head start on your competitors.

Reversing assumptions

Sometimes the assumptions we make about a problem, business challenge or scenario seem so basic, so fundamental, that we never think to challenge them. Yet at the core of all innovation is a challenge of some assumption – maybe more than just one. This is what is meant by the cliché *'thinking outside the box'*.

In the 1950s, it was common for Walt Disney's animators to ask, 'how would Walt think?' The nine-dot puzzle (a topographical puzzle that had been around for at least a century) presented an example of how you had to think 'outside the box' to solve it, just like Uncle Walt supposedly did. 'Outside the box' refers to the process required to link the nine dots with no more than three straight lines which will cross through them all, and without lifting your pencil.

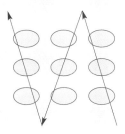

Figure 1.5 Thinking outside the box

We make two inherent assumptions when we first frame this challenge: first, you must not extend beyond the outside dots, and second, the lines must pass through the centre of each dot. But neither of these constraints was explicitly stated in the problem. Once you challenge those assumptions, the problem is easily solved. At Disney Studios, each dot had a meaning and the two points outside of the box were labelled as 'the Vision' and 'the Method'.

Properly framing a challenge is the first step (and an essential step) in coming up with a solution to the problem. *Any assumption can be challenged.* We tie ourselves to assumptions about the way things work for two reasons: first, often we have spent a lifetime gaining the experience that underlies these assumptions, and thus are reluctant to let them loose, and second, it is easier to cling to an incorrect assumption than to face the

uncertainty of challenging it. Thus we take most assumptions for granted, as no one has the time or need to challenge every assumption. For those who are willing, though, all sorts of opportunities arise which may not be apparent to your competitors.

In your *Assumption Reversals* innovation workout, chose a product or service that is already on the market and do the following:

1. Frame the major challenges that you need to overcome to meet your marketing objective.
2. Identify the assumptions you have implicitly made about what makes this product marketable.
3. Challenge one or more your fundamental assumptions by reversing it: for example, if it was assumed that customers only want cars in black, reversal means that you now say 'customers only want cars that *are not* black'.
4. Ask yourself how to accomplish each reversal, what the resulting product would look like, and how you would go about marketing it.

For example, Apple in brainstorming the iPod challenged that assumption that customers wanted a device that could play their music collection. Instead, they reversed the assumption and stated that 'customers want access to a music collection, and are willing to pay for a device that can give them that access'. The resulting device was just 50 per cent of the business model: the other half was iTunes, the music collection that customers wanted to access.

Reversing assumptions is about challenging prevailing beliefs and assumptions by looking at them from the customer's, or some other stakeholder's, perspective. Many of the greatest breakthroughs in management have been the direct result of assumption reversals. Alfred Sloan took over General Motors when it was on the verge of bankruptcy and turned it around. His genius was to take an assumption and reverse it into a 'breakthrough idea'. For instance, it had always been assumed that you had to buy a car before you drove it. Sloan reversed this to mean you could buy it while driving it, pioneering the concept of installment buying for car dealers.

Reversing an assumption helps you escape

from looking at your challenge in exactly the same way as your competitors. Markets in which every competitor sees the challenge in exactly the same way are called *commodity markets*; these are markets in which the lowest-priced supplier wins (at least as long as it remains solvent).

Reversing your assumptions also forces you to think provocatively, and is guaranteed to liven up product development and problem-solving meetings. Assumption reversals are the basis for great debates and striking breakthroughs – like the iPod.

C A S E   S T U D Y

Apple's (iPod + iTunes) innovation

In 2005, *Business Week* reported a Boston Consulting Group survey of 940 senior executives in 68 companies, asking them to rank the most innovative companies in the world (Table 1.1). Apple ranked number one, with nearly twice the votes of second ranked, 3M. Apple's most innovative product was the iPod. How CEO Steve Jobs brought Apple back from near death a decade earlier, and in the process crafted the iPod into a hugely profitable cult icon, is the story of our first case study in this book.[21]

The intellectual roots of the iPod MP3 player date back to the birth of the digital audio player (DAP) market, which started with the introduction in 1982 of the compact disk (CD) for music and computer data storage, followed shortly by portable CD players.

Shortly after the birth of the World Wide Web in 1993, MP2 (MPEG-1 Audio Layer 2) files appeared on the internet. Initially the only encoder available for MP2 production was the Xing Encoder, accompanied by the program CDDA2WAV, a CD ripper that transforms CD audio tracks to waveform audio files. The Internet Underground Music Archive started online music downloads, hosting thousands of authorized MP2 recordings before MP3 or the web was popularized.

MP3 was the culmination of a project managed by Egon Meier-Engelen of the German Aerospace Centre, and a collaboration of European researchers which began in 1987 and was formalized in 1992 as part of MPEG-1 standards published in 1993 and further enhanced in MPEG-2 published in 1995. On 7 July 1994 the Fraunhofer Society released the first software MP3 encoder called l3enc. The filename extension .mp3 was chosen by the Fraunhofer team on 14 July 1995 (previously the files had been named .bit). With the first real-time software MP3 player Winplay3 (released on 9 September 1995), many people were able to encode and play back MP3 files on their PCs. Because of the relatively small hard drives back in that time (around 500 MB), the technology was essential to store music for listening pleasure on a computer. MP3 is a pulse-code modulation compression format which reduces audio data to a much smaller size by discarding portions that are considered less important to human hearing (similar to JPEG, a lossy compression for images). A number of techniques are employed in MP3 to determine which portions of the audio can be discarded: in particular, psychoacoustics. Acoustical engineer Karlheinz Brandenburg used a CD recording of Suzanne Vega's song 'Tom's Diner' to assess and refine the MP3 compression algorithm (Suzanne Vega came to be known as 'The mother of MP3'). 'Tom's Diner' was chosen because of its softness and simplicity, making it easier to hear imperfections in the compression format during playbacks.

By the late 1990s, MP3 files were flourishing on the internet, thanks to software packages like Nullsoft's Winamp (released in 1997), mpg123, and Napster (released in 1999). Those programs made it very easy for the average user to play back, create, share and collect MP3s.

The first solid state MP3 DAP in the world was created by SaeHan Information Systems in 1997, followed in 1998 by Diamond Multimedia's US$200 Rio PMP300, with a form factor surprisingly similar to the modern iPod. Even with its high price and paltry 32MB of memory, the Rio PMP300 was popular enough to prompt a lawsuit from the record industry, claiming that any MP3 player facilitated piracy. In October 1998 the Recording Industry Association of America filed a lawsuit in the Ninth US Court of Appeals in San Francisco, claiming Diamond's Rio PMP300 player violated the 1992 Audio Home Recording Act. The three-judge panel ruled in favor of Diamond, paving the way for the development of the MP3 portable player market. *This removed the major legal barrier to entry for the MP3 standard.*

Diamond's defence referred to Sony Corp. v. Universal City Studios (1984, the 'Betamax case'), where the US Supreme Court determined home videotaping to be legal in the United States since there were *substantial non-infringing uses.* Most importantly, the Betamax could be used to 'time shift' television programmes so that owners could watch them at a more convenient time. Diamond argued that its MP3 player allowed *space shifting* of broadcast content so that owners could enjoy them wherever they went. (Incidentally, the Betamax precedent was also later invoked in MGM v. Grokster (2005), where the high court agreed that the same 'substantial non-infringing uses' standard applies to authors and vendors of peer-to-peer file sharing software.)

All of this occurred at a time of explosive growth in the internet. MP3, already the standard for hard disk recording of music, became the de facto standard for internet peer-to-peer file sharing (the 'peer' being an individual's personal computer as opposed to an easy to police network server). Peer-to-peer music sharing, made possible by services such as Napster, became a euphemism for the widespread piracy of music, and kicked the MP3 player business into high gear, depriving the recording industry of substantial revenues.

Jobs, a consummate habitual innovator and the CEO of Apple Computers, initiated the iPod design, but not as a me-too MP3 player trying to cash in on Apple's brand. Rather the iPod business was an inadvertent extension of Apple's digital hub strategy, which intended to place iMacs at the center of a hub of consumer digital devices such as cameras, video recorders, game consoles and MP3 players. The 'i' stood for 'individual' or 'independence' or other words that would complement Apple's 'Think different' campaign, launched in conjunction with the first iMac. Apple's strategy assumed that the iMac connected to the WWW would serve as an exchange network and storage entrepot for digital content which would keep consumer electronics devices occupied, or would allow their content to be readily uploaded and shared with others or displayed on websites.

At the time that Apple was searching for devices for the digital hub, Asian consumer electronics manufacturers offered a wide range of high-quality digital cameras and camcorders. But Jobs felt that existing digital music players lacked quality (partly because of the previous copyright infringement controversies, manufacturers were wary of the music player market), and decided to develop Apple's own MP3 player. Apple's team of engineers designed and built the first iPod in less than a year, integrating the core firmware from PortalPlayer with the user interface library developed by Pixo, which had previously developed the Apple Newton, a personal digital assistant. The iPod was unveiled by Jobs on 23 October 2001 as an iMac-only compatible product (to promote the digital hub model which was about selling iMacs rather than iPods) with a 5GB hard drive that put '1000 songs in your pocket'. The original iPod cost US$399, and was considered prohibitively costly (just like the US$200 Rio at an earlier time), but the iPod proved an instant hit in the marketplace, quickly overtaking earlier hard drive MP3 players.

Shortly thereafter, Jobs used his film and music industry influence to create the iTunes market – a legal alternative to Napster's peer-to-peer music download business, greatly expanding the market. Jobs (the consummate Hollywood and music industry insider) was able to hammer out contracts which had eluded the other players, giving him a larger, more affordable library of music than his competition.

To bind the iPod hardware to the iTunes service and software, Apple developed FairPlay from technology created by the company Veridisc. FairPlay is designed to help the CD industry. As of the start of 2007, according to Jobs there were 20 billion CD tracks, compared with 2 billion iTunes tracks. The record companies completely control the CD industry, whereas iTunes tracks are shared between Apple and the music industry. FairPlay is a digital rights management (DRM) technology built in to the QuickTime multimedia technology used by the iPod, iTunes and the iTunes Store. FairPlay allows a protected track to be used in the following ways:

- ▸ The protected track may be copied to any number of iPod portable music players.
- ▸ The protected track may be played on up to five (originally three) authorized computers simultaneously.
- ▸ The protected track may be copied to a standard audio CD any number of times.
- ▸ The resulting CD has no DRM and may be ripped, encoded and played back like any other CD. However, CDs created by users do not attain first sale rights and cannot be legally leased, lent, sold or distributed to others by the creator.
- ▸ The CD audio still bears the artifacts of compression, so converting it back into a lossy format such as MP3 may aggravate the sound artifacts of encoding.
- ▸ A particular playlist within iTunes containing a protected track can be copied to a CD only up to seven times (originally ten times) before the playlist must be changed.

Jobs' stroke of genius in creating the (iTunes + iPod) business was to make all music available at a fixed price (99¢ per tune). Indeed he has done this over the vigorous objections of the music companies. The traditional CD production model for successful bands involved bundling a set of a dozen or so tunes together on a CD. Perhaps two or three of these tunes (less than 20 per cent) would take 80 per cent of the budget to record, and the remainder of the CD would be less popular 'fillers'. By unbundling tunes on the CD, iTunes forced the music industry to take the same revenue from costly tunes as from cheap ones. Furthermore, download volumes for the costly tunes were typically several times that of the 'filler' tunes (which also sold for 99¢).[22] To make this more palatable, all of the revenues and even a small subsidy from iTunes were passed on to the music companies.

Table 1.2: *iPod unit sales*

Year	Unit sales
2002	381,000
2003	939,000
2004	4,416,000
2005	22,497,000
2006	45,138,000
Total	73,371,000

Apple actually loses money on iTunes in order to ensure an unlimited supply of 'content' for its iPod players. The players are simply overpriced commodity hard drives or flash memory with proprietary software and packaging. Manufacture of iPods simply adds a few production steps to inexpensive Asian hard drive and flash memory production lines. Apple's (iPod + iTunes) franchise is enormously profitable because of the high mark-up and relatively short product life of its players, which were already cheap to produce to begin with.

Apple has more recently expanded its product offerings to television programming, commercials and other video content. Essentially this has put the iPod rather than the iMac at the centre of its digital hub, and Apple has even dropped the iMac name from its new Intel-based computers. Thus Apple has progressed from selling iPods as an incentive to buy into

C A S E   S T U D Y

the iMac standard, to selling iTunes as an incentive to buy into the iPod standard. Jobs' insider position in Hollywood (he is currently the major shareholder of Disney, which purchased his Pixar Studios) will allow him a substantial edge in the access to content for the foreseeable future, allowing him to vanquish any pretenders to the 'iPod Killer' title. By the end of 2007, the iPod dominated digital music player sales in the United States, with over 90 per cent of the market for hard-drive-based players and over 70 per cent of the market for all types of players.

(iPod + iTunes) case study: questions for review

1. Describe Apple's iPod business model. Where does Apple make money? What are its costs?

2. Many once innovative companies suffer from the 'Not Invented Here Syndrome' (NIHS), in which the firm's labs insist on developing all components in-house, to the detriment of competitiveness and product quality. How do you think Apple has managed to avoid the NIHS problem?

3. How did Apple use adaptive execution to develop the (iPod + iTunes) business? What firm competences does Apple possess that made it a successful competitor in the MP3 player market?

4. What was innovative about the iPod versus other MP3 players? How did this help its commercialization?

5. What role does the industrial design of the iPod play in its success?

6. What role does software play in the success of the iPod business? Describe how Apple reused and repurposed software designed for another function in order to make the iPod a success.

7. What role does the WWW play in the success of the iPod business?

8. Challenge one of the fundamental assumptions of iPod's business model by reversing it. Then define an 'anti-iPod' product and business model that satisfies your reversed assumptions

9. What are the commercially important attributes that make iPod's business model successful and sustainable?

10. Split just one of the attributes in question 8 into three sub-attributes. How could you alter each of these sub-attributes to create a new product?

11. Describe customer activity at each step of iPod purchase and usage. Do you see any opportunities for new businesses?

CHAPTER QUESTIONS FOR REVIEW

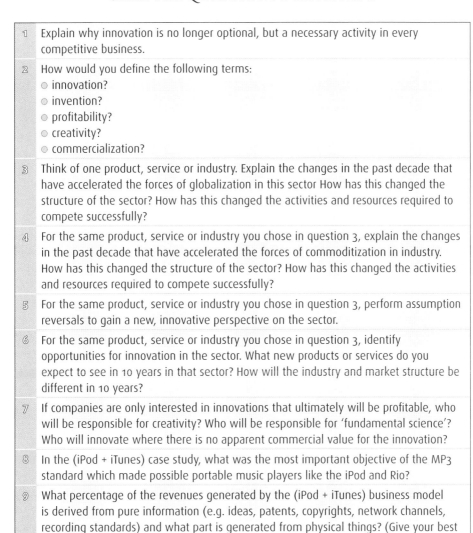

1	Explain why innovation is no longer optional, but a necessary activity in every competitive business.
2	How would you define the following terms: ○ innovation? ○ invention? ○ profitability? ○ creativity? ○ commercialization?
3	Think of one product, service or industry. Explain the changes in the past decade that have accelerated the forces of globalization in this sector How has this changed the structure of the sector? How has this changed the activities and resources required to compete successfully?
4	For the same product, service or industry you chose in question 3, explain the changes in the past decade that have accelerated the forces of commoditization in industry. How has this changed the structure of the sector? How has this changed the activities and resources required to compete successfully?
5	For the same product, service or industry you chose in question 3, perform assumption reversals to gain a new, innovative perspective on the sector.
6	For the same product, service or industry you chose in question 3, identify opportunities for innovation in the sector. What new products or services do you expect to see in 10 years in that sector? How will the industry and market structure be different in 10 years?
7	If companies are only interested in innovations that ultimately will be profitable, who will be responsible for creativity? Who will be responsible for 'fundamental science'? Who will innovate where there is no apparent commercial value for the innovation?
8	In the (iPod + iTunes) case study, what was the most important objective of the MP3 standard which made possible portable music players like the iPod and Rio?
9	What percentage of the revenues generated by the (iPod + iTunes) business model is derived from pure information (e.g. ideas, patents, copyrights, network channels, recording standards) and what part is generated from physical things? (Give your best guess!)
10	In the (iPod + iTunes) business model, what percentage of the cost generated is from pure information, and what percentage is from tangible and physical things?

CHAPTER 1: KEY POINTS

▷ Innovation = Invention + Commercialization.

▷ Creating new businesses = Entrepreneurship (it can happen either inside or outside a corporation).

▷ Rates of return on successful innovations typically average over 50 per cent, compared with those of traditional businesses, which average in the range of 15 per cent. Improved profits come with elevated risk – business and technological – which needs to be managed.

▷ The US asset base today consists of around 40 per cent intellectual assets (patents, copyrights and the like). A bit more than 15 per cent of US GDP consists of the production of tangible goods; the other 85 per cent represents ideas and services.

▷ The rapid pace of globalization and technology development ensure that in the future most new businesses will be innovation businesses.

▷ Successful innovators are action-oriented.

▷ When moving fast (innovating) complexity creates confusion and delay; innovators order and simplify complexity by:
  ◦ identifying generic business models and action strategies for innovation businesses
  ◦ stretching their own innovation skills
  ◦ exercising their ability to capitalize on uncertainty and take calculated risks.

▷ Innovations require the development of new businesses that are predicated on new inventions, and which often require new business models (entrepreneurship).

▷ Disruptive innovations are even riskier; they demand that you educate investors, customers and other stakeholders.

▷ Things that distinguish successful innovators:
  ◦ passionately seek new opportunities
  ◦ pursue opportunities with discipline
  ◦ pursue only the best opportunities
  ◦ focus on execution
  ◦ engage the energies of everyone in their domain

▷ There is no checklist.

▷ Incremental improvement of existing products or business models is insufficient. You need to really make a difference.

NOTES

1 Chandler, A. DuPont (1962) *Strategy and Structure: Chapters in the History of the American Industrial Enterprise*, Cambridge, Mass.: MIT Press.

2 Alfred Chandler obituary, *Economist*, 10 May 2007, p. 87.

3 Clark, P. and Staunton, N. (1993) *Innovation in Technology and Organization*, London: Routledge. Gundling, E. (2000) *The 3M Way to Innovation: Balancing people and profit*, New York: Kodansha International.

4 Source: adapted from Friedman, T. L. (2005) *The World is Flat*, New York: Farrar, Straus and Giroux, pp. 341–5.

5 Pear Sheene, M. R. (1991) 'The boundness of technical knowledge within a company: barriers to external knowledge acquisition', paper presented at R&D Management Conference on the Acquisition of External Knowledge, Kiel, Germany.

6 'Maxing out', *Economist*, 1 March 2007.

7 Xie, A. (2007) 'Pouring cold water on global prosperity?', *South China Morning Post*, 17 March 2007, p. A13.

8 Chesbrough, H. W. and Teece, D. (1996) 'When is virtual virtuous? Organizing for innovation', *Harvard Business Review* Jan–Feb, 11, pp. 65–73.

9 Wolfe, R. A. (1994) 'Organizational innovation: review and critique and suggested research directions', *Journal of Management Studies* **31**(3), pp. 405–31.

10 Porter, M. E. and van Opstal, D. (2001) 'U.S. Competitiveness 2001: strengths, vulnerabilities and long-term priorities' , Washington, DC: Council on Competitiveness, p. 35. Original source: Porter, M. E. and Stern, S. (1999) *The New Challenge to America's Prosperity: Findings from the Innovation Index*, Washington, DC: Council on Competitiveness.

11 Byron, K. (1998) 'Invention and innovation', *Science and Public Affairs*, Summer, Royal Society; Badden-Fuller, C. and Pitt, M. (eds) (1996) *Strategic Innovation*, London: Routledge.

12 Mintzberg, H. (1978) 'Patterns in strategy formulation', *Management Science* 24, pp. 934–48; Pavitt, K. (1994) 'Sectoral patterns of technological change: towards a taxonomy and theory', *Research Policy* 13, pp. 343–73.

13 Tushman, M. L. (1977) 'Communication across organizational boundaries: special boundary roles in the innovation process', *Administrative Science Quarterly* 22, pp. 587–605; Tushman, M. L. and Nadler, D. (1978) 'An information processing approach to organizational design', *Academy of Management Review* 3, pp. 613–24.

14 Slevin, D. P. and Covin, J. G. (1990) 'Juggling entrepreneurial style and organizational structure: how to get your act together', *Sloan Management Review*, Winter, pp. 43–53; van de Ven, A. H. (1986) 'Central problems: the management of innovation', *Management Science* **32**(5), pp. 590–607.

15 The idea of action-oriented innovation is promoted, for example, in Jones, O. (1992) 'Postgraduate scientists and R&D: the role of reputation in organizational choice', *R&D Management* 22, p. 4; Katz, D. and Kahn, R. L. (1966) *The Social Psychology of Organizations*, New York: Wiley; and Langrish, J., Gibbons, M., Evans, W. G. and Jevons, F. R. (1972) *Wealth from Knowledge,* London: Macmillan.

16 Kondratieff, N. D. (1935/51) 'The long waves in economic life', *Review of Economic Statistics* 17, pp. 6–105 (1935), reprinted in *Readings in Business Cycle Theory*, Irwin, Homewood, Ill. (1951).

17 Henry, J. and Walker, D. (eds) *Innovation*, London: Sage/Open University Press, Chapter 2, pp. 18–27; Perrow, C. (1970) *Organizational Analysis: A sociological view*, London: Tavistock.

18 Mayer, N. Zald (ed.) *Power in Organizations*, Nashville, Tenn.: Vanderbilt University Press; Henry, J. and Walker, D. (eds) (1991) *Managing Innovation*, London: Sage/OU Press.

19 Porter, M.E. (1990) *The Competitive Advantage of Nations* (p. 780), New York: Free Press; Roberts, E. B. and Fushfield, A. R. (1981) 'Staffing the innovative technology-based organization', *Sloan Management Review*, Spring, pp. 19–34.

20 Source: adapted from Friedman, T. L. (2005) *The World is Flat*, New York: Farrar, Straus and Giroux, pp. 341–5.

21 'Apple: the third act' and leader, *Economist*, 7 June 2007, pp. 63–7.

22 Nonaka, I. and Kenney, M. (1991) 'Towards a new theory of innovation management: a case study comparing Canon, Inc. and Apple Computer, Inc.', *Journal of Engineering and Technology Management*, 8, pp. 67–83.

UNDERSTANDING INNOVATION

LEARNING OBJECTIVES

After finishing this chapter, you will

▶ understand **features**, **constraints** and **figures of merit**

▶ understand how **'long tail' effects** foster innovation in digital markets

▶ understand the **components of innovation**

▶ understand how the profitability of innovation is influenced by **competences**, **complements**, **architecture** and **components**

▶ understand **science**, **technology** and **innovation**, and the inherent **risk** at each stage of **maturity**

▶ be able to classify innovations based on the degree of impact on firm operations

▶ be able to identify the main **mistakes** made by firms that fail in their attempts to innovate.

After reading the *innovation workout*, you will be able
to perform **attribute segmentation** to gain a new and
innovative perspective on a product, market or service.
After reading the Ford Model T *case study*, you will be able to identify
the roles of **knowledge clusters**, **luck**, **barriers to entry**, **theory**
and **customer understanding** in the success of the Model T.

Note: Further information, class slides, test questions and other
supporting material are available on our companion website at

www.palgrave.com/business/westland

THE SHIFT FROM RESEARCH TO DEVELOPMENT[1]

In the waning days of the Second World War II, Vannevar Bush, the senior science advisor to US President Franklin Roosevelt, laid out the blueprint that would dictate organizational and technological innovation for the next half-century. This blueprint saw separate roles for academia and industry. Universities *researched* 'basic science', publishing it in journals that industry could access to *develop products* for the market. In Bush's words, 'basic research is performed without thought of practical ends'.[2] Research & development (or R&D for short) was defined as two distinct activities. Organizations developed along the lines perceived by Bush, keeping research scientists safely apart from the more pragmatic engineers. The approach spawned numerous successful university research groups as well as commercial labs like Xerox PARC, AT&T Bell Labs and IBM's Zurich Research Laboratory. These were places where basic science was done, to later be handed over to industry by the production and marketing departments.

Modern technology firms are much less vertically integrated than the quasi-monopolies of AT&T, IBM and Xerox were in their heydays. Modern firms also face shorter product cycles than companies in the 1950s and 1960s, when new computers, telephone handsets or switches might appear every 5 years, rather than every 5 months. In contrast, Google epitomizes the contemporary R&D doctrine, where CEO Eric Schmidt contends that you cannot isolate researchers. The 'smart people on the hill' method no longer works. 'Researchers have become intellectual mercenaries for product teams: they are there to solve immediate needs.'[3] Failure is an essential part of the process, and employees are encouraged to 'please try to fail very quickly' so that they can try again.

How innovation affects consumer prices

Even in a single country, a monetary value measure is a difficult thing to tie down. For example, since 1900 average consumer prices in the United States have grown 20-fold, or an average of about 3 per cent a year. Additionally, the variations are large between products. Goods or services that have benefited from large productivity gains, thanks to technological improvements and mass production, have seen large price falls in real terms. The prices of telephone, electricity, bicycles and cars have all fallen. In 1900 a car, then hand-made, cost over US$1,000. Henry Ford's original Model T, introduced in 1908, cost US$850, but by 1924 it cost only US$265: he was using an assembly line, and in a virtuous circle, was also selling far more cars. Over the century, the real price of a car fell by 50 per cent. The figures also overstate the true increase in unit price, because they do not take account of

improvements in quality. The automobiles of 2000 were much more comfortable, reliable and faster than cars of 1900.

Substitutes have given consumers choices that they did not have in 1900. For example, a consumer might have been tempted to take his car to an orchestral concert in 1900; in 2000, he might be tempted to download the MP3 files for the same musical renditions at a fraction of the cost of the original concert.

Where such substitutes are not an option, as in labour-intensive services – for example hotel rooms and orchestra seats – prices have increased in real terms.

The computer did not exist in 1900. From 1990 to 2000, the price of a personal computer came down 40 per cent annually, and the cost of a unit of computer processing power fell nearly 100 per cent over the decade.

As the breadth of research areas available in science has expanded, so has the potential to spend money on research that will never yield tangible benefits. As a consequence, firms are increasingly blurring the distinction between 'R' and 'D' into a continuum which directs basic research towards product teams who work with the scientists to move those technologies out of the lab and into the marketplace. Not surprisingly, researchers who matured during the years that 'R' and 'D' were distinct activities find it hard to adjust to this new reality.[4] It is one thing to come up with blockbuster products when you can over-engineer with an unlimited budget; it is another to innovate within the given budgets and timeframes of commercial product life-cycles.

The new 'R' and 'D' continuum requires smart, energetic and flexible minds that can innovate on the fly. It also requires flat organizations that communicate quickly and widely, and outsource as soon as it is clear that the requisite expertise and resources reside outside their own laboratory. As a consequence, research policy at IBM, Hewlett-Packard and Microsoft are directed towards avoiding the inefficiencies resulting from hand-outs. Paul Horn, who oversees IBM's research, asserts that 'technology transfer' is a bad phrase at IBM, where researchers are expected to stay with their ideas all the way through manufacturing.

There are two problems with technology transfer (the formal handover of ideas from laboratory scientists to manufacturing engineers).[5] First, this handover of responsibility provides many opportunities for delay and attribution of blame for any problems in the technology. And second, it reinforces a false and archaic hierarchy of 'pure science' over product engineering, to the detriment of modern firms, which tend to be flat and egalitarian. These problems bedevil university laboratories and science parks as well, a topic we shall revisit in Chapter 13.[6]

Flat management structures and short product cycles are partly responsible for the blurring of 'R' and 'D', but a greater impetus comes from the trend towards innovating in software rather than hardware.[7] For example, in the 1980s a new model of single lens reflex (SLR) camera might innovate on the shutter, focus screen, film advance mechanism, or numerous other tangible physical components. But a comparable camera in 2007 lacks a physical shutter, a focus screen or any film at all. It is essentially a small standardized computer, image chip and lens, with components shared across competing manufacturers.[8] Market-differentiating innovation occurs in the software and firmware, where development times are fast, and the internet is expected to deliver any updates to the existing base of consumers who have purchased a particular brand. Corporate innovation today demands that basic research be reflected in the product before, during and even after its sale.[9]

Source: 'The price of age', *The Economist*, 23 December 2000, pp. 91–3.

INNOVATION FOR MARKETABILITY: FEATURES, CONSTRAINTS AND FIGURES OF MERIT

This book asks you to take a big leap of faith, and accept that innovation is not about zippy 'new' technology, design or marketing. It is instead all about new combinations and configurations of *features*, limited only by the *constraints* imposed by existing technology.[10] Economist Paul Romer has observed that the big advances in our standard of living have always come from 'better recipes, not just more cooking'.[11] The overall desirability of these collections is measured by a *figure of merit*. A figure of merit is a quantity used to characterize the performance of an item relative to other products or services of the same type. It is often used as a marketing tool to convince consumers to choose a particular brand.[12]

Thinking about innovation in this way frees us from a host of inbred biases about what is 'new' or 'high-tech' or 'cool and interesting'. It forces us to focus on what some set of customers will want, what some set of technologies can produce, and how we are supposed to know when we've finally developed the best product or service possible. Almost every failure of a promising innovation can be attributed to the inventor's inability to honestly maintain this sort of focus on the innovation goal.[13]

A product or service feature is a prominent or distinctive aspect, quality or characteristic; one that potential consumers would consider to be particularly attractive or to provide an inducement to purchase. The process of developing an innovation is fundamentally the process of deciding which combination of features to bundle into a product or service, and what priority each feature has in the overall product design.

Innovation would be easy if all that was necessary was the selection of desirable features. Unfortunately, *each feature carries with it both desirable and undesirable characteristics*. The undesirable characteristics constrain what we can do with a feature. Of foremost concern is the *cost constraint* – there is often a direct correlation between desirability and cost. Cost-conscious consumers will of necessity limit their purchase of a costly product or service, no matter how otherwise desirable it is, if only because they are constrained by their own limited budgets. Constraints will also arise from *technology* – for example, if battery power is limited – or by prior legal claims – an innovation may infringe on *copyrights* and *patents* owned by others.

THE LONG TAIL

Innovations provide the primary means for differentiating a product from its competitors. This was not always so. In the days before affordable global logistics, and the internet's instantaneous free information transfer, consumers had little knowledge of competitors' products, and less of a chance to buy, even if they truly wanted to. Companies could grow rich on brand loyalty, local monopolies and control of retail distribution. But the globalization and informatization of the world economy has steadily chipped away at local monopolies, leaving producers little choice but to differentiate.

Chris Anderson, editor of *Wired* magazine and author of *The Long Tail*,[14] complains that local monopolies subject consumers to 'the tyranny of lowest-common-denominator'. The problem is that most decisions about consumer choice are actually the result of poor matching of supply and demand; they are a market response to poor logistics and inefficient distribution. The problem is that we live in the physical world, and until recently most of our product information and entertainment did so as well. That constrains products to local audiences. An average cinema will not show a movie unless it can attract at least 1500 people over a two-week run; that's essentially the rent for a screen. An average record store needs to sell at least two copies of a CD per year to make it worth carrying; that's the rent for a half inch of shelf space. There are similar calculations to be made for DVD rental shops, video game stores, booksellers and news stands. In each case, retailers will carry only content that can generate sufficient demand to pay its rent, drawing from a limited consumer population – perhaps a 10-mile radius for a typical cinema, less than that for music and bookstores, and even less for video rental shops.

Shelf space and the long tail

Robbie Vann-Adib is CEO of Ecast, an online music company which offers more than 150,000 tracks. Vann-Adib was interested in finding what percentage of his top 10,000 titles would rent or sell at least once a month. Most people would guess 20 per cent, because we've been trained to think in terms of the 80–20 rule, formally known as Zipf's law, after the Harvard linguistics professor who popularized the concept. In the physical world this is true: only 20 per cent of major studio films, television shows, games and mass-market books will be hits. The odds are worse for major-label CDs, where fewer than 10 per cent are profitable, according to the Recording Industry Association of America.

In contrast, Vann-Adib says that 99 per cent of his top 10,000 titles sell or rent. Each month thousands of people pay for songs that no traditional record store has ever carried. With no shelf space to pay for, purely digital services, no manufacturing costs and hardly any distribution fees, a miss sold is just another sale, with the same margins as a hit. A hit and a miss are on equal economic footing, both just entries in a database called up on demand, both equally worthy of being carried. Suddenly, popularity no longer has a monopoly on profitability.

When retailing migrates to the internet, physical constraints imposed by shelf space and transportation costs disappear, leading to interesting developments in consumer behaviour. Rhapsody, a subscription-based streaming music service owned by RealNetworks, currently offers a selection of more than 735,000 MP3 format music tracks. A look at the demand statistics for individual tracks shows an exponentially decreasing demand curve that looks much like any record store's, with huge demand for the top hits, tailing off quickly for less popular music. A physical music store carries from 4000 to 25,000 CDs, or 40,000 to 300,000 songs, with the amount of fluid inventory – the songs carried that will eventually be sold – of around 40,000. Beyond this point, the Wal-Marts of the world simply stop carrying any more music.

The Rhapsody demand, in contrast, keeps on going. Not only is every one of Rhapsody's top 100,000 tracks streamed at least once each month, the same is true for its top 200,000, top 300,000 and top 400,000. As fast as Rhapsody adds tracks to its library, those songs find an audience, even if it's just a few people a month. This is the 'long tail'. Its implication is that there is a paying, reachable customer base that allows for an infinite degree of product differentiation. Innovation, and lots of it, is the way to reach customers on the long tail. There is every indication that as customers are presented with more choice, more innovation and personal customization, they come to demand this of their retailers. Physical music stores can no longer compete against the extensive selection offered by Rhapsody, iTunes or Amazon stores.[15]

Apple Computer's chief designer talks about innovation management

Jonathan Ive says:

I think one of the things we are good at as a team is gently moving these fragile ideas along a bit so they become just a little more robust and you can actually start to see what they are. So we go from those sorts of discussions and then we just make lots and lots of prototypes. Then we spend a lot of time at the manufacturing sites. We'll be there right to the end when we're in production.

If you are going to design something that's going to be truly innovative, my experience has been that this will require the company that's going to make it to change – often to change fundamentally – in its approach to how it develops products, how it evaluates them, how it makes them, and how it markets them. We try very genuinely to design products that solve problems. They are not about self-expression. What we are trying to do is design something that when you

see it you really wonder if it's been designed at all because it seems so obvious and so inevitable and so simple.

We don't make very much stuff. That's a very important part of our approach to what we do, which is to not do a lot of unnecessary stuff but just to focus and really try very sincerely to care so much about the few things that we do.

We love taking things to pieces and understanding how they are made. We will figure something out that seems relatively interesting and we'll spend some time in Northern Japan talking to the master about how we can form metal in a certain way. As you truly understand that, that obviously informs your design rather than it just being an arbitrary shape.

Source: Interview with Jonathon Ive, Radical Craft Conference, Art Centre College of Design, Pasadena, 25 March 2006.

From the producer's perspective, this makes some of the old business models redundant, and creates pressure to innovate to provide a range of new products, business models and distribution channels. How can we do this profitably? It requires improving supply and demand matching. On the supply side, producers need to understand their core competences and limitations; on the demand side, they need to know their customers intimately. Innovation on the supply side creates new *inventions*. Innovation on the demand side creates new *commercial opportunities*: new solutions, new learning, new channels, new customer bases.[16]

WHEN DO YOU HAVE AN 'INNOVATION'?

By its very definition, you are very likely to know when you stumble across an innovation – the fact that what you have found is new to you, your customer or your employer makes it an 'innovation'. But because of its newness, you are just as unlikely to know its value.

Innovations are often conceived in terms of new product market opportunities. But to be successful, they must align with the competences and assets of the firm (see Figure 2.1). The consequences of misalignment are poor production and channel efficiency; and the prospect of rivals outdoing the firm.[17]

No innovation has value until it is 'completed' and 'complemented' in various ways through the various processes of innovation management. Figure 2.2 shows the essential components required for product innovation.

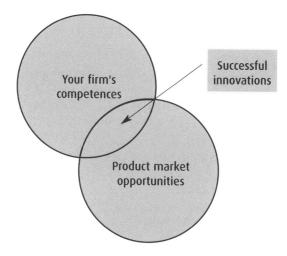

Figure 2.1 Competences and opportunities

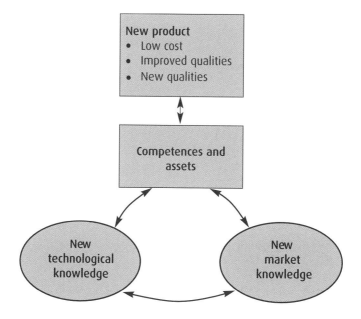

Figure 2.2 Elements of product innovation

THE NATURE OF INNOVATION

A widely used definition of innovation is that it is *an invention that has been commercialized* (a definition first articulated by Chris Freeman and Luc Soete in their book *The Economics of Industrial Innovation*).[18] The 'innovation = invention + commercialization' characterization immediately offers several insights. First, new ideas may arise in either the technology behind the invention, or the marketing, logistics, networking and design strategy behind the profitable sale of that invention. Second, to succeed requires a holistic perspective on management of the innovation process: innovations will not come about by R&D staff inventing whatever they fancy, then throwing it over the fence for Production to make, and Marketing to sell.[19] All specialities in the firm are needed at all phases of the innovation's life-cycle if it is to be a success.[20] Finally, the factors that can make your innovation a success – either marketing or technological – may be neither under your control, nor available at all times. Successful innovation demands that the firm be sensitive to 'windows of opportunity' where competitive dynamics give it firm a chance to promote a new product, and where technology is advanced enough to make it possible to design an attractive product at an attractive price.[21]

Figure 2.3 shows how the life-cycle of an innovation follows a curve that is known as the Foster S-curve. The early part of the S-curve is a period of idiosyncratic development, before standards or deep understanding of the technology exist. There are typically many competing theories and trajectories, promoted by strong and volatile egos, making any investments highly risky. As understanding evolves, standards are established, and technology advances incrementally, generally through sober research, investment and hard work. Depending on the inherent complexity of the technology, several situations confront the investor in innovation, as shown in Figure 2.4.

The physical limits of the S-curve are constrained by the limits of scientific knowledge; often technology alone cannot push it back. For example, it has been predicted for some time that the advance of computing will stall as chip architecture scales down to a level where quantum effects prevail, ostensibly some time before 2020. In order to continue to double computing power every two years, as we have since the 1930s, we need a breakthrough. The next breakthrough seems likely to come from experiments with quantum computing. In the past, major breakthroughs in computing pushed back physical limits about every 20 years, first when gears and solenoids were replaced

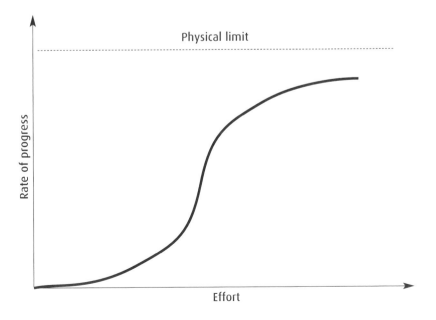

Figure 2.3 The life-cycle of an innovation (the Foster S-curve)

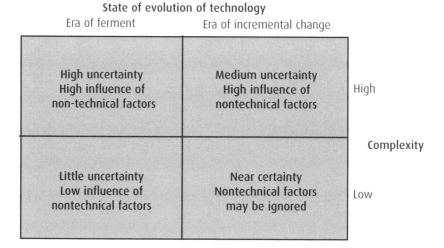

Figure 2.4 Uncertainty and the evolution of technology

by vacuum tubes in the 1940s, then with transistors in the 1960s and large-scale integration in the late 1970s.[22] The result is a series of stacked S-curves (see Figure 2.5).

What is necessary here is fundamental science, where the objective is discovery. Technology's objective is more focused on delivering usable inventions to consumers (whoever they may be). Some of the most important consumers of technology are the scientists themselves, who benefit from automation and better measuring tools.[23] For example, the sequencing of the human genome was one of the great breakthroughs of

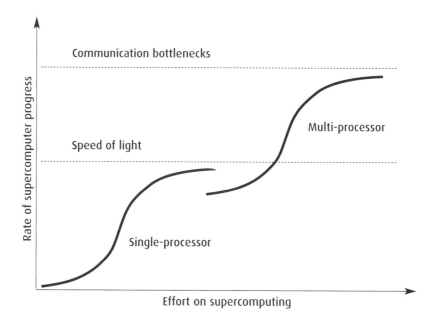

Figure 2.5 Stacked S-curves yield exponential performance growth over time

the twentieth century, and was made possible by the development of robotic chemists to do the physical work, aided by powerful supercomputers to do the sorting, matching and storage of gene sequences and proteins. Science and technology feed each other in the virtuous cycle shown in Figure 2.6.

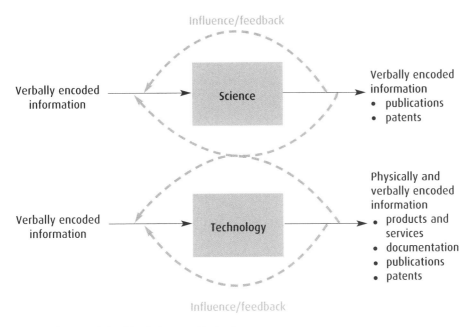

Figure 2.6 The interrelationship of science and technology

Science generates commercial technologies in three phases. The first 'fluid' phase marks the prototyping of laboratory technologies for custom applications in highly profitable areas such as the military. At this stage, there are still unanswered questions in the underlying science, and standards have not been established. Quantum computing, in its current development, is more or less at this stage. The second 'transitional' phase begins standardizing components, and defining consumer–producer relationships that will ultimately lead to a dominant design. In 2006, Sony's Blu-Ray optical recording technology based on blue diode lasers could be considered to be in the 'transitional' phase. In the last 'specific' phase, a dominant design has emerged and proliferated, with mostly incremental innovation around this dominant standard. DVD optical technology is at this stage.

In a series of studies of the profitability of business innovations, William Baumol of New York University found that on average only around 20 per cent of the value generated by innovations through improved productivity and lowered cost was realized by their inventors; the remainder was passed on to the consumer. Variance was high between markets, and markets with stiff price competition tended to pass most of their profits on to consumers. Competition was not the only factor in this result. Many innovations depend on complementary assets in order to be attractive to customers. Automobiles are only attractive where there are roads, petrol stations and safety provided by rules of the road; sports cars may be unattractive where speed limits are restricted; MP3 players are more attractive where online stores provide a wide selection of downloadable tracks; desktop computers are useful only if software exists to run on them. These complementary assets may be tightly controlled by their owners – for example, iTunes by Apple and WindowsXP by Microsoft. Other complements, such as roads, may be offered as public goods paid for through excise taxes. Figure 2.7 shows how complementary assets affect the profitability of an innovation.

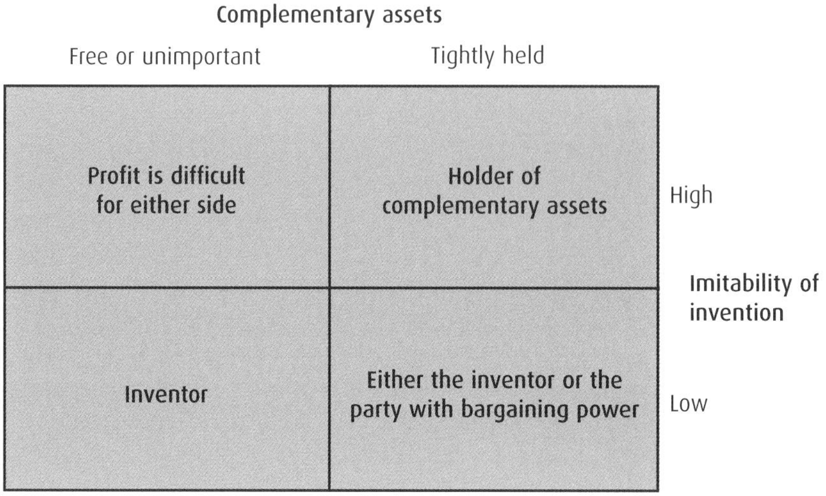

Complementary assets

	Free or unimportant	Tightly held	
	Profit is difficult for either side	Holder of complementary assets	High
	Inventor	Either the inventor or the party with bargaining power	Low

Imitability of invention

Figure 2.7 Who profits from innovation

Even without competitors, there are some inventions that are better suited for some companies than others. This is because every organization has certain things that it does better than its competitors, others that it does adequately, and others that it doesn't do well at all. The degree to which a company has 'competence' in an area determines its set of 'core competences'. Specific inventions will do better at companies with specific competences: in the laboratory, marketing, production or another area. The 'coreness' of an innovation's needs determines how well it is likely to do at a particular firm, as is shown in Figure 2.8.[24]

If there is no match between the innovation's needs and the core competences of the firm, then the firm cannot expect to compete in this innovation. If there is a match, then the profitability of the innovation will be determined by barriers to entry – how easily the product can be imitated.

There may, in addition, be interactions between the technology and the market. This interaction is covered at length in the chapter on disruptive innovation, but for now it can be summarized in the Abernathy–Clark categorization of types of innovations as niche, incremental, revolutionary, and architectural (see Figure 2.8).

Abernathy and Clark were concerned with the impact that particular innovations have on firms' core competences and their markets. Incremental innovations (such as that from Windows 2000 to Windows XP) preserve both competences and markets;

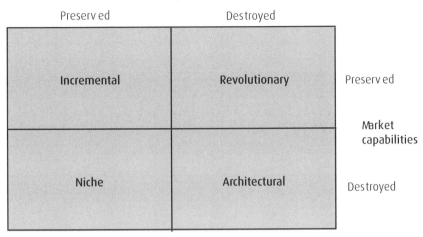

Technical capabilites

Preserved   Destroyed

| Incremental | Revolutionary | Preserved |
| Niche | Architectural | Destroyed |

Market capabilities

Figure 2.8 The Abernathy–Clark classification of innovations

Source: *Abernathy and Clarke (1985).*

revolutionary innovations create new markets, leaving old ones behind. Where a firm's market capabilities are destroyed, the firm's technology may still serve a niche community (for example, high-end audio still has demand for vacuum tube amplifiers, despite the general move to solid state technology). Where both core and niche markets are destroyed, the firm needs to shift rapidly to survive (as did Kodak's film business in response to the move to digital photography).

Henderson and Clark looked at how innovations affect the firm's processes for making and marketing a product (that is, its architectural knowledge) and its knowledge of the components of the product (its component knowledge) (see Figure 2.9).[25]

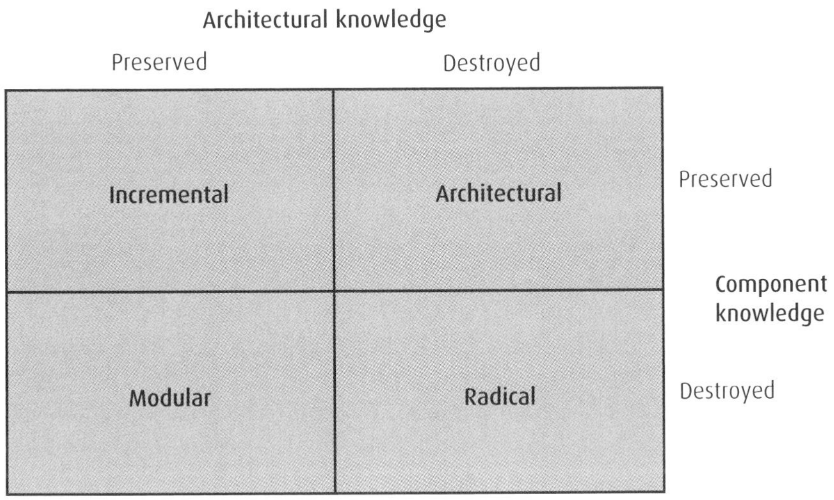

Architectural knowledge

Preserved   Destroyed

| Incremental | Architectural | Preserved |
| Modular | Radical | Destroyed |

Component knowledge

Figure 2.9 The Henderson–Clark classification of innovations

Incremental innovations preserve both aspects of the firm's production and market-ing; radical innovations destroy both, forcing the firm to move on to new products. In between, there are modular innovations which keep production and marketing chan-nels intact, so long as the firm can acquire the component expertise needed to produce the innovation – for example when Microsoft externally acquired technology from Sybase in order to remain competitive in database technology. Architectural innova-tions may arise in response to the loss of demand for products, when the organization rearranges components to come up with an ostensibly different product serving a dif-ferent customer base. For example, Niklas Zennstrom and Janus Friis, the entrepreneurs who created the peer-to-peer music sharing site Kazaa, repurposed their technology after legal pressures forced them to rethink the market for music downloads. The result was the popular Skype Internet telephone service which was then sold to eBay.

HOW BUSINESS GETS INNOVATION WRONG

One source of the high level of risk in innovating arises from some common failures to accurately identify the nature and role of innovation in business. This is almost always a product of too restrictive a view of innovation. Where decision making is constrained by organizational 'stovepipes' (that is, departments that compete with each other for resources rather than collaborating towards the success of a business) and vanities of the 'not invented here' kind (a lazy attitude which dictates that the firm should not look outside its own people for new ideas), these risks can run rampant.[26] Table 2.1 describes common myths about innovation; and Table 2.2 describes the manner in which department activities can become confused with innovation.

Table 2.1: *Common myths about innovation*

Myth	Reality
1. Innovation is about creating exciting new products	Much of the world's innovation goes unseen (though not unappreciated). For example, the process of drying consumes around 10 per cent of the world's energy, and innovation has improved efficiency dramatically in the past two decades. You are unlikely to hear much about these innovations, because they are architectural. They make production more efficient and controllable, offering consumers lower prices and higher quality.
2. Innovation requires 'crazy' creativity	This myth of the 'mad scientist' is enduring, and promoted by some of the more successful innovators. But it belies the reality of hard-nosed management required to create a truly exciting customer experience.
3. Innovation is expensive and takes time	Some fields, like pharmaceuticals, take time and money; others are not as resource intensive. In either case, not innovating is even more expensive in the long run.
4. Innovation requires hundreds of product ideas because failure rates are high	Every innovation has its own 'life-cycle' of application. Effective innovation management assesses the maturity and profitability of innovations at every phase and eliminates or sidelines projects that cannot contribute. Good managers will concentrate on just a few of the most profitable innovations to avoid losing focus.

Table 2.1: *Common myths about innovation* (continued)

Myth	Reality
5. Metrics, financial and otherwise, can assure the right innovation and technology choices	Only in the broadest sense. Accounting and financial metrics were designed for industrial economies with heavy physical resource usage. We still do not have good metrics for managing innovations; this is one significant source of innovation risk.

Source: *Rothwell, R. (1992) 'Successful industrial innovation: critical factors for the 1990s', R&D Management, 22(3), pp. 221–39.*

Table 2.2: *How to confuse innovation with something it isn't*

Mistake	Reality
Innovation with R&D	A common mistake in old-line corporate bureaucracies, which see R&D as the innovation 'stovepipe' and the people who will make the company innovative. It is also called 'the not invented here' syndrome, or just NIH. In fact, R&D departments typically develop less than 10 per cent of the products that ultimately go on to become blockbuster innovations.
Consumer understanding with consumer marketing	Marketing is mainly about conveying messages to consumers; in contrast, understanding consumers' activities, needs and dynamics can suggest product innovations. Marketing has few tools to directly assess the needs of innovators.
Design with design strategy	Design looks and feels nice; design strategy conveys a message – often subtle – about the company's product. Design strategy uses design as a tool to achieve an end.
Innovation with technology	Innovation = invention + commercialization. New technology may underlie invention, but it is only a small part of innovation.
'Out of the box' thinking with innovation	Like technology, 'out of the box' thinking underlies new inventions and approaches to commercialization; but it is only a part of the process of innovation management. As Thomas Edison once noted, invention is 2 per cent inspiration and 98 per cent perspiration.

Source: *Rothwell, R. (1992) 'Successful industrial innovation: critical factors for the 1990s', R&D Management, 22(3), pp. 221–39.*

Attribute segmentation

Reductionism is the attempt to explain complex phenomena or structures by reducing them to simpler parts and principles, such as by asserting that life processes or mental acts are instances of chemical and physical laws. We accomplish this through segmenting ideas into smaller and smaller component ideas.

Complexity is created by the character of a product or service, and this in turn is influenced by the numerous attributes on which character is assessed, and the difficulty of making trade-offs between these attributes. For example, in choosing a new watch, we might trade off accuracy for stylishness (in choosing a watch with a mechanical movement), thickness for functionality (as in choosing a thin Swatch or Movado over a bulky chronometer), and so forth. Marketing research analyses these trade-offs in terms of attributes of the watch – bezel, band, crystal, movement, face and hands. Together these attributes form a watch; separately they can be refined into sub-attributes, each with its own characteristics. To change the consumer's perception of the character of this watch, the designer doesn't start from scratch, but alters individual attributes – material used, cost, error tolerances and so forth. The ability to list the various attributes of a problem and work on one attribute at a time is the key to successfully tailoring a product (such as a watch) to a given consumer market.

Different individuals will define attributes differently. When listing the attributes of a design or problem, think of them simply as a general list of components. You may have to revise your list several times before you are satisfied that you have captured the real character of a product or service. To help in this process consider various ways to organize and differentiate attributes:

▸ descriptions: substance, structure, colour, shape, texture, sound, taste, odour, space and density

▸ activities: marketing, manufacturing, selling, function and time
▸ values: responsibilities, politics and taboos
▸ economic factors: cost to manufacturer, delivery cost, profit per unit, marginal cost.

For example, the attributes of a retail bank may be perceived in terms of activities (internet banking, private banking, commercial banking) or in terms of economic factors (low interest rates for depositors, zero-balance account handling, overdraft coverage). HSBC, Wells Fargo and Chase aimed for mass market (activities) banking using highly integrated internet banking operations in pursuit of low-cost (economic) computer interfaces at transaction processing; Rothschild & Cie Banque has grown through private investments in Eastern Europe, taking on high-risk investments (economic) by working the Rothschild family business networks (activities).

By examining the individual attributes that make up a bank, we can devise many alternative business models for making money in the banking industry. See if you can quickly devise three more combinations of attributes that would define a specific banking market. How might a changed economic environment force each bank to change its business model?

Blueprint

1. Frame the challenge.
2. Analyse the challenge and list as many attributes as you can.
3. Take each attribute, one at a time, and try thinking of ways to change or improve it. Ask, 'How else can this be accomplished?' and 'Why does this have to be this way?'
4. Clearly articulate your product, service or business model as a smoothly integrated collection of attributes.

Case study: Ford's Model T

The automotive industry evolved in the centre of a 'knowledge cluster'. Detroit had grown to become America's premier motor and machine tool centre over the 19th century as a result of the Great Lakes shipping industry. Ships laden with iron ore from Duluth would travel through the St Lawrence Seaway, delivering their cargo to smelters in Pittsburgh (next to Pennsylvania's coal fields). They stopped halfway at Detroit, where a burgeoning industry built up around steam, then diesel, engines on the ships. The development of 'portable' versions of these engines was a natural move in Detroit.

Nearly 300 different cars were made and marketed in 1908 (often little different from each other). In 1909, 18 new firms began building cars; in 1910, 18 went bankrupt. Financiers worried about the exposure, as most were run by technicians rather than businesspeople. By 1914 there were only 50 auto companies; by 1925, the year that Walter Chrysler started his company, over half of the cars sold were either Ford or GM; and the bursting of the stock-market bubble in October 1929 winnowed the automotive field to these three.

Henry Ford's technology was not radically different from that of his 300 competitors, and he started late as well (not unlike Bill Gates and Microsoft). But what catapulted him from relative unknown to kingpin was his defiance of the Selden Cartel. In 1895 George Selden, a Rochester, New York lawyer who had never built a car, applied for and received US patent number 549160 for an internal combustion engine. The patent was purchased by a consumer watchdog group, the Selden Patent Group, which operated as a trust, similar to the Edison and Eastman cartels trying to regulate the newborn cinema. It used the patent to collect royalties, and to decide who could build cars, and how many they could build if permission was granted. Cantankerous Midwest farm boy that he was, Henry Ford refused to pay their royalties, or to let the Selden Cartel regulate his firm's production, prompting a lawsuit in 1903 which Ford eventually won in 1910. The trial and his widely reviled adversaries gave Ford a public relations coup that made him an immediate folk hero.[27]

The Model T was not only a better car in 1915 than it was in 1908; it also sold at half the original price. There was no obvious increase in material, labour or overhead invested in each car (in fact, the latter two obviously dropped). Instead, Ford's systemization and automation of production followed the principles of Fred Taylor's scientific management.[28] Fred 'Speedy' Taylor, father of the stopwatch-and-clipboard approach to factory management, showed Ford and his managers during 1913 the time and motion techniques that had been implemented with so much success by Isaac Singer (sewing machines), Cyrus McCormick (reapers) and Samuel Colt (firearms). 'Speedy' Taylor's *ideas* about the production of cars *replaced materials, labour and overheads* that had previously been required to produce a Model T. In Ford's 'Taylorized' Highland Park plant, one man could now do what three or four had done before. This knowledge leaked off to his competitors in no time. Within 10 months, Willie Durant (again with the help of Taylor) adapted the assembly line to assembling Chevrolets in Flint, Michigan.[29]

A Ford Model T (originally painted in red, green, blue and grey varnishes, but in black after Henry Ford discovered in 1914 a superior Japanese paint which only came in black) cost US$850 (a teacher's salary) in 1908. It came without speedometer, windshield wipers or even doors, and the gas gauge was a long thin stick that the owner had to find for himself and insert into the tank. By 1915, assembly lines had allowed Henry Ford to incorporate speedometers, wipers and doors, and still lower the price to $440. It was down to $295 by 1925.

'Taylorized' mass production made farm boy Henry Ford so rich that in 1914, embarrassed by his riches, he took 20 per cent off the retail price of a Model T. When the result was even more sales, he announced that if 300,000 Americans bought Model Ts in 1914 he would return US$50 to every buyer – a gesture that ultimately cost him $15 million. Next he raised the pay of his 13,000 workers from $2 per day to $5 per day. The raise was so steep (GM paid around $2.35 per day) that the *New York Evening Post* exclaimed it 'a magnificent act of generosity'. In contrast, the *Wall Street Journal* accused Ford of 'economic blunders if not crimes' by injecting 'spiritual principles into a field where they do not belong'.[30]

Much of the move toward mass production in those days involved standardizing parts and processes; it was a process of making transactions routine. Alfred Sloan, the legendary boss of GM, learned one of his first lessons in efficiency as a GM supplier at Sloan's Hyatt Company, which made roller bearings. The dressing down came from Henry Leland, founder of Cadillac, for the tolerances he allowed in his roller bearings. With calipers in hand, Leland showed Sloan the discrepancies in bearing diameters, commenting, 'You must grind your bearings even though you make thousands, the first and the last should be precisely alike.'[31] Leland walked Sloan over to a window, showed him a pile of rejected Weston-Mott axles, and told him that unless he could guarantee bearings ground to within a thousandth of an inch in accuracy, the Hyatt products would also end up on the scrap heap. Only precision to within a thousandth of an inch made parts interchangeable.

Ford Model T case study: questions for review

1. Describe how the early automotive industry parallels other more recent technologies.

2. Why do you think that the automotive industry developed in a 'knowledge cluster'? How might this drive the pace, and provide investment for the new auto companies?

3. How was the US patent system used to stifle creativity?

4. Why do you think Ford as a company prevailed despite the fact that it did not possess better technology? How did it benefit from a combination of good marketing, good technology, sound production and luck?

5. Much of Ford's success resulted from replacing materials, labour and machines with knowledge. Describe this process.

6. The benefits from the technology accrued mainly to customers (in better quality and lower prices) and workers (in higher wages). Why?

7. Ford's manufacturing innovations made the industry more competitive and less profitable. Do you think that this contributed to the bursting of the stock market bubble in 1929?

8. Efficiency improvement through automation was largely a procedure of standardizing parts and processes – in other words, making transactions routine. How does routinization bring about reduced costs, faster and more efficient production?

9. Ford's substitution of technology for human effort was not a one-to-one replacement of man by machine; rather, it was a more subtle process whereby three people could do the task formerly allocated to four. Is this typically the way automation impacts firm economics, or is it unique to Ford?

CHAPTER QUESTIONS FOR REVIEW

1	Describe the differences between research, development, production and commercialization. How is each complementary or supplementary to the others?
2	Choose three items within your field of view at this moment, and provide for each the 'figure of merit' that best conveys what makes that item good or bad.
3	The box 'How innovation affects consumer prices' looks at how the purchase price of various goods and services has changed over the century. Can you think of any single characteristic that would explain in general why there have been declines and increases in purchasing power?
4	What accounts for the S-shape – slow performance increases, followed by acceleration, followed by levelling off – in the performance of particular technologies? Consider the countervailing forces of (1) consumer demand for products using the technology; and (2) idea generation for improvements in the technology.
5	The initial (flat) part of the S-curve has sometimes been called the 'era of ferment', whereas the rapidly increasing centre of that curve has been called its 'era of incremental change'. How does uncertainty in understanding and applying the technology to practical problems influence the evolution of that technology's performance?
6	In what ways are science and technology complementary disciplines?
7	Choose two items within your field of view at this moment. Consider for each the impact of complementary products, imitability of the product, and the technical and market capabilities of the firm that makes these products. How much unit profit do you think is made on each unit? Would you describe either of these as a luxury product? A commodity product?

CHAPTER 2: KEY POINTS

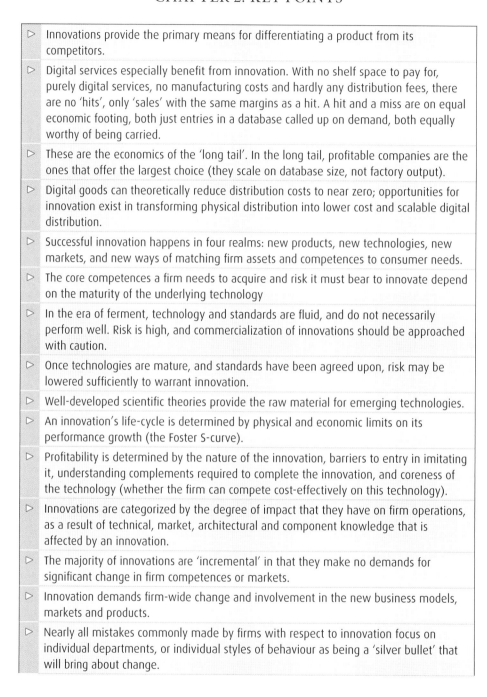

▷ Innovations provide the primary means for differentiating a product from its competitors.

▷ Digital services especially benefit from innovation. With no shelf space to pay for, purely digital services, no manufacturing costs and hardly any distribution fees, there are no 'hits', only 'sales' with the same margins as a hit. A hit and a miss are on equal economic footing, both just entries in a database called up on demand, both equally worthy of being carried.

▷ These are the economics of the 'long tail'. In the long tail, profitable companies are the ones that offer the largest choice (they scale on database size, not factory output).

▷ Digital goods can theoretically reduce distribution costs to near zero; opportunities for innovation exist in transforming physical distribution into lower cost and scalable digital distribution.

▷ Successful innovation happens in four realms: new products, new technologies, new markets, and new ways of matching firm assets and competences to consumer needs.

▷ The core competences a firm needs to acquire and risk it must bear to innovate depend on the maturity of the underlying technology

▷ In the era of ferment, technology and standards are fluid, and do not necessarily perform well. Risk is high, and commercialization of innovations should be approached with caution.

▷ Once technologies are mature, and standards have been agreed upon, risk may be lowered sufficiently to warrant innovation.

▷ Well-developed scientific theories provide the raw material for emerging technologies.

▷ An innovation's life-cycle is determined by physical and economic limits on its performance growth (the Foster S-curve).

▷ Profitability is determined by the nature of the innovation, barriers to entry in imitating it, understanding complements required to complete the innovation, and coreness of the technology (whether the firm can compete cost-effectively on this technology).

▷ Innovations are categorized by the degree of impact that they have on firm operations, as a result of technical, market, architectural and component knowledge that is affected by an innovation.

▷ The majority of innovations are 'incremental' in that they make no demands for significant change in firm competences or markets.

▷ Innovation demands firm-wide change and involvement in the new business models, markets and products.

▷ Nearly all mistakes commonly made by firms with respect to innovation focus on individual departments, or individual styles of behaviour as being a 'silver bullet' that will bring about change.

NOTES

1   'The rise and fall of corporate R&D', *Economist,* 3 March 2007, pp. 69–71.

2   Quoted in Tiberius, R. (2002) 'Educational abstracts', *Academic Psychiatry,* 26 (June), pp. 128–30, June 2002.

3   Schmidt, E. and Varian, H. (2005) 'Google: ten golden rules', *Newsweek*, 2 December.

4   Rothwell, R. (1976) 'Innovation in the UK textile industry: some significant factors in success and failure', Science Policy Research Unit, Occasional paper series 2, June; Slevin, D. P. and Covin, J. G. (1990) 'Juggling entrepreneurial style and organizational structure: how to get your act together', *Sloan Management Review*, Winter, pp. 43–53.

5   Katz, D. and Kahn, R. L. (1966) *The Social Psychology of Organizations*, Wiley, New York; Langrish, J., Gibbons, M., Evans, W. G. and Jevons, F. R. (1972) *Wealth from Knowledge,* Macmillan, London.

6   See also Bell, D. (1999) *The Coming of the Post-Industrial Society*, New York: Basic Books reissue edition (May) for an early prediction of the rise of these problems.

7   Henry, J. and Walker, D. (eds) *Innovation*, Sage/OU Press, London, Chapter 2, pp. 18–27; Perrow, C. (1970) *Organizational Analysis: A sociological view*, Tavistock, London.

8   Tidd, J. (2000) *From Knowledge Management to Strategic Competence: Measuring technological, market and organizational innovation*, Imperial College Press, London.; Tidd, J., Bessant, J. and Pavitt, K. (2001) *Managing Innovation*, 2nd edn, Wiley, Chichester.

9   Van de Ven, A. H. (1986) 'Central problems: the management of innovation', *Management Science*, **32**(5) pp. 590–607; Wolfe, R. A. (1994) 'Organizational innovation: review and critique and suggested research directions', *Journal of Management Studies*, **31**(3), pp. 405–31.

10 Burgelman, R. A. (1983) 'A process model of internal corporate venturing in the diversified major firm', *Administrative Science Quarterly*, 28, pp. 225–44; Porter, M. E. (1985) *Competitive Advantage*, Boston, Mass.: Harvard University Press.

11 Romer, Paul (1990) 'Endogenous technological change', *Journal of Political Economy*, **98**(5), pp. 71–102.

12 Allen, T. J. (1977) *Managing the Flow of Technology*, Cambridge, Mass.: MIT Press; Baumol, William (2002) *The Free Market Innovation Machine*, Princeton, N.J.: Princeton University Press.

13 Mintzberg, H. (1978) 'Patterns in strategy formulation', *Management Science*, 24, pp. 934–48; Pavitt, K. (1994) 'Sectoral patterns of technological change: towards a taxonomy and theory', *Research Policy*, 13, pp. 343–73.

14 Anderson, C. (2006) *The Long Tail*, New York: Hyperion. In his book, Anderson attributes the term to a paper by MIT professor Erik Brynjolfsson, who used it in reference to the right-skewed probability distribution of consumer choice as product choices proliferate.

15 Source: *Wired*, issue 12.10, October 2004.

16 Tidd, J. (2001) 'Innovation management in context, organization and performance', *International Journal of Management Reviews*, **3**(3).

17 Chesbrough, H. W. and Teece, D. (1996) 'When is virtual virtuous? Organizing for innovation', *Harvard Business Review*, Jan–Feb, 11, pp. 65–73.

18 Freeman, C and Soete, L. (1997) *The Economics of Industrial Innovation*, 3rd edn, Cambridge, Mass. MIT Press. Freeman and Soete's definition is widely adopted among academics studying innovation.

19 Jones, O. (1992) 'Postgraduate scientists and R&D: the role of reputation in organizational choice', *R&D Management*, 22, p. 4.

20 Tushman, M. L. and Nadler, D. (1978) 'An information processing approach to organizational design', *Academy of Management Review*, 3, pp. 613–24; Utterback, J. M. (1975) 'The process of technological innovation within the firm', *Academy of Management Review*, 12, pp. 75–88.

21 Rothwell, R. (1976) 'Innovation in the UK textile industry: some significant factors in success and failure', Science Policy Research Unit, Occasional paper series 2, June; Slevin, D. P. and Covin, J. G. (1990) 'Juggling entrepreneurial style and organizational structure: how to get your act together', *Sloan Management Review*, Winter, pp. 43–53.

22 Tushman, M. L. (1977) 'Communication across organi-zational boundaries: special boundary roles in the innovation process', *Administrative Science Quarterly*, 22, pp. 587–605.

23 For example, see comments in Sheene, M. R. (1991) 'The boundness of technical knowledge within a company: barriers to external knowledge acquisition', paper presented at R&D Management Conference on the Acquisition o' External Knowledge, Kiel, Germany.

24 Henderson, R and Clark, K. B. (1990) 'Architectural innovation: the reconfiguration of existing product technologies and the failure of established firms', *Administrative Science Quarterly*, 35, pp. 9–30.

25 Clark, P. and Staunton, N. (1993) *Innovation in Technology and Organization*, London: Routledge; Gundling, E. (2000) *The 3M Way to Innovation:*

Balancing people and profit, New York: Kodansha International; Heilemann, J. (2000) 'The truth, the whole truth, and nothing but the truth, *Wired*, November, pp. 68–127.

26 A number of examples are provided in Mayer, N. Zald (ed.) (1970) *Power in Organizations*, Nashville, Tenn.: Vanderbilt University Press; Henry, J. and Walker, D. (eds) (1991) *Managing Innovation*, London: Sage/OU Press.

27 Roberts, E. B. and Fushfield, A.R. (1981) 'Staffing the innovative technology-based organization', *Sloan Management Review*, Spring, pp. 19–34.

28 Taylor, F. (1947) *Scientific Management*, New York: Harper & Row. Despite his popularity as a 'business guru', Taylor continued to provide such services at his customary fee of US$35 per day.

29 Madsen, A. (1999) *The Deal Maker*, New York: Wiley, p. 92.

30 Madsen, A. (1999) *The Deal Maker*, New York: Wiley, p. 83.

31 Madsen, A. (1999) *The Deal Maker*, New York: Wiley, p. 112.

ASSESSING THE POTENTIAL OF AN INNOVATION

LEARNING OBJECTIVES

After finishing this chapter, you will

▸ understand that your **core capabilities consume your resources**; that your **innovations are responsible for generating future resources** to support the acquisition of future capabilities

▸ understand the steps for **assessing the potential demand** for an innovation

▸ be familiar with the **innovator's mindset**, and understand that innovation is seldom radical and completely new

▸ recognize that most innovation is **incremental**, **reconfiguring** and **redifferentiating** existing services, business models and products

▸ be familiar with the innovator's *analysis toolkit* consisting of:
  ▸ **quizzing**, and organization of resulting insights through **mind maps**
  ▸ the **consumption chain**
  ▸ the **feature map.**

After reading the *innovation workout*, you will be able to perform **mind mapping** to organize quizzing insights gained about a product, market or service.
After reading the Viagra *case study*, you will be able to identify the roles that **commercialization strategies play in reconfiguring** the market for an existing product.

Note: Further information, class slides, test questions and other supporting material are available on our companion website at

www.palgrave.com/business/westland

THE MYSTERY OF DEMAND

The greatest unknown in any innovation is consumer demand. Demand forecasts are better seen as tools that help decide between alternatives than any real prognostication of future wealth. That is not all bad – an understanding of the way in which decisions are made needs to precede any informed assessment of a new innovation.

The ideal consumer in economic models is a rational economic being who carefully weighs the beneficial features of a product against its cost. In practice, of course, this is not what happens; consumer behaviour departs from 'rationality' because of individual quirks in our thinking processes. Some of these are atavisms: useful when we lived as hunter-gatherers, less so in the modern world. Human decision makers suffer from limited processing capabilities, emotional swings which impact decisions, and tend to be motivated by appearances as well as outcomes.[1]

Investment decisions have been studied the most (this is where the money is) focusing on three particular 'irrationalities' which are systematic and robust:

- ▸ overconfidence
- ▸ loss aversion
- ▸ salience.[2]

When investors are overconfident, they tend to overestimate the precision of their knowledge and their abilities. Overconfidence has several implications. Overconfident investors believe their own valuations and worry less about the beliefs of others, leading to speculation and a high volume of trading. Overconfident investors overweight their personal signals, and when those signals are correlated (as might be expected), this increases volatility and makes prices less informative. Overconfident investors trade more than 'normal' investors and lose money. Men are in general known to be more overconfident than women, and do worse than women on their investments: on average men earn 6.9 per cent less than the market, while women earn only 4.1 per cent less.[3]

Loss aversion and regret avoidance occur because it usually hurts a consumer more to lose $1000 than it gives pleasure to gain $1000. Loss aversion tends to cause investors to sell winning stocks too soon and hold losing stocks too long; collect a gain now, but put off taking a loss until later.[4] In product markets, regret avoidance motivates consumers who have already purchased a product to look for and read only material that confirms the 'wisdom' of their prior purchase. Disconfirming evidence is ignored. This can be a problem for new entrants in a product market.

Fender's tube amplifiers: second life for a winning sound

Old technology can sometimes have hidden attractions which are not noticed until consumers begin to deal with their technologically more sophisticated replacements. Leo Fender – famous for his eponymous guitars and amplifiers – developed products with just such attractions. In the 1950s, to complement his then 'radical' electronic instruments, he built portable amplifier-speaker consoles. He didn't design his amplifiers in the 1950s with any thought of the controlled and sustained overdrive, nor any of the other vacuum tube amp qualities that guitar players have come to crave. In fact his first amp designs were straight out of the RCA vacuum tube handbook.[5]

With the help of field tests with musicians, Leo Fender created a physically and electronically reliable design to withstand use and abuse by touring performers. It just happens that the combination of his robust design, and the natural overdrive characteristics of tubes, produces the trademark Fender sound we came to love.

Electronics subsequently evolved into more robust, compact and powerful transistor platforms. Unfortunately, early solid-state amplifiers became infamous for their harshness and limited dynamic range, caused almost entirely by the super-clean sound and wide frequency response up to their maximum output, after which the onset of clipping occurred quite abruptly and harshly. The attack of notes (that bit immediately after the note is struck) pushes the amplifier briefly into the clipping region, producing a 'squashy, spitting' sound at the start of each note. If the amplifier is overdriven well into the clipping region, the type of overdrive was typically very dirty and unmusical.

Russell Hamm, in his seminal study 'Tubes versus transistors: is there an audible difference?'[6] found that bass and guitar amplifiers are often severely overloaded by signal transients. The transistor characteristics that guitarists and bassists dislike are buzzing, white-noise sound and the lack of 'punch'. The buzz is directly related to the 'edge' (like the edge of a square wave) produced by overloading on transients (like the high-amplitude attacks on individual notes). This white noise contains edge harmonics like the seventh and ninth which are not musically related to the fundamental.

Vacuum-tube amplifiers differ from transistor amplifiers because they can be operated in the overload region without adding objectionable distortion. The combination of the slow rising edge and the open harmonic structure of the overload characteristics forms an almost ideal sound recording compressor. Within the 15 to 20 dB 'safe' overload range, the electrical output of the tube amplifier increases by only 2 to 4 dB, acting like a limiter.

Tubes also sound louder and have a better signal-to-noise ratio because of this extra subjective head room that transistor amplifiers do not have. Tubes get punch from their naturally brassy overload characteristics. Since the loud signals can be recorded at higher levels, the softer signals are also louder, so they are not lost in tape hiss and they effectively give the tube sound greater clarity. The feeling of more bass response is directly related to the strong second and third harmonic components which reinforce the 'natural' bass with 'synthetic' bass. In the context of a limited dynamic range system like the phonograph, recordings made with vacuum-tube preamplifiers will have more apparent level and a greater signal to system noise ratio than recordings made with transistors or operational amplifiers.

So why is this important? The sound of a tube power amplifier moving into and out of its clipping region is the sound that many bassists and guitarists crave. Additionally, musicians perceive vacuum tube-based instrument amplifiers to be noticeably louder than the same-power solid state amplifier. This occurs because of the logarithmic response of our hearing. For example, a 100 watt amp sounds only a little more distorted when trying to deliver 110 watts. This means that you can drive the amp quite hard with a 'musically pleasant' amount of overdrive which sustains a volume level at the amplifier's maximum power capability. As the note decays, the volume level changes little while the sound gradually cleans up (sometimes referred to as a 'warm bloom').

How ironic that in an era of blistering computational power in cheap boxes, we are still trying to capture the analogue sonic character of Leo Fender's classic early amps. Leo's designs gave a characteristic full and punchy sound, suitable for many styles of the day, and later. Steel and country players like the chime-like clean sounds, and blues players were quick to discover the classic way the sound breaks up when the amp is pushed hard. The Fender company to this day counts vacuum tube amplifiers among its most successful product lines, despite the availability of cleaner, cheaper, more powerful transistor designs.

Consumer avoidance of disconfirming evidence is related to a third 'irrationality', which concerns the evidence that investors choose to accept as true. People generally tend to anchor on salient evidence. They overweight evidence that is vivid and captures attention; they prefer stories rather than data. They tend to be less critical of the source of information if they like the message. And they tend to overweight evidence that supports their existing belief and do not collect disconfirming evidence.[7]

Recent research by Thomas Griffiths and Joshua Tenenbaum[8] provides evidence that decision making under uncertainty is decidedly Bayesian, with priors drawn from a small set of conjugate distributions. Anecdotal evidence abounds for a Bayesian basis for human decision making among computer scientists trying to design software with human-like intelligence. Bayesian reasoning lies at the heart of leading internet search engines and automated 'help wizards', and assumptions are often made that the brain copes with everyday judgements in the real world in a Bayesian manner. Griffiths and Tenenbaum found that Gaussian (normal), Poisson, Erlang and power-law prior distributions lay at the root of much human decision making – including the decisions that eventually influence and constitute consumer demand. Contrary to assertions suggesting it is impossible to model irrational decision making, Griffiths and Tenenbaum suggest that the 'irrationality' we see in the consumption of goods and other human decision making follows specific distributions and methods, and that Bayesian models of decision making are an effective tool for predicting both 'rational' and 'irrational' consumer behaviour.

Where corporations acquire their technology

Innovations and new technology can be acquired from many sources. Traditionally internal development was the most popular approach, because it assures close tailoring of the resulting products to the firm's product lines and production strengths, and helps the firm gain ownership of the technology. Today, many innovations require technologies that are so complex (this is especially true in biotechnology) that licensing technology from multiple sources is unavoidable, and increasingly critical components for innovation are licensed from outside the firm.

Table 3.1: *Sources of new technology in large corporations c. 1985*

Method of acquisition	Process innovation	Product innovation
Independent R&D	1	1
Licensing	2	3
Publications or technical meetings	3	5
Reverse engineering	4	2
Hiring employees of innovating firm	5	4
Patent disclosures	6	6
Conversations with employees of innovating firm	7	7

Source: R. E. Levin, 'Appropriability, R&D spending, and technological performance', *American Economic Review* (May 1988), pp. 424-8, a survey of 650 executives in 130 industries on the methods that US firms use to acquire new technology on process and product innovations.

Griffiths and Tenenbaum allude to statistical tools that are beyond the scope of this book. Nonetheless, their basic presumption is the motivation for much of the remainder of this chapter – that consumer irrationality can not just be understood, but products can be optimized to take advantage of the peculiarities of consumer decision making. The next sections present a methodological approach to designing products, complementary services and consumer experiences that – irrational as they may be – will maximize the profitability of the innovation.

EXPLORING POTENTIAL DEMAND FOR AN INNOVATION

An invention does not become an innovation until its commercial potential is developed – a process with many steps which may extend over years. During the time that the organization is exploring the potential demand and profitability of a new business model, product, idea or other invention, that invention resides in its opportunity register – a log book of ideas that are not yet complete products or services.[9]

Thomas Edison pioneered the opportunity register in the 1870s, first at his New York laboratory, and then at his expanded Menlo Park (New Jersey) facility. Edison would jot down idea after idea in his personal notebooks – many only half thought-through in barely legible scrawls (shown in Figure 3.1). His subordinates would be offered a percentage of the profits on any commercial products that they were able to pull out of these notes, of course with the promise of Edison's reputation and market clout to help them along. It was one of the first examples of corporate profit sharing in the world.[10]

The first steps towards understanding whether an innovation has commercial potential (and thus whether it should be pursued or left in the opportunity register until such commercial opportunities arise) require asking questions about the customers' potential use and perception of this invention. We accomplish this through a process of successive refinement – by means of a series of tasks – of feature set, complements and market niches which hold commercial potential.[11]

Phase I: Quizzing: cursory *feature mapping* to identify market-differentiating features of the innovation; mind maps to cluster and prioritize the features that will influence potential customers.[12]

Phase II: Consumption chain analysis: identification of *target demographic groups* and particular activities that would involve the innovation.

Phase III: Detailed feature map for each *feature x demographic group x activity* to identify necessary product features for the innovation.[13]

Innovations may be conceived in terms of new product market opportunities, but to be successful, they must align with the competences and assets of the firm (see Figure 3.3).[14] The consequences of misalignment are poor production and channel efficiency; and the prospect of rivals beating the organization.[15]

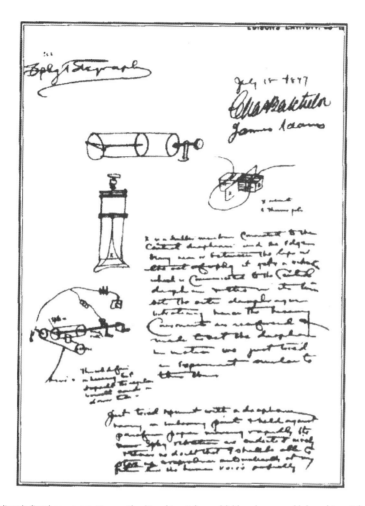

Figure 3.1 Edison's first known notation on the 'Speaking Telegraph' (the phonograph) from his notebooks

Source: Niel Baldwin (1995) *Edison*, Chicago University Press, p. 81.

To this point, we have focused on the character of innovation, as well as misconceptions and biases that may keep individuals and firms from achieving their greater creative potential. Thus armed with a sound theoretical understanding of innovation, we can move on to studying some tools and techniques that can help us generate innovations that satisfy specific pairs of firm competences and market opportunities. In this section we introduce three tools: quizzing, consumption chain analysis and feature mapping, for testing new ideas and inventions against existing market and supply realities.

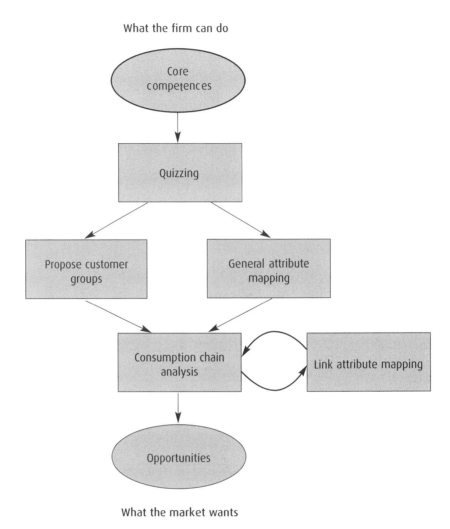

What the firm can do

What the market wants

Figure 3.2 Tools for assessment of potential customer demand

QUIZZING

> I keep six honest serving-men
> (They taught me all I knew);
> Their names are What and Why and When
> And How and Where and Who.
> I send them over land and sea,
> I send them east and west;
> But after they have worked for me,
> I give them all a rest.
>
> Rudyard Kipling following the story 'Elephant's child' in *Just So Stories*

Quizzing offers the innovator an unstructured, open-ended approach for making a comprehensive analysis of customer usage and decision making regarding a product.

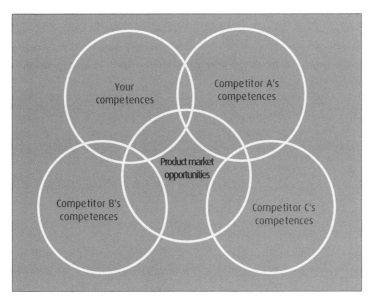

Figure 3.3 Mismatch of markets and competences

The goal is not just to understand a customer group, but to identify new potential users. The approach takes a free-form, 'stream of consciousness' contemplation of a potential customer's perspective via a series of questions. The stream of consciousness approach is closely identified with the Bloomsbury Group in English thought, which championed investigation through the set of constantly changing inner thoughts and sensations that an individual has while conscious. The Bloomsbury Group sought to describe an individual's point of view by giving the written equivalent of the character's thought processes. May Sinclair transferred 'streaming's' context from psychology to the literary context, where figures such as Virginia Woolf, E. M. Forster and Clive Bell in literature, Vanessa Bell, Duncan Grant, Dora Carrington and Roger Fry in art, John Maynard Keynes and Leonard Woolf in economics and Saxon Sydney-Turner in music, sought to apply it to the widest range of topics.

Quizzing brings these elitist concepts into our pragmatic world of products and customers. It is our first attempt to understand where we can innovate; our first attempt to understand potential customers and their experiences using proposed products and services. Specifically it looks for ideas that hold the power to change your customers' experience.[16] Because experience is dynamic, so must be the questions in quizzing. The basis for quizzing is a simple sequence of questions: what, who, when, where, how and why:

▶ What is the problem?
▶ Who (which individual in the case) is responsible for solving the problem and making a decision?
▶ Where is the money (the value generated by the solution)?
▶ When does the problem need to be solved?
▶ How will you measure success?

▶ Why did you have this problem, and what will you do to prevent it in the future?

▶ Who is with customers while they use the product?

▶ How much influence do they have?

▶ If you could arrange it, who would you want the customers to be with?

▶ What do your customers experience?

▶ What else might customers have on their minds??

▶ When do your customers use this?

▶ Where are your customers when they use this?

▶ How do customers learn to use the product?

Quizzing, properly done, will generate an avalanche of insights, ideas and modifications to the invention, and the addition of features that had not been initially obvious. But this embarrassment of riches also brings a need to bring order to chaos; to prioritize and reduce the choices the innovator needs to make. The innovation workout for this chapter explains how to organize the output of quizzing through a method popular among Silicon Valley technology firms: the mind map, which has been promoted by top design consultancies such as Ideo.

It is at this point that the firm must make a fundamental calculation – will the product compete only on price (that is, will it be a commodity product), or will it be differentiated in some other way from competitors that will allow the firm to charge a premium? Unless your firm is the sole holder of a new cost-reducing technology, or is very rich with world-class production or logistics, it is unlikely that competition on price will be attractive. The innovator's challenge is to differentiate the goods from the competitor's to gain a competitive advantage – even if only temporary, and even if only with a niche customer group.

3M and Norton[17]

Minnesota Mining and Manufacturing (3M) began life in 1904 as a failure – two years of mining for gem-grade rubies and sapphires had yielded only common corundum. 3M's owners spent that winter pondering just what to do with their investment, before finally moving into the decidedly less glamorous grit-and-sandpaper business (one of the few uses for common corundum). For the next decade, 3M struggled with low margins, excess inventory and cash flow crises. In 1914 it promoted William McKnight, an accountant turned sales manager still in his 20s, to be general manager. One of McKnight's first investments was in a sink and glue bath for a small storage room, thereby turning it into the firm's 'laboratory'. Steady experimentation yielded the first success in a cloth abrasive named 'Three-M-Ite' (which remained in 3M's product catalogue for the next 75 years). This and other successes developed in McKnight (and 3M as well) an unrelenting curiosity and drive for progress through innovation, which has become the hallmark of the company today, but back then was a determined, one could say desperate, drive to keep the company in business.

McKnight, knowing that he would one day step down, sought to design an organization that would continually evolve and innovate.[18] Among the quotes attributed to him are:

Listen to anyone with an original idea, no matter how absurd it might sound at first.

Encourage; don't nitpick. Let people run with an idea.

Hire good people, and leave them alone.

If you put fences around people, you get sheep. Give people the room they need.

Encourage experimental doodling.

The extensive questioning of customer experience achieved through quizzing establishes a context in which the innovator can understand, predict and explore the customer's experience. Quizzing can help you find new business by suggesting differing demographics, different activities, and different features in the product, service and customer experience.

3M and Norton (part 2)

Norton was founded in 1885, when a group of seven investors bought a grinding-wheel company from Frank Norton to capitalize on the growing market for grinding wheels for the expanding machine tools industry. The company was always successful, multiplying its capital 15 times in the first 15 years of its existence; by 1990 it was and has remained the largest abrasives company in the world. Norton's success grew from its good management through classical planning and control approaches. It determined what it did well (its competences); grew its asset base around those competences, and dominated a market that is in many ways not that much changed from a century ago.

Military theorist Karl von Clausewitz once observed that 'detailed plans fail, because circumstances inevitably change'. Thus you might be forgiven for asking, 'what if?' What if Norton's customers suddenly found an abrasive-free, laser-powered,

environmentally friendly industrial smoothing process which made Norton's technology obsolete overnight? This sort of disruptive change has happened so often in other industries that it might just be possible that Norton was lucky all along.

But Norton failed in one way. Its conservative stance caused it to miss out on substantial new markets as they arose. As Figure 3.4 shows, from 1914 until the Second World War 3M made only a fraction of the sales that Norton did. But its willingness to take on new challenges paid off handsomely in a growth spurt that has continued uninterrupted to the present day. Norton's failures have been 'opportunity costs' – cost of not gaining the markets and accompanying profits that might have been. With 3M for comparison, we have a relatively clear picture of what could have been for Norton as well, if only it had been more adventurous and innovative.[19]

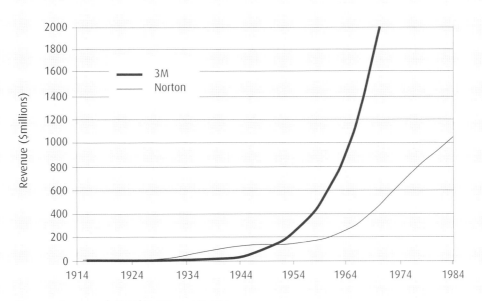

Figure 3.4 Revenues of 3M and Norton, 1914 to 1984

3M and Norton (part 3)

Jim Collins and Jerry Porras in their book *Built to Last* (1997) contend that what made 3M different from Norton, and ultimately able to expand far from its roots, was the 'ticking clock' that McKnight instilled in the company. McKnight's 'ticking clock' transcended the reigns of McKnight and managers that succeeded him.[20]

Give it a try – and quick!

When in doubt, vary, change, solve the problem, seize the opportunity, experiment, try something new (consistent, of course, with the core ideology) even if you can't predict precisely how things will turn out. Do something. If one thing fails, try another. Fix. Try. Do. Adjust. Move. Act. No matter what, don't sit still.

Accept that mistakes will be made

Since you can't tell ahead of time which variations will prove to be favourable, you have to accept mistakes and failures as an integral part of the evolutionary process. Even though 3M failed in the car wax business, if it had never entered it, it probably wouldn't have invented Scotch tape. Charles Darwin might have recommended 'multiply, vary, let the strongest live, and the weakest die' in order to have healthy evolution. Try enough experiments (multiply) of different types (vary), keep the ones that work (let the strongest live), and discard the ones that don't (let the weakest die).

Take small steps

It's easier to tolerate failed experiments when they are just that – experiments, not massive corporate failures. Small incremental steps can form the basis of significant strategic shifts. Try becoming an 'incremental revolutionary', harnessing the power of small, visible successes to influence overall corporate strategy.

Give employees the room they need

When you give people a lot of room to act, you can't predict precisely what they'll do. Visionary companies hire and promote the best people, decentralize more, provide greater operational autonomy and allow people to be persistent.

Leadership tone is just the start

You need to translate intentions into tangible mechanisms. Good intentions or setting the right 'leadership tone' by themselves simply won't succeed.

For example, if you're a division manager, you achieve the 30 per cent new product goal. If you want to become a technical hero at 3M, you need to share your technology around the company. You need to continually create a successful new ventures with actual products, satisfied customers and profitable sales. If you cannot, then you should consider a different position either inside or outside the company.

WALKING THROUGH THE CUSTOMER EXPERIENCE

Quizzing and mind maps establish a context in which your invention will be polished, fine-tuned, and made attractive to potential customers. Through them, you will decide, first, for which customer demographic groups you will chose to design your product, services, marketing, production and logistics; and second, what features will differentiate your product from competitors, and how to prioritize by relative importance each of the features you have chosen.

Once you have honed in on the particular customers you are trying to impress, the next step is to walk through the customers' experience with each variation (that is, each unique permutation of the features you feel are important).

Figure 3.5 provides an example of a consumption chain for the purchase of an

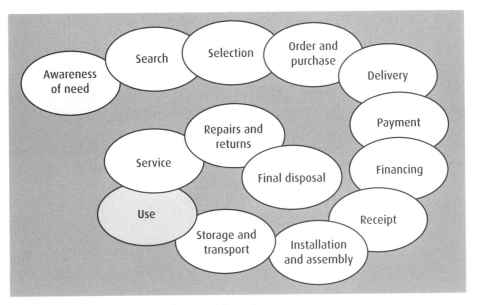

Figure 3.5 Customer consumption chain for automobile purchase

automobile. Each step of the chain represents an activity resulting in a choice: either the customer moves on to the next link, or he or she ceases to be interested in the product, in which case none of the subsequent links are visited. Moving the customer on to the next link requires that your product meet minimum product standards, and that it is differentiated from your competitors' products so that the customer gives it attention, and perhaps is excited enough about the innovation that it becomes a 'must own' product.

There will be a separate consumption chain for each potential customer group identified in the quizzing process. Walking through the consumption chain allows an evolutionary revision of the firm's business model and capabilities, through a continual tweaking and redesign of product and services offerings that so appeal to target customers at every stage of the process that they feel compelled to buy from you. Peter Drucker remarked that the purpose of a business is to create a customer; think of the purpose of the consumption chain as a way to create, attract and keep that customer along every step of your business model.

THE FEATURE MAP

There will be a distinctive set of features that define each step of a customer's experience. Customers may perceive a feature to be attractive (making it more likely that they will proceed to the next link of the consumption chain) or unattractive (leading them to lose interest in your product). This gives the innovator a chance to mould not only the product, but the entire consumption experience. This will help craft a collection of product features for the innovation that will ensure a higher likelihood that the customer will move on to the next link in the consumption chain. Feature maps and consumption chains formalize the documentation of customer activity in a way that allows it to be explored, to see how altering the design of the product can ensure maximum profitability of sales.

The enabler

Over the past few years, we've talked about technology as if it were a stand-alone product – something that either does or doesn't 'sell well'. But it is really an enabler for an awful lot of the great products that have made life better for all of us, including cars, computers, PDAs and phones.

Because technology enables these things, any broad recovery will be felt immediately in the technology arena. Tech is the sweetener in the lemonade, you might say.

Hector de J. Ruiz, chief executive officer, Advanced Micro Devices[21]

For each link in the consumption chain, innovators need to consider both the demand impact and the supply impact of a given feature. Two feature maps allow this to be studied on an ad hoc basis. The feature demand map is a 3×3 table that locates the customer's perception of the feature in terms of whether it is expected in such a product (that is, something basic); if it will somehow help to differentiate the product from competitors (a discriminator); or it will single-handedly galvanize a customer to make a decision about moving onto the next consumption chain link (an energizer).

Perceptions of features can be positive, negative or neutral. Ideally, a feature worth pursuing will be a *differentiator* (that is, discriminator that influences a positive move to the next stage in consumption) or an *exciter* (an energizer that incites a positive move to the next stage in consumption). *Dissatisfiers* and *enragers* are features either to be avoided; or if that is difficult, to be managed so that customers see them as tolerable.

Table 3.2: *Feature demand map*

	Basic	Discriminator	Energizer
Positive	Non-negotiable	Differentiator	Exciter
Negative	Tolerable	Dissatisfier	Enrager
Neutral	So what?	Parallel	

The feature supply map is a 2×2 table which 'reality checks' the incremental cost of adding the feature to the product. If the feature is compatible with the firm's current core capabilities (that is, its assets plus its competences) then any cost increases must be justified by assurances that customers are willing to pay a premium for the feature. If adding the feature requires non-core capabilities, the company will need to outsource these or acquire them itself. Both are expensive propositions involving infrastructure and organizational learning.[22] Typically they are only justified for radical innovations, and are likely to incur a high risk of failure.

Table 3.3: *Feature supply map*

	Core	Non-core
Increases cost	Incremental value must exceed incremental cost	Generally avoided
Decreases cost	Optimal	Cost reduction must be substantial to offset cost of acquiring capabilities

Most innovations add value and cost incrementally to products and services around which firms have built their core capabilities. Despite the disproportionate press given to radical innovations, the majority of innovations are mundane (and consequently not of great interest to the media). That does not absolve the firm of its responsibility for either radical or incremental innovation – it merely puts in perspective the proportionate effort the firm needs to spend on each type of innovation. Radical innovations set up temporary barriers to the entry of competitors until they can figure out how to duplicate the success. Incremental innovations, in contrast, keep firm personnel thinking, and make sure they are continually attuned to the needs of their customers. Radical innovations are risky, because technologies may prove unreliable, and customers need education about their value; their payoff is high. Incremental innovations exercise the creativity of the firm on a daily basis, with lower risk and easily managed failures.

CREATIVE TENSION

Even if you create marvellous inventions, your customers will not care unless those inventions are precisely what they think they will need. Business customers are especially impatient with any product that fails to help them gain competitive advantage. At the same time, your own firm cannot expect to maintain its competitive advantage unless the services and products, and all the complementary processes, lie mostly within the firm's core capabilities – its existing corporate inventory of assets and competences. Firms establish their core capabilities by investing in their people, investing in their assets and facilities, and firmly identifying and focusing on their mission. Core capabilities consume your resources; innovative services and products generate more resources. The creative tension within an innovative firm continually reviews and balances one against the other.

Mind maps

If Sherlock Holmes had a modern incarnation, it would be Inspector Rebus – the detective in Ian Rankin's whodunit *The Naming of the Dead*.[23] Rebus uses mind maps to chase down clues to crimes in a fashion similar to Holmes's use of 'deductive reasoning' to track down the bad guys.

Mind maps have, in one form or another, been used for centuries. Some of the earliest examples of mind maps were developed by Porphyry of Tyros in the third century to graphically visualize the concept categories of Aristotle.[24] Their modern incarnation is the (re)invention of pop-psychologist Tony Buzan, and is designed to draw people away from traditional outlines that require readers to scan left to right and top to bottom, instead of free-associating in a non-linear fashion, as

Buzan contended the brain actually works. Buzan emphasized the thinking *process* as opposed to the content. When you map a challenge, you can emphasize either individual thoughts or the challenge as a whole. Mind maps provide a technique for organizing your thought process. They create a geographical layout of the way your mind records, stores and manipulates information about a challenge; they help you see relationships between different parts of the problem.

Tony Buzan suggests using the following technique for mind mapping:[25]

1. Start in the centre with an image of the topic, using at least three colours.
2. Use images, symbols, codes, and dimensions throughout your mind map.

Figure 3.6 A mind map

3. Select key words and print using upper or lower-case letters.

4. Each word/image must be alone and sitting on its own line.

5. The lines must be connected, starting from the central image. The central lines are thicker, organic and flowing, becoming thinner as they radiate out from the centre.

6. Make the lines the same length as the word/image.

7. Use colours – your own code – throughout the mind map.

8. Develop your own personal style of mind mapping.

9. Use emphasis and show associations in your mind map.

10. Keep the mind map clear by using radial hierarchy, numerical order or outlines to embrace your branches.

Scholarly research[26] has found that the mind map technique results in a limited but significant increase in recall. To test the efficacy of mind maps in generating new insights, set yourself the challenge of developing a new pharmaceutical drug which you think will be able to generate more than $1 billion in revenues per year. What would this drug have to do to be a 'blockbuster'?

Case study: Viagra

In 1991, inventors Andrew Bell, Dr David Brown and Dr Nicholas Terrett (who were also employees at the Sandwich Kent European headquarters of Pfizer, the American pharmaceuticals firm) discovered that chemical compounds belonging to the pyrazolopyrimidinone class were useful in treating heart problems such as angina. Terrett was named in the 1991 British patent for sildenafil citrate (later tradenamed Viagra) as a heart medicine, and some experts consider him as the father of Viagra. Pfizer claims that hundreds of inventors were involved with the creation of Viagra and there was not enough room on the patent application to name them all, so only the department heads were listed. Dr Simon Campbell, who until recently was the senior vice president of medicinal discovery at Pfizer and oversaw Viagra's development, is considered by the American press to be the inventor of Viagra. Campbell himself preferred to be known as the father of Amlodipine (a cardiovascular drug), deferring to Terrett in this honour. 'I'm like Columbus,' commented Campbell (never the modest type), on Viagra's development.

Sildenafil's disputed paternity took a more interesting turn as doctors began noticing a remarkable side-effect. Though it had only been a mediocre reliever of angina, sildenafil was a reliable initiator of erections. Whatever questions surrounded the paternity of Viagra, the marketable product was undoubtedly the offspring of William C. Steere, Jr., the son of the prominent botanist William C. Steere, Sr. Steere was named to head the prescription drug division of Pfizer in 1985. Unlike his father, William Jr. had little inclination towards the academic, and had made his way to the top through the marketing ranks. A brilliant salesman and marketing tactician, Steere came to the job with a strong prejudice that the church-and-state division between marketing and R&D had outlived its usefulness (a conclusion drawn by most of Big Pharma in the free market environment of the Reagan years). Steere's modest aspiration was to make Pfizer, a perennial also-ran, into the largest pharmaceutical company in the world, an aspiration goaded by the fact that Merck was the perennial 800-pound gorilla of pharmaceuticals.

At a time when the reengineering movement was gaining traction, Steere reengineered Pfizer's drug pipeline around two new kinds of management teams for every new drug developed by the company: an Early Candidate Management Team and an Advanced Candidate Management Team. Out was the idea that the cloisters of R&D should be free from market guidance, or free to throw a drug over the fence, expecting marketing to take it from there. In-house synergies between marketing and R&D would ensure a pipeline of successful drugs. The Early Candidate Management Team would ensure that R&D knew the marketing prospects of candidate drugs as they were developing and testing them. This team would include representatives from research, marketing and sales, to maintain a steady dialogue that would direct diseases to which drugs might be applied, dosages, trials and so forth. Once the drug was ready for FDA submission, the first team would hand the portfolio over to the second, which was chaired by a marketing person. Steere explained that 'our goal was to communicate earlier on products to make sure that their development was such that when they entered the market, they'd be instant successes'.

Instant successes! Size matters! These were Steere's passions throughout the 1990s when Pfizer aspired to outperform its perennial rival Merck. Then came Viagra.

Never one to miss an opportunity, Steere put the compound through a crash screening process to come up with a marketable drug. Essentially, he asked marketing to 'find' a 'disease' that regarded an erection as a 'cure'. Marketing coined a condition with the uninspiring name 'erectile dysfunction' (ED) (what else would a doctor call the failure to get a woody?). Sildenafil was rechristened Viagra.

Unfortunately, there were details still to be worked out before Viagra could become an instant success. One of the stickier parts of FDA approval was that a drug was approved only for treatment of the specific malady specified in the FDA approval. Any other use (for example, of an angina drug for treating ED) would be considered 'off-label' and was strictly prohibited. Nor was there much chance that general practitioners were going to confuse angina and ED.

Fortunately, once the felicitous effects of Viagra were identified, Steere's in-house synergy worked brilliantly. The Medical Affairs Division funded studies on ED, and underwrote seminars on the subject. The salespeople were tutored on the biology of smooth muscle tissue (Erectile Anatomy 101), the physiological target of Viagra, as sildenafil was now called.

'Viagra crystallized some things I'd been thinking about' Steere told *Fortune* at the time. 'It struck me that a quality-of-life drug for aging would be a real winner. Look at the volume in cosmetics, which are basically nostrums that really don't do anything.' From Pfizer's standpoint, Viagra was a miracle drug: it cured a 'disease' of rich, pill-happy seniors, with only a few side-effects, none which couldn't be easily doctored.

Pfizer had also recently gained a powerful new tool in its marketing arsenal: direct-to-consumer advertising had been allowed by the FDA. In the 1980s, drugs in the United States were prescribed under the advice of physicians, and patients were carefully guarded from knowing anything that might possibly hurt them. This fitted well with the physicians' own view of their profession; as counsellors, rationers and demi-gods lording over patient health.

But Viagra, coming as it did after the FDA relaxed its rules on direct-to-consumer advertising, was not just a commercial success, but a cultural revolution in a pill. Where the baby boomers had oestrogen, 'the pill', in the 1960s, their older selves now had Viagra and Austin Powers to keep the revolution alive. Viagra changed the billion-dollar porn industry, which changed internet entertainment marketing. Viagra's presence was so huge, its medical legitimacy established so rapidly, that teenage ravers worldwide were popping 'V' with their 'X' (although why a bunch of 18-year-old males needed any help is anyone's guess, least of all Pfizer's R&D department).

Viagra's impact on Pfizer was (we can only use one word) huge. First-year sales were US$400 million (a then unheard-of figure). In the United States alone, physicians were writing 275,000 prescriptions for it a week. By 2000, worldwide sales were $1.5 billion. Large investors started calling Pfizer the best company in the industry; other companies were expected to perform as well. Bill Steere was a happy man (take that, Merck!).

None of this would have been possible in the old pre-Steere Pfizer, where R&D developed the product and threw it over to marketing for sale. Steere's synergies had propelled an also-ran – both the firm and the drug – to the front of the industry's ranks.

Not all was smooth sailing though, as many lawsuits surrounded Viagra, including a suit filed for $110 million on behalf of Joseph Moran, a car dealer from New Jersey, who claimed that he crashed his car into two parked cars after Viagra caused him to see blue lightning coming from his fingertips, at which point he blacked out. Moran was driving his Ford Thunderbird home from a date at the time. Yet Joseph Moran's unfortunate black-out was little more than a bump on the very profitable road to fulfilment.[27]

Questions for the Viagra case study

1. Some might say that the marketing strategy for Viagra, no matter how successful it ultimately was, severely tested some ethical principles. Would you agree? If so, what should Pfizer have done differently? How would they explain this action to their stockholders?

2. How many drugs or food products can you think of that might be amenable to Pfizer's strategy of asking marketing to 'find' a 'disease' that regarded that particular food or drug as a cure?

3. Can you make a case for the new tool in its marketing – the direct-to-consumer advertising that had been allowed by the FDA?

4. Can you make a case for not allowing direct-to-consumer advertising, and letting drugs only be prescribed under the advice of physicians? How then would you market drugs?

CHAPTER QUESTIONS FOR REVIEW

1	What do we mean by recognizing the potential of an innovation?
2	'Not-invented-here (NIH) syndrome,' 'I already know it (IAKI),' 'Prove it to me (PITM)' and 'How on earth could my firm possibly do that?' have been said to be innovation's worst enemies. Do you agree? Why or why not?
3	It has been suggested that the United States is more innovative than Asia or Europe. Do you agree or disagree? What is behind a national culture of innovativeness?

CHAPTER 3: KEY POINTS

▷ Core capabilities consume your resources; innovations are responsible for generating future resources to support the acquisition of future capabilities. Because of this strategy, companies must keep a resource-based perspective.

▷ These are the steps for assessing the potential demand for an innovation:
- For each customer segment sketch the consumption chain.
- Identify the trigger events that precipitate customer movement from link to link.
- Put in place procedures to alert you when the trigger is pulled (and plan your response).
- Quiz to assess needs that may not be met currently.
- Create a feature map for each significant link in the consumption chain.
- Use your knowledge of customer experience to create blockbuster services and products.
- Put the ideas you generate into your opportunity register.

▷ The innovator's mindset:
- Successful innovators are action-oriented.
- When moving fast (innovating), complexity creates confusion and delay.

▷ Innovators order and simplify complexity by:
- identifying generic business models and action strategies for innovation businesses
- stretching their own skills
- exercising their ability to capitalize on uncertainty and to take calculated risks.

▷ Innovation is seldom radical and completely new. Typically it is incremental, reconfiguring and redifferentiating existing services, business models and products, by reconfiguring existing value maps, or introducing entirely new kinds of solutions.

▷ Reconfiguration is about breaking down the barriers (technological, regulatory or organizational) that set limits on the features you can offer, or on the way that consumption chains can be configured. It builds on your insights from the consumption chain analysis and feature map, looking to remove the limitations imposed by existing core capabilities.

▷ Reconfiguration takes advantage of opportunities arising from the knowledge that underpins new innovations, the commercialization of those innovations, and the value flows generated.

▷ The analysis toolkit consists of:
- quizzing, and organization of resulting insights through mind maps
- the consumption chain
- the feature map.

NOTES

1 Smith, C. M. and Alexander, P. L. (1988) *Fumbling the Future*, New York: William Morrow.

2 Fiske, S. T. and Taylor, S. E. (1991) *Social Cognition*, New York: McGraw-Hill.

3 Von Hippel, E. (1994) '"Sticky information" and the locus of problem solving: implications for innovation', *Management Science* 40(4), pp. 429–39. The story of Singer's invention of the electronic cash register is based on 'The rebuilding job at National Cash Register: how Singer got the jump on the industry's top supplier', *Business Week*, 26 May 1973.

4 Hill, C. W. L. and Jones, G. R. (1995) *Strategic Management: An integrated approach*, Boston, Mass.: Houghton Mifflin, p. 352.

5 Gross, N., Coy, P. and Port, O. (1995) 'The technology paradox', *Business Week*, 6 March, p. 78.

6 Hamm, R. O. (1972) 'Tubes versus transistors: "is there an audible difference?"' *Journal of the Audio Engineering Society*, 14 September.

7 Lawrence, P. R. and Lorsch, J. W. (1967) *Organization and Environments: Managing differentiation and integration*, Homewood, Ill.: Irwin; March, J. G. and Simon, H. (1958) *Organizations*, New York: Wiley.

8 Griffiths, T. L. and Tenenbaum, J. B. (2006) 'Optimal predictions in everyday cognition', *Psychological Science* 45, pp 56–63.

9 The term 'opportunity register' was introduced by Rita Gunther McGrath and Ian MacMillan in their book *The Entrepreneurial Mindset* (Cambridge, Mass.: Harvard Business School Press, 2000).

10 Baldwin, N. (1995) *Edison*, Chicago, Ill.: Chicago University Press, pp. 79–89.

11 Howell, J. M. and Higgins, C. A. (1990) 'Champions of technological innovation', *Administrative Science Quarterly* 35, pp. 317–41; Iansiti, M. (1993) 'Real-world R&D, jumping the product generation gap', *Harvard Business Review*, May–June, pp. 138–47.

12 Allen, T. (1984) *Managing the Flow of Technology*, Cambridge, Mass.: MIT Press.

13 Christensen, C. M. and Bower, J. L. (1996) 'Customer power, strategic investment and failure of leading firms', *Strategic Management Journal* 17, pp. 197–218.

14 Hamel, G. M. and Prahalad, C. K. (1994) *Competing for the Future*, Boston, Mass.: Harvard Business School Press; Bettis, R. A and Prahalad, C. K. (1995) 'The dominant logic: retrospective and extension', *Strategic Management Journal* 16, pp. 5–14.

15 Clark, D. and Strecker, W. D. (1980) 'Comments on `the case for the reduced instruction set computer', *Computer Architecture News* 8(6), pp. 34–8; Clark, K. B. and Wheelwright, S. C. (1994) *Managing New Product and Process Development*, New York: Free Press; Clark, P. and Rutter, M. (1979) 'Task difficulty and task performance in autistic children', *Journal of Child Psychology and Psychiatry* 20, pp. 271–85.

16 Hambrick, D. C., Geletkanycz, M. A. and Fredrickson, J. W. (1993) 'Top executive commitment to the status quo: some tests of its determinants', *Strategic Management Journal* 14, pp. 401–18.

17 Collins, J. C. and Porras, J. I. (1994) *Built to Last: Successful habits of visionary companies*, New York: HarperBusiness.

18 The importance of this is reiterated many places in the literature: for example see Galbraith, J. R. (1982) 'Designing the innovating organization', *Organizational Dynamics* 10, pp. 5–25; Galbraith, J. R. (1974) 'Organization design: an information process view', *Inter-faces* 4, May, pp. 28–36.

19 Source: adapted from Collins, J. C. and Porras, J. I. (1994) *Built to Last: Successful habits of visionary companies*, New York: HarperBusiness.

20 Collins, J. C. and Porras, J. I. (1994) *Built to Last: Successful habits of visionary companies*, New York: HarperBusiness.

21 Overholt, A. (2002) 'Technorecovery?' *FastCompany* 60 (June), p. 61.

22 Cohen, W. M. and Levinthal, D. A. (1989) 'Innovation and learning: the two faces of R&D', *Economic Journal* 99, pp. 569–96.

23 Rankin, I (2006) *The Naming of the Dead*, London: Orion.

24 *Porphyry the Philosopher to Marcella*, Kathleen (1987) trans. W. O'Brien, place?: Society of Biblical Literature.

25 Buzan, T. (1991) *The Mind Map Book*, New York: Penguin.

26 Farrand, P., Hussain, F. and Hennessy, E. (2002) 'The efficacy of the "mind map" study technique', *Medical Education* 36(5), pp. 426–31.

27 References and quotations in this case study were provided by Critser, G. (2005) *Generation Rx: How prescription drugs are altering American lives, minds, and bodies*, New York: Houghton Mifflin.

BUSINESS MODELS

LEARNING OBJECTIVES

After finishing this chapter, you will

► be able to define a **business model** and know where the concept is applied in assessing an innovation

► understand what a '**scientific method**' for business analysis of innovation means, and that this is different from **strategy**

► understand that business models fail because they fail either to tell a convincing story or to support that story with convincing financial numbers

► understand the components of value mapping and how they are used to support a story, and generate financial projections of costs and revenues for an innovation.

After reading the *innovation workout*, you will be able to use **morphological boxes** to explore all the permutations of a product, market or service.
After reading the the Mad Catz *case study*, you will be able to identify the roles that **different components** play in **generating costs and revenues**.

Note: Further information, class slides, test questions and other supporting material are available on our companion website at

www.palgrave.com/business/westland

A 'SCIENTIFIC METHOD' FOR BUSINESS

Business modelling is the managerial equivalent of the scientific method – you start with a hypothesis, which you then test in action and revise when necessary. Unfortunately in practice, 'business model' and 'strategy' can be among the most sloppily used terms in business. Too often they are stretched to mean everything, but end up meaning nothing. They suffer from a fundamental lack of formal language.[1]

Business models earned a somewhat dodgy reputation during the dot-com era, where loosely knit promotional stories were used to justify huge wealth transfers from unsuspecting investors.

Beam me up

Entrepreneur Jay Walker invented Priceline.com, a reverse auction for airline tickets, going on to extend his concept to hotels, groceries and petrol. The 'story' as Walker told it was that consumers would tell him how much they wanted to pay for, say, a flight to Bali. Consumers could specify the price but not the airline. Priceline.com wanted to be a power broker for individual consumers. By representing the demand of millions of consumers, it would negotiate discounts and then pass on the savings to its customers, taking a fee in the process.

Through most of the dot-com years, Priceline's official spokesperson was *Star Trek*'s William Shatner, who agreed to do the spots for free in exchange for stock in the company. He was later 'replaced' by his *Star Trek* co-star, Leonard Nimoy (although Shatner still appeared in spots, running into Nimoy as his replacement). The arrangement turned out to be quite lucrative for Shatner, who sold most of his Priceline stock shortly before its value plummeted in the dot-com bust.

So what is wrong with 'the story'? The biggest problem was Walker's assumption that companies such as American Airlines – which had made huge investments in its own proprietary Sabre pricing, reservation and seat inventory system – would actually be interested in playing by Priceline's rules, and losing huge sums of money in the process. Airlines retaliated by collaborating on the prices they sent Priceline, effectively undermining its price search model. Walker's 'story' was myopic. It failed to see beyond the consumers' problem; it specifically failed to account for the complex of investments and dynamics on the vendor side. Walker's story was incomplete, and ultimately Priceline was forced to move to a traditional sales model where travellers are presented with prices which they can take or reject. Priceline's offerings in groceries and petrol (through partially owned affiliate WebHouse) were even less successful. In October 2000, WebHouse ran out of cash at the same time that it ran out of investors who were willing to put any more money into 'the story'.

What's in a name?

Motorola's Iridium satellite system was originally to have 77 active satellites, and as such was named for the element iridium, with a nucleus surrounded by 77 electrons. But to reduce cost, that number of active satellites was reduced to 66 early in planning. The element with atomic number 66 is called dysprosium, which in Greek means 'hard to get in contact with'. Understandably, the company was less than enthused with either the name dysprosium or its translation, and stuck with its original name.

In case anyone thinks internet entrepreneurs have a monopoly on flawed business models, think again. We tend to forget about ideas that don't work out, but business history is awash with 'stories' that on deeper inspection made little sense. Motorola invested US$3.5 billion in the Iridium system (the company incurred more than $6 billion in losses in its short life). Motorola's 'story' was that customers would pay a premium to be able to make phone connections anywhere at any time. To the delight of Motorola's engineers, Iridium more or less pulled off that technological feat, beginning operations in late 1998.

Nothing about the Iridium system was particularly innovative. The main patents on the system were in the area of mass production of satellites, designed by the same engineer who set up the automated factory for Apple's Macintosh, each contained a cluster of seven of the Macintosh's PowerPC 603E 200MHz CPU chips. But with a $3,000 price for a massive Iridium phone, plus international calling rates of up to $14 a minute, the company brought in only 15,000 customers before declaring Chapter 11 bankruptcy on 13 August 13 1999.

In late 2000, a group led by ex-airline executive Dan Colussy paid $25 million for the entire network (about 0.4 per cent of its original cost) which now primarily serves the US Department of Defense. After Iridium filed for bankruptcy it cited its 'difficulty in gaining subscribers'. These 'difficulties' were elaborated by CNN writer David Rohde when he detailed how he applied for the Iridium service and was sent information kits, but was never contacted by a sales representative, encountered programming problems on Iridium's website and a 'run-around' from the company's representatives. Apparently the engineers felt that putting their satellites in orbit was all that was required for a successful business – end of 'story'. Ultimately, business models like these fail because they are built on faulty assumptions about customer behaviour. They are solutions in search of a problem.

What's in a name? (part 2)

Auctionweb was founded in San Jose, California on 4 September 1995 by computer programmer Pierre Omidyar, as part of a larger personal site that belonged to his consulting firm, the Echo Bay Technology Group. The company officially changed its name to eBay in September 1997. Omidyar had tried to register the domain name EchoBay.com but found it already taken by Echo Bay Mines, a gold mining company, so he shortened it to his second choice, eBay.com.

The irony of a careless employment of business models is that when used correctly, they force managers to think rigorously about their business. Business models are beneficial implements that articulate the activities, players and resources required of a business proposal, and describe how they work together as a value-creating system. Even during the internet boom, executives who understood the language of business models outperformed the naïve.[2]

Meg Whitman was candid in her reasons for joining eBay in its early days – she was struck by what she described as 'the emotional connection between eBay users and the site', and realized that that the communities and services eBay had originated simply 'couldn't be done off-line'.[3] Whitman saw these two characteristics lying at the core of the eBay business model, one that could be translated into an engine of value. Ever since, Whitman has enshrined 'the emotional connection between eBay users and the site' as a key competence in eBay's business, taking full advantage of the psychology and the economics that draw collectors, bargain hunters, community seekers and small-business people to eBay. This helps eBay to make decisions about the scope of its activities that result in a profitable cost structure. Compare this with the pretext of Priceline, which naively assumes that consumers are only concerned with price and that sellers are unconcerned about loss of revenue. In fact, the reverse is the actual case.

STRATEGY AND BUSINESS MODELS

Sound business models, whether articulated or not, underlie every corporate success story. Nonetheless, a business model is not the same thing as a strategy (although the terms are sometimes used without distinction). Business models describe the systems view of a business – its operations and its relationships with the world of consumers and vendors. Strategies, in contrast, derive from a military perspective which expects an action plan for winning in the rivalry with competitors, either current or foreseen.[4]

Business strategy

As overused as the word strategy is today, its provenance as a business term is remarkably recent. Perhaps the first widely read treatise that incorporated strategy as a business concept was historian Alfred DuPont Chandler's 1962 book *Strategy and Structure*, which profiled the relationship between the strategy and corporate departments at General Motors and Sears. A scion of the DuPont family, Chandler used his pedigree and access to determine how the department and organizational structure of a firm relate to its mission – its 'strategy'. Chandler presciently devoted chapters to technological and market innovation and to the roles of functional departments. (The latter had a defining influence on the curriculum and departmental structure of today's business schools.)

Historian and economist Peter Drucker also began his studies of business strategy at General Motors as a consultant. Drucker's 1964 book *Managing for Results*[5] was originally called *Business Strategies*. Both Drucker and his publisher rejected this title after informal test marketing. Drucker explained in the preface to a later edition that he was repeatedly told that 'strategy belongs to military or perhaps to political campaigns, but not to business'.

The work of both Chandler and Drucker was strongly influenced by both men's personal ties to General Dwight Eisenhower. Drucker worked closely with Eisenhower at Columbia University to set up the business school there, and Chandler was Eisenhower's biographer. It seems apt that historians, with their focus on governments and power, introduced strategy to business.

Competitive strategy ultimately requires you to do something better than your opponents; it requires you to differentiate yourself in some way, with products, service, cost, or whatever else registers on your customers' radar.[6] Businesses can only outperform others when they are unique; when competitors are forced to innovate in order to enter their competitive space. Any barrier to market entry is at most temporary. To erect new barriers against competitors, products and services need continual differentiation and redifferentiation. Continually evolving the basis for differentiation can only be done through innovation.

STORYTELLING

At heart, business models are stories – stories that explain how enterprises work. A good business model illustrates the intricacies of an enterprise by painting a mental picture. It may be elaborate, or simple and abstract; it may be still life, landscape, portraiture, or combinations of several on a single canvas.[7] It should answer fundamental questions about how money is made in this business, and what the underlying economic logic is that will attract customers and revenue commensurate with the competences and resource usage.[8]

The prophet of post-industrialism

Sociologist Daniel Bell is best known for three particularly influential books: *The End of Ideology* (1960), *The Cultural Contradictions of Capitalism* (1976) and *The Coming of Post-Industrial Society* (1973).[9] In *The End of Ideology*, Bell argued that the influence of both history and ideology had been subsumed by market forces (foreshadowing the influence of the storytelling of 'pop culture' and 'spin politics') and that genuine political debate would give way to technocratic guidance from social and cultural elites (foreshadowing political decision making guided by the storytelling of consultants, lobbyists and think tanks), substituting consensus for moral discourse. In *The Coming of Post-Industrial Society*, he outlined a new kind of society – the post-industrial society – arguing that post-industrialism would be information-led and service-oriented, and would replace the industrial society as the dominant system. The post-industrial society would be marked by a shift from manufacturing to services, the centrality of new science-based industries, the rise of new technical elites and the advent of a new principle of social stratification.

Storytelling used to be simple; in fact until the 1960s a business school education was usually little more than time spent listening to retired executives tell stories (which they called case studies). The first half of the 20th century was dominated by businesses that were easy to understand – they were retailers, utilities, banks or whatever, with straightforward business models and goals unique to each industry. But the growth of services and especially information industries that populate the post-industrial society spawned an ecological explosion of new species of business, often setting up barriers to competition based simply on the complexity of their business models.[10] Globalization and outsourcing flattened competitive environments, and shortened life-cycles, making business models even more dynamic and varied. Telling a story – at least one that conveys an accurate portrait of the firm's operations and competitive landscape – is no longer simple. It takes technical skill as well as artistry to portray a realistic story of a modern business's value proposition. In comparison with good business storytelling today, the stories we told a decade ago come off as stilted, flat and drab as hieroglyphics on an ancient tomb. No wonder this crude storytelling got us into trouble during those heady dot-com days.

The story behind a successful business model represents a better way to create value than existing alternatives. It may offer more value to a discrete group of customers. Or it may completely replace the old way of doing things and become the standard for the next generation of entrepreneurs to beat. It may subtly fine-tune the internal operations of a business to such a degree that competitors find it hard to duplicate, as is the case with Wal-Mart. It may consistently create customer experiences that are so trendy and exciting that competitors find them hard to duplicate, as in the case of Apple. And all the while it leaves competitors to scratch their heads wondering what exactly is the business model behind this magic.

Numbers guys

Michael Milken was the undisputed champion of the junk bond, and a ponytailed computer programmer made it all possible. Milken headed the New York-based non-investment-grade bond (junk bond) department when Drexel merged with Burnham and Company in 1973, an operation that earned a remarkable 100 per cent return on investment. By 1976, Milken's income was estimated at US$5 million a year, giving him the influence to move his operation to his home town, Los Angeles, where he had swanky offices on Beverly Hills' Rodeo Drive.

Dan Bricklin's experiences analysing case studies at Harvard Business School with his primitive Texas Instruments calculator convinced him that there had to be a better way. Working with some of his old MIT professors, he adapted an old table-driven chalk-and-blackboard approach to production scheduling which had been in use since the 1930s to work on one of the new personal computers. Tests on the Pepsi-Cola case study convinced him that he had a winning business analysis tool, which he soon parlayed into a company: Software Arts, selling VisiCalc (Visible Calculator). If VisiCalc was the 'killer application' for the new PC, then Milken certainly must have to be considered the killer applicant.

Michael Milken once commented that Bricklin's invention had single-handedly paved the way for the 1980s corporate megadeals. It certainly did the job for Milken, who remodelled his Beverly Hills offices in the early 1980s around a large X-shaped desk lined with personal computers loaded with spreadsheets. Prior to this time, bonds salespeople received all of the analysis for dealing in securities on documents prepared by their New York-based research department. Securities inventories, prices, customers, profit margins and so forth might at best be updated daily, or more likely weekly or monthly. With PCs, spreadsheets and data on inventories, market prices and customers at their fingertips, bond salespeople were no longer reliant on the static reports of a distant research department. Instantly tying numbers to their telephone narrative, salespeople could buy and sell, restructure deals and process new market information while they were speaking with customers, or across the X-shaped desk when talking with Drexel traders.

Milken's payoff was a rapid expansion of the use of junk bonds in corporate finance and mergers and acquisitions, which fuelled the 1980s leveraged buyout boom. Drexel went from $1.2 million in fees to over $4 billion in 1986, making it the most profitable firm on Wall Street. A single transaction in 1989 sold $5 billion of high-yield bonds to help finance Kohlberg Kravis Roberts & Co.'s purchase of RJR Nabisco Inc. Because the perceived risk of default made investors skittish, the firms that could find buyers for junk bonds had the power to dictate their own terms to participate in the largest deals. Hostile takeovers often hinged on whether Milken issued a letter saying he was 'highly confident' of being able to provide the financing. With Bricklin's spreadsheet, he could usually assure himself of being on the winning side of even the riskiest trades.

At some level, business models, just like stories, are variations on a few archetypes giving voice to universal themes underlying all human experience. Business models are variations on the economics of supply and production underlying all businesses (which in turn are just reflections of human behaviour). On the one side are stories about the activities associated with making something – designing it, purchasing raw materials, manufacturing – the costs and resource usage narrative. The other side is associated with selling something – finding and reaching customers, transacting a sale, distributing the product or delivering the service – the revenue generation narrative. A new business model's plot may turn on designing a new product for an unmet need, or it may turn on a process innovation. There is one big difference between stories and business models: business models tell investors where they make their money.[11]

TYING NARRATIVE TO NUMBERS

Before PC spreadsheet programs became widespread, business planning usually meant producing a single, base-case forecast. At best, people did a little sensitivity analysis around the projection. The spreadsheet ushered in a much more analytical approach to planning, because every major line item could be pulled apart, its components and subcomponents analysed and tested. People could ask what-if questions about the critical assumptions on which their business depended. They could model the behaviour of a business.

This was something new. Before the personal computer changed the nature of business planning, most successful business models were created more by accident than by design and forethought. The business model became clear only after the fact. By enabling companies to tie their marketplace insights much more tightly to the resulting economics – to link their assumptions about how people would behave to the numbers of a pro forma profit and loss (P&L) projection – spreadsheets made it possible to model businesses before they were launched.

Of course, a spreadsheet is only as good as its underlying assumptions or its model. It is easy to get lazy and assume that the business model or whatever can be modelled on a spreadsheet – nothing more or less. But this is an increasingly tenuous assumption as businesses grow more convoluted, complex and intangible. What exactly is Google's business model; or eBay's? Both are profitable companies. Value creation in both business models is driven by social networks and customer experience; try plugging those into a spreadsheet.[12]

To generate reliable and meaningful numbers, business modelling needs a rich and dynamic language to model how the entire business system works, and compare that with real outcomes as they develop. The success of decisions, strategic initiatives, income and financials provides feedback on whether the model is working. Business modelling is, in this sense, the managerial equivalent of the scientific method – you start with a hypothesis, which you then test in action and revise when necessary.

Coca-Cola finds that competitors can be devious

Coca-Cola failed both its story and numbers tests when it concocted a sweeter drink, unofficially dubbed New Coke. New Coke was formulated in response to Pepsi's highly successful 'Pepsi Challenge' advertising campaign which took place in malls, shopping centres and other public locations. A Pepsi representative would set up a table with two unmarked cups, one containing Pepsi and one (old) Coke. Shoppers were encouraged to sip both colas, and then select which drink they preferred. Pepsi regularly won the 'Challenge' simply because parched, weary shoppers preferred the sweeter drink. If customers were asked within a minute of comparing drinks, they would usually respond that they preferred the illusion of glucose jolt from sipping the sweeter one. If they were allowed a few more minutes, controlled laboratory tests revealed that they complained the sweeter drink left them queasy, with a bad taste in their mouth. Additionally, some participants recalled that the Pepsi was served chilled while the Coke was at room temperature. But the Coca-Cola Company didn't know that, at least not before it replaced its flagship soda with a sweeter Pepsi-bashing 'New' Coke in 1985.

Public reaction to the change was devastating. New Coke quickly entered the pantheon of major marketing flops. The subsequent reintroduction of Coke's original formula led to a significant gain in sales, with Coca-Cola learning a painful lesson along the way: that it should do its own marketing research in the future rather than relying on the advertising campaigns of its competitors.

When a business model fails, it is because the story doesn't make sense, or the numbers don't make sense. *Stories* fail to make sense when they make unrealistic assertions about technology, production capabilities or consumer behaviour. Rough tests of the story can be made fairly quickly using *consumption chain analysis* and *attribute maps* (see Chapter 3).

The *numbers test* is more difficult, because of the risk inherent in the new, on both the demand and supply sides. On the demand side, it is likely that whatever is new in an innovation will not be appreciated by customers.

Finding an innovation's value proposition

The context of the business model for an innovation is established by the firm's *value proposition*, which ultimately drives its business model as well as its strategy and technology choice.[13]

The value proposition is the business' *raison d'être* – the justification for committing people and resources to the operations. The ecology of the market may allow different business models to find their own niche within the competitive environment. Swatch

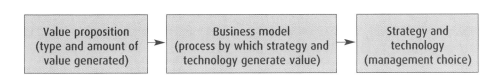

Figure 4.1 The value proposition for the innovation

makes low-cost watches whose styles are updated weekly; Patek Philippe makes expensive watches which the company claims are 'timeless'. Each can be considered different solutions to the generating of retail profit in the consumer watch market. Each demands different technology and strategy to generate value. Yet the direction of influence is the same in both businesses: only once the idea or objective of the business – that is, the value proposition – has been articulated can management go about designing the business processes.

Once business processes have been settled upon, management can make strategic or technology choices, although sometimes the processes will be selected to take advantage of a firm's particular strategic or technological advantages. The approach is Platonic: the value proposition has a permanency that is wanting in the ephemeral worlds of business processes, strategy and technology.

VALUE MAPS

One of the earliest comprehensive value map methods to enter the business mainstream was a conceptual model of the value transformation in firms which was introduced by Michael Porter in his 1985 book *Competitive Advantage*.[14] Porter's idea derived from the economic intuition of production, that every firm is a collection of activities that are performed to design, produce, market, deliver and support its product. All these activities can be mapped using a value map. A firm's value map and the way that it performs value-adding activities reflect its history, its strategy and the underlying economics in the market.

Thematic maps

Edmond Halley, patron of Newton, student of magnetism, Latin poet and cartographer, is best remembered today as the 17th-century astronomer who predicted the periodic return of Halley's comet. But his greatest contribution to science was the introduction of the first 'thematic map' – a map that illustrates a set of facts and figures in a geographic format. Halley's map was the culmination of his two-year voyage as captain of the *Paramour*, mapping the variations in the magnetic compass from true north. It ushered in the very modern notion that anything that can be measured – abstract or not – can be mapped.

In Porter's view there were eight sorts of activities in a typical value map. There were four types of primary activities – logistics, operations, delivery and marketing – and four types of supporting activities – procurement, R&D, human resources and infrastructure. *Competitive Advantage* was written in the early 1980s; the PC had just been introduced, and information technology was limited mainly to back-office accounting systems. The modern pantheon of corporate activities – especially knowledge-intensive ones – has evolved substantially since then. Today's value map must map a rich, complex and inherently knowledge-based set of primary and supporting activities. The rate at which new technology adds competitive niches means that any definition must be open-ended, creating an entirely different environment from the one Porter faced two decades ago.

In knowledge-intensive businesses, an updated perspective may be more suitable. In this perspective transaction flows circulate around the core processes in the firm's value map. *Core processes* directly involve the creation and delivery of a product or service, and are those essential to value creation. *Supporting processes* add cost, and ostensibly make core processes more efficient. There are usually many different options for supporting core activities – make or buy, vertical integration, outsourcing and so forth. As a consequence, the inherent cost of the supporting activities is often be difficult to assess. Generally though, they may be considered to fall into four categories:

- transportation, coordination and communication activities
- administrative activities; administrative systems are support activities that improve the efficiency of core activities
- quality control activities
- activities that promote process efficiency.

Porter's value map perspective has proved popular, and consultants and academics have over the years incorporated it into varying formal methodologies – from extensions to XML called Value Chain Markup Language to extensions of Michael Hammer's Semantic Modelling, which were the basis of the reengineering vogue a decade ago.

Value-generating processes on the value map transform the transactions to generate value for the firm. This value is assessed by the ultimate consumer of the product or service, and – from the firm's point of view – can be assumed to be the aggregate of revenues, costs (both capital assets and expenses), and adjustments to risk (for example, hedges such as are common in commodity-intensive businesses such as chocolate and grains).

This approach makes the relationships between events and the value they generate much more transparent. Consider the tactics used by telecommunications company Qwest to inflate income through accounting for offsetting sales and purchases of bandwidth. In the first six months of 2001, Qwest sold US$857 million worth of bandwidth to other telecom companies which was accounted for as revenue; at the same time it also bought $450 million from some of those same companies, which was accounted for as an asset. This accounting fiddle pushed Qwest's revenue growth for the six months from 7.5 per cent to 12.0 per cent, at a time when insiders were selling off substantial stakes in the company at inflated stock prices.[15]

THE MECHANICS OF VALUE GENERATION

'One picture is worth a thousand words' goes one incarnation of an advertisement created by Fred R. Barnard for the trade journal *Printers' Ink* in 1921,[16] where he suggested that advertisements with images are more effective than those without. Our minds seem to be able to take in more information at a glance with pictures, and here we use that fact to advantage by showing how to depict business models graphically.

Figure 4.2 presents the components of a graphic business model (value map) – the environment box, the strategy-owner bubble and the value flow. At the centre of a value map is the network of business processes that are owned by a firm, and are the focus of its strategy. These are processes over which the firm has a high degree of control. That

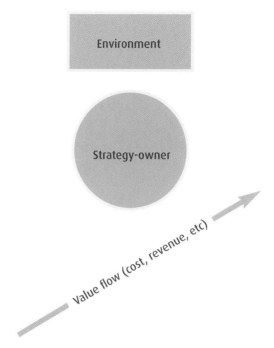

Figure 4.2 Value map components for diagramming a business model

control comes at the cost of ownership of the process, and the risks that come with it. These are connected to one another through value flows which represent transferred costs and revenues. The environment boxes define the competitive environment with which the firm interacts. These boxes represent things like customers, vendors, competitors, government regulators, and other groups or entities that can only be controlled indirectly by the firm.

How standards help or hurt a business model

The Pythagorean philosopher Archytas of Tarentum (5th century BC) is the alleged inventor of the screw. Screws came into common use around the 1st century BC. These were the wooden screws that were used in wine presses, olive oil presses and for pressing clothes. Metal screws and nuts only appeared in the 15th century.

Sixteenth-century screw-making was a cottage industry. The threads, filed by hand, were imperfect and shallow, and screws were so expensive that they were sold individually. In the 18th century, industrialization brought consumers mass-produced screws at cheaper prices, but they still had one drawback: the machinery of the day couldn't file

a screw to a point. Workers had to drill a hole into material to get the blunt screw-end started. The familiar machine-made, pointed self-starting screw didn't appear until the mid-19th century.

In 1906, Canadian Peter Robertson hit on a head design with a square recess that is still a favourite among many woodworkers. Robertson patented his square-headed driver and screw system in 1908, and not long after, the Fisher Body Company (famous for constructing the Ford Model T) decided to use Robertson head screws in its production line. Today, around 85 per cent of the screws sold in Canada use the Robertson head as opposed to about 10 per cent of those sold in the United States.

In contrast, the Phillips head emerged as the choice of the international community. Henry F. Phillips, a Portland, Oregon businessman and former travelling salesman, hit on the idea of an X-shaped socket head. Phillips' design was initially rejected, but eventually accepted by the American Screw Co., which persuaded General Motors in 1936 to use the Phillips-head screw in manufacturing Cadillac cars. The car industry soon embraced it, setting the stage for even wider acceptance by the military during the Second World War. Carmakers liked the fact that there is a degree of cam-out or slippage inherent in the Phillips design which allows automated screw-driving machines to pop out once the screw is tight.

The acceptance of the Phillips head over the Robertson head in the United States came about because the tool industry originally standardized around the design with the lowest royalties – the Phillips head. This lead to adoption by the auto industry, and subsequently the US military. The relative merits of one design over the other were peripheral to the influence of industry standards.[17]

The value-flow, strategy-owner and environment constructs are borrowed from the formal diagramming methods of dataflow diagrams.[18] The rigorous methodology of dataflow diagrams offers a formal language to capture the structure of the value map, and of the competitive and strategic environment in which it functions. Dataflow diagrams have been shown to provide a complete and unambiguous language for the description of interrelated processes. Because of this, dataflow diagrams can provide us with an unequivocal language to describe innovation strategy, firm operations and the competitive environment. Such rigour is useful in assuring that decisions and forecasts are unique and unambiguous – in other words, that they provide a scientific basis for decisions and forecasts involving innovations.

Value maps show the flow of value of major parties that own, or have claims to or influence over, the value created in a firm – what are commonly termed the 'stakeholders' in an innovation. These are the 'principalities' of the map, where 'value flows' are the rivers traversing the map and connecting the principalities. The major stakeholders with claims to value are *owners* (concerned with maximizing wealth), *customers* and *vendors* (concerned with price and timing), *creditors* (concerned with downside risk), *managers* (concerned with their jobs) and *competitors* (concerned with market share).

The value of an idea or innovation is seldom localized to one setting or owner. In a competitive market, it is the customers that are likely to benefit most from an innovation; other stakeholders will share whatever is left over. Additionally, the wealth generated by an innovation is seldom storable like gold or other commodities; value in the innovation economy arises from 'ideas in action'. Knowledge assets in themselves are little more than curiosities until they are put to work. In the traditional 'stocks and flows' perspective of corporate systems, inventories and assets have played a central role in corporate systems. But with innovations, assets, if they exist at all, are just another cost of doing business. Often less is more, leading to decisions to outsource whatever activities lie outside the firm's core competences.

In addition there are *inductive processes*, which consume resources and modulate the operation of key processes in one way or another. These may support *key processes*, as is the case with the traditional 'cost centres' of the firm – information processing, legal, accounting, administration and so forth. They may be internal or external to the firm, and are often the subject of outsourcing decisions because of their non-central character. Historically, rules of thumb have suggested that inductive processes consume between 50 and 90 per cent of a firm's operating budget.

Value 'quanta'

Our fundamental definition of innovation = invention + commercialization makes the implicit assumption that we are interested in innovations that generate value, and are profitable (this is the commercialization part of the equation). Valuation is a problem in even the simplest of business models. We address it in the more complex models required for analysing innovations by segmenting value into its components, and analysing each subcomponent individually. (For an example, see the innovation workout on attribute segmentation in Chapter 2)

Costs and revenues are both lumpy – computer scientists refer to this as 'granularity' – and usually they come in lumps of significantly different size. For example, consider the fundamental unit by which software is measured, as perceived from either the supply side or the demand side. On the supply side, the unit of work is the packaged software product. This will take many person-years of effort to produce, but once produced, the firm can make an unlimited number of copies to sell. Thus the value is the full cost of production, less the projected life-cycle revenues, less the projected life-cycle support for each software package produced. From the demand side, the logical unit is a single copy, the unit used for measuring sales. From a value-modelling standpoint, adopting the 'quantum' to be the packaged software product makes more sense than to treat it as a single copy of the software. Management's strategy and policy are applied uniformly across all sales, but are unique to the project. Thus the appropriate level of granularity for 'quanta' or 'transactions' is at the software project level. All measurements throughout the value map should be expressed in terms of unique software products (whether they are versions of a given product, or customized installations or whatever).

Value flows in the value map are pipelines carrying packets of value called 'transactions'. Transactions originate as discrete economic events arising either outside or within the firm, which either consume or generate value. In traditional accounting, journal entries capture the transactions specified on the chart of accounts, and all value is measured in the cash equivalents exchanged in arm's length transactions. The value map, in turn, consists of the key value-generating processes in which the firm has invested and the transactions running through them.

One key problem with ascertaining 'value' is that the units of value – dollars, euros and so forth – are priced through markets themselves. There is no 'absolute' global value metric. Any particular business operates in a specific region, purchasing particular commodities, selling its products in exchange for specific currencies. The knowledge economy clearly exacerbates problems with monetary denomination. Many knowledge products have no market, nor is there a clear way to value them (for example, consider a patent or copyright).

1884: The measurement crisis in geographical mapmaking

During the last two decades of the 19th century, colonialism caused cartographers to reflect on the shortcomings of their discipline in its ability to generate a world map. By late 1884, less than one-ninth of the land surface of the globe had been surveyed or was being surveyed. This patchwork of surveying had been confounded by a variety of standards of measurement. Each country had gone its own way, developing its own traditions from a chauvinistic perspective.

Without standardization, map making could never provide an unambiguous language. England had a semblance of standards: Henry I decreed that the yard was the distance from the tip of his nose to the end of his thumb; the length of a furlong (furrow-long) was established by the Tudors as 220 yards, and Elizabeth I declared a mile to be 8 furlongs (increasing the Roman mile of 5000 feet to the modern mile of 5280 feet). France was in much worse shape, having different standards from province to province. The most commonly used measure on maps was the *toise*, which equalled six French feet (which were slightly longer than English feet), and was derived from half the width of the main gate of the Louvre.

Yet it was ultimately the French Academy of Sciences that developed the 'metric' standard (from the Greek metron = 'a measure'), and it was this that prevailed. A metre was one ten-millionth of the meridian distance between the pole and the equator; a gram was the mass of a cubic centimetre of water; a litre was the volume of a cubic decimetre.

The immediate effect of the metric system on map making was to introduce a simple, universal language for expressing map scale. In October 1884 the US government invited 25 nations to the first International Meridian Conference, in which France and England agreed that the prime meridian would run through the Observatory at Greenwich, England, in exchange for the British adopting France's metric system. Only then did map making embrace a universal and unambiguous standard of measurements necessary for mapping the world.[19]

In the environment of the knowledge economy, then, how can we distinguish good management, good business models and good accounting from simple good luck? This was a major problem in the 1990s dot-com bubble. It was difficult to know what a 'good' business model was, because so many of the models were novel and untested. Money and effort chased after business models that didn't make sense, but were – for a while – very lucky. And when their luck ran out, managers in some firms (read: Enron and WorldCom) augmented the gap in their revenues with creative accounting (read: fraud). These sorts of problems will only grow more widespread and common as the knowledge economy grows, and business becomes even more complex.

To deal with these uncertainties, it is probably best to take a non-denominational and opportunistic approach. Value flow units (that is, the fundamental 'quantum') may be either monetary or non-monetary 'transactions'. At least for our purposes, this will sidestep problems with monetary units which arise in four areas:

- ▶ inflation/deflation: they are unstable over time
- ▶ erratic exchange rates: they are unstable across global operations
- ▶ market failures: they fail to capture value where there is a ready market for goods that are either thinly traded or non-existent
- ▶ rapid depreciation: historical cost fails to properly assess value where there is rapid depreciation of goods, an especial problem where technology is accelerating rapidly.

Non-monetary bases for valuation, as well as graphic maps of processes, have been used in several valuation approaches over the past half-century. The cost accounting techniques that arose around Taylor's factory accounting and efficiency movements after the First World War provided an 'equivalent units of production' (EUP) technique for putting all processes throughout the factory on a common metric – essentially units of finished and saleable product.[20]

Activity based costing (ABC), which was popular in the 1990s, extended cost accounting concepts to a broader base, including a broader scope of non-monetary bases (that is, 'activity bases') than cost accounting's 'finished goods'. ABC laid out the organizational ownership and control structure in a value map, similar to the value map prescribed in this chapter.[21] On a much grander scale, the Soviet Union's Soviet State Planning Committee (Gosplan) ran national economic policy for nearly seven decades on a non-monetary basis. Russian production quotas were set by the state through a series of five-year plans. By design, supply and demand generally adjusted to meet these quotas. Money became redundant, and all accounting up and down the supply map was done in units comparable to the cost accountants' EUP. The Russian experiment would, no doubt, be a disaster for consumers and producers wherever supply and demand are volatile (in fact, it was a disaster in Russia, resulting in waste, obsolete inventories and massive queues). But under free markets, such a system is still useful to the planners and managers, even if it does do a terrible job of defining the schedules and preferences of consumers and producers.[22]

The legacy of Gosplan has been a modern Russian industrial complex that conducts from 40 to 70 per cent of its internal trade via barter. A barter economy must base value on ad hoc assessments for each exchange, which potentially require an enormous amount of information processing (and thus create enormous overhead costs) when transaction volumes become large. The modern solution is to set reference prices which can be used to determine transaction ratios. Gosplan's databases (now on computer) evolved into the reference prices for Russia's free markets. These are the de facto market economics imposed on any society when price controls are enacted. For example, consider the United States in the 1960s and 1970s under Richard Nixon's price controls.

VALUE FLOWS

The interaction between the details of transactions, cost and revenues in a single transaction flow can actually be quite complex, but it is at the core of many successful models of innovation. Thus any useful value mapping needs to be able to incorporate methods of capturing this added complexity to:

▸ allow for the creation of independent models of **value** as well as modelling **volumes** of transactions
▸ incorporate specific **strategy and technology models**: that is, the explicit or implicit models underlying management's strategic choice and the consequent future value creation
▸ incorporate **growth models** implicit in the life-cycle of the technology underlying the business model.

Earlier in the chapter, we showed how something that can be defined as *value* can be delivered in discrete containers called *transactions*. Transaction *price* measures the value delivered; transaction *volume* measures the quantity of number of transactions processed in a given time period (the default accounting time unit is one year); *value flow* is total value generated in a given time period. In practice, the distributions of business's account balances tend to be highly kurtotic (fat-tailed) and right-skewed (because negative values are prohibited). These tendencies are the result of commingling different value-generating processes in the same account.

More importantly, particular management strategies may tend to affect one component differently from the other. Let's assume that management is assessing the merits (in this context, the impact on future value flows) of a high volume/low margin product (think Saturn automobile) or of a low volume/high margin product (think Ferrari). The first strategy raises volume while lowering unit value; the second strategy raises unit value while lowering volume. If only value, and not its components, is considered, the two might well be seen as equivalent. But if instead we think in terms of volume and value components, the comparative impact of different strategies on potential losses, risk and error become explicit.[23]

Very little research has been conducted into asset market volumes. Where it has been done, the influence of volume and liquidity on price volatility is most often addressed. Thus there tends to be a significant asymmetry in the amount of research done on market prices and on trading volumes, and we cannot necessarily look to that research for guidance in our current task. Fortunately, within a firm or project context, we know a good deal more about transaction volumes because they are so central to capacity planning, utilization and discretionary budget. Managerial strategy and policy are most important in ascertaining transaction volumes; market forces are most important in ascertaining transaction prices.[24]

GROWTH, CHANGE AND RISK

Traditional discounted cash flow financial analysis commonly assumes an ad hoc two-stage growth model for forecasting future cash flows (the so-called Gordon growth model, introduced in a popular finance text back in the 1960s[25]). This assumes that there is an initial stage of rapid growth in a firm, some constant rate of growth which applies up to the forecasting horizon, which is typically set 10 to 15 years in the future. Past that horizon, convention uses two approaches to calculate a so-called 'terminal value' – first, perpetuity, and second, price/earnings multiple approaches. The *perpetuity* approach assumes that the cash flows beyond the forecast horizon act like an annuity payable indefinitely. This approach assumes – primarily for sake of argument – that the firm reaches a steady state of operations. Alternatively, if the firm's business model is stable (a big 'if' in the knowledge economy) the *price/earnings multiple* approach assumes that the market will ultimately value the firm at some multiple of earnings. Industry averages may be used, or for lack of better numbers, it is common practice to use a multiple in the range from 5 to 15.

Lacking information to the contrary, it seems reasonable to assume constant growth (or shrinkage, although this seems suspiciously rare in practice) based on prior trends in the objective historical data. With additional information – seasonal cycles, market trends and so forth – a wide range of econometric and time-series statistical tools have been developed in economics to improve forecast accuracy.

Henri Pagès[26] suggests that Gordon's growth model is inherently incompatible with non-stationary growth of firm or project value. A more glaring problem arose during the dot-com bubble – there is little justification for the 'kink' that occurs in growth between the first and second stages. This kink often took extreme values in financial plans that appeared during the late-1990s dot-com bubble, where it was not uncommon to see 80–120 per cent of the firm value in the terminal valuation.

A more transparent and defensible approach to growth involves discarding the planning horizon altogether. Growth is seen as resulting from two sources: first, growth induced by managerial strategy, and second, growth induced by the external supply and product market factors – what we call the business environment.

Channels

Marketing and supply channels coordinate the succession of functions that are required to bring a product from factory to customer. Where a service is being sold, the channel controls contracting and settlement.

Marketing channels emerge as a part of the natural evolution of hierarchies and markets in an industry. Although producers may provide many of the channel functions required to stimulate and satisfy demand for their goods and services, economies of scale and access to multiple competing products may make some channel functions better suited to third parties. Channel intermediaries provide a link between buyers and sellers, lowering the costs of transactions and making most goods and services cheaper. They may consolidate particular channel operations from a variety of producers, thus achieving economies of scale. For example, few magazine publishers actually distribute their own products or handle their own subscription services – these services are provided by one or two large subscription processors.

Channel intermediaries smooth the flow of goods and services, helping the producer to better plan and control production, by creating possession, place and time utilities. They do this by representing a large number of producers supplying complementary goods and services. Four benefits are realized by working through intermediaries – *breaking bulk, creating assortments, reutilization of transactions* and *efficient search.*

At least seven generic functions must succeed for a channel to work, regardless of who, or what, is performing that function – *physical possession, ownership, promotion, negotiation, provision of market information, financing, payment,* and *risk bearing.*

Physical possession of inventory in a warehouse or on consignment is required at one or more points in the channel. How much of this inventory is stockpiled depends on the cycle times required to produce, replenish, distribute and sell a particular product. The warehousing and distribution management functions are dedicated to transferring physical possession between channel members, and finally to the consumer.

Ownership is distinct from physical possession in that it is a legal concept. Ownership is a contentious issue in the information age. Laws have more or less focused on ownership of real and tangible properties. Intellectual assets have only recently received the attention they deserve. Without a clear judgement on ownership, sales are difficult. Unit sales of pirated media, for example, are estimated to be double legitimate sales. Since there is a significant price differential between pirated and legitimate copies of intellectual property (for instance, a movie that sells for US$10 on the legitimate market may sell at a tenth that price on the black market), it is difficult for legitimate channels to maintain any sort of competitive advantage.

Where ownership of property is ambiguous, legitimate channels may be able to maximize their revenues by dealing with pirates. For example, a British textbook publisher found that, for a variety of reasons, it was impossible for it to publish legitimately in Turkey's market. Yet pirates were able to obtain Xeroxed copies of nearly any British text on short notice, including the publisher's own. Publishers typically distribute textbooks at marginal cost in many developing economies to thwart pirates. In the case of Turkey, this publisher simply agreed not to prosecute the pirates in return for the pirates maintaining the quality of their copies. The pirates essentially acted as local printers. The pirates made a profit; the publisher found the pirates to be faster and more efficient than its legitimate channels in that area; and the publisher's text maintained a presence in the Turkish market, which opened up future opportunities for expansion in the market.

Particularly where items are large and unique, specific channel intermediaries have arisen to facilitate ownership and title transfer of goods. For very unique transactions, this may require the services of a skilled lawyer. For less unique products – say, houses – title transfer has been routinized and become considerably less expensive as a result.

Promotion of a product often demands specific talents, in addition to a wide range of customer contacts. The use of the World Wide Web for electronic commerce has spawned a hi-tech cottage industry of graphic artists, multimedia and communications experts, and advertising types to construct online web pages which project the producer's corporate image, promote the producer's products, and provide feedback on customer needs.

Negotiation is required for many big-ticket products, where price, options, customization and after-market service can be tailored to the needs of each individual customer. Automobile and home purchases are the most prominent examples of products in which negotiation is a central function in the channel.

The ordering function has seen the most dramatic applications of information technology over the past two decades. Electronic data interchange, electronic commerce, web order forms, telephone direct orders, and numerous other applications of computer and communications technology make it possible to place orders conveniently, with costs savings passed on to consumers.

Market information is essential for production planning, and minimizing stockouts and other forms of risk which must be borne by channel members. Although existing applications in electronic commerce are only beginning to realize the potential for accumulation of market information, this has been an important application for computers over the past two decades. For example, Wal-Mart has dedicated a worldwide telecommunications network and powerful Teradata supercomputers to provide the company and its suppliers with statistical synopses of demand patterns on a near real-time basis.

Financing is also required for expensive products, and is likely to be a significant factor in negotiation. Automobile and home purchases demand specialized financing. Sales of less expensive products, especially impulse sales, may be facilitated through routine transactions financed with credit cards. Credit cards make the transfer of funds straightforward. They can also smooth individuals' cash inflow from income with the cash outflow from purchases.

Payment must be collected if producers and channel intermediaries are to stay in business. Payment presents an increasing problem as developed economies move away from cash transactions. Credit and debit cards have greatly facilitated this move, and have standardized and routinized transaction payments. Unfortunately, their use on open networks such as the internet is still suspect. A considerable portion of the expense passed on to consumers and producers using credit cards for payment is needed to cover criminal abuse of credit cards. It may be difficult to protect against this abuse because of restrictions on consumer credit monitoring.

Risk bearing and *insurance* are important when products have a long production cycle (as do houses), where there is significant investment in inventories (as with jewellery), or where there are significant responsibilities incurred through warranties and for after-market servicing. Sales contracts typically state who bears the risk for performance of a product. This influences both price and marketability. For example, an automobile sold 'As is' will be worth less than one sold with a '3-year 50,000 mile warranty'.

Morphological boxes

The morphological research method – or more simply the graphical perspective that we call *morphological boxes* – is an orderly way of making complex decisions involving large numbers of features and business model components. Its aim is to achieve a schematic of all of the possible solutions of a given large-scale programme. This innovation workout draws on the brainchild of Fritz Zwicky, a former professor of astrophysics at Caltech. In 1933, Zwicky employed the morphological method to discern that a 'considerable fraction of the mass had been missed' in measuring the velocities of certain galaxies. This was the first known observation of the 'missing mass' of the universe – what later became known as 'dark matter'.

Morphological boxes offer a way to combine the parameters of a challenge into new ideas (parameter here meaning characteristic, factor, variable or aspect). You choose the number and nature of the parameters with an objective of selecting the combination that best represents your innovation – young, edgy, conservative, iconoclastic and so forth.

Blueprint

Specify the objectives you have set for your innovation.

Select the components: the criterion for selecting a parameter is whether that particular parameter affects your objectives.

List characteristics, values, or states that each component can take: these could be colours, shapes, materials or anything else that might influence the ultimate goals of your innovation.

Try different combinations. Make random runs through your 2x2 matrix of components and characteristics, selecting one or more from each column and then combining them into entirely new formulations for the innovation. You may find it helpful to randomly examine the entire box, and then gradually restrict yourself to portions that appear particularly fruitful.

Consider the following challenge that might face Mad Catz, the company in this chapter's case study: to design a video game console with morphological boxes, then write its business model and estimate the value from commercializing your video game console innovation. Consider the features that your capabilities allow you to produce. These could be either particular components (chosen from the columns in Table 4.1) or a given feature set (chosen from the rows in Table 4.1).

Each characteristic of a component adds some market value (a consumer willingness to pay or W-to-P in Table 4.2) and some production cost (also shown in Table 4.2).

With this information, Fritz Zwicky's morphological boxes can be used to build products for different markets, to different price points. We shall look at this further in the Mad Catz case study below.

Describing your innovation in a set of morphological boxes simplifies and condenses a complex problem, making possible informed decisions where there are simply too many components for the human mind to track. The myriad of unrealized opportunities and designs possible for restructuring the business represent the 'dark matter' of any innovation. Firms that fail to explore this unseen mass of opportunities may very well be surprised when they show up in a competitor's product – or worse, in the angry reviews of disgruntled customers.

Table 4.1: Possible features for a video game console with morphological boxes

Characteristics	Components				
	Package	Console casing	Electronics	Screen	Connectivity
	Recycled paper	Cheap plastic	Basic	NTSC TV	Wired
	Coloured plastic	Hard plastic	+Vibration	PAL/multi	Infrared
	Cloth case	Lexan	+Motion sensor	1024x768	Wi-Fi
	Hard shell	Brushed metal	+Television	1280x1024	+Internet
	Metal with velvet cushion	Two-tone clamshell	+Body suit	1080i (i.e. 1920 x 1080/2 interlaced)	+Other consoles

Table 4.2: Market value and production cost for feature options

	Package			Console casing			Electronics			Screen			Connectivity		
	Type	W-to-P	Cost	Material	W-to-P	Cost	Features	W-to-P	Cost	Resolutions	W-to-P	Cost	TV and Internet	W-to-P	Cost
1	Recycled paper	3	1	Cheap plastic	3	1	Basic	0	15	NTSC TV	30	10	Wired	10	1
2	Coloured plastic	12	1.5	Hard plastic	7	2	+Vibration	3	25	PAL/multi	40	10	Infrared	25	5
3	Cloth case	24	3	Lexan	12	6	+Motion sensor	16	40	1024X768	40	40	Wi-Fi	30	25
4	Hard shell	45	15	Brushed metal	35	12	+Television	35	160	1280 x 1024	40	60	+Internet	45	30
5	Metal with velvet cushion	50	34	Two-tone clamshell	120	24	+Body suit	120	600	1080i (i.e. 1920 x 1080/2 interlaced)	45	100	+Other consoles	60	30

Case study: Mad Catz Interactive, Inc.

In 1987 a small group of engineers saw the 40 per cent annual growth of the global video gaming industry as a unique opportunity to invest in what they predicted was destined to become the world's premier entertainment industry. By 1989 they had founded Mad Catz, with production facilities in Shenzhen, P.R. China managed from their Hong Kong office, and design and marketing in Southern California, bringing them closer to their target gaming audience.

For several years, Mad Catz operations revolved around a half-dozen employees, generating aftermarket peripherals and accessories with innovative stylistic twists for Nintendo, Sony, Sega Dreamcast and Xbox game consoles.

By the late 1990s Mad Catz had grown to over 100 employees making controllers and other video game accessories under the Mad Catz and GameShark brand names, and selling through about 12,000 retailers globally. The United States accounted for more than 80 per cent of sales, with much of that being sales at Toys'R'Us, where Mad Catz also OEMed[27] its 'TRU High Frequency' store brand of video game accessories. Toys'R'Us was impressed enough with the quality and innovativeness of Mad Catz controllers that in 1997 Mad Catz was its Vendor of the Year (receiving, for its efforts, an effigy of the Toys'R'Us mascot, Geoffrey the giraffe).

Total industry revenue for the game console aftermarket was about US$400 million in 2006, with Mad Catz accounting for about one-quarter of the market. Three competitors made up the remainder: Take Two Interactive with around 20 per cent, the privately held NYKO Technologies with 50 per cent, and the privately held Bigben Interactive at 5 per cent. Competition was intense, and all of the companies were losing money in 2006. One of Mad Catz's priorities was to revise its business model in a fashion that would ultimately assure profitability.

The Mad Catz value map (Figure 4.3) consists of three relatively independent phases that add to value in the final game controller product – the electronics, the plastic casing with buttons and joysticks, and the packaging. Mad Catz visualizes these in terms of their demands on planning (in other words, their lead time), the degree of influence on the customer's purchase decision (that is, value added in terms of willingness to pay and impulse to buy), and the cost contributed to production, including allocation of fixed and discretionary costs.

A glance at Table 4.3 might convince you that there is little justice in business, since cost and value generation by component are inversely correlated. The most expensive component of Mad Catz's controllers, the electronic assembly, has the least influence on the buying decision of customers; the least expensive component, the packaging around the controller, has the greatest influence, being a big motivator of impulse buying.

This can best be understood in the context of the feature map (discussed in Chapter 3: see Table 4.4).

Game controllers are 'experience goods' – you need to use them before you really know whether you like them, even where gamers may have strong preconceptions about what they are buying. Electronics are a basic feature of controllers – love 'em or hate 'em. The plastic cases, with their unique location, look and feel of buttons, joysticks and the way they fit in the hand, are differentiators, and if well (or poorly) received by the gaming community may even be exciters. Packaging, though, is the first thing a consumer sees, and in most cases is the only thing he or she is able to 'experience' prior to purchasing. For relatively inexpensive controllers such as Mad Catz's, the packaging is the 'deal closer'.

C A S E   S T U D Y

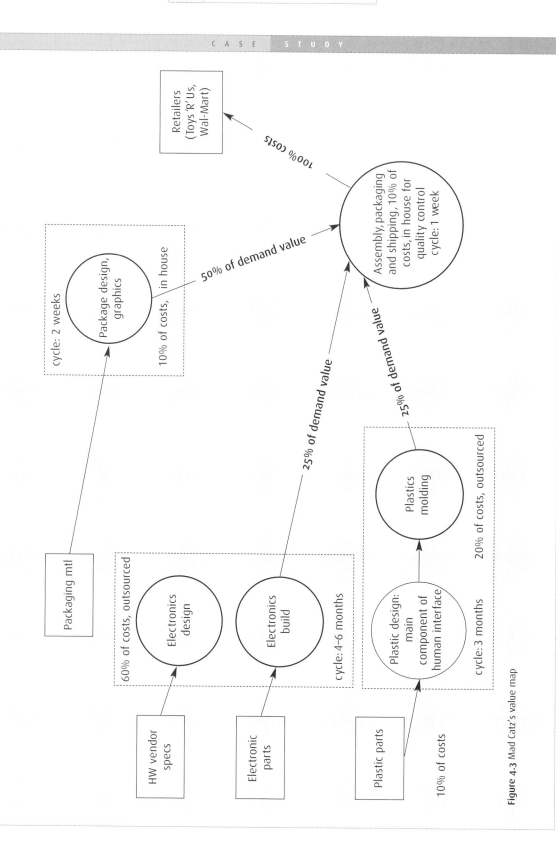

Figure 4.3 Mad Catz's value map

Table 4.3: *Value and cost generated by game controller components*

	Value added %	Cost added %	Lead time
Electronics	0–20	60	4–6 months
Case	30–40	20	3 months
Packaging	40–70	10	2 weeks

Table 4.4: *Feature map of game controller*

	Basic	Differentiator	Exciter
Plus	Electronics	Case	Packaging, case
Minus	Electronics	Case	Packaging, case
Neutral	Electronics	Case	

Repeat purchases are different. After gamers have had a chance to use the controllers for a few days, they are likely to form a strong opinion about the *case* of the controller – they are either excited or enraged. You can't please everyone, and every controller will have some users in each category. In the short run (before the original purchase) the *energizing features* are those of the package – often the art on the box the controller comes in. In the longer run (before a repurchase of the Mad Catz brand controllers) the case will become the energizer. Electronics, on the other hand, are often outsourced, and Mad Catz electronics may end up being the same as those used by its competitors. Electronics are neither differentiators nor energizers; because they are expensive, they are the ante that firms must pay upfront to get into the game.

Package and case features are entirely directed towards manipulating the *human interface* – visually, tactilely and psychologically. Advances in plastics moulding and digital photography have greatly expanded the options available for manipulating that interface through package and case design. The great challenge is how to choose the right mix of components to satisfy a given market.

Finding out what a market wants from a controller, on the other hand, may yield to more direct solutions. It will lie in the particular games they want to play with the controller. *Grand Theft Auto* players might describe their ideal controller as 'edgy and violent', while *Dance Revolution* players might go for 'glitter'. *Madden NFL* players might go for home team logos, while fantasy games enthusiasts would opt for a mystical 'amazons and lizards' look and feel.

Where innovative minds may really meet their challenge is in designing controllers for entirely new markets. By 2007, broadcast television audiences had rapidly dwindled and moviegoing had stagnated, being replaced by internet-enabled gaming, which emerged as the new pillar of the media world. With new game consoles, and new computer-based games continually entering the market, Mad Catz has ample latitude to innovate in the coming years.

Questions for the Mad Catz case study

1. Given the split of costs in the Mad Catz business model, see how many different products you can 'invent' in your mind that are amenable to Mad Catz business model. Can you think of any that are not in the gaming industry?

2. Review the Mad Catz innovation example given in the Morphological Box innovation workout. Assume that marketing has determined that unit demand for the Mad Catz innovation has been computed from historical data and market tests by your accounting department. Overall price influences (reduces) sales volume by the following formula: Volume (units) = ($700 − Sales Price) $*$ 10,000. What is the most profitable combination of components for the product?

CHAPTER QUESTIONS FOR REVIEW

1 Business models can be described on several different levels. In the chapter, three forms were described: a story, a story with financial projections, and a graphical bubble-arrow-box model:

   a. Describe the situation in which each might be appropriate.
   b. If you were given one minute to present your innovation to a wealthy investor, which form of business model would be best? Why?
   c. If you were given one hour to present your innovation, which form would be best? Why? Is there anything that you might add if you had a full hour to sell your 'business model' for the innovation?

2 Typically 50 to 90 per cent of the cost of running a business represents routinized 'operations' – legal, accounting, information systems, and so forth – that are not specific to the innovation:

   a. How do you 'sell' investors on the routine, non-innovation related costs of your business?
   b. What options do you have to control the cost of operations?

3 One of the most difficult aspects of designing an appropriate business model for an innovation is the choice of marketing channel.

   a. What factors influence your choice of marketing channel?
   b. Is it best to choose only one channel, or select more than one channel for marketing? In what situations would you recommend one channel versus many channels? Why?
   c. Market intermediaries (middlemen) have been criticized for generating unnecessary cost and delay for consumers. Think of three reasons that the cost add by market intermediaries is justified by the value that they add to the product.

CHAPTER 4: KEY POINTS

▷   Business modelling is the managerial equivalent of the scientific method.

▷   Business models supporting an innovation are composed of first, a story, and second, financial analysis tied to the story components.

▷   Stories behind successful business models have been getting progressively more complex:
   - as technology evolves and offers more distinct types of opportunities
   - as competition becomes more intense
   - as competitors get better at innovation.

▷   Business models, like fictional stories, are variations on a few archetypes giving voice to universal themes underlying all human experience.

▷   Complexity in today's business models requires an innovative response to providing financial support for the story supporting a new innovation.

▷   Value propositions motivate the entire business model:
   - they are the first choice that needs to be made in commercializing an innovation
   - there may be separate value propositions for each customer group for an invention.

▷   Value maps graphically depict the core and supporting (inductive) processes of a business, while value flows describe how their value is generated.

▷   The environment box describes the outside parties (customers, vendors, competitors etc.) with which the firm needs to interact.

▷   The fundamental unit of value is the transaction, which is a packet that carries costs, revenues and unit quantities.

NOTES

1 Clark, K. B. and Fujimoto, K. (1991) *Product Development Performance: Strategy, organization, and management in the world automobile industry*, Boston, Mass.: Harvard Business School Press; Porter, M. E. (1991) 'Towards a dynamic theory of strategy,' *Strategic Management Journal* 12, pp. 95–117.

2 Eisenmann, T. R. (2002) *Internet Business Models and Strategies: Text and cases*, New York: McGraw-Hill; Gulati, R. (1998) 'Alliances and networks,' *Strategic Management Journal* 19, pp. 293–317.

3 Boyd, J. (2002)' In community we trust: online security communication at eBay,' *Journal of Computer Mediated Communication* 7(3) (April).

4 Clark, K. B. and Fujimoto, K. (1991) *Product Development Performance: Strategy, organization, and management in the world automobile industry*, Boston, Mass.: Harvard Business School Press; Oster, S. (1999) *Modern Competitive Analysis*, New York: Oxford University Press; Ghemawat, P. (1991) *Commitment: The dynamics of strategy*, New York: Free Press; Porter, M. E. (1996) 'What is strategy?' *Harvard Business Review*, Nov–Dec, pp. 61–78.

5 Drucker, P. F. (1964/1993) *Managing for Results*, Collins.

6 Priem, R. and Butler, J. E. (2001) 'Tautology in the resource-based view and the implications of externally deter-mined resource value: further comments,' *Academy of Management Review* 26, pp. 57–67.

7 Magretta, Joan (2002) *What Management Is: How it works, and why it's everyone's business*, New York: Free Press.

8 This concept is at the centre of the resource based view of strategy, presented for example in Priem, R. and Butler, J. E. (2001) 'Is the resource-based "view" a useful perspective for strategic management research?' *Academy of Management Review* 26, pp. 22–41; Collis, D. J. and Montgomery, C. A. (1995) 'Competing on resources: strategies for the 1990s,' *Harvard Business Review*, July–Aug, pp. 118–28; Barney, J. B. and Arikan, A. M. (2001) 'The resource-based view: origins and implications,' working paper, Fisher College of Business, Ohio State University; Barney, B. (2001) 'Is the resource-based "view" a useful perspective for strategic management research? Yes,' *Academy of Management Review* 26, pp. 41–57.

9 Bell, D. (1960) *The End of Ideology*, Glencoe, Ill.: Free Press; Bell, D. (1976) *The Cultural Contradictions of Capitalism*, HarperCollins; Bell, D. (1973) *The Coming of Post-Industrial Society*, New York: Basic Books.

10 Oster, S. (1999) *Modern Competitive Analysis*, New York: Oxford University Press, p. 2.; Saloner, G., Shepard, A. and Podolny, J. (2001) *Strategic Management*, New York: Wiley, p. 279.

11 Bowman, E. H. and Helfat, C. E. (2001) 'Does corporate strategy matter?' *Strategic Management Journal* 22, pp. 1–23; Drucker, P. (1994) 'The theory of strategy,' *Harvard Business Review*, Sept–Oct, pp. 95–105.

12 See Dyer, J. H. (1996) 'Specialized supplier networks as a source of competitive advantage: evidence from the auto industry,' *Strategic Management Journal* 17, pp. 271–92; Dyer, J. H. and Nobeoka, K. (2000) 'Creating and managing a high performance knowledge-sharing network: the Toyota case,' *Strategic Management Journal* 21, pp. 345–67.

13 See Grant, R. M. (2002) *Contemporary Strategy Analysis: Concepts, techniques, applications*, Oxford, U.K.: Blackwell, p. 307; Gulati, R, Nohria, N. and Zaheer, A. (2000) 'Strategic networks,' *Strategic Management Journal* 21, pp. 203–15; Barney, J. B. (2002) *Gaining and Sustaining Competitive Advantage*, Reading, Mass.: Addison-Wesley, p. 6.

14 Porter, M. E. (1985) *Competitive Advantage: Creating and sustaining superior performance*, New York: Free Press; McGahan, A. M. and Porter, M. E. (1997) 'How much does industry matter? Really?' *Strategic Management Journal* 18 (summer special issue), pp. 15–30; Porter, M. E. (1998) *On Competition*, Boston, Mass.: Harvard Business School Press.

15 Grover, R, Palmeri, C. and Elstrom, P. (2002) 'Qwest: the issues go beyond accounting,' *Business Week*, 25 March, pp. 66–8.

16 The journal has since changed its name to *Marketing/Communications*.

17 Rybczynski, W. (2001) *One Good Turn: A natural history of the screwdriver and the screw*, New York: Scribner / First Touchstone.

18 Adler, M. (1988) 'An algebra for data flow diagram process decomposition,' *IEEE Trans. Software Engineering,* Feb.

19 Wilford, J. N. (2002) *The Mapmakers*, London: Pimlico, p. 253.

20 Thompson, A. A. and Strickland, A. J. (2003) *Strategic Management: Concepts and cases*, New York: McGraw-Hill, p. 3; Chandler, A. D. (1962) *Strategy and Structure: Chapters in the history of the industrial enterprise*, Cambridge, Mass.: MIT Press, p. 13.

21 Our value map borrows symbols and terms from Dataflow Diagrams (DFD), whereas ABC typically used an IDEF0 modelling tool, with more involved terms and modelling techniques. Both can be shown to be equivalent to Petri nets, and thus provide the same language richness. DFDs are simpler and more intui-

tive, thus the choice was made to pattern value maps on the DFD modelling approach. (This short section is based on *Business Process Improvement* v.1.0, Office of Information Technology (AIT), Federal Aviation Administration, Washington, DC, 30 November 1995.)

22   Barney, J.B. and Arikan, A. M. (2001) 'The resource-based view: origins and implications', working paper, Fisher College of Business, Ohio State University, 2001; Barney, B. (2001) 'Is the resource-based "view" a useful perspective for strategic management research? Yes', *Academy of Management Review* 26, pp. 41–57.

23   Rumelt, R. (1991) 'How much does industry matter?' *Strategic Management Journal* 12, pp. 167–85.

24   These themes play an important role in Michael Porter's work, including (1996) 'What is strategy?' *Harvard Business Review*, Nov–Dec, p. 68; (1980) *Competitive Strategy: Techniques for analysing indus-tries and competitors*, New York: Free Press; (1990) *The Competitive Advantage of Nations*, New York: Free Press; (1979) 'How competitive forces shape strategy', *Harvard Business Review*, March–April, pp. 137–56.

25   From the once popular finance textbook by Gordon, M. (1962) *The Investment, Financing and Valuation of the Corporation*, Homewood, Ill.: Irwin.

26   Pagès, H. (1999) 'A note on the Gordon growth model with nonstationary dividend growth', Bank for International Settlements Working Paper no. 75, Basle, Switzerland.

27   Original equipment manufacture (OEM) is a term used to describe companies that manufacture (and often design, too) products that are sold under a different company's brand name (such as Toys'R' Us). The term is so widely used that it is common to hear it as both noun and verb.

ASSESSING AND MANAGING CAPABILITIES

LEARNING OBJECTIVES

After finishing this chapter, you will

▶ understand how **capabilities** (assets + competences) constrain the space in which we can compete effectively

▶ understand the difference between radical, progressive, creative and intermediating **industry innovation trajectories**

▶ understand that **acquiring capabilities** can expand your opportunities for innovation, but that they are limited by the money and people at your disposal

▶ have learned that successful innovation requires the collaboration of five very different types of people: **idea generators**, **boundary spanners**, **evangelists**, **coaches** and **project managers**

▶ recognize two **sources of innovation**, functional and circumstantial

▶ recognize that innovations may be created in a firm's own laboratories, but more often are **procured from a combination** of competitors' laboratories, universities and government laboratories.

After reading the *innovation workout*, you will be able to perform **forced splits** to force a more detailed perspective on a product, market or service. After reading the Paxil *case study*, you will be able to understand the roles of **risk avoidance**, **redifferentiation**, **story line**, **sponsored research** and **marketing** in launching a successful innovation.

Note: Further information, class slides, test questions and other supporting material are available on our companion website at

www.palgrave.com/business/westland

CAPABILITIES AND COMPETENCES

Our capabilities are defined by our competences (what we do well; perhaps better than any of our competitors) and our assets (the physical and intellectual property we own that erects barriers against entry by competitors). This fundamental equation (capabilities = competences + assets) determines the space in which we can compete effectively.

The first step in managing capabilities is to assess whether your existing capabilities are sufficient to enable you to remain competitive in your market.[1] Obviously, 'sufficiency' is a moving target; the entry and exit of competitors, new product and service offerings, and new technologies will keep an innovator's market in flux. This, then, is more often a question of whether the firm is evolving its capabilities as the industry in which it compete evolves. It is the interplay of the capabilities of the firm and the competitive marketplace that directs direct strategy and investment.[2]

The descent of strategy

Drucker originally perceived strategy as a battle waged with competitors in the marketplace. Managers were able to draw directly on parallels from military strategy. Predictably, flaws in the metaphor raised immediate objections from several quarters. Wars are limited to a relatively short time frame, while firms may muddle on for decades.

In the 1970s James March and Richard Cyert promoted behavioural concepts of organizational slack and managerial bounded rationality in describing the limits of strategy in practice, and why firms so often chose sub-optimal strategies.[3] In the 1980s Oliver Williamson suggested that sub-optimal behaviour was a matter of degree, and in the long run, the fittest will win out, subject to industry and market specific transaction costs.[4]

In the 1990s, sociologists like Mark Granovetter promoted the idea that culture strongly influences firm-specific strategy, as well as the optimal strategy in a market.[5] For example, competition in Asia could be predicted to vary considerably from that in the United States because of the fundamental differences in culture. More recently managers have grown fond of integrating all of the considerations into a resource-based view of strategy which recognizes that firms possess a unique 'personality' influenced by culture, transaction costs and bounded rationality, but also influenced by a firm's specific history, managerial personalities, and in general its unique capabilities. Activities in both vendor and consumer markets are constrained and moulded by the firm's capabilities in the resource-based view.[6]

A RESOURCE-BASED VIEW OF STRATEGY

The dominant view of strategy and strategy formulation today is the resource-based view (RBV) of firms' decision making. The RBV suggests that a firm's unique resources and capabilities provide the basis for a strategy. Strategies should be chosen to allow the firm to best exploit its core competencies relative to opportunities that arise in the external environment[7] (see Figure 5.1).

Chapter 2 presented several models that took an RBV in describing the consequences of industrial change on the capabilities demanded of a competitive firm. Three of these specifically address the challenges that arise when the largest profits to be made in an industry are moving away from the core capabilities that the firm currently possesses.

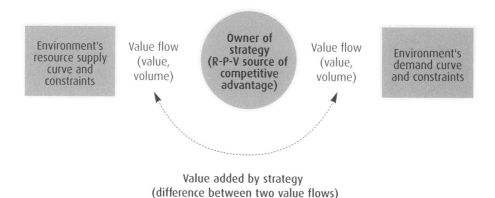

Figure 5.1 A resource-based view of strategy

Vacuum tubes: the market for niche innovations

Vacuum tube amplification has been around for a long time. Thomas Edison first observed in 1883 that a current flowed between the filament of an incandescent lamp and a plate in the vacuum near it when the plate was connected to the positive end of the filament, but not when the plate was connected to the negative side. In 1899, J. J. Thomson showed that this *Edison effect* was due to a stream of negatively charged particles – electrons – which could be guided by electric and magnetic fields. Further developments led Lee de Forest to patent the Audion triode vacuum tube (also known as a 'valve'), which was immediately put to use in audio amplifiers. For more than a half-century, these devices were the preferred choice for amplifying music.

Audio amplifiers based on transistors became practical with the wide availability of inexpensive transistors in the late 1960s, but they took a long time to reach that stage of development. The first patents for the transistor principle were registered in Germany in 1928 by Julius Edgar Lilienfeld. On 22 December 1947 William Shockley, John Bardeen and Walter Brattain succeeded in building the first practical point-contact diode transistor at Bell Labs for use in radar units (early tube-based technology did not switch fast enough for radar). Problems creating a working transistor triode needed for audio amplification required Bardeen to develop an entirely new branch of surface physics to account for the 'odd' behaviour of transistors.

From a design standpoint, transistors are much more flexible than tubes. They can put very high power in a very small package. They don't inherently draw much power nor create much heat, nor require high voltages. Myron Glass, an engineer at Bell Labs once quipped that 'nature abhors a vacuum tube', and went on to list the advantages of transistors for amplification:

- small size
- highly automated manufacture
- low cost, low power dissipation, low operating voltage
- no warm-up period (vacuum tubes need 10 to 60 seconds to function)
- high reliability and physical ruggedness
- much longer life
- complementary devices allow much more flexibility in circuit design
- ability to control large currents (even one ampere tubes are large and costly)
- much less microphonic (vibration can create ugly noises in amplifiers).

Yet, with all of these benefits, there are to this day still high-end audio aficionados who prefer tube-based amplifiers, claiming they have a 'warmer' sound due to a more linear V/I characteristic. Since these amplifiers cost 2 to 10 times the price of comparable transistor amplifiers, this constitutes a serious market for *niche innovations* in vacuum tube technology.

We shall discuss later in the chapter the options available to realign the firm's capabilities with the market, but for now, let's consider the outcomes when industry changes threaten the firm.

'Coreness' and 'imitability' of the firm's capabilities determine the profitability of innovations dependent on those capabilities.[8] This provides one explanation of why incumbents may outperform new entrants in the face of 'radical' innovations. There are actually two kinds of knowledge that underpin an innovation: *technological* and *market* (see Figure 2.8). An innovation is incremental (regular) if it conserves the manufacturer's existing technological and market capabilities; niche if it conserves technological capabilities but uses obsolete market capabilities; radical (revolutionary) if it makes obsolete technological capabilities, but enhances market capabilities; and architectural if both technological and market capabilities become obsolete. The point to note is that market knowledge is just as important as technological knowledge.

Some incumbents have great difficulty with apparently incremental innovations which involve seemingly small changes which could easily be handled by their capabilities. For example Xerox, the pioneer of the copier industry (albeit through its acquisition of Chester Carlson's technology), stumbled for years before developing a small plain-paper copier to challenge Japanese products. This can be explained by the fact that innovations are invariably built up of components, and thus building them requires two kinds of technical knowledge – technology underlying individual components, and architectural knowledge about how to link components together (see Figure 2.9). If the innovation enhances both component and architectural knowledge, it is incremental; if it destroys both, it is radical; if only architectural knowledge is destroyed, the innovation is architectural; where only component knowledge is destroyed (for one or more components) the innovation is modular.[9]

The prototype database

Ichiro Asai is one of the best motorcyclists in the world, most recently winning the coveted 2001 SuperSports 600cc class FIM Asia Road Racing Championship. He also has one of the most daunting 'day jobs' in the world – as a test rider for Yamaha Motorcycle's prototypes at the factory's Sugo racetrack near Sendai, Japan. The soft-spoken Asai described his job one afternoon during some free time at the Sugo track:

> The bikes need to be driven at 110 per cent of their capabilities. We really push the bikes past their limits. The test driver's job is to discover design flaws, whether it is in the chassis, motor, suspension, ergonomics or any of a thousand other aspects of the bike.[10]

None of this seems particularly surprising until Asai relates the terms of his contract with Yamaha.

'I have my job up until the first time that I crash the motorcycle. Any damage to their prototype and I will be fired immediately.' This is a bracing revelation in light of the fact that motorcycles, unlike most other forms of transportation, suffer what engineers call 'capsize instability' – they fall over.

Yamaha spends millions of dollars on R&D, prototyping and homologation which can take up to ten years and tens of thousands of test laps in a typical design. Its prototype is an extremely expensive individual unit, and one that is not easily replicated. Once the design is stable, production is simply a matter of stamping out the finished motorcycles. In motorcycles and many other tangible goods, the majority of cost is incurred upfront, in the generation of ideas – not at the end, when materials are being used.

A firm may find itself unable to introduce its particular innovations, no matter how much they may benefit the firm and fill out its product or service offerings, because it lacks the capabilities to effectively deliver them. The firm then faces a choice: either to acquire more capabilities (which can be expensive) or to discontinue commercialization of the innovation (which in the long run might be even more expensive).[11]

Industries, products and services follow distinctive change trajectories, and proper assessment of the particular trajectory on which it is competing is essential for an effective investment in capabilities. If the entire industry is in the midst of radical change, there will be an eventual need to dismantle old business models and acquire capabilities that are aligned with the emerging order. On the other hand, if the industry is experiencing incremental change, continual investment in redirecting and expanding capabilities is in order. The need to understand industry change trajectories may seem obvious, but such knowledge is not always easy to come by. Companies misread clues and arrive at false conclusions all the time. Management and investment in capabilities demands, first, complete and up-to-date business models describing the company's operations and markets, and second, knowledge of the particular trajectory along which the sector in which the company competes is moving.[12]

Cisco kids

Cisco Systems has a reputation for expanding its capabilities through acquisitions. Shortly after going public in 1990, Cisco (the name is an abbreviation of San Francisco, and Cisco's logo is a stylized Golden Gate bridge) went on a buying spree, acquiring 73 firms from 1993 to 2000. By late March 2000, at the height of the dot-com boom, Cisco was the most valuable company in the world, with a market capitalization of more than US$500 billion.

This had not always been the case. During its first decade after it was founded in 1984 the company acquired no businesses at all, sticking to selling routers and only routers. The market was growing rapidly, and Cisco went public in 1990. But three years later, a faster and cheaper piece of hardware – the switch – threatened its business. Cisco engineers scrambled to produce their own switch, but realized that they could not acquire the capabilities to produce one any time soon. Thus came the first acquisition in 1993 of Crescendo Communications for $95 million, which got the firm into switches – fast. Cisco's engineers grumbled that they could have produced their own switch in time, but the deal worked. Cisco got into the market ahead of the competition, most of Crescendo's

executives stayed with the company, and switches became a core Cisco business. The switching unit today generates nearly $10 billion in annual revenues.

Since then, acquisitions where they are unable to develop internal capabilities quickly enough to be competitive, and partnering with other companies, have enabled Cisco to retain its market dominance. Cisco has made inroads into many network equipment markets outside of routing, including Ethernet switching, remote access, branch office routers, ATM networking, security and IP telephony.

What began as a one-off response in an emergency soon evolved into a long-term strategy, an essential part of the Cisco culture. While most big tech companies rely heavily on R&D to create products and business lines, after the Crescendo purchase Cisco decided to use strategic acquisition to expand its capabilities. In 1995 it acquired its way into firewalls and cache engines; in 1998, internet telephony. In 2003, with the acquisition of Linksys, a home-networking company, Cisco made its first big move away from corporate customers into the consumer market, and in 2006 it continued by acquiring Scientific Atlanta, a set-top box manufacturer.

Anita McGahan of Boston University began ongoing research in the early 1990s into how industry structure affects business profitability. She found that industries evolve along four distinct trajectories, which she called radical, progressive, creative and intermediating.[13]

ALIGNMENT OF COMPETENCES AND ASSETS

Where a firm's strategy (its plan for achieving a return on investments in capabilities) failed to align with the industry's change trajectory, profitability suffered commensurately. In particular, these trajectories set bounds on the types of innovation that will successfully contribute to the firm. Failure resulted from obsolescence of the firm's products or services arising from two directions: first, a threat to the industry's core competences, and second, a threat to the industry's core assets – the resources, knowledge, and brand capital that have historically differentiated the firm.[14]

It is critical for firms evaluating their investments in capabilities to be aware that there is a significant misalignment between the type of industry change and the need for innovation normally described in the business press, and those that are important in reality. As Figure 5.2 shows, even though most stories of innovation and change concern radical change, it is intermediating and progressive change that dominates capabilities reengineering in practice. Firms strategizing for radical change, when what

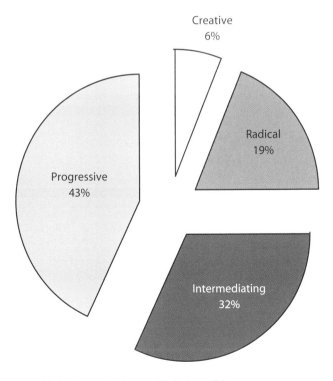

Figure 5.2 Percentages of industries undergoing a particular type of change

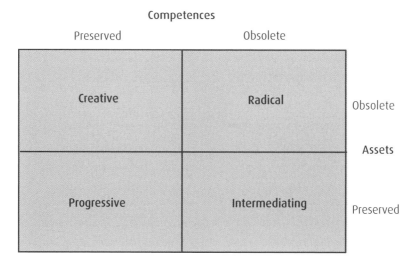

Figure 5.3 Trajectories and the threat of obsolescence

they need to address is the need for intermediating or progressive change, are likely to misallocate resources, and acquire the wrong sorts of capabilities.

Let's look at the four types of change, and the innovation and capabilities required for the firm to effectively meet the challenges presented by these changes in their industry.[15]

Cisco kids (part 2)

The vast majority of Cisco's acquisitions have been targeted technology purchases: small start-ups with 50 or fewer engineers whose products link back to Cisco's core competencies, routers and switches. If there is a secret to Cisco's success, it is this: Cisco has come to realize that the acquisition of technology really isn't just about technology. 'For us,' says Ned Hooper, vice president of business development, whose former company LightSpeed was acquired by Cisco in 1998, 'the people are the most strategic asset.' If, after the acquisition, Cisco loses the technologists and product managers who created, say, the Linksys router, then it has lost the second and third generations of the product that existed only in those employees' heads. That, says Hooper, is where the billion-dollar markets lie. And that is where Cisco's acquisitions are aimed. 'We need the expertise,' he says. 'We need the people.'

In the classic mergers and acquisitions world, if you can't measure it, you don't trust it, but that's not how Cisco operates. In addition to balance sheets and business models, Cisco scrutinizes would-be acquisitions' cultures and visions. The group holds meetings with everyone from junior engineers to top execs, observing who speaks and for how long, gauging how open the company is to debate and discussion, and watching how team members treat one another. 'We look for cultures that empower people,' says Hooper. Cisco doesn't do hostile takeovers, but it also doesn't want to buy a company whose people will head for the exits. Sometimes an acquisition is torpedoed because of a simple gut feeling. Hooper adds:

> I've had relatively junior people come to me and say, 'I don't like the people,' and we've walked from the deal. With Cisco, the acquisition is not the end but the beginning. The people we're acquiring have to feel the same way: It's the beginning of the next generation of that company.[16]

Radical change occurs when an industry's core assets and core activities are both threatened with obsolescence. Businesses fail because of disruptive innovations that substitute for their core products and undermine their business models. The music and network television industries have undergone radical innovation because of the internet-enabled mobility of digital media such as MP3s and DivX files, and emerging competitor technologies such as video games. Under radical change, knowledge and brand capital built up in the industry erode, and so do customer and supplier relationships. During the 1980s and 1990s, roughly 20 per cent of US industries went through some stage of radical change. When neither core assets nor core competences are threatened, the industry's change trajectory is progressive. Over the past 20 years, this has been by far the most common trajectory; about 43 per cent of US industries were changing progressively, including economically significant businesses of long-haul trucking and commercial airlines. In those industries, the basic assets, activities and underlying technologies remained stable. Innovators like Yellow Roadway, Southwest and JetBlue succeeded not because the incumbents' strengths became obsolete but because of a better understanding of how to take advantage of new technologies and squeeze more efficiencies out of their networks.

The other two change trajectories – creative and intermediating – have received less attention. *Creative change* occurs when core assets depreciate quickly but core competences are stable. Some industries, for example the news media, have always dealt with this scenario. But over the past decade, many new industries have faced the challenge of rapid asset obsolescence, and have needed to continually find ways to restore their assets while protecting ongoing customer and supplier relationships. For example, telephone equipment maker Ericsson saw its competences threatened by competition from consumer electronics firms; it solved this by transferring the most difficult product affected, its handsets, to consumer electronics giant Sony, leaving it free to concentrate on the more lucrative operator equipment market. About 6 per cent of all US industries are estimated to be on the creative change trajectory.

Intermediating change occurs when core competences are threatened with obsolescence, while core assets retain the capacity to generate value. For example, in the 1990s Swiss watch makers watched their sales decline rapidly as consumers became convinced that analogue clocks were considered obsolete. They joined forces with designers from many countries to reinvent the Swiss watch. The result was that they managed to considerably reduce the number of components and production time of an analogue watch. In fact the watches they designed were so cheap that if a watch broke it was cheaper to throw it away and buy a new one than to repair it. The watch makers founded the Swiss Watch company (Swatch) and called on graphic designers to redesign a new annual collection. The enormous success of Swatch was fuelled by new competences of clever industrial and graphic design. In the 1980s and 1990s, around 32 per cent of industries went through some form of intermediating change.[17]

The business press has historically focused on radical innovation in industry, where the relevance of an industry's established capabilities and resources is diminished by some outside alternative, and relationships with buyers and suppliers come under severe attack. In industries being radically transformed, most companies are eventually thrown into crisis. However, radical industry evolution is relatively unusual. It normally occurs following the mass introduction of some new technology, such as digital cameras in place of film cameras. It can also happen when there are regulatory changes (as in the telecommunications industry of the 1970s) or because of changes in taste (in the developed world, the decline in smoking).

An industry on a radical change trajectory is entirely transformed – but not overnight. It usually takes decades for change to become clear and play out. The end result is a completely reconfigured and downsized industry. The photographic industry – traditionally a chemical industry – has been transformed into a specialized discipline in the consumer electronics/computer sector, with much of the benefit of the transformation going to consumers.

Four phases of radical innovation

In the summer of 2003, digital cameras finally outsold film cameras, a day that the film camera industry had been predicting for decades. The major film producers Kodak and Fuji first attempted to transfer their competence in imaging to other fields such as image software and copying; subsequently they collaborated on the APS film system, which combined digital information with chemical imaging. But fundamental advances in digital imaging steadily drove down prices while elevating resolution. Chris Anderson of *Wired* magazine documented four critical phases marking radical change in the photographic industry[18] – the critical phase when the alternative camera technology became price competitive; critical mass, when complementarities set off a growth in interest in the alternative technology; the displacement of film cameras as the new digital cameras finally outsold film cameras, and the continued decline of digital camera prices to zero, causing cameras to be placed in every product imaginable (in 2006 Nokia was the world's largest seller of cameras by volume).

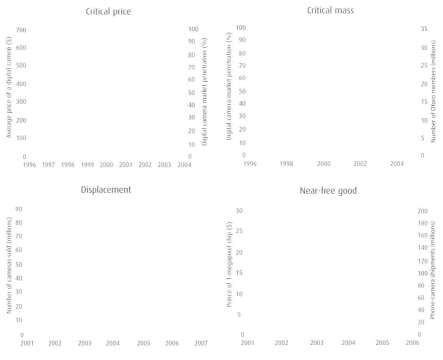

Figure 5.4 Phases of radical innovation in the camera industry

ACQUIRING NEW CAPABILITIES

Capabilities are often a constraint on innovation and market entry not only because it is expensive to acquire them, but also because it is difficult to determine the value of what has been acquired when a firm invests in particular capabilities. We shall defer the financial analysis of capabilities and innovations until a later chapter, but briefly touch on the investments that are required in order to expand capabilities.

Coach Schmidt

Eric E. Schmidt, CEO of Google, has been around the block. Formerly chief technology officer and corporate executive officer at Sun Microsystems, and CEO of Novell, he also worked at Xerox PARC, at Bell Laboratories and at Zilog. Google's youthful founders, Larry Page and Sergey Brin, recruited Eric Schmidt to run their company in 2001 under pressure from venture capitalists John Doerr and Michael Moritz. Google's S-1 filing notes that Schmidt, Page and Brin run Google as a triumvirate, but Schmidt possesses the legal responsibilities typically assigned to the CEO of a public company, and focuses on management of the vice presidents and the sales organization. More importantly, the dull, punctilious and austere Schmidt serves as a counterbalance to his exuberant founders and staff, working to help them achieve their objectives while reassuring investors and management that they are (in Schmidt's words) 'building the corporate infrastructure needed to maintain Google's rapid growth as a company and on ensuring that quality remains high while product development cycle times are kept to a minimum'.

Assets are easier to buy, sell and value than are people; and competences reside almost entirely in the firm's employees. At least five types of individual are needed to expand a firm's capabilities into a new area of product or service innovation – idea generators, boundary spanners (or gatekeepers), evangelists (or champions), coaches (or sponsors) and project managers.[19] Each class of individual has unique personality characteristics which make them good at what they do. Some may already exist in your organization. (In fact every firm has an obligation to develop and promote individuals in each category who are good at what they do.). *Idea generators* are good at sifting through large quantities of technological and market data to identify 'innovations'. *Boundary spanners* are conduits for knowledge from other firms and labs. They are likely to be social and gregarious, happy to attend professional meetings and travel around the firm. *Evangelists* are the champions who 'get' the invention and are happy to sell the innovation to the firm. They are enthusiastic, gregarious and tell a good story. They are also the first to 'get' the business model that will propel the invention to success. *Coaches* are the mentors for the team that will bring the invention to market. They are often also sponsors, senior-level managers who provide behind-the-scenes support, access to resources and protection from political foes. Finally, *project managers* inject the discipline to complete the detail work, and may serve as a one-stop decision-making shop for the innovation.

No discussion of the acquisition of capabilities would be complete without some indication of where to shop for them. Economist Eric von Hippel has suggested that innovations arise historically in one of two ways – by thinking about either functional or circumstantial activities surrounding the innovation. Functional innovation requires capabilities that can address the functional relationships between groups and individuals (such as customer and manufacturer). In contrast, circumstantial innovation requires capabilities that can address the circumstances in which a product (innovation) will be encountered (such as a cooking innovation when it is consumed in a restaurant).

Most innovations do not arise from inside the producing firm. This fact has implications for capabilities that the firm needs to acquire, because if other individuals or organizations possess the capabilities to produce an innovation, there is potential for outsourcing and buying capabilities on the open market, or for acquiring them through alliances. Both are less risky than direct acquisition, although they may ultimately be less profitable as well.[20] Innovations can be created in a firm's own laboratories, but they may also be procured indirectly from competitors' laboratories. For example, when Toyota markets a new model of car, the engineering department of German car maker BMW is likely to be one of the earliest purchasers. These cars will be completely disassembled, measured, chemically tested and so forth until BMW's engineers are thoroughly familiar with Toyota's latest innovations. The same sort of engineering may be procured on the open market. For example, Porsche has for many years offered consultancy services to various other car manufacturers. Studebaker, SEAT, Daewoo, Subaru and Yugo have consulted Porsche on engineering for their cars or engines, and Porsche also helped Harley-Davidson design the engine in its V-Rod motorcycle. There are also substantial resources invested by governments in university laboratories and science parks, which are increasingly important as sources of innovation.

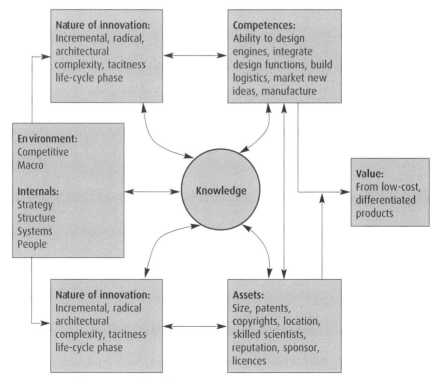

Figure 5.5 Factors in the acquisition of capabilities

Forced splits

Methodological reductionism – or more simply, forced splits – is the idea that developing an understanding of a complex system's constituent parts (and their interactions) is the best way to develop an understanding of the system as a whole. Richard Dawkins[21] introduced reductionism to describe the view that complex systems can be described with a hierarchy of organizations, each of which can only be described in terms of objects one level down in the hierarchy. He provides the example of a computer, which under hierarchical reductionism can be explained well in terms of the operation of hard drives, processors, and memory, but not on the level of semiconductor logic, or on the even lower level of electrons in a semiconductor medium.

The approach can be used to master complex design decisions through a process of 'forced splits' – taking each component in a complex product, system or innovation and subdividing it into a system of two or more subcomponents. These in turn may be subdivided. Aristotle used the method to develop taxonomies for everything from the animal kingdom to astronomy, and influenced the character of science for nearly two millennia.

The advantage of an innovation analysed in terms of forced splits is that the subcomponents at each layer can in theory be recombined in different ways to create any number of alternative inventions.

Reduction of complex systems, problems or things into subcomponents and subproblems is often the only way that you can effective manage a complex task. Forced splits give you a formal method for doing this that adds a layer of discipline to your creativity.

Blueprint

▸ Describe each component of your innovation, and identify how each relates to the overall objective. For example, if you have designed a shoe polisher, describe how each part helps achieve shiny shoes.

▸ Split each component into two subcomponents. These splits can be on character, function, concept, or anything else that is useful. Continue the process for a third (and in the extreme a fourth) split. You will end up with a tree whose branches are subcomponent systems.

▸ Don't be concerned about correctness or accuracy of subcomponents. The objective of this exercise is to look at your innovation in a new way – one that potentially uncovers new insights and variations.

▸ Let your diagram sit for five minutes, then revisit it, but this time going from the most detailed level of components up to the most integrated.

▸ Try reassembling subcomponents in new ways as you move from the most detailed to the most integrated.

Paxil

Jan Leschly is a fierce competitor, ready to unload on colleagues with exhortations like 'If you're not keeping score, you are just practising' or 'Never step on the court without expecting to win.' The son of a brewer, he wouldn't have been considered a Big Pharma type in the 1980s, but after a highly successful stint at Squibb where he built the drug Capoten into a $700 million a year bestseller (unheard of in that day), Leschly was in demand. He left Squibb in 1990 to reassess his priorities (with a sojourn in Princeton's graduate programme in philosophy), emerging to take a job as the right-hand man to Jean-Paul Garnier, CEO of SmithKline.

Risks of overdose in tricyclics

Studies in the 1990s in Australia and the United Kingdom showed that between 8 and 12 per cent of drug overdoses were the result of tricyclics, and it was thought that tricyclics might be involved in up to 33 per cent of all fatal poisonings, second only to analgesics. Tricyclics were often the choice of suicides, because of their pleasant mode of action.

But many of the overdoses are accidents, the result of what doctors call the 'narrow therapeutic index' of these drugs: that is, the therapeutic dose is close to the toxic dose. Doubling the prescribed dosage may result in poisoning, with uncertainties that increase the risk of toxicity include advancing age, cardiac status, and concomitant use of other drugs and alcohol.

Leschly's perspective on the drug business had evolved during his sojourn among the Princeton philosophers. He had come to see pills not as chemicals, but as *software*. Moreover, he saw this as a rationale for the escalating prices of drugs. He would explain to visiting journalists:

> Suddenly information technology was so essential that we realized we are an information company more than we are a pill company. Because it's the software, all the research, networking, marketing, that's so important in that pill. The pill is a piece of software!

As he told a group of fellow CEOs at a Harvard roundtable:

> I'm restructuring my work habits. I now spend about ninety per cent of my time on strategic issues and ten per cent on operational issues. I am almost totally disengaged from day-to-day, tactical implementation.

Every successful software company looks for a killer-app (that is, a software application that everyone simply must have). Leschly's was an antidepressant called paroxetine, with the brand name Paxil. It was one of a number of drugs available for treating mood disorders; Lilly's Prozac was one, Pfizer's Zoloft another. None was new – they had all had been around since the 1970s. Like Prozec and Zoloft, Paxil was not really any better than previous generations of drugs (called tricyclics) at alleviating depression. But it had one huge advantage from a marketing standpoint: it was almost impossible to overdose on it, and that made it easy to sell to (generally risk-averse) general practitioners in an era of rapidly escalating malpractice liability.

Paxil was a powerful cultural product tailored to a generation of young, obsessive, upwardly mobile professionals who were not keen to relive their parents' experience with Valium. Valium, which had been touted as a non-addictive successor to the tranquillizer Librium in the 1960s, turned out in fact to make its users addicted. Valium's troubles had hobbled the tranquillizer industry ever since.

Leschly knew that he could avoid the opprobrium surrounding Valium only by telling the Paxil 'story' SmithKline's way, using the new direct-to-consumer advertising recently approved by the US Food and Drug Administration. Leschly's story was a new-age parable, illustrated with brightly coloured diagrams and cartoon characters, that unfolded like this:

> Paxil works on a different brain chemical system than did older drugs. The name of this 'natural' brain chemical was serotonin. In some depressed patients, this chemical was lowered in volume because a certain brain synapse was 'overactive'. Paxil, by 'naturally' blocking reuptake of serotonin led, it was touted, to relief from depression.

Was the 'story' true? Well, every component had elements of truth. But no one really knows what 'serotonin balance' is. It has rarely been measured (and then only in dead people), and it would certainly never be measured in any patient coming to a general practitioner (the procedure involves a spinal tap!). Indeed, it was known that in different populations, both low and high levels of serotonin had been associated with depression. Yet all this misses the point: the 'story' was a simplification provided to help resistant physicians explain a complex and poorly understood biological process to recalcitrant patients.

Paxil sailed through FDA trials, being approved for sale as an antidepressant in the United States in early 1993. While trials were in process, Leschly had made sure that the marketing department talked with the company's pharmacologists. Indeed, the marketing people came away with something useful. They found out from the pharmacologists that Paxil only affects some particular neurotransmitter systems, not all of them. It is technically a 'selective serotonin reuptake inhibitor'. From this information the marketing department took away the knowledge simply that it was 'selective', connoting a sort of 'cleanliness' which distinguished it from previous generations of 'dirty' drugs. This made Paxil seem somehow better. Marketing promptly commissioned a set of advertisements (which have become legendary in medical marketing) depicting a pool table, to show how other antidepressants were 'scattershot' and Paxil was the clean, winning eight ball in the side pocket.

One of the stickier parts of FDA approval was that a drug was approved only for treatment of the specific malady specified in the approval documents. Any other use (for example, of an antidepressant drug for treating panic attacks) would be considered 'off-label' and was strictly prohibited. Such prohibitions were often difficult to enforce, because doctors could diagnose a particular set of symptoms as any one of a number of maladies.

Off-label proscriptions were a concern as Leschly's product development group thought about new outlets for Paxil, trying to enlarge their base of potential 'customers' by selling it as a cure for a number of related psychiatric disorders. There was the notion of a 'panic disorder', a highly agitated state of mind that might have specific or non-specific causes. Psychiatrists were pressed to define exactly what a 'panic disorder' was, beyond the fact that they once used to prescribe Valium for it. There was also the better studied phenomenon of obsessive-compulsive disorder, which might include sub-disorders like bulimia, anorexia and so forth. Although the disorder was rarely seen (at least in the early 1990s), there were likely to be many undiagnosed cases out there, and it was just a matter of alerting and educating general practitioners to this lurking threat to mental health. And even another opportunity raised itself: a phenomenon known as 'social phobia disorder'. This was another bona fide psychiatric disease, a debilitating lack of social confidence which led its sufferers to lives of isolation, loneliness, and inability to perform many of the simplest tasks of everyday life. As traditionally measured, it affected very few people in the United States or Europe (in fact it was known mainly as an 'Asian disorder'). But again marketing determined that there could be many undiagnosed cases, waiting for a prescription for Paxil.

To prepare the stage for Paxil's social phobia launch, Leschly's marketing department commissioned a huge publicity campaign to raise awareness of the disease, one that set the pattern for many to follow both at SmithKline and in the industry as a whole. The first step involved the hiring of a public relations agency to produce a free video on the disease and distribute it widely for use by network affiliates and independent television stations. (Health stories of any sort guarantee a minimal audience, and the fact that these were 'free' health stories was just icing on the cake.) The second step was to underwrite studies by experts in the field, who were intended to conclude that the disorder was debilitating and probably afflicted many more than had originally been suspected. Finally, while awaiting FDA approval for a new use, Smith-Kline underwrote a few small-scale studies off-label (that is, where the drug is used for other than its approved purpose, which in Paxil's case was adult depression). Through these, SmithKline became aware of even more promising new markets in child and adolescent depression.

By 2000 Paxil's unrelenting expansion of 'markets' (in other words, diseases) treatable with Paxil had proved brilliant: Paxil was FDA approved for depression, panic disorder, obsessive-compulsive disorder and social anxiety disorder (the latter of which was routinely described on night-time television as affecting tens of millions of people in the United States alone). At the end of 2000, Paxil had sales exceeding US$2.1 billion per year. This was not bad for a drug that had languished on the shelves of SmithKline's labs for most of the 1970s and 1980s.[21]

Paxil case study: questions for review

1. Describe SmithKline's Paxil business model. Where does SmithKline make money? What are its costs?

2. How did SmithKline use adaptive execution to develop its SSRI antidepressant business? What firm competences does SmithKline possess that made it a successful competitor in the antidepressant player market?

3. What was innovative about Paxil compared with other tricyclics? How did this help its commercialization?

4. With complex products, an important part of 'product design' is telling the 'story' about the product, its use and its benefits. Describe how Leschly made the Paxil story the innovation.

5. Challenge one of the fundamental assumptions of Paxil's business model by reversing it. Then define an 'anti-Paxil' product and business model that satisfies your reversed assumptions.

6. What are the commercially important attributes that make Paxil's business model successful and sustainable?

CHAPTER QUESTIONS FOR REVIEW

1. What is the difference between a competence, a capability and an asset? How do you go about investing in (that is, allocating resources to) each of these?

2. Describe the 'resource-based view' of firm strategy. What other perspectives exist on firm strategy? Choose a single firm, and consider which of the strategy perspectives presented in the chapter is most appropriate for describing and prescribing firm decisions.

3. In what way do coreness and imitability of a firm's capabilities the profitability of innovations dependent on those capabilities?

4. Industries in transition – for example, the camera industry several years ago as it moved from film to digital cameras – experience one of four types of change associated with the transition – creative, intermediating, progressive and radical. Most research and reporting focuses on radical change, even though it tends to be rare. How do you think that this research and reporting bias misleads firms that are going through intermediating and progressive change rather than radical change?

CHAPTER 5: KEY POINTS

▷ The fundamental equation – capabilities = competences + assets – determines the space in which we can effectively compete.

▷ Industries evolve along four distinct trajectories called radical, progressive, creative and intermediating.
  - Radical change occurs when an industry's core assets and core activities are both challenged; around 19 per cent of US industries in the 1990s faced radical change.
  - When neither core assets nor core competences are threatened, the industry's change trajectory is progressive; about 43 per cent of US industries were changing progressively in the 1990s.
  - Intermediating change occurs when core competences are threatened with obsolescence, while core assets retain the capacity to generate value; in the 1990s about 32 per cent of industries underwent intermediating change.
  - Creative change occurs when core assets depreciate quickly but core competences are stable. It is rare: in the 1990s only 6 per cent underwent creative change.

▷ Capabilities are often a constraint on innovation and market entry not only because it is expensive to acquire capabilities, but also because it is difficult to determine the value of has been acquired when a firm invests in particular capabilities.

▷ Assets are easier to buy, sell and value than are people.

▷ Competences are nearly always human resource-based.

▷ Five categories of people with distinct personalities are required to implement competence in a specific area:
  - *Idea generators* are good at sifting through large quantities of technological and market data to identify 'innovations'.
  - *Boundary spanners* are conduits for knowledge from other firms and labs.
  - *Evangelists* are the champions who can sell the innovation.
  - *Coaches* will sponsor and support politically those individuals essential for the success of the innovation.
  - *Project managers* attend to the details of making the innovation a success.

▷ Innovation is structured in two ways:
  - Functional relationships are between groups and individuals (such as customer and manufacturer).
  - Circumstantial innovation requires capabilities that can address the circumstances in which a product or service (innovation) will be encountered.

▷ Innovations can be created in a firm's own laboratories, but they may also be procured indirectly from their competitors' laboratories, universities, government laboratories or other sources. Corporate laboratories are responsible for comparatively few innovations used by a typical firm.

NOTES

1   Prahalad, C.K. and Hamel, G. (1990) 'The core competence of the corporation', *Harvard Business Review* **68**(3), pp. 79–91.

2   Hill, C. W. L. and Jones, G. R. (1995) *Strategic Management: An integrated approach*, Boston, Mass.: Houghton Mifflin.

3   Cyert, R. and March, J. (1963) *Behavioral Theory of the Firm,* Oxford: Blackwell.

4   Williamson, O. (1983) *Markets and Hierarchies: Analysis and antitrust implications*, New York: Free Press.

5   Granovetter, M. (1973) 'The strength of weak ties', *American Journal of Sociology* **78**(6) (May), pp. 1360–80.

6   Sources: Bowman, E. H. and Helfat, C. E. (2001) 'Does corporate strategy matter?' *Strategic Management Journal* 22, pp. 1–23; Drucker, P. (1994) 'The theory of strategy', *Harvard Business Review Sept–Oct*, pp. 95–105; Magretta, J. (2003) *What Management Is,* New York: Profile Business; Williamson, O. (1975) *Markets and Hierarchies,* New York: Free Press, p. 21.

7   Hamel, G. M. and Prahalad, C. K. (1994) *Competing for the Future*, Boston, Mass.: Harvard Business School Press, p. 203; Whittington, R. (2000) *What Is Strategy and Does It Matter?* London: Thomson Business Press.

8   Peteraf, M. A. (1993) 'The cornerstones of competitive advantage: a resource-based view', *Strategic Management Journal* **14**(3), pp. 179–91.

9   Porter, M. E. (1985) *Competitive Advantage: Creating and sustaining superior performance*, New York: Free Press; Barney, J. B. (1997) *Gaining and Sustaining Competitive Advantage*, Reading, Mass.: Addison-Wesley; Stabell, C. B. and Fjeldstad, O. D. (1998) 'Configuring value for competitive advantage: on chains, shops, and networks', *Strategic Management Journal* 19, pp. 413–37.

10 Source: conversation with author.

11 Henderson, R. and Clark, K. B. (1990) 'Architectural innovation: the reconfiguration of existing product technologies and the failure of established firms', *Administrative Science Quarterly* 36, pp. 9–30.

12 Conner, K., and Prahalad, C. K. (1995) 'A resource-based theory of the firm: know ledge versus opportunism', *Organization Science* 7(5), pp. 477–501.

13 McGahan, A. M. (2004). *How Industries Evolve: Principles for achieving and sustaining superior performance*, Cambridge, Mass.: Harvard Business School Press.

14 Von Hippel, E. (1988 *The Sources of Innovation*, Oxford: Oxford University Press; Von Hippel, E. (2005) *Democratizing Innovation*, Boston, Mass.: MIT Press.

15 Conner, K. and Prahalad, C. K. (1995) 'A resource-based theory of the firm: knowledge versus opportunism', *Organization Science* 7(5), pp. 477–501.

16 Source for Cisco information: Burrows, P. and Khar, O. (2005) 'Cisco's consuming ambitions', *Business Week*, 5 August, p. 13.

17 Abernathy, W. and Clark, K. B. (1985) 'Mapping the winds of creative destruction', *Research Policy* 14, pp. 3–22; Nonaka, I., Takeuchi, H. and Umemoto, K. (1996) 'A theory of organizational knowledge creation', *International Journal of Technology Management* 11, pp 833–45.

18 Anderson, C. (2006) *The Long Tail: Why the future of business is selling less of more*, New York: Hyperion, p. 72.

19 Schon, D. A. (1963) 'Champions for radical new inventions', *Harvard Business Review* 41, pp. 77–86.

20 Teece, D. J. (1986) 'Profiting from technological innovation: implications for integration, collaboration, licensing and public policy', *Research Policy* 15, pp. 285–306.

21 References and quotations in this case study were provided by Greg Critser (2005) *Generation Rx: How Prescription Drugs are Altering American Lives, Minds, and Bodies*, New York: Houghton Mifflin. Other sources are: 'Drug makers see "branded generics" eating into profits', *Wall Street Journal*, 18 April 18 2003, p. Al; 'Delicate balance needed in uniting of drug companies,' *New York Times,* 27 April 2004, p. Cl; 'An overdose of bad news,' *Economist*, 15 March 2005, pp. 73–5; 'Merck to pay $253 million after losing Vioxx suit,' *Financial Times*, 21 August 2005, p. 1.

SERVICE INNOVATIONS

LEARNING OBJECTIVES

After finishing this chapter, you will

► understand how the same concepts and features that are used to analyse product innovations can be applied to **service innovations**

► understand service innovations in the finance field, and how they are developed and sold

► understand service innovations in logistics and supply chain management.

After reading the *innovation workout*, you will see some of the unanticipated problems that arise because of the dynamics of service operations, and the additional dimension of features that need to be considered in service innovation.
After reading the Amazon *case study*, you will be able to understand the importance of **adaptive execution of strategies** over the life of the business model.

Note: Further information, class slides, test questions and other supporting material are available on our companion website at

www.palgrave.com/business/westland

SERVICE INNOVATION

Slick, user-friendly products usually come to mind when consumers and corporations think of innovation. But leading companies, innovation consultants and academic researchers have expanded their definition of innovation to from products to services. The initial impetus for the shift was the service nature of many of the dot-coms in the late 1990s. Over the next decade, services are expected to eclipse products as the main venue for innovation.[1]

The Federal Express story

In 1965, as a Yale undergraduate, Fred Smith, the future president of Federal Express, wrote a term paper which concluded that the passenger route systems used by the US Post Office were ignoring an important market – overnight delivery. Smith conjectured that he could turn Post Office economics upside-down. Post Office delivery optimized distance travelled where time was not a critical value, and package handling was cheap. He wanted to compete for customers using new technology – transportation networks that took advantage of the increasing size and speed of jets to restructure the geography of space, time and wealth. Smith saw that new air technology could let him ignore distance travelled, and instead, optimize speed and handling to create new market value. Such a system would be designed specifically for airfreight, which could accommodate time-sensitive shipments such as medicines, computer parts and electronics.

The paper was returned with the teacher's comment, 'The concept is interesting and well-formed, but in order to earn better than a "C", the idea must be feasible.'

Undaunted, after a stint in the military Smith bought a controlling interest in Arkansas Aviation Sales, located in Little Rock, Arkansas, and officially began operation as Federal Express on 17 April 1973, with the launch of 14 small aircraft from Memphis International Airport. On that night, Federal Express delivered 186 packages to 25 US cities – from Rochester, New York to Miami, Florida.

Memphis, Tennessee was selected as the headquarters since it was the geographical centre of the original target market cities for small packages. In addition, the weather in Memphis was excellent, in that the airport rarely closed as a result of climatic conditions. Memphis International Airport was also willing to make the necessary improvements for the operation and had additional hangar space readily available.

A major part of the initial business was overnight flat letter delivery. Smith used his first-mover advantage, and linked and leveraged products off one another – taking advantage of network economies in the process – to 'lock in' customers. Yet advances in technology undermined this business, as Group III facsimile – which used standard telephones to transmit images of flat mail at the speed of light – substituted for overnight delivery at very competitive prices. Within three years of its introduction, Group III faxes accounted for about 60 per cent of international telephone calls. In the days before widespread email, businesspeople increasingly took advantage of the asynchronicity of Group III fax to overcome global time differences. Federal Express quickly reengineered its business around package shipping, especially for inventory expediting out of their Memphis base.[2]

Figure 6.1 shows the numbers of US workers involved in four types of work – innovation, industrial work, service work (typically meaning customer-facing services such as retailing, telemarketing and so forth) and agriculture – over the 20th century, and their approximate wages circa 2003.

The growth of innovation in the 20th century was intimately tied to the growth of

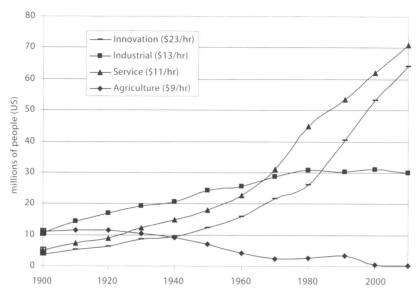

Figure 6.1 The rise of services

Sources: US Census Bureau, US Bureau of Labour Statistics, and Florida, R. (2003) *The Rise of the Creative Class: And how it's transforming work, leisure, community and everyday life*, New York: Basic Books.

the service worker. Work restructuring involved some 'outsourcing' of tasks, and when a sufficient market grew for these outsourced tasks to support it, another service job was created. Often these tasks were deskilled and formalized: jobs that previously required specialized skills were structured and standardized so that they could be given to the lowest-cost worker. For example, a hamburger stand in the 1950s would have depended on the speed, judgement and skill of a short-order cook to satisfy customers' orders. A modern hamburger stand would limit the menu, purpose-build kitchen equipment for specific items, allow cooks and order takers to change jobs at a moment's notice, and generally minimize any specialized knowledge needed for any specific task. Even communication tends to be standardized around polite, pre-scripted phrases: 'Welcome to our restaurant, may I take your order.'

7-Eleven (Hong Kong) innovates in electronic retailing

Retailing has been a great generator of service jobs over the past two decades. Dallas based 7-Eleven is one example of such retail service providers, operating over 18,000 convenience stores worldwide, with roughly 70 per cent located outside the United States. In Hong Kong, China and Singapore, 7-Eleven stores have been run since 1981 by Bermuda-based Dairy Farm International Holdings Ltd, with around 150 stores across tiny Hong Kong's 1100 square kilometres of land. Total annual sales in 2006 were around US$0.75 billion, and average store sales transactions averaged US$1.25; virtually all sales are cash. In consequence, cash-handling costs are around 15 per cent of sales price, which adds a substantial amount to variable selling and administrative costs. Management recognized that volume, pricing, server efficiency and net income would all improve significantly by a move to adopt new electronic commerce services – indeed, many in management felt that the only way to sustain sales growth was through innovations in automated payment, operations and sales services.

To reduce the costs of currency and coin handling, 7-Eleven examined suitable electronic payment methods. Credit cards tended to be costly for small transactions. This had resulted in the development of several alternative payment methods – Mondex, Visa Cash and Octopus – in the late 1990s which were specifically designed for small cash purchases typical of 7-Eleven convenience stores. Although 7-Eleven experimented with several systems from 2000 to 2003, the Octopus contactless cash card was the most popular of the small payment methods from the start. The move to automated payment significantly reduced costs by reducing the need for checkout staff, and reducing back-office administrative costs.

Since 2000 7-Eleven has engaged various employees and outside consultants in focus groups to invent and assess other convenience store service innovations which might open new markets and customer sets. Innovations appropriate for 7-Eleven's Hong Kong stores tended to be unique, first because high land costs meant stores were smaller, busier and more densely stocked than anywhere else in the world, and second, because customer profiles and tastes differed from the rest of Asia. By 2003, a list of eight retail service automation projects (see Table 6.1) were mooted at a company meeting.

The new services that were adopted were generally successful, generating a modest sales growth. 7-Eleven saw the success of these programmes as a 'proof of concept', and to the current day rely on similar focus groups to suggest and critique potential new services.[3]

Table 6.1: *Potential retail automation service projects for 7-Eleven Hong Kong*

Automated retail service innovation	Marginal cost	Marginal benefit	Adopted?	Comment
Mark Six (lottery) vending machine	Medium	High	No	Legality issues; HK government does not allow online betting on lottery
Concert ticket vending machine	High	High	Yes	Adopt, high growth potential, attracts customers who buy other items
Colour photo development	High	Medium	Partly	Feasible, but store space concerns may limit to only a few of the larger stores
All-in-one electronic purchase platform (for all of store's stock)	Very high	High	No	Risk of failure is too high
Digital bus route (information only)	Low	Medium	Yes	Phone inquiry terminal was added to kiosk; draws customers into store who buy other items
Entertainment kiosk (MP3s, etc.)	Medium	High	Yes	Limited success to date
Internet access terminal	Low	Medium	No	Store space concerns
Self-customized greeting cards	Low	Medium	No	Store space concerns

This is all very reminiscent of factory line standardization under the scientific management of Fred Taylor,[4] father of the stopwatch-and-clipboard approach to factory management. 'Taylorization' cut the cost of Henry Ford's Model T in half; it yielded similar gains for Isaac Singer (sewing machines), Cyrus McCormick (reapers), and Samuel Colt (firearms).

Taylor's *ideas* about the production of cars *replaced materials, labour and overhead* that had previously been required to produce a Model T. In Ford's 'Taylorized' Highland Park plant, one man could do what three or four had done before, and Taylor later did the same at Chevrolet's plant in Flint. The rise of innovation has created many more opportunities to 'Taylorize' every aspect of our life, segmenting and deskilling labour-intensive tasks, and transferring them to the lowest-cost provider. The rise of the internet, and cheap global communications and logistics, often make it possible for such segmented and deskilled jobs to be transferred to low-cost bidders halfway around the world.[5] The net effect of such task restructuring, deskilling, segmentation and global outsourcing has sometimes been socially unsettling. But it is also a fundamental part of the growth of service innovation which ultimately enriches our lives, and provides us with enormous market choice.[6]

Services now provide the primary settings for innovation among executives at high-profile companies in the technology industry.[7] Many developed economies have ceased to generate much GDP from goods – rather they have become service economies. The ten industries with the most dramatic salary growth are all in this service-providing sector, ranging from employment services to education to health care. In the United States, it has been estimated that manufacturing employment will drop 5 per cent and goods-producing industries will decline 13 per cent from their 2003 levels by 2014.[8] This reflects a global trend stemming from the relentless exponential increase in manufacturing productivity. Globally, service workers now outnumber farmers for the first time in history.[9] A study of the ten largest non-energy firms in the United States in 2005 discovered that they obtained 65 per cent of 2005 revenues and 85 per cent of 2005 profits from services.[10] Despite the greater challenges in service industries, these numbers underline the importance of corporate investment in service innovation.

Services have in the past tended to be provided locally, because the expertise behind the service resided in individuals, workshops, or stations on a transportation network. The rise of two-way communications networks – first telephones, then the internet – combined with desktop computing power changed this, though. Starting in the 1980s, software innovators used desktop computers to offer the services of professionals through their software. For example, Intuit encapsulated the expertise of tax accountants and financial planners in its TurboTax and Quicken software, and PGMusic offered piano and guitar lessons interactively through its Master Class software. The growth of the World Wide Web in the 1990s offered the ability to connect everyone in the world to services provided by an individual on location, or through servers with computing power much greater than a desktop PC. For instance, eBay and Craigslist offered the same advertising services as local newspaper classifieds, but not limited by local circulation; large web retailers now provide customers with live instant-messaging with a consumer representative while shopping online.[11]

Internet bandwidth and desktop computing power continue to grow exponentially, making possible the delivery of almost any 'local' service to a global customer base. The revenue potential is similarly global, but without incurring rapidly increasing costs. Add to this levels of standardization and control that are not possible in locally provided services, and service innovations are truly revolutionary.

At the time of writing, two service industries are probably being changed fastest by service innovations – financial services and the medical profession. Searching for a loan, buying insurance and trading stocks are all 'local' services that have migrated to the web. Stock trading sites were consistently the fastest growing dot-coms in the mid-1990s.[12]

The medical profession is silently being transformed through outsourcing and the shift towards self-service. The outsourcing of prescriptions from proprietary branded drugs to generics sold across borders (for example, from Canada to the United States) has shown the potential to dramatically lower drug prices, albeit with some risks that go with less intense monitoring. Sites such as WebMD and Wikipedia offer health information online which many patients use both to flag health problems and to provide a second opinion.

Definitions and practice in service innovation are still in flux, with many conflicting opinions on how to innovate. An internet search on 'service innovation' retrieves mostly financial and supply-chain innovations. In this chapter I shall try to relate some of the advances that have been made in these services, looking closely at services in finance, and operations, where recent innovations have contributed significantly to firm competitiveness.

DEFINING 'SERVICES'

Services are processes that in some way or another solve a customer's problem, perform an activity that the customer cannot do personally, or benefit the customer in some other intangible way. Services are often personally tailored to a customer's needs, and often demand face-time – face-to-face interaction with the customer and substantial exchange of information between customer and server. The nature of work involved in providing a service will be heavily influenced by the sort of contract, relationship, mission or circumstances under which it is conducted. We differentiate between:

- ▶ *business to consumer* (B2C) services such as financial services, retailing and leisure services
- ▶ *business to business* (B2B) services such as consulting, office equipment support and communications
- ▶ *internal services,* such as information technology, accounting and human resources
- ▶ *public services* such as police, education and health services
- ▶ *not for profit services* such as churches and charities.

Up to this point, we have strategized mainly in terms of innovative products that incidentally require that we tailor some production, sales and support processes to make the innovation a success. In service industries, we are interested in innovative activities that may incidentally require a product for success (for instance, a doctor providing vaccination will need the vaccine), but where strategy, implementation and success are all about the conduct of the activity.

Service activities must be *scalable* – for example, there might be only ten retail customers coming into a store today, but it needs to be prepared to have 100 tomorrow, and should prepare to keep the store running efficiently and effectively over many years. For this reason, the aim is to make the service *routine* – in fact, delivering this as routine in a way that makes every customer feel uniquely treated is one of the great challenges of service of all types today.

Two aspects define services: first, they are activities rather than tangible products, and second, they are customer-facing, involving direct and repeated interaction with customers at a face-time level. Otherwise, services should be analysed in the same way that we have analysed products and processes in this book – as a bundle of features with market appeal, production constraints and financial constraints.

FINANCIAL SERVICES

Financial service innovation has earned more recent recognition than any other area in service innovation. That is only reasonable, as the most substantial amounts of money are in the finance sector, and that sector has been restructuring almost continually since the early 1980s. Perhaps no other sector has been so influenced by the World Wide Web, and the global flattening that it has enabled.

Finance deals entirely with information – with products that are easily converted to bits and bytes. The industry's products are universally directed towards contracts that transfer money at some time, place and contingency, often in connection with an asset. For example, home mortgages transfer money for the purchase of a house, secured by the house, and contracting with the owner to pay in instalments over some future time period. Corporate stocks are contracts that share in the ownership of a firm, and for which elaborate secondary markets are constructed and operated.

Although the underlying components of financial services are comparatively limited, innovation in these markets can become very involved, because of payment timing, conditions on payment (such as bond covenants or derivative terms) and contingencies that affect contracts. Financial specialists have developed an involved colloquial language to articulate the features that characterize their products; innovations are conceived in terms of the restructuring and reengineering of these features.

Any list of features from the finance industry (or any other industry for that matter) will necessarily be very incomplete, but a short list will provide a flavour of what innovators in financial services actually have to manipulate to define new products. A few of the most prominent features of financial products are, for example:

▶ risk: the measurable loss potential of an investment
▶ return: the earnings made on an investment
▶ liquidity: the speed of trading, price stability, depth and breadth of the market in a particular asset
▶ face value: the nominal amount printed on the face of a security
▶ spot price: the price at which an asset is quoted on the market, for immediate delivery.

Banking services

From the 1950s to the 1970s, world banking was dominated by US banks, while in the 1980s Japanese banks expanded substantially. The race for size in banks was understandable: not only could large banks finance any deal, they also could cross-sell an entire portfolio of services efficiently. Much of the innovation in banking services has involved figuring out how to make size a barrier to entry at the same time that it is a source of operating efficiency.

In 2005, the world's largest bank (with assets of US$2.0 trillion) was created from the merger of Japan's Mitsubishi Tokyo Financial Group (MTFG) and UFJ. Citigroup (United States) was second, with $1.5 trillion in assets. Of the world's ten largest banks, three were American (Citigroup, JP Morgan Chase, and Bank of America), two were Japanese, and one each British, German, French, Dutch and Swiss. Size is important in banking because with deregulation, each bank must increasingly compete with foreign banks

at home and abroad to be successful. Global banks must be able to meet the rising financial needs for lending, underwriting, currency and security trading, insurance, financial advice, and other financial services for customers and investors with increasingly global operations. (In other words, they must provide one-stop banking for global corporations.)

But size is not everything in banking, and once a bank is, say, one of the ten largest in the world, efficiency is what matters the most. Global banks must also be highly innovative, and introduce new financial products and technologies to meet changing customer needs. Overcapacity – too many banks chasing too few customers – will also increase competition. Large US banks are strong on innovations, and with the repeal of the 1933 Glass-Steagall Act (which prevented them from entering the insurance and securities fields), they are now able to compete with foreign banks more effectively at home and abroad.[14]

The success of financial innovations is measured by their ability to jointly meet the needs of borrowers and investors. Ideally the amounts of money available will be equal, although this is difficult to assess in advance of marketing. Investors, and borrowers or businesses that need money for assets and projects, are likely to have a wide divergence of needs, risks and timing requirements; only some of these will be known in advance. Although financial markets exist to determine precisely how to price a given financial innovation to clear the market, they are predicated on the existence of financial products that can generate sufficient interest on both the buying and selling side. For this reason, as with other sorts of innovation, the ability to assess the viability of an innovation in advance of development and marketing is just as essential as it is for a tangible physical innovation.

SERVICE INNOVATIONS THAT ENGINEER FINANCIAL RISK

Contracting for services often involves substantial risk – risk of non-performance, poor-quality performance, failure to follow up with maintenance, liability arising from the service and so forth. If the risk is too great, sales will suffer. Auctioneer eBay knows this, and offers seller ratings, escrow services, financial services, fraud investigation services and many other services that reduce the risk of an eBay transaction. EBay charges for these services, in addition to its basic transaction charges.

Many recent innovations in financial markets have similarly involved clever engineering of risk to make certain financial services more saleable; the resulting financial instruments are called *derivatives*. A derivative is any financial innovation whose valuation at a point in time is derived from some asset other than itself. For example, the option derivative that gives the holder the right to sell a share of Google stock at a fixed price, say $400 per share, will have a sales value that depends on the current spot price of Google's stock (the *underlying asset*). The value of a derivative will be some mathematical function of the current and future values of the underlying asset, and because the future values of that asset are unknown and the ultimate source of financial risk, it is common to refer to derivatives as *risk management instruments*. There are potentially as many unique derivative innovations as there are unique mathematical functions on the current and future values of the underlying asset. The purpose of a derivative is to allow both the seller and the buyer to tailor their investment risk to meet the needs of their particular business model and planned projects.

Derivatives are a relatively recent innovation. In the late 1970s, Wall Street's finance community suffered from multiple crises. The New York Stock Exchange ended fixed commissions. This took place during a severe recession and the oil price shock after-effects of Iran quadrupling oil prices in the early 1970s, and many major banks hovered on the edge of bankruptcy. The increased risks borne by banks initiated a furious rate of innovation in financial derivatives, ushering in the first interest rate swaps, currency swaps, zero coupon bonds, and variable rate financing started to appear on financial markets.

The option adjustable rate mortgage

One of the most successful financial innovations in recent years in the home mortgage market is the *option adjustable rate mortgage*, or option ARM. Option ARMs offer flexibility at the expense of complexity and risk. They allow new home buyers to afford a home in a rising market with a minimum of downpayment. The critical features that sold the option ARM innovation were:

▸ *Assumptions*:
  – House values will rise enough to make refinancing worthwhile.
  – The borrower's income will rise enough to cover the increased cash payments.
▸ *Low payments* in the first one to five years (which benefits the home owner).
▸ High home owner *refinancing costs* (which benefits the mortgage lender).
▸ High *fees/commission* (which benefits the mortgage lender).
▸ The lender is allowed to *claim the full monthly payment as revenue* on its books even when borrowers choose to pay much less (which benefits the mortgage lender).

▸ Interest rates and up-front fees might be determined by a *hedge fund* (which benefits the mortgage lender).

Option ARMs accounted for as little as 0.5 per cent of all mortgages written in 2003, but rose to 12.3 per cent by 2006. They made up one-third to one-half of mortgages in the high-priced markets of California and Florida. Their initial low payments are only temporary, and the less a borrower chooses to pay upfront, the more is tacked on to the balance. This creates a risk for lenders of customer default if the borrowers are not able to come up with cash later in the loan cycle. The banking system (in theory) insulated itself reasonably well from ARM default. Poorly performing option ARMs (where home owners have stopped paying their loans) can be packaged with other, better loans and resold in chunks to investors – about half of ARMs are dealt with in this way. Banks sell substantial amounts directly to hedge funds and other big investors with big appetites for risk.[14]

Swaps are financial derivatives where one party contracts to swap cash flows with another. For example, a bank may have a large number of fixed-rate mortgage loans, while another bank may have a pool of variable-rate mortgage loans. Assume that each of the banks would prefer to have the other type of loan. Rather than cancel their existing loans (which would be difficult if not prohibitively expensive given a large pool of mortgage loans) the two banks could achieve the same end by agreeing to 'swap' cash flows. The first bank pays the second based on a floating-rate loan, and the second pays the first based on a fixed-rate loan (in practice, the two will net out the amounts). By swapping the cash flow, each has 'swapped' one type of loan – and one source of risk – for another.

Such swaps are just one example of a mortgage-based derivative. Because of the huge size of the global housing market, the repackaging of mortgage loans, and associated risks of homeowners defaulting on their payments, has not only been a huge business, but has also provided an arena for innovation in new derivative instruments. The previously discussed swap can trade off the risk of a change in interest rates, but buyers are necessarily limited to other banks who may have similar (large) cash flows derived from home owners. To swap risk with a larger market of investors (in other words, to devise a derivative with more market liquidity), banks may turn to collateralized mortgage obligations (CMOs: see Figure 6.2), a derivative first created in June 1983 by investment banks Salomon Brothers and First Boston. A CMO has a pool of home mortgage loans which provide collateral, a set of tranches (tranche is the French word for 'slice') and a set of rules that dictate how money coming in from the collateral will be distributed to the tranches. Investors purchase certificates of a tranche.

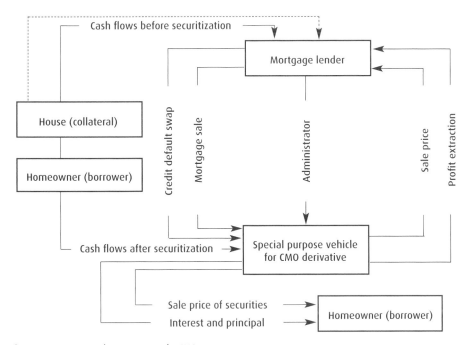

Figure 6.2 Features and components of a CMO

Although the terminology used to describe the features of derivatives can seem arcane, the underlying concepts invoked in designing financial products are identical to those that would be invoked in building, say, a new consumer electronics device. Consumer demand and producer competences ultimately dictate what can or cannot be successfully introduced into the marketplace – whether that marketplace is for mortgages or cameras.

INNOVATION IN LOGISTICS AND SUPPLY-CHAIN OPERATIONS

Innovations in information processing and communication have had an enormous impact on logistics and supply-chain operations. The latter consume 10 to 20 per cent of global GDP, and have grown substantially over the past few decades. Supply-chain innovations, though, are usually not noticed by any but those directly involved in the supply chain. The average customer sees them only as a slightly lower price, or faster order processing – the rest of the work is largely invisible to the consumer.

The force of new ideas that has pushed productivity in semiconductors, software and transportation has similarly benefited service operations. Shipping logistics were responsible for moving some 250 million containers around the world in 2006, a quantity that is increasing by around 15 per cent annually, while cost per container continues to decline as a result of continuing innovations in scale and scheduling efficiencies.

Outsourcing design and manufacturing: Flextronics' Peabody mobile phone

Flextronics International, with US$15 billion in annual sales and 100,000 employees in 2006, offers turnkey manufacturing services to the world's leading electronics companies, including Alcatel, Dell, Ericsson, Hewlett-Packard, Juniper Networks, Microsoft and Siemens. The company's services range from design engineering, through manufacture and assembly, to distribution and warehousing. It manufactures and assembles printed circuit boards, electromechanical components, subsystems and complete systems for a wide range of makers of networking and telecommunications equipment, computers, consumer electronics and medical instrumentation.

Flextronics is an original equipment manufacturer (OEM) for consumer electronics that are marketed under another brand (such as Microsoft's Xbox360). Its services fall into two main categories. First is contract manufacturing (CM), where companies send designs and prototypes of consumer electronics products to Flextronics, which takes care of production set-up, supply-chain management, product quality control, and the first stages of the distribution channel. This category accounts for 40 per cent of Flextronics' contracts.

The second service is contract design and manufacturing (CDM), where companies outsource product objectives, requirements and interface-usability guidelines to Flextronics' R&D. Once the product is designed and approved by the outsourcing firm, Flextronics is responsible for production and other downstream operations. This category accounts for 50 per cent of Flextronics' contracts.

By 2003, Flextronics was designing and producing mobile phones for the major brands. Engineers in Flextronics' R&D repeatedly pointed out flaws in either requirements or designs that they received from clients; they also became convinced that they could develop and produce a much better telephone in-house than anything that currently existed in the market.

It was at the suggestion of R&D that Flextronics embarked on its original design and manufacturing (ODM) project to produce the Peabody mobile telephone. The design was initially mooted with the intention of selling it to one of the firm's clients, and then marketing and distributing through the client's channels. There was also discussion of developing the Peabody or Flextronics brand from scratch. The main attraction of the latter approach was the high mark-up on retailing of mobile phone handsets (versus the extremely low margins in contract manufacturing).

Potential clients initially balked that the Peabody phone was too sophisticated, and that there was no way that Flextronics could complete the design prototype and produce the items in less than one year. Flextronics countered by completing the design prototype in six weeks, and offering to commence production and delivery within another six weeks. Clients were impressed, but then fell back on more pedestrian complaints – that the Peabody phone was not invented in their own labs, that it did not fit into their current product line, or that there could be interoperability problems (although this seemed not to be a problem with CDM phones contracted to Flextronics).

Flextronics CEO Michael Marks was more candid in his assessment, noting that the ODM business was significantly different from manufacturing services:

> With manufacturing, our customers don't really care who else we work with ... rarely ask for an exclusive relationship. With design, we're getting much closer to what our customers care about ... they don't want us selling the same product to others in the market. If we do an exclusive deal with one customer, the others get upset. Finding the right strategy in this market is probably the most interesting intellectual issue I have faced in my business career.

Thus the prospect of selling the Peabody phone to one of their clients confronted Flextronics with concerns from other customers about exclusive deals on proprietary technology. These concerns could be followed up by customers withholding their key technology, or contracts, from Flextronics, and potentially switching their business to competitors like Hon Hai, Sanmina-SCI or Solectron who lack channel conflicts.

The prospect of Flextronics marketing the Peabody itself was not even considered, as Flextronics lacked both brand recognition in the mobile phone market, as well as any marketing channels or selling expertise. An updated Peabody prototype was vetted at the 3GSM World Congress in 2005, and Microsoft showed some interest in selling it under its own brand, but to date the Peabody mobile phone remains a prototype only.

Despite the excellent reviews Flextronics received on its Peabody design, its troubles in making the transition from low-margin contract manufacturing to high-margin branded retailing highlights the fact that the biggest profits are earned, and the strategic battles are fought, at the distribution channels and at the customer interface – not on the factory floor or in the design labs.[15]

CONSUMER EDUCATION, WARRANTY AND AFTERMARKET SERVICES

Even physical products are attached to a bundle of services, which may represent a substantial portion of cost. As products grow more complex, the set of features and user interface tends to grow complex as well. Consumers require services that will educate them on use and on the advantages of a particular product – otherwise the product would not be usable, and thus not saleable. Education can be delivered before the sale – for example, via advertising for drugs, or demonstrations and trial offers for software, games and so forth – or it can be delivered after the sale – say, as help desk support for consumer electronics or software problems, and on-site service for computers. If physical services on a product are required, such help desks will tell customers how to receive this service. In many cases, information is the product – legal advice or medical diagnoses can be expensive, and only involve the transfer of information between a professional and client or patient.

Manjushree Infotech's call centre

Sam Swaminathan, CEO of Manjushree Infotech (part of the B.K. Birla Group) set up a call centre in 2000 in Kolkata, India to serve a single health maintenance organization (HMO) in Tampa, Florida, USA. The plan was to build a small set-up consisting initially of 25 employees, which could be scaled up as business picked up and new clients were acquired. With an eye towards rapid expansion, Swaminathan determined that the initial call centre platform absolutely had to be scalable by at least two orders of magnitude in order to handle expected business at targeted service levels.

Companies like to locate call centres in India because of the employees. Employees have excellent English (even to the point of being able to speak with US regional accents) and can be hired for 10 per cent of the cost of comparable employees in the United States. Still, wages in India were rapidly increasing, chipping away at the labour price advantage. Even with a ten to one cost advantage, cheap labour can only scale so far. Swaminathan needed to innovate if he was to stretch his resources to scale by at least two magnitudes of call volumes.

Call centre operations are essentially designed to deliver educational services. Education may involve solving a problem, discovering a feature, or discovering whether the product is defective. The traditional call centre dialogue is two-way verbal between the customer and a call centre employee over a wide area voice telephone network. This suffers from all of the inefficiencies of traditional conversation – misunderstood phrases, linear presentation of facts and issues, and speed limited by the articulation of the speaker.

Thus Swaminathan planned initially to build and debug operations consisting only of human responses to questions, but via an integrated data/voice/video wide-area telephone network. As more firms were added, the intent was to add voice recognition and response for a set of perhaps 20 to 50 of the most

common queries for any given product, with the automated system turning control over to a human operator if it could not satisfy the customer's query. Once working, such a system could automate close to 95 per cent of call responses, at close to zero marginal cost per call.

The third phase of expansion would add the ability to respond either automatically, or with human intervention, to queries typed through the client's webpage. Again, once working, such a system could automate close to 95 per cent of web query responses, at close to zero marginal cost per call. Where the automated response system could not handle a query, it would be turned over to a call centre/help desk employee for response. Unlike voice calls, web response could not be immediate, but Swaminathan was targeting an average response time of 4 hours for queries, with 99 per cent response within 24 hours.

A voice over internet protocol (VoIP) system was deployed at the Tampa Florida call centre, which routed calls to India. It began operations on 4 January 2000 and within a year handled around 1600 incoming calls a day. To assess the efficacy of operations, Swaminathan worked with the HMO to compare Manjushree Infotech's customer satisfaction for inquiries with those of the industry. Industry data was purchased from a clearinghouse that gathers a number of measures about customer satisfaction and call centre technical and business performance, and distils them into a seven-point satisfaction rating.

Comparing their company with the benchmark average and a select best-in-class group, the company's management team could see that customer satisfaction with its support services (gathered by an unbiased industry source) was above average, but that there was still room for improvement. (See Figure 6.3.) The steady monitoring of the customer satisfaction distribution as new technologies were brought on line would help Manjushree Infotech to optimize its operations.[16]

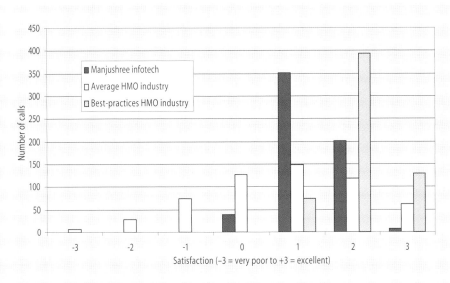

Figure 6.3 Manjushree Infotech customer satisfaction ratings

Because so many services are dedicated purely to conveying information between firms or professionals and consumers, firms increasingly look to information technology for the innovations that can improve productivity. Information technology seeks to encapsulate expertise and deskill work. Product expertise initially resides in the heads and notes of a few designers and engineers – people unlikely to staff call centre phones. One of the first steps in setting up the aftermarket call operations is to transcribe this knowledge to a user manual on a computer database. The more information on the database, the less technically skilled need be the call centre employees, which is the reason that such databases are said to 'deskill' jobs.

It is easy to forget and consequently undervalue the importance of warranty and aftermarket services. Brands can fail solely as a result of poor aftermarket service. Rather that failing because of poor quality, failure is too often the result of users failing to understand a product, thinking it too complex, and thus becoming discouraged with it. As products grow inherently more complex, the need for effective consumer education and aftermarket support is an essential differentiator in crowded markets.

John Sterman's beer game

(Note: this workout uses the Java programme that can be accessed at the book's website.)

The beer game – developed by MIT Professor John Sterman as a 'flight simulator' for management education – is a staple of introductory Operations Research classes, where it is used to provide students with insights into supply-chain management. Interestingly enough, its intent was not try to optimize the supply chain. Instead the purpose of the model is to mimic human behaviour and attempt to help it, in this case by increased knowledge down the supply chain (visibility).

I want you to use it here to experiment with possible delivery service innovations. If you really think that a computer is the answer to supply chain problems, then give it a try. Remember that any automated computer, any innovation, any change in the status quo is ultimately implemented within the ongoing dynamics of the existing management and operations group, the existing inventory and supply systems, and the existing customer and supplier environment. Your innovation might not look as attractive once you have 'flight tested' it.

Rather than playing this as a traditional board game (the way it was designed), the website for this book includes one of the many computer programs available for implementing this game (or if you don't like the one provided with the book, you may visit John Sterman's site at MIT to find references to other computer implementations).

Playing the game

The supply chain consists of four components (suppliers): retailer, wholesaler, distributor and factory. The customer makes an order to the retailer. The retailer (and the rest of the supply chain in turn) performs these tasks:

1   Get new stock from previous pending orders (variable name: received).
2   Get new requests for beer from downstream (variable name: demand).
3   Supply beer for the request and backorders (variable name: supply).
4   Make an upstream order based on inventory (variable name: ordered).

It takes one time slot (1 week) for an order to be received by the upstream supplier, and two time slots (2 weeks) for an order to be filled by that supplier, thus there is a 3-week lag in all. These pending orders are remembered by each agent (variable name: pending).

Scoring is done by cost: Inventory cost is stock on hand * $0.50, but backorder cost (when you cannot supply enough thus have the demand unfulfilled, carrying over to the next move) is more expensive: $2.00 per unfulfilled request.

Each supplier shows its inventory in a box just below its building. It turns red when the inventory is negative, showing the existence of backorders. Similarly, supplied orders are red if they are part of the backorder (that is, they are less than the requested number of cases of beer).

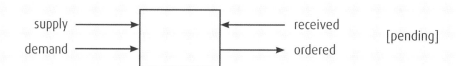

Figure 6.4 Four tasks in the beer game

Amazon's identity crisis

Amazon.com was born in 1995. The name reflected the vision of CEO Jeff Bezos, to produce a large-scale phenomenon like the Amazon river; today it sells over US$10 billion worth of goods each year. Amazon's original goals set the standard for the dot-com boom – grow at any cost, reach a critical mass at which network externalities kick in, and finance that growth through equity market and bank capital. This strategy was often referred to as 'competing for eyeballs', the scramble for customers' attention which would create the virtuous cycle of positive feedback which in turn would fuel growth.

Amazon's initial market was books, and its competitors were book superstores run by chains such as Barnes & Noble. On paper, the Amazon model certainly looked superior (see Table 6.2).

But as with many other dot-coms, it didn't work out as well as anticipated. By around the year 2000 some analysts were predicting Amazon's bankruptcy. Bezos hustled to reinvent the company, and to this day, his reinvention has not paused.

The problem that confronted Bezos in 2000 was that his internet-disintermediated business model – which he had predicted would be ultra-efficient – turned out actually to be more expensive than that of traditional retailers such as Circuit City and Best Buy. Once the sums included the company-wide costs of fulfilling orders, promoting sales and finding new customers, the margin in Amazon's consumer electronics business became a negative 42 per cent. Every $1 of consumer-electronics revenue shipped out of the door cost Amazon $1.42. Compare that with profits and gross margins at Best Buy, which are 3 per cent and 23 per cent; at Circuit City Group they are 2 per cent and 21 per cent. Gross margin for the consumer electronics business at Amazon was 8 per cent.

The problem was simple. At a store, the customer actually has the merchandise in hand, and once past the cash register, the store has no more involvement with that inventory (except perhaps to restock). But Amazon's work would just begin once the customer made a purchase; it faced the logistical problems of any delivery service or mail-order house. Amazon's business was plagued with high levels of split shipments and long hauls, resulting in higher-than-expected fulfilment inefficiencies.

Table 6.2: *Amazon versus Barnes & Noble (c. 1998)*

	Amazon	Barnes & Noble
Number of stores	1 website	1011
Number of employees	1600	27,000
Titles per superstore	3.1 million	175,000
Total sales	$542 million	$3.1 billion
Sales per employee per year	$375,000	$100,000
Sales growth (last quarter of 1998)	306%	10%
Book returns	2%	30%
Inventory turnover per year	24%	3%
Operating income in 1998	-$29.2 million million	$147.3 million

In the fiscal year 2000, Jeff Bezos gave up on 'network effects'. FedEx may have loved Amazon's network, but the payoff to Bezos was less certain. Amazon's share of the market was simply too small to take advantage of any network effects. This was also the year that Amazon suffered its identity crisis – the firm that had once been the darling of dot-com investors, and had established the ground rules for internet competition, was struggling just to survive.

Bezos quickly shifted his view of the Amazon business model to that of a 'fee for service' model. The more interesting question concerned who actually would be billed the fee – who Amazon saw as a paying customer. Of course there were the retail customers that would seek out books, CDs, consumer electronics and so forth. But Bezos also followed eBay's lead in encouraging small retailers to use its services. Particularly on books and CDs, the price of used or discounted titles from Amazon's partners was displayed along with Amazon's own price, and Amazon, for a fee, would handle all parts of its partners' transactions. Amazon also began to provide its services to other large retailers with a recognized brand, but no internet presence – Toys'R'Us was the most prominent of these recognized brands. The approach was beginning to look like traditional retailing in the age of 'big box' stores – offer the maximum selection of merchandise (in Amazon's case perhaps 6 to 7 million items) under one roof.

In its 2005 annual report, Amazon describes the services it provided, many above and beyond traditional retailing services, which allowed the company to stay competitive:

> We work to earn repeat purchases by providing easy-to-use functionality, fast and reliable fulfilment, timely customer service, feature rich content, and a trusted transaction environment. Key features of our websites include editorial and customer reviews; manufacturer product information; Web pages tailored to individual preferences, such as recommendations and notifications; 1-Click® technology; secure payment systems; image uploads; searching on our websites as well as the Internet; browsing; and the ability to view selected interior pages and citations, and search the entire contents of many of the books we offer with our 'Look Inside the Book' and 'Search Inside the Book' features. Our community of online customers also creates feature-rich content, including product reviews, online recommendation lists, wish lists, buying guides, and wedding and baby registries.

From 1998 onward, Amazon had adopted another characteristic of physical retailers – an obsession with performance metrics. Bezos called it a 'culture of metrics'. He made sure that responsible employees had the latest inventory availability information, delivery date estimates and options for expedited delivery, as well as delivery shipment notifications and update facilities – and furthermore that they were evaluated on how well they managed these statistics. This focus on the customer has translated into excellence in service, with the 2004 American Customer Satisfaction Index giving Amazon.com a score of 88, which was at the time the highest customer satisfaction score ever recorded in any service industry, online or offline.

Rather than guessing, Bezos also developed an obsession for customer satisfaction metrics for the Amazon website. Each site was closely monitored with standard service availability monitoring (for example, using Keynote or Mercury Interactive) site availability and download speed. Interestingly it also monitored per-minute site revenue upper/lower bounds. These effectively constituted an alarm system similar to those in a nuclear power plant. If Amazon's revenue from a site fell below $10,000 per minute, alarms would go off. Furthermore there were internal performance service level agreements for web services where a certain percentage of the time, different pages must return in a specific number of seconds. As with employees, the web service providers were responsible for these targets and could be dropped when they failed to meet them. This obsession with 24/7 service was Amazon's online and mail order counterpart to Wal-Mart's greeters, associates and cleaning personnel – they were essential to making Amazon an attractive place to shop.

By 2003, Bezos's culture of metrics was pursued with a vengeance. A fully online business like Amazon could record every move a visitor made, every last click and wobble of the mouse. As the data piled up, it could potentially analyse all sorts of consumer behaviour, and even conduct controlled experiments by altering website algorithms, changing pricing or suggestions and so forth, and profiling how customers responded.

Amazon began by developing a 'Creator Metrics' tool – essentially a flexible report generation tool. But soon it realized that standard statistical packages would better suit the needs of experimentalists with massive customer behaviour datasets that would be the envy of any marketing professor. Bezos began pushing managerial decision making to a new paradigm which he termed 'automation replaces intuitions', in which 'real-time experimentation tests are always run to answer these questions since actual consumer behaviour is the best way to decide upon tactics'. By 2005 Amazon had evolved a culture of experiments of which so-called A/B tests are key components. If an employee suggested that decision A was the best decision, this would never be taken at face value – the employee would initiate limited market testing on certain websites to see whether customers liked A or B better (thus A/B testing). And if the firm decided to go with decision A, then that decision would be monitored after implementation, as customer satisfaction could be temporary. Amazon has found that as its users evolve in their online experience, the way they act online changes. This means the company has to constantly test its features and make them evolve.

The result is a system where humans are progressively being drawn further out of the decision-making loop. Statistical algorithms handle the critical and strategic decisions for Amazon, and monitor the activities implemented as a result of those decisions to see that they stay on track.

So successful has been this approach that Jeff Bezos is formulating future strategy around 'selling the store'. Through its partner programmes Amazon is already running retail websites for many other companies, and now it is promoting a complete package of retail services like its own for anyone who wants to put up a store. And it is selling unbundled computing services through its data storage initiative, and a virtual service system call Elastic Compute Cloud. Because Amazon already has a huge server capacity and retailing tools finely honed by years of metrics analysis, it feels that these are services that it can potentially sell for more than other services providers.

In a sense, this represents yet another in Amazon's series of identity crises. Perhaps Amazon doesn't quite know what it wants to be when it grows up. But it seems to be maturing innovatively, and with a style that keeps everyone around it excited.[17]

Case study: questions for review

1. Why do you think that Amazon's (and many other dot-com's) pursuit of network effects – what it called competing for eyeballs – was such a failure? Are network effects illusory? Or do network effects only apply to certain business models, and retailing is not one of them?

2. When in 2000 Amazon made its transition into being more of a traditional mail-order retailer, do you feel that this represented a viable model for the company, or was Jeff Bezos just trying to justify his investment in company infrastructure (services, bandwidth, warehouses and so forth)?

3. Can you see problems with a 'culture of metrics'? Can human judgement be better than decisions based on statistical algorithms? Why do you think the culture of metrics worked at Amazon?

4. Why don't more companies A/B their decisions?

5. Is there any danger in taking humans out of the decision-making loop in a company? Do you think that Amazon will suffer (or perhaps already has suffered) from some of these problems?

6. Why would any company use Amazon's retailing computer services rather than just renting them from a low-cost internet service provider? Is there any problem with a retailer giving up its customer data to Amazon?

7. What do you think is the best business for Amazon to move into in the future?

CHAPTER QUESTIONS FOR REVIEW

1	Outline the main features of a financial service, and how these may be manipulated in innovation.
2	Outline the main features of a logistics service, and how these are manipulated to produce viable innovations.
3	Are there businesses that could be considered intermediate to purely physical 'products' and purely dynamic 'services' – businesses that combine the challenges of both?

CHAPTER 6: KEY POINTS

▷ Services are activities that are sold for profit.
▷ We differentiate between: ○ *business to consumer* services such as financial services, retailing and leisure services ○ *business to business* services such as consulting, office equipment support and communications ○ *internal* services, such as information technology, accounting and human resources ○ *public* services such as police, education and health services ○ *not for profit* services such as churches and charities.
▷ The fastest growth in US wealth creation over the past two decades has occurred in service industries with high rates of innovation (computer and network services, financial services).
▷ Innovation in service industries has been studied most actively in logistics and supply-chain management, finance and marketing.
▷ Financial innovations have radically altered the character of financial markets over the past 30 years. In particular they have increased the speed of market transaction execution, and have shifted the industry's focus towards the management of risk.
▷ Defining business models to analyse service innovations is both complex and difficult. It is also a source of significant competitive advantage for firms.
▷ Services firms such as Amazon.com are likely to change their business model every few years, as options provided by new technologies open up new opportunities.

NOTES

1   Freeman, C. (1982) *The Economics of Industrial Innovation*, Cambridge, Mass.: MIT Press; Griffiths, T. L. and Tenenbaum, J. B. (2006) 'Optimal predictions in everyday cognition', *Psychological Science* 45, pp. 56–63; Gross, N., Coy, P. and Port, O. (1995) 'The technology paradox', *Business Week*, 6 March, p. 78.

2   Hammer, M. and Champy, J. (1993) *Reengineering the Corporation. A manifesto for business revolution*, New York: HarperBusiness; Tidd, J. and Hull, F. M. (eds) (2003) *Service Innovation: Organizational responses to technological opportunities and market imperatives*, London: Imperial College Press; Allen, T. (1984) *Managing the Flow of Technology*, Cambridge, Mass.: MIT Press.

3   Westland, J. C. and Lang, K. (2002) 'Electronic delivery of convenience: a service innovation at the 7-Eleven retail chain in Hong Kong', *Journal of Information Technology Cases and Applications* (JITCA) 2(3), pp. 77–86..

4   Despite his popularity as a 'business guru', Taylor continued to provide such services at his customary fee of US$35 per day.

5   Documented in Friedman, T. (2005) *The World is Flat*, New York: Farrar, Straus and Giroux.

6   Hill, C. W. L., and Jones, G. R. (1995) Strategic Management: An integrated approach, Boston, Mass.: Houghton Mifflin, p. 352; Cohen, W. M. and Levinthal, D. A. (1989) 'Innovation and learning: the two faces of R&D', *Economic Journal* 99, pp. 569–96.

7   Jana, R. (2007) 'Service innovation: the next big thing', *Business Week*, 29 March.

8   Florida, R. (2003) *The Rise of the Creative Class: and how it's transforming work, leisure, community and everyday life*, New York: Basic Books, p. 253.

9   International Labour Office (2007) *Global Employment Trends*, January.

10 Rae, J. M. (2007) *Innovating Services in the Post-Six Sigma Era*, Peer Insight, Keynote speech at 2007 BMA annual conference.

11 Christensen, C. M. and Bower, J. L. (1996) 'Customer power, strategic investment and failure of leading firms', Strategic Management Journal 17, pp. 197–218; Hamel, G. M. and Prahalad, C. K. (1994) Competing for the Future, Boston, Mass.: Harvard Business School Press.

12 Hambrick, D. C., Geletkanycz, M. A. and Fredrickson, J. W. (1993) 'Top executive commitment to the status quo: some tests of its determinants', *Strategic Management Journal* 14, pp. 401–18; Johne, A. and Storey, C. (1998) 'New service development: a review of the literature and annotated bibliography', *European Journal of Marketing* 32(3/4), pp. 84–251; Johnston, R. and Clark, G.. (2001) *Service Operations Management,* London: Financial Times Prentice Hall; Lawrence, P. R. and Lorsch, J. W. (1967) *Organization and Environments: Managing differentiation and integration*, Homewood, Ill.: Irwin.

13 Sources: 'Competition rises in global banking', *Wall Street Journal*, 25 March 1991, p. Al; 'International banking survey', *Economist*, 30 April 1994, pp. 1–42; 'Congress passes wide-ranging bill easing bank laws', *New York Times*, 5 November 1999, p. 1; 'In face of growing U.S. Rivals, Europe's banks balk at talk that consolidation is needed', *Wall Street Journal*, 29 June 2004, p. CI ; 'The world's biggest bank opens in Japan', *Free Republic*, 3 January 2006, p. 1.

14 Hovanesian, M. D. (2006) 'Nightmare mortgages', *Business Week,* 11 September 2006.

15 Source for Flextronics information: Rutkowski, E. J. (2005) '3GSM World Congress 2005 coverage: Microsoft and Flextronics announce Peabody', [online] msmobiles.com, 14 February 14 (accessed 10 October 2007).

16 Das Gupta, S. (2002) 'Building a call centre', *Network Magazine*, December.

17 Sources: SEC (2005) United States Securities and Exchange Commission submission form 10-K from Amazon for the fiscal year ended 31 December 2004; Demery, P. (2003) 'Getting personal', *Internet Retailer*, October, p. 416; Demery, P. (2004) 'The new Wal-Mart?' *Internet Retailer*, May, p. 2; von Hippel, E. (1994) '"Sticky information" and the locus of problem solving: implications for innovation', *Management Science* 40(4), pp. 429–39; Ward, M. and Dranove, D. (1991) 'The vertical chain of research and development in the pharmaceutical industry', mimeo, Northwestern University; Howell J. M. and Higgins, C. A. (1990) 'Champions of technological innovation', *Administrative Science Quarterly* 35, pp. 317–41; Marcus, J. (2004) *Amazonia. Five years at the epicenter of the dot-com juggernaut*, New York: New Press.

PROTECTING INNOVATIONS

LEARNING OBJECTIVES

After finishing this chapter, you will

- ▸ understand the motivation and history behind **intellectual property (IP) laws**

- ▸ understand the function and applicability of a **patent**

- ▸ understand the function and applicability of a **copyright**

- ▸ understand the function and applicability of a **trademark**

- ▸ understand the function and use of **trade secrets**

- ▸ know how to get started in setting up an **IP strategy**.

After reading the *innovation workout*, you will gain
valuable insights into managing trade secrets.
After reading the Hitachi *case study*, you will gain valuable
insight into how a major Japanese electronics manufacturer
developed and implemented its IP strategy.

Note: Further information, class slides, test questions and other
supporting material are available on our companion website at

www.palgrave.com/business/westland

LAWS

Our laws reflect society's standards, values and expectations. They establish the 'rules of the game' in our personal interactions and business dealings, assuring us that we are being treated fairly (and ensuring that we treat others fairly in return). Laws establish our responsibilities and our rights, to help us avoid or resolve problems before they become unmanageable.

Specific sections of the law govern our rights and responsibilities regarding new ideas. Our society's 'values' regarding ideas are currently in flux – churned by ever-evolving technologies for storing, communicating, searching, associating and advertising information, ideas and innovations. Our 'rules of the game' are evolving along with our values, which leads to a higher level of uncertainty and change in intellectual property (IP) statutes than nearly any other area of the law. Still, there are basic strategies and facts that innovators need to know to protect their ideas; this chapter covers those basics.

Stealing the whole company

At first it seemed to be nothing more than a routine case of counterfeiting in a country where faking it has become an industry. In mid-2004, managers at the Tokyo headquarters of the Japanese electronics giant NEC started receiving reports that pirated keyboards and blank CD and DVD discs bearing the company's brand were on sale in retail outlets in Beijing and Hong Kong. NEC hired a Hong Kong forensics firm, International Risk, to investigate the possible theft of its intellectual property – its brand, its designs, its electronic circuits, its patents. After two years and thousands of hours of investigation in conjunction with law enforcement agencies in China, Taiwan and Japan, their firm discovered something much more sinister than a few impromptu workshops turning out inferior copies of NEC products. The pirates were faking the whole company.

Evidence seized in raids on 18 factories and warehouses in China and Taiwan showed that the counterfeiters had set up what amounted to a parallel NEC brand with links to a network of more than 50 electronics factories. Production included home entertainment systems, MP3 players, batteries, microphones, DVD players and so forth, manufactured in mainland China, Hong Kong and Taiwan. The counterfeiters erected phoney NEC signs outside their factories, shipped their products packaged in 'authentic' boxes and display cases, carried NEC

business cards, commissioned product research and development in the company's name and signed production and supply orders which were paid by the real NEC. Using the company's name, the pirates were not content just to copy NEC products; they even developed new ranges of consumer electronic products that would sell under NEC's brand.

Steve Vickers, a former senior Hong Kong police officer and now CEO of International Risk, observed that the pirates required factories to pay royalties for 'licensed' products, and went so far as to issue official-looking warranty and service documents – with the real NEC receiving complaints and warranty service requests for these counterfeit products. Criminal networks coordinated all of the manufacturing and distribution, and collected all of the proceeds for goods which ultimately found their way onto retail shelves in Taiwan, China, Hong Kong, Southeast Asia, North Africa, the Middle East and Europe, right alongside legitimate NEC products.

'These entities are part of a sophisticated ring, coordinated by two key entities based in Taiwan and Japan, which has attempted to completely assume the NEC brand', observed Fujio Okada, the NEC senior vice president and legal division general manager, in written answers to questions:

> Many of these entities are familiar with each other and cooperate with each other to develop,

manufacture and sell products utilizing the NEC brand. On the surface, it looked like a series of intellectual property infringements, but in reality a highly organized group has attempted to hijack the entire brand.

Mr Vickers noted that 'the reality is that factories in China will produce what they are asked to produce .... The challenge is finding out who placed the orders and who funded it.'

Once aware of the full extent of the fraud, NEC acted quickly to disrupt the supply chain and market channels of the counterfeiters. Prosecutors in the southern Taiwanese city of Kaohsiung issued warrants for the local police to raid a warehouse and offices in the area, where investigators seized 60 pallets of counterfeit goods, mostly audio products, carrying the NEC brand. Evidence collected in these raids also implicated factories in China, leading to late-night raids which were extensively covered in the Taiwan media, with television reports at nine factories in the cities of Guangzhou, Zhongshan, Zhuhai and Shenzhen in Guangdong Province of China.[1]

In this chapter we shall cover the parts of this law that are most commonly invoked to protect innovations, and show how – and how not – to incorporate these into a general strategy for protecting your innovation. This chapter confines itself to US IP law. The laws of most countries adopt similar principles, and it is common for intellectual property to be licensed in the United States as well as any other jurisdictions in which it might be sold or used, simply because of the large size of the US market.[2]

INTELLECTUAL PROPERTY LAW

If you have come this far, you probably already have a very good understanding of your innovation and how you plan to develop it into a profitable business. Yet there is a risk – substantial in an era when information can be communicated globally a with the flick of a few keys – that someone else will beat you to the implementation of your idea, or that someone with more resources will crowd you out of your potential markets before you have a chance to implement your plans. This is where your knowledge of IP law and the strategies for correctly using it can make the difference between success and failure.

The first patents

Patents originated in Venice in 1474, where inventions, once they had been put into practice, had to be communicated to the Republic in order to obtain the right to prevent others from using them. This definition was conveyed through British law to the US colonial lawyers who drafted the Articles of Confederation. Thomas Jefferson was viscerally opposed to any sort of patent monopoly, but at the time of the Constitutional Convention was serving as ambassador to France. Alexander Hamilton is credited with including a patent and copyright clause in Article II of the US Constitution. The first US patent was issued on 31 July 1790 on a process for the making of potash.[3]

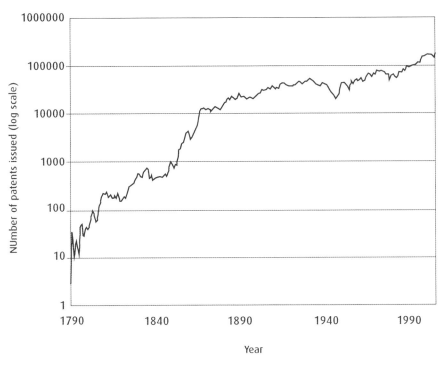

Figure 7.1 Total number of US patents issued by year, 1800 to 2006

Data source: US Patent Activity, 1790–Present (Historical and Extended-Year Set Statistics) annual counts of utility (invention) patents. http://www.uspto.gov/web/offices/ac/ido/oeip/taf/reports.htm#by_hist (retrieved December 2007).

Qualcomm's CDMA patent

Irwin Jacobs and six others founded Qualcomm in 1985 to build on the pioneering work of Austrian actress and polymath Hedy Lamarr, who perhaps is more famous for her nude appearance in the film *Ekstase* (1933) and other Hollywood films than her later work as a radio-communications inventor who assisted the United States in the Second World War.

Qualcomm's patent for Code-Division Multiple Access (CDMA) – No. 4,901,307 – Spread Spectrum Multiple Access Communication System Using Satellite or Terrestrial Repeaters – set the stage for the growth of CDMA, which now has more than 180 million users worldwide with a host of wireless solutions, ranging from internet access to global positioning technology. Today, Qualcomm designs and manufactures digital processors which are central to cell phones and cellular networks. The company has 1900 patents in the United States and has applied for 3200 more. Qualcomm does not disclose terms of deals with its 135 licensees, but recently said its standard fee is under 5 per cent of a handset's wholesale price. That amounts to roughly US$10 a phone.

Roughly half of the company's employees are legal staff dedicated to assuring that Qualcomm realizes all of its potential royalty revenue. Licensing accounted for a third of Qualcomm's $7.53 billion in revenue in 2006 and three-quarters of its pretax profits of $3.16 billion. CDMA is now used in about 20 per cent of the world's mobile phones through carriers such as Verizon Wireless and Sprint Nextel Corp. in the United States, and throughout much of Asia.

Gemstar's aggressive patent strategy

On 12 March 2001, an owlish Henry C. Yuen graced the cover of *Business Week* magazine, which asked the provocative question, 'Will Henry Yuen take control of your TV set?' With a PhD in mathematics, Henry Yuen became a research scientist in 1989 at California Institute of Technology, where he came up with VCR Plus+, a programme that made him a millionaire. That technology ultimately went in nearly all VCRs, making it easier to programme the recorders.

Yuen didn't stop there, going onto acquire 90 more patents, all of them ostentatiously displayed on his office walls. He rode the market's enthusiasm for interactive TV to enormous power in the industry, developing the Gemstar-TV Guide interface and menu system for interactive TV. This channel-surfing interface – necessary for the hundreds of channels offered on cable TV – became the standard across the industry.

To make sure he profited from his patents, Yuen went on to earn a night-school law degree alongside his maths PhD. And he developed a penchant for suing his competitors over alleged patent infringement. He became so aggressive that one magazine described him as a 'patent terrorist'. Yuen's only response was, 'I am no terrorist. A terrorist is someone who breaks the law. I am only doing what the US Congress and patent law allow.'

Cable executives saw it differently. 'He scares the hell out of us,' said one. 'He can force his way onto our system because we need the guide, and he seems to be the only way to get one.' Cable giants

John Malone and Rupert Murdoch launched a $2.8 billion hostile takeover of Gemstar in 1998, but Yuen countersued and ultimately forced a merger of interests. His opponents conceded that they 'could litigate for 50 years with Henry, or get half the company'.

By 2003 Henry Yuen had the entire cable industry under his sway, including some of the most notoriously aggressive deal makers in any industry. Along the way he made powerful enemies who felt trapped by his restrictive contracts and aggressive litigation. And that is about the time Gemstar-TV Guide began to unravel.

Someone tipped off the US Securities and Exchange Commission that Gemstar's revenues didn't add up. It appeared the company was overstating revenues by at least $248 million, and Henry Yuen appeared to be profiting from stock sales at inflated prices. The SEC took Yuen to court, and on 8 May 2006 it found him guilty of receiving $10,577,692 in ill-gotten gains from his fraudulent conduct. This consisted of $3,022,452 in gross bonus compensation received by Yuen during the period of the fraud, and $7,555,240 in excess trading profit he received by selling Gemstar stock during the period of the fraud. The court ordered Yuen to pay a total of $22,327,231 in disgorgement, penalties and interest, and entered a permanent injunction against future securities law violations and a permanent bar on his serving as an officer or director of a public company.[4]

The origin of copyrights

Copyrights are a product of a specific invention – Gutenberg's moveable type printing press. Prior to the press, copying manuscripts involved painstaking and expensive work by literate servants or slaves; the expense alone ensured that distribution was limited. With the availability of cheap copies, printers began lobbying for protection of their property from illicit copying – basically a 'copy right' for themselves. In Britain, this led to the Licensing Act of 1662 which

established a register of licensed books and required a copy to be deposited with the Stationers Company. Subsequent extensions of copyright laws have built on the publisher's perspective, which gives it the right to make copies, and excludes others from making copies. This was enforceable when copying involved expensive typesetting and hot metal presses, but has grown troublesome as technology has pushed the cost of copying to near zero.

Under the law, an innovator has at his disposal four types of IP protection – patents, copyrights, trade secrets and trademarks. All provide specific rights to use material (rights of publicity) and to exclude it from use (privacy or exclusion). These rights come with obligations, some of which can be expensive. At the core of rights and enforcement of those rights is the idea of *excludability* – the ability to exclude others from use of the property – generally through 'tollbooths' which artificially congest access to the property (but also saddle the industry with input and coordination costs). Advances in technology over the past several decades have steadily eroded the ability to create and operate such 'tollbooths', in many cases (as with the music industry) completely subverting the ability of companies and the industry to enforce IP protection.

PATENTS

A patent is a temporary legal right granted by the government as a reward for a unique invention, giving the inventor the right to exclude others from using the invention. An invention is defined as a technological advancement that is useful, new and is not obvious to a person with ordinary skill in the field. Inventions can take many forms, from a machine or device to a method or process. They can be new compositions for an old product, or perhaps new uses of an old product. They can be an artificially created organism, or even a discovery about how plants and animals express their genes.

The three types of patents under US law are:

▶ *utility patent*: protects a machine, manufactured article or process, and is granted for 20 years (before 8 June 1995 the duration was 17 years)
▶ *design patent*: covers a new and original ornamental shape or surface treatment, which need not have any utility; granted for 14 years
▶ *plant patent*: covers characteristics of plants that have been asexually reproduced, and is granted for 20 years.

To obtain a patent, you need to file an elaborate application that completely describes your invention, and indicates how it differs from other patented inventions (available at www.uspto.gov). The form is filed with the US Patent and Trademark Office (USPTO), and is followed by a wait for approval averaging two years. On approval, you pay a fee, and are given rights to 'exclude' others from using your invention.

Unfortunately for patent holders, exclusion is not free. A patent is really just a licence to sue someone; and lawyers and lawsuits cost money. The substantial sums involved in defending patents may lead some innovators to look for buyers for their patents – ones with lawyers on retainer and deep pockets. For this reason, if you are dealing with a chemical or process invention, or any other improvement that does not need to be exposed to the general public and can be kept secret, trade secrets may be a better choice than a patent.

For this reason, there are other types of IP protection that may be more suitable for a particular business situation. After all, the purpose of IP protection is to ensure that the innovator is protected enough to take strategic advantage of an innovation.

Patent law is currently at the centre of controversy, partly because corporate patent strategies have proven so successful over the past several decades, and partly because of the rapid advances in technology. The World Trade Organization (WTO) has attempted to align the patent systems around the world, particularly with regard to certain controversial issues, such as what can be protected by patents and the issue of compulsory licences in cases of national need. A more fundamental issue was raised by law professors Michael Heller and Rebeka Eisenberg in a 1998 *Science* article.[5] They argue that current patent law can fragment IP rights so widely that, effectively, no one can take advantage of them, as to do so would require an agreement between the owners of all of the fragments. In fact this appears to be an increasing problem in the biotechnology and pharmaceutical industries, where complications involving the myriad patents covering gene expression, drugs, laboratory methods and so forth have squelched promising technologies.

The Selden patent

One of the earliest recorded patent strategies played a pivotal role in the birth of America's car industry. Inspired by George Brayton's mammoth internal combustion engine displayed at the 1876 Centennial Exposition in Philadelphia, George Selden filed for and received a series of patents for technologies underpinning the design of the automobile, ultimately selling them to a group of lawyers under the name of the Association of Licensed Automobile Manufacturers (ALAM). Despite never having built a working automobile, ALAM forced royalties out of nearly every car maker in Detroit – every one but Henry Ford, owner of the Ford Motor Company. Ford's legal fight lasted 8 years, generating a case record of 14,000 pages. The case was heavily publicized in the newspapers of the day, and ended in a victory for Selden. Ford appealed and on 10 January 1911 won his case; a win based at least partly on his challenge to Selden to build a working car based on the patent. The resulting Selden car started up, chugged forward 5 feet, and promptly stopped, never to start again.

Jeff Bezos and 'One-click'

Jeff Bezos, founder of the online retailer Amazon.com, patented Amazon's 'one-click' checkout process, a process that was considered by many to be both trivial and obvious. Following the granting of this patent, Bezos used the Amazon.com website to argue that the patent process was flawed because – among other things – it was granting patents to 'trivial and obvious' processes like 'one-click'. Bezos went on to argue that software and software-based processes should not be patentable at all; that patent life should be shortened from the current 17 years to varying lengths that would reflect the innovation's life-cycle; and that the USPTO, rather than trying to handle all aspects of patent review itself, should create a centralized, searchable database of 'prior art' and give all competitors and interested parties six months to review patents pending for infringement. The searchable database has since been created on Google Patent Search.[6]

COPYRIGHTS

Although derived from the same constitutional mandate as patents, copyrights resemble them only superficially. A copyright is a temporary right giving control over the use of an original work of authorship – texts, graphics, plastics, musical pieces, dramatic works, movies, audio programmes or visual creations. Copyrights protect the form in which an idea is presented, not the idea itself. Copyrights do not extend to abstractions, or to technical designs. An idea for a movie is not copyrightable; the written script is.

Computer programs are copyrightable, giving programmers and the computer industry an effective security tool. Copyrights in computer programs over the choice of words or lines of computer code and their respective positions in an instruction represent the creative portion of the program and are critical to its operation. Patents are also available for computer code to protect innovative processes within a given program, but are much less used in the industry than are copyrights.

It's a Wonderful Life

The American Film Institute called it one of the best films ever made – *It's a Wonderful Life* (1946) directed by Frank Capra and based on an original story *The Greatest Gift* written by Philip Van Doren Stern in 1939. Capra bought the script for $10,000 from RKO Pictures, which was so anxious to unload the project that it gave Capra three more scripts for free.

Shot in the spring of 1946, *It's a Wonderful Life* opened to moderate commercial and critical success. Over time, various mergers and acquisitions eventually put the film in National Telefilm Associates' library, where through a 1974 clerical error the copyright was not renewed. Once it entered the public domain, many television stations began airing the film without paying royalties.

The stations were in fact in error in believing that *It's a Wonderful Life* was out of copyright – it was more properly half in and half out. Although the film's images had entered the public domain, the film's story was still protected by virtue of it being a derivative work of the published story *The Greatest Gift*, whose copyright had been properly renewed by Philip Van Doren Stern in 1971. By the 1980s (the beginning of the home video era) the film had become a perennial Christmas favourite and was shown multiple times on multiple stations throughout the holiday season.

The film's accidental public domain success is often cited as a reason to limit copyright terms. Frank Capra commented that:

> it's the damnedest thing I've ever seen. The film has a life of its own now and I can look at it like I had nothing to do with it. I didn't even think of it as a Christmas story when I first ran across it. I just liked the idea.

Copyright laws have been the subject of intense debate over the past decade as paper declines as a recording medium. With the advent of high-resolution computer screens and desktop printers, paper increasingly became an archival medium – used for long-term storage, but not for display. The attractiveness of search engines such as Google has eliminated the appeal of paper even for archives. The US Digital Millennium Copyright Act (1998) rectified some problems associated with internet servers, communications and data storage. Internet service providers are protected from prosecution for copies of copyrighted works that they might have on their servers, since it is recognized that this is a necessary part of their services over which they have little control.

Significant challenges to copyright (and patent) law have arisen from the success of free software such as GNU/Linux, Mozilla Firefox and the Apache web server. These projects have demonstrated that successful businesses can be created despite the absence of a copyright-enforced monopoly rent (see the box on *It's a Wonderful Life*). These products use copyright to enforce their licence terms, which are designed to ensure the free nature of the work, rather than securing exclusive rights for the holder for monetary gain.

Some interesting complexities arise in categorizing products as either copyrightable or patentable in the computer industry, where the distinction between ideas and their physical implementation is often blurred. In particular, separate laws have been written to address photolithographic mask work – the two or three-dimensional layout of an integrated circuit of transistors, interconnections, resistors and so forth which is photo-etched onto silicon substrate. Because of their functional nature, mask designs cannot be protected effectively under copyright law. Similarly, because individual lithographic mask works are not clearly protectable subject matter, they also cannot be protected effectively under patent law. Separate laws grant exclusive rights to mask work owners which are more limited than those granted to copyright or patent holders. For instance, modification (derivative works) is not an exclusive right of mask work owners. Similarly, the exclusive right of a patentee to 'use' an invention would not prohibit an independently created mask work of identical geometry. Furthermore, reproduction for reverse engineering of a mask work is specifically permitted by the law. As with copyright, mask work rights exist when they are created, regardless of registration, unlike patents, which only confer rights after application, examination and issuance.

Shifting time and space

In the early 1980s Sony's Betamax videotape technology was perceived to be a significant threat to the television broadcasters' business model. It allowed viewers to tape their shows, and then fast-forward through sponsors' advertisements. The US lawsuit *Sony Corp. v. Universal City Studios* (1984, the 'Betamax case'), ultimately went to the US Supreme Court, which determined home videotaping to be legal because viewers were deemed to be using it for 'time shifting' of TV shows (for instance, watching late night shows during the following day). This precedent was later successfully invoked in October 1998, when the Recording Industry Association of America (RIAA) filed a lawsuit against Diamond Multimedia – maker of the Rio PMP300, the second portable consumer MP3 digital audio player. Diamond successfully argued that MP3 players would be used for 'space shifting' of music on CDs (for instance, ripping them off the CD so they could be carried around on the Rio player). The 'Betamax case' was later invoked in *MGM v. Grokster* (2005), where the high court agreed that peer-to-peer file sharing software was useful for time and space shifting.

Unlike a patent, there is no need to file for a copyright. Copyright attaches automatically as soon as the work is shown in a perceptible and reproducible form without the need for any formal application. As soon as a book is printed, a song is played or picture is hung, it is copyrighted. But, if you want to sue someone for infringement (or someone sues you), you need to prove that it's actually your original work. This is a lot easier if you have registered your copyright with the Copyright Office (a division of the Library of Congress) and submitted a copy as proof of authorship. Copyright lawsuits are similar to patent lawsuits, but quicker and less expensive.

Copyrights are long lived, and became even longer after the overhaul of the US Copyright Act in 1978. Copyrights assigned to the original authors of a work last for 70 years after the death of the last author; if the authors are hired to write, or write anonymously, it is 95 years from publication or 120 from creation (the copyright extends through 31 December on the year of its expiration).

COMMERCIAL IDENTIFIERS

Trademarks are just one type of IP protected by the USPTO under the rubric of *commercial identifiers*. These are used to distinguish a company, its products and services from those of its competitors. It goes without saying that these sorts of property – brands, names, logos and so forth – may over the long run be the company's most important assets. It is a mistake to treat them as the poor stepchildren of patents and copyrights. The three basic types of commercial identifiers are:

▶ *company identifiers* such as a legal name or logotype that graces letterheads and offices
▶ *service identifiers* that identify the services offered to customers, such as McDonald's 'supersize it' and the arched 'M' on their buildings
▶ *product identifiers* which include trademarks: brand names like Kleenex and logos like the Nike 'swoosh'.

Commercial identifiers offer a huge breadth of coverage, from colours of automobiles to MP3 players. Textures, container shapes, and other subtle or not so subtle design features are all potentially protected. But that protection may be limited to the specific markets in which a brand is known. For example, a well-known burger chain would have difficulty suing McDonald's Plumbing Supply over infringement, especially if the owner's name were McDonald.[7]

Commercial identifiers are the IP rights that are most neglected, misunderstood and underestimated by innovators. Often the aspects of a product or business covered by commercial identifiers will be much more crucial to the success of the business than risky patent applications. 'What's in a name?' More than you think – often those non-verbal cues that entice and attract, without customers knowing exactly why, add to reputation and quality image, and help to convey what the product and company is about without the need for advertising. Commercial identifiers cover all of the subtle parts of an innovation that can make or break success more certainly than winning a patent lawsuit.

TRADE SECRETS

The last sort of IP protection is distinctly one-sided – there is no publicity, only privacy and exclusion. These are the laws that protect trade secrets, a particularly important and inexpensive IP right. But not every commercially advantageous material or process can safely and practically be kept under lock and key.

Secret ingredients

The oldest trade secret still under protection by US law is Merchandise 7X – the 'secret ingredient' in Coca-Cola, which has remained a secret since its invention in 1886. In 1925, the only written copy of its formula Coca-Cola admits to having was retrieved from a New York bank (where it had been held as collateral on a sugar loan) and reverently laid in a safe deposit box in SunTrust Bank in Atlanta, Georgia. That same year the company set a policy whereby no one could view the formula without written permission from the board, and then only in the presence of the president, chairman, or corporate secretary. Furthermore, the rule dictated that only two company officials would be allowed to know the recipe at any given time, and their identities were never to be disclosed for any reason.

The company has admitted to tinkering with the formula over the years (glycerin was added as a preservative, cocaine was eliminated, caffeine was greatly reduced, and citric acid was replaced with phosphoric acid). The formula was also changed in 1935 with the help of Rabbi Tobias Geffen of Atlanta to allow it to be certified kosher. Rumour has it that the 1925 copy of the formula now resides in a safe at Coca-Cola's Atlanta headquarters.

Merchandise 7X joins two other trade secrets in being fixtures of popular speculation – McDonald's secret sauce, and KFC's secret blend of 11 herbs and spices. KFC's security measures for the latter include blending those 11 herbs and spices at two different locations and combining at a third location prior to basting the chicken with them.

OTHER CONTRACTUAL IP RIGHTS

The rights and obligations offered by these four IP laws don't necessarily fit the needs of everyone. In particular, many innovators may simply not have the resources to defend their IP in court. Thus there are various categories of legal contracts that are specifically intended to deal with IP rights. They provide contractual IP rights to all parties. For example, a company may acquire the contractual right to manufacture a patented product while the inventor obtains rights to royalties (a portion of the sales). Third parties in addition to the inventors can obtain exploitable rights; inventors can sell or lease their patent, copyright or commercial identifier rights to others. *Franchising* is a specific type of business that sells contractual rights to intellectual property. (Companies such as KFC and McDonald's deal in franchises for their brands.)

THINKING STRATEGICALLY ABOUT IP

An IP acquisition and protection strategy is necessary for a business of any type or size. It is often even more important for innovators, because the only property they may own, and the core of their competences, will often be IP.

There are three valid reasons for investing in IP protection:

▶ gaining and maintaining competitive advantage in your market
▶ creating a new revenue source
▶ enhancing the value of existing revenue streams.

IP strategy starts by taking an inventory listing: what assets (ideas, knowledge, processes, inventions, channels and so forth) are actually important to your business? Begin by looking at the following.[8]

1. Innovations in products or manufacturing methods that the company, its associates and employees have developed during the last two years (older innovations will already have fallen into the public domain).
2. Gather up any software, instruction manuals and promotional literature developed or published for the last five years (the grace period given to challenge any infringement).
3. Inventory all of the company's commercial names and logos, including business identities and product brands.
4. If you don't already have one, implement a record-keeping system to document innovations. You will need this for patent applications, but it is good policy anyway.

To help you with this task, you should revisit your *business model* (see Chapter 4) which defines the assets you will need to compete in the market, and consider your *strategy model* (see Chapter 11) which defines the assets that will generate value, and how they will generate that value. Once you have your inventory, your next step is to decide whether IP protection by copyright, patent or trademark makes the most sense for each type of asset; and how much you expect that protection to cost annually.[9]

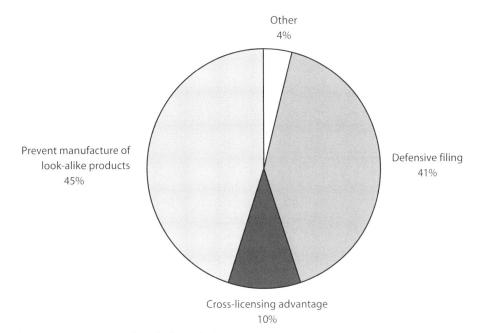

Figure 7.2 Reasons Japanese firms file for a patent

Source: Corporate Intellectual Property Right Trends, JPO, March 1998.

Computing your risk for keeping a secret

Trade secrets are assets only as long as the firm and its employees can keep that secret. In times past, when a merchant accumulated a pile of gold, the customary way to protect such assets was to hide them by burying them or stuffing them in a vault. But it is impossible to bury an idea; at best you can keep it secret. And not all secrets are equally easy to keep. This workout shows you how to evaluate your secret, its complexities and its risks.

The nature of your secret

(Type) What are you keeping private (or secret)? Things that you would want to keep private fall into one of three basic categories.

1 information: (previous events, memories, and other information)
2 physical objects: (mementos, valuables or other objects)
3 activities (current and/or future).

Figure 7.3 provides a visual representation of the risk associated with particular types of secrets and secret holders.

(Who) Who will be searching for your secret? You may be keeping your secret from most of the known world – but generally speaking, only a few people would be truly interested enough in it to spend time trying to find it out. Determine who these people are. All of the people from whom we want to keep things private fall into one of three categories.

1 general public: (strangers, casual acquaintances, the world at large)
2 close friends/relatives/spouses
3 officials: (includes newspapers, government, employers, police or anyone with official standing in the community).

(Time) How long will you be keeping your secret (say on a scale of 1 to 3, being short to long duration)? Generally speaking, the longer you try to keep a secret, the more opportunity someone will have to discover it.

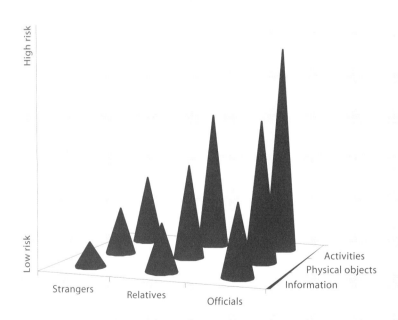

Figure 7.3 Relative risk of various factors involved in keeping a secret

(People) How many people are actively involved in keeping the secret? The ideal number of people required to keep a secret is one.

(Resources) What quantity and quality of resource are available to those who would try to find out your secrets – resources being everything from time and energy, to money, to emotional resilience?

1 average (the standard for most situations)
2 above average (for those with access to extra help, money, time, etc.)
3 official (the highest risk rank is reserved for 'official' groups).

(Suspicion) What is the level of suspicion from those whom you are keeping your secret (on a scale of 1 to 4, from least to most suspicion)?

(Motivation) What is the level of motivation of those from whom you are keeping your secret (on a scale of 1 to 4, from least to most motivation)?

The risk scorecard

What are the chances that you will be able to keep your secret successfully? Your numerical response to the six questions above allows you to compute your relative risk:

Relative Risk = (Type + Who) x Time x People x Resources x Suspicion x Motivation

Relative risk score	Risk of divulging secret
Less than 25	Low
25 to 50	Average
50 to 100	High
Above 100	Impossible to keep this secret

Adjust your assumptions (and the associated numbers) to see how to optimally keep your secret and lower your risk score.

Hitachi's patent strategy

Hitachi's first president, Namihei Odaira, was once quoted as saying 'Inventions are an engineer's lifeblood.' Since Odaira's days, Hitachi has made patent strategy central to its business planning, and among all Japanese firms in the 1990s, Hitachi's patent strategy was by far the most successful. Hitachi earned US$455 million in patent royalties in 1996. In the same year, it paid some $91 million in patent licensing fees. Thus, it made a profit of about $364 million that year in its patent trade, and patents made an important contribution to the company's bottom line.

After 1945, Hitachi aggressively sought out and imported foreign technology in an effort to jump start its industry. Gaining access to such basic technologies as those used in semiconductor manufacture, computer production, television manufacture and nuclear power generation, Hitachi focused on reverse engineering (that is, dismantling items and finding out how they worked), then improving commercially important technologies in order to compete globally. It then aggressively sought to patent these improvements in Japan, the United States and Europe. Hitachi, and Japan's industry in general, sought to ensure that Japan had its own technology, patented by its own people. To this end, Hitachi dedicated a staff of specialists to work solely on patents. Technical people were encouraged to apply their engineering skills to inventing things. This focus, common across industry, was highly beneficial to the Japanese economy, and by the early 1950s production surpassed prewar levels. Between 1953 and 1965, GDP expanded by more than 9 per cent per year, and in manufacturing by 13 per cent annually.

From the early years, Hitachi was one of the most aggressive filers of patents. In 1970 alone it filed 20,000 patent applications. All of the company's technical achievements were reported to the patent department, which then checked them and filed the appropriate applications. The emphasis was on sheer number more than the quality of each patent. (Hitachi was not alone in this as most Japanese companies competed fiercely in the patent arena, each company filing huge numbers of applications.)

Significantly, in 1970, Hitachi adopted the policy of opening its patents. At that time it was losing money on all of this patent filing. In 1970 it earned $5 million but incurred expenses in excess of $95 million in licensing fees. To reverse these losses, Hitachi became the first Japanese company to go shopping for cross-licensing and royalty deals.

In 1979, Hitachi faced its first major patent challenge when Westinghouse charged the company with patent infringement and petitioned the US International Trade Commission (USITC: an 'independent', quasi-judicial federal agency that provides trade policy advice to both the legislative and executive branches of government) to block the import of circuit breakers from Japan (Westinghouse eventually lost the suit).

Hitachi decided to counterattack by directing its patent division to look for Japanese patents (not just Hitachi's but those of other Japanese companies as well) that Westinghouse might be infringing. Hitachi had dozens of US patents for electrical power transmission equipment, but it found that they were all patents for detailed features distinctive to Hitachi products. Hitachi's engineers were not particularly adept at developing the broad, basic patents on fundamental technology that the company needed to countersue competitors such as Westinghouse. Although Hitachi owned huge quantities of patents, these tended to be so narrowly focused on specific implementations of technology that other companies found it easy to get around them with only minor product redesign.

This was a bitter lesson for Hitachi, which initiated a goal in 1981 to double the number of 'strategic' patents it filed each year. Hitachi's idea was to pre-emptively build a 'fence' of strategic patents around each of its major product lines – both current and planned. The idea was that if a competitor wanted to enter into an industry claimed by Hitachi, it would have no choice but to license some of Hitachi's strategic patents. There is no point in obtaining a mountain of patents if they fail to give the company competitive leverage.

Hitachi divided its strategic patents into three categories, designated gold, silver and bronze. Those that other companies could not get around and that covered world-class, basic technology were in the gold category. Hitachi was one of the first companies to recognize the value of strategic patents, to scale up its patent investments, and to make patents central to corporate strategy.

The emphasis on strategic patents was crucial to Hitachi's success over the next few years. By 1985 the entire patent operation had become profitable, as Hitachi saw royalties and licensing income expand.[10]

Hitachi ran into more patent problems in 1986. During that time Micron Technology formally accused the Japanese semiconductor industry of 'dumping' (that is, selling below cost to gain market share) and filed along with Texas Instruments a US$300 million antitrust lawsuit against six Japanese electronics companies. This eventually led to the signing of the Semiconductor Trade Agreement between the United States and Japan in 1986, which established 'fair prices' for Japanese memory chips. Texas Instruments used the period to renegotiate its licensing fee with Hitachi – it wanted to set the licensing fee for DRAM manufacturing technology at 10 per cent of sales. It then filed suit with the US ITC and with the Texas courts. Hitachi counter-sued in the Texas courts and in Japan, charging Texas Instruments with infringing some of its strategic patents. In the end, Texas Instruments settled out of court, at a licensing fee considerably less than it had originally asked. This represented the first major victory of Hitachi's strategic patent campaign.

1985 also saw Hitachi embarked upon a new campaign to – once again – double the number of strategic patents that it filed annually. In contrast to the previous programme, though, this was a programme to patent basic technology that might otherwise be overlooked or taken for granted. A third campaign was launched in 1990, to double the number of strategic patents yet again. Working under a 'patent first' slogan, this was an effort to patent the basic technology that would be needed to meet emerging market requirements and open up new technology streams.

This strategy paid off again when Motorola tried to force Hitachi out of the microcomputer market in the early 1990s. Hitachi was able to use its patents on 'overlooked' technology to counter Motorola's market entry.

A fourth campaign to once again double the number of strategic patents was initiated in 1995. This was slightly different from previous initiatives, because it was mainly concerned about obtaining global coverage for the company's strategic technologies.

CASE STUDY

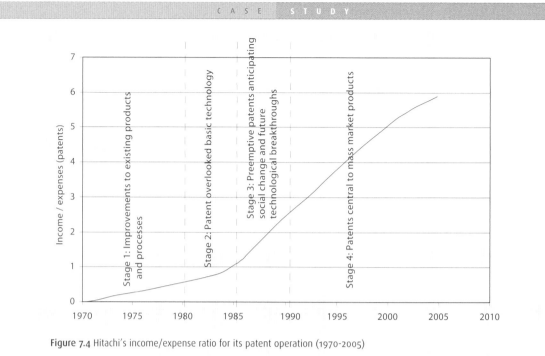

Figure 7.4 Hitachi's income/expense ratio for its patent operation (1970-2005)

Source: Hisamitsu Arai (2000) *Intellectual Property Policies for the 21st Century: The Japanese experience in wealth creation*, Publication 824(E),Geneva: WIPO , chapter 4.

Questions for the Hitachi case study

1. What role does secrecy play in Hitachi's IP strategy?

2. Why do you think that Hitachi's stage 1 strategy was unsuccessful?

3. Do you think software should be patentable? Why?

CHAPTER QUESTIONS FOR REVIEW

1. Describe the motivation and history behind IP laws. Will these same factors be attributable to IP in the future? Why or why not?

2. Outline the function and applicability of a patent.

3. Outline the function and applicability of copyright.

4. Outline the function and applicability of a trademark.

5. Outline the function and use of trade secrets.

6. What is an IP strategy? Are strategies directed to owning patents and copyrights the best IP strategy? Why or why not?

7. Why are many research organizations against the patenting of life forms?

8. Why are discoveries not patentable?

9. Discuss some of the limitations of the patent system.

10. Explain with the use of examples when it would be appropriate to use trademarks and copyright to protect a firm's intellectual property.

11. Explain why the patent system may not be working as originally intended.

CHAPTER 7: KEY POINTS

▷ Laws establish our responsibilities and our rights to help us avoid or resolve problems before they become unmanageable. They are the basic business 'rules of the game.'

▷ Intellectual property is covered by four types of legally recognized property rights:
  ○ patents for novel ideas
  ○ copyrights for artistic works
  ○ trademarks for brands and logos
  ○ trade secrets for secret formulae.

▷ At the core of rights and enforcement of those rights is the idea of excludability
  ○ the ability to exclude others from use of the property
  ○ through 'tollboths' which artificially congest access to the property.
  ○ Advances in technology over the past several decades have steadily eroded the ability to create and operate such 'tollbooths'.

▷ IP strategy recognizes that the management of property rights is both imperfect and expensive. Good strategy aligns costs of legal rights with the benefits they provide – sometimes in complex ways, as in the evolution of Hitachi's patent applications away from specific products and processes, towards general patents that could be used for strategic lawsuits and cross-licensing agreements.

NOTES

1   Source: Lague, D. (2006) 'Next step for counterfeiters: faking the whole company', *New York Times*, 1 May 2006, p. B6.

2   Borg, E. A. (2001) 'Knowledge, information and intellectual property: implications for marketing relationships', *Technovation* 21, pp. 515–24.

3   Derwent (1998) *Derwent World Patents Index*, Derwent Scientific and Patent Information: www. Derwent.com; and graphic courtesy of www.uspto. gov.

4   Source: Grover, R. (2004) 'A spotlight on Gemstar and Pixar', *Business Week*, 4 August 2004.

5   Heller, M. A. and Eisenberg, R. S. (1998) 'Can patents deter innovation? The anticommons in biomedical research', *Science* 280(1 May 1998), pp. 698–701.

6   Sources: 'Gene is out of the bottle', *Financial Times*, 30 October 1997, p. 15; Graham, N. (1998) 'Inventor cleans up with profits', *Sunday Times*, 1 March, pp. 4, 16; Rowan, D. (1997) 'Signing up to a patent on life', *Guardian*, 27 November, p. 19.

7   Badenhausen, K.(1995) 'Brands: the management factor', *Financial World*, 1 August, pp. 50–69; Bainbridge, D. I. (1996) *Intellectual Property*, 3rd edn, London: Pitman.

8   Alpert, E. (1993) 'Breadth of coverage for intellectual property law: encouraging product innovation by broadening protection', *Journal of Product and Brand Management* 2, p. 2.

9   Arias, J. T. G. (1995) 'Do networks really foster innovation?' *Management Decision* **52**(5), 15 December, pp. 33, 9.

10 Doyle, P. (2001) 'AIDS and the pharmaceutical industry', *Guardian*, 10 March; 'The knowledge monopolies: patent wars', *Economist*, 8 April 2000, pp. 95–9.

ENTRANCE STRATEGIES FOR INNOVATIONS

LEARNING OBJECTIVES

After finishing this chapter, you will

- ► understand that as **markets and technologies change and evolve**, your capabilities need to evolve to keep up with the changing demand for products and services

- ► have learned how to decide where you will **acquire new capabilities** (assets and competences) based on an analysis of your existing and planned products/services by growth, profit and revenue size

- ► have learned to use **real options analysis** to factor risk into your decisions on where capabilities will migrate in the future

- ► understand the use of three particular options in developing an entrance strategy: **positioning options**, **scouting options** and **stepping-stone options**

- ► have found out how to optimize entry through **early engagement** of the potential customers; the 'first three customers' rule.

After reading the *innovation workout*, you will be able to perform force-field analysis to analyse the dynamics of your entry into a competitive market.
After reading the Triumph and Victory Motorcycle *case study*, you will be able to understand the roles of image and brand history in packaging new technology.

Note: Further information, class slides, test questions and other supporting material are available on our companion website at

www.palgrave.com/business/westland

ASSESSING THE COMPETITIVE
TERRAIN FOR AN INNOVATION

Successful innovation requires that the firm attain and retain strategic focus in two ways. First, strategy needs to choose competitive terrain, selecting those business arenas to compete in that represent the best chances for profitable growth. Second, strategy must set priorities on the perceived competitive opportunities in each of the selected arenas – these will largely be determined by the product and service ideas you have come up with. You are likely to be most successful by choosing intermediating or progressive change in the firm's capabilities when charting the current terrain; then use that as a basis for selecting the future arenas.[1]

These tasks are made more difficult as the need arises to invest in new capabilities, and dispose of old ones, as consumer markets evolve. Figure 8.1 depicts this migration in pursuit of changing markets. Clearly there are many markets in which the firm might compete; one objective of strategy is to make a decision on which market will actually be pursued.

Not all the customers the firm serves today, the products or services it sells today, the distribution channels it uses today, or the geographical areas in which it operates today are going to fit with the new business domains you are creating. Identifying opportunities to stop investing in a particular activity is every bit as important as coming up with

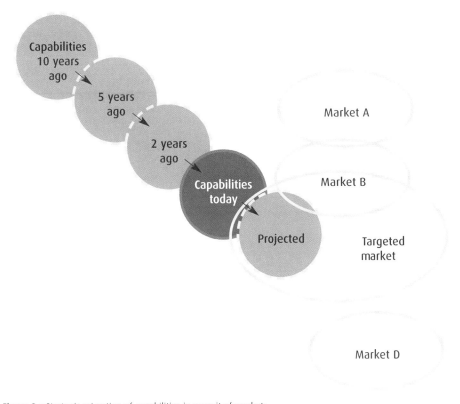

Figure 8.1 Strategic migration of capabilities in pursuit of markets

innovations to propel future growth.[2] Unfortunately, firms often pay insufficient attention to the need to prune outdated operations as they become obsolete. Every budget line, skilled person, good technologist, or expert sales or service person dedicated to the pursuit of a business arena without a good chance at profitable growth is a resource going to waste.[3]

The best place to start is to develop simple *stratification maps*, which highlight the contributions of business activities to the firm's current performance. Stratification maps analyse the contribution that each component of the business is making to current performance. The most attractive of these components will be the key to deciding on future markets; the least attractive are the candidates for pruning.

Table 8.1: *Business segment portfolio ranking*

Business segment	Revenues ($000)	Contribution ($000)	Cumulative % of revenue	Cumulative % of profit	Annual growth
Segment 1	89	28	51.45%	32.56%	4.00%
Segment 2	54	63	31.21%	73.26%	8.00%
Segment 3	25	5	14.45%	5.81%	15.00%
Segment 4	5	−10	2.89%	−11.63%	8.00%

ANALYSING YOUR CURRENT BUSINESS PORTFOLIO

Each of your current business segments represents an investment in assets, competences and people that is directed towards making a profit from particular products. Some classes are more profitable than others. Your options for migrating your capabilities are commensurate with the opportunities for improving this portfolio. The problem is inherently more complex than managing a financial portfolio because the relevant arena for you might not be return on investment; rather it could be products, customer segments, geographical areas, branches, distributors or brokers (in a distribution-intensive business), or services. Your chosen categories will be your strategy drivers – the factors you deem most important in the evolution of your business.[4]

To analyse your business portfolio, first collect data on how much revenue each business arena has generated in the past year. You then rank your business segments by building a table of the contribution of each segment to revenue, profit and growth. For example, Table 8.1 provides a comparison of the revenue, profit and growth for four segments of a hypothetical company. The firm's future support for any particular segment will be determined by its ranking, which will differ depending on whether revenue, profit or growth are considered most important.

Your portfolio ranking will provide you with a concise, relatively unambiguous portrayal of your business's business segments. From Table 8.1, we can see that this company would be likely to have grounds for divesting itself of business segments 3 and 4; the money, management attention and capabilities freed up could then be reallocated to segments 1 and 2 which are contributing the major share of profits and revenue. Consideration might be given, though, to the qualitative assessment given to segment 4, which describes it as a loss leader. If, for example, it is like the iTunes service, provided at loss in order to sell iPods (see the case study at the end of Chapter 1), it would not be possible to eliminate it without considering the complementary segment. On the other hand, if this were the case it could be argued that the businesses were not segmented properly to begin with, and that this segment should have been included with the complementary segment.

One other factor that needs to be considered is growth in the market. Smaller segments may often have the capacity for growing quickly, although prior years' performance is no guarantee of future performance (as they say). In Table 8.1, segment 3 is experiencing 15 per cent annual growth. The smaller contribution may be because of start-up costs if it is a new product, or more intense competition in the market.[5]

Action steps for an innovation and investment

The action steps that follow are meant to get you started on the concepts and processes discussed in the chapter. Elaborate on them in any way that fits with your innovation, competition and firm environment.

Step 1: Decide on the appropriate business segments for the ranking (products, services, customers, geographies or other types of business). Develop your equivalent of Table 8.1. Review the basic recommendations for each cell in the map, paying particular attention to how the business categories have shifted in the past.

Step 2: Revisit the opportunity register and categorize opportunities according to whether their potential is in building new arenas or in model-transforming arenas.

Step 3: For the most appealing arena-building opportunities, assess their upside potential, risk, and adoption characteristics.

Step 4: Determine the revenue, profit and growth potential of future arena-building opportunities associated with the innovations in your opportunity register.

Step 5: Carry out projection of the ranking into the future. Determine which opportunities and existing businesses are worth further serious consideration and which should be restructured or sold.

Step 6: Determine where the capital, people, and capabilities will be obtained for any new business segment investments.

Step 7: Identify the people and groups that will be needed to make an innovation and associated new business segment work. Start planning your strategy for managing the actors in each cell.

This sort of analysis only provides insight in how to prune unproductive business segments. You need to look in your opportunity register to determine where to add new business segments with the potential to provide new markets and new opportunities for investment in core capabilities.

Your portfolio ranking also provides you with targets for revenue, profit and growth in new business segments. Your opportunities have to measure up to your current portfolio, or they will need to wait in the opportunity register for another day.

COMPETITIVE OPTIONS

Eliminating activities from your agenda is as important as adding new ones. Looking at both sets of activities – the new and the existing – is essential in gaining control of your innovation portfolio.[6]

Now we have described an approach to prioritizing the innovations from your opportunity register that are most likely to contribute future growth and profit, the next challenge is to figure out how to allocate resources appropriately to those opportunities that you elect to pursue. We recommend an approach to building a portfolio of projects that draws on real options, a modification of a highly successful financial technique that can be applied to non-financial investments in things such as labour, time and technology. *Real options* are inherently project oriented, directed towards operations that require management and resources, whereas *financial options* are normally limited to assessing financial contracts.

An important distinction rarely made explicit is that the purpose and nature of financial and real options are not the same. Real options actually provide a richer language for innovators than their financial counterparts. That is because real options take into account the manner in which management learns about an innovation, and the particular steps that are taken to manage that risk of the life of the product or service. Thus real options come in three different forms – *positioning*, *scouting* and *stepping-stone* options. You will find that you manage them differently and expect different things from them.

Positioning options

Positioning options create the right to *wait and see*. Investments that put the company in a position to capitalize on uncertain external events, should they occur – such as the emergence of a new market on the internet or of a successful technology that has been competing for market dominance – are positioning options. Such options are useful when the uncertainty faced is mostly out of the company's control but it needs to be positioned to act in case fortune turns its way.[7]

Positioning is appropriate when several competing outcomes could satisfy high potential market demand, but it is not yet clear which outcome will dominate. Take mobile telephony in Asia. As of the time of writing, there are three different communication standards and massive uncertainty about which will ultimately become the standard. The plausible scenarios include:

- ▸ a lock-in on one of the three standards
- ▸ preservation of the current multi-standard system
- ▸ the emergence of some new standard or way of communicating that makes the current mobile concept obsolete.

Given such uncertainty, a sensible route for an interested organization may be to make modest investments that will prepare it for any of the three scenarios; committing itself entirely to one or the other would not be prudent. We see this, of course, in practice, as telecommunications companies engage in a vast array of mergers, acquisitions of smaller firms, and joint ventures and alliances with larger firms while also aggressively lobbying regulatory agencies and investing in the development of standards.[8] The reason to select a positioning option is to make the smallest possible investment and still buy time and flexibility to pursue the best course of action once it becomes clear.[9]

The father of Sudoku

Chain-smoking, unkempt, in jeans and dowdy sweater, Maki Kaji is an unlikely corporate success story. He readily admits that he would rather spend his days hanging out at the racetrack than sitting in his president's chair at Nikoli, the Tokyo-based company (named after the winning horse in 1980's Irish 2000 Guineas race) that developed the hugely successful puzzle game Sudoku.

Kaji's education certainly didn't prepare him for success. In the early 1970s he began studying literature at one of Japan's most prestigious private colleges, but found it boring. He spent most of the time gambling and playing tennis, quitting college after his first year. He tried being a waiter, a roadie and a construction worker before setting up a small publishing business which indulged his love of gambling and chance.

Sudoku came from an earlier puzzle – Number Place – that Kaji saw in a US magazine in 1984; he rearranged the numbers and grids and released it in Japan. It was picked up more than a decade later by Wayne Gould, a retired Hong Kong judge whose promotion of the game led to an international craze. Now the game appears in more than 600 newspapers, on thousands of webs and in dozens of books in about 70 countries. In 2006, 20 nations took part in the first Sudoku world championship in Italy.

Sudoku's success caught Kaji as much by surprise as anyone else. 'We have no idea what makes something popular, so we try them out on the readers. About once every five years, one suddenly takes off. It's as big a surprise to us as anybody else.'

Sudoku has not made Kaji rich. Nikoli's team of 22 employees edits and refines the 1000 puzzles that flood into the company every month, from their cramped quarters in an unfashionable business district of Tokyo, generating a modest US$4 million of revenue. The company has never used a distributor or advertised in its 27-year history, depending on publications and a roster of 300 games to build awareness. Like Daisuke Inoue, the amateur inventor who constructed the first karaoke machine, Kaji didn't bother to patent his discovery. And like Inoue, he seems mostly unconcerned. 'More than the money, it's gratifying to see the explosive worldwide growth of our puzzles. That makes me very happy.'

Creativity at Nikoli happens mostly elsewhere – in bedrooms, kitchens and commuter trains across Japan. Nikoli's puzzle writers design 90 per cent of the games and work for a flat fee. Kaji draws them from a cross-section of ordinary Japanese: teenagers, housewives, company employees and pensioners. Two-thirds of them are high school and university students; the oldest is an 81-year-old retired teacher. It's from this diffuse network of individuals with time on their hands that recent successes, including Kakuro and local hit Slitherlink, have emerged.

When he gets time away from the firm, Kaji likes to be at the racetrack, describing the excitement of a race as similar to solving a puzzle. In 1986 he wanted to find out the fate of the Irish-born horse Nikoli that had inspired his little company. Eventually, Kaji found him in Uruguay. 'He was retired and taking it easy after a lifetime of entertaining people. I thought that was cool.' It is easy enough to imagine Kaji one day similarly retiring and taking it easy after a lifetime of entertaining people.[10]

Positioning options tend to be most useful when the level of technical uncertainty is high but the company has some idea of what markets and segments it eventually wants to serve. The uncertainty may stem from the lack of a dominant design or standard, a lack of knowledge about the technical feasibility of a given solution set, or issues such as the regulatory acceptability of certain technologies. Since the major uncertainties have to do with alternative technological solutions, the idea is to take a limited number of positions at the lowest possible cost to hedge against making a single wrong bet, thus containing the damage done by any one position that does not work out.

For example, from about 1998 to 2003, AT&T spent billions of dollars on taking attractive positions, acquiring cable companies such as Tele-Communications and

MediaOne. It entered into joint ventures with British Telecom and Japan Telecom, and worked with Microsoft for set-top box software, all in pursuit of a convergence of telephone, internet, gaming and television services on top of one technological platform. This is a market that AT&T could possibly dominate with its network position, but Microsoft, Sony and Nintendo may be in a better consumer position with their game consoles. For AT&T, billions of dollars is a reasonable price to pay for a positioning option when you consider the size of the potential industry, which may represent hundreds of billions of dollars in annual revenue.

Scouting options

A second class of options, scouting options, can be considered as entrepreneurial experiments. They are investments made with the intention of discovering and/or creating markets for products and services by deploying capabilities that a firm has (perhaps recently) developed in potential new arenas. Through these options, it can explore new terrain from a current competence base, gathering information on its most attractive locations.[11]

Scouting options differ from positioning options in that they extend existing competences in directions that the firm believes will allow it to capture significant market opportunities. This kind of option might emerge from insights that large opportunities can be within reach if it breaks a barrier (see Chapter 5). Scouting options are also used to discover opportunities to break through barriers. The reason for selecting a scouting option is thus to deploy or develop competences that allow a company to ferret out high-potential markets that are highly uncertain.

Scouting options can take many forms. The most familiar is the sacrificial product or probe from which firms seek to determine the market's reaction to a bundle of attributes. These are options that are conscientiously managed as scouts – exploratory small investments made without necessarily expecting an immediate pay-off, and designed to maximize what is learned about a market or particular technology. They are used to learn, to gather information. The idea is to send out scouts using the smallest investment possible and be ready to redirect your efforts once promising paths are found.

Scouting options tend to be used when people are not sure what combination of attributes the market will eventually prefer. By staking out several contrasting positions in a market, for example, a firm can systematically pretest the market acceptance of an innovation. A similar line of thinking allows it to test its coverage for adverse contingencies. Scouting options can also provide information concerning what data needs to be tracked, and help develop the scanning and intelligence systems that will ultimately be needed when the product or service comes to market.

Later in the chapter, we shall investigate in detail one particular scouting option that puts the offering into the hands of customers in order to aggressively get feedback on their reactions to its features.

It pays never to assume that you know what the customer wants. Customers can be remarkably inarticulate about their real concerns are. This can be frustrating, but it is often necessary to observe the customer in a buying or using situation to gain the insights needed.[12]

Genghis Khan's entrance strategy

In the 12th century, Mongols were known for dramatic entrances. Under Genghis Khan, their army was incomparably superior to any other force on earth, wiping out, in their time, most of the European nobility, and subduing the powerful armies of the Caliph of Baghdad. Genghis was a great innovator in psychological warfare, generating his own propaganda which exaggerated the brutality and decisiveness of his conquests to frighten future opponents. He instituted a professional class of bookkeepers to inventory his spoils and to impose harsh but efficient taxation on the vanquished. He thrived through superior strategy and mobility, which allowed his army to cover thousands of miles in weeks, and conquer and keep large areas of territory even though often it was vastly outnumbered. There was no Mongol infantry to slow them down. Horses outnumbered people five to one in Mongolia, and everyone was born into the cavalry.

Much of their superiority lay in their technology. Almost all of it was borrowed, but Genghis Khan improved each piece, integrating it into the development of Mongol tactics. Unlike European knights, Mongols were not burdened by heavy steel armour, but wore a silk shirt covered in light cloth armour in front, and none at the back (which discouraged troops from retreat). When armour-clad knights were struck by powerful Mongol arrows, they were faced with the difficult task of removing the arrow embedded in their armour and their flesh. In contrast, when struck by an arrow the Mongolians' silk shirt would be carried into the wound by the arrow. Tugging gently on the silk around the arrow could free it with minimal additional wounding to the soldier.

The Mongolian horses, unarmoured themselves and carrying soldiers clad in light armour, had much more endurance than the horses ridden by the opposing medieval knights. Mongols in battle would suddenly retreat, travelling miles into their own territory to wear out heavily armed opponents, only to turn back on them when they were thoroughly worn down.

Technologically advanced siege machines built by Chinese technicians were used in attacking fortified cities. Between battles they were disassembled and carried on horses to be rebuilt at the site of the battle. Chinese fireworks were modified to produce brass cannon to shoot balls which could breach city walls and demoralize opposing troops. Greek fire was thrown from trebuchets to burn down cities and demoralize residents. Once the main battle and city siege was over, the Mongol army would follow the enemy leader until he was killed in order to prevent him from becoming a rallying point for his army.

The Mongol logistical system was distinguished by its mobility and practicality, living off the land heavily, much as General Sherman did in his march to Atlanta. Heavier equipment was brought up by well-organized supply trains. An essential feature of Mongolian tactics was the use of 'kharash'. During a battle the Mongols would drive a crowd of local residents as a human wall, who would erect siege machines around the walls, forcing the king to attack his own subjects. Genghis Khan's cavalry was a highly efficient, disciplined organization, with superior military intelligence of a form not seen again until the 18th century. Operating in massive sweeps, extending over dozens of miles, the Mongol army combined shock, mobility and firepower unmatched in land warfare.[13]

Large companies commonly do worse at scouting that do small entrepreneurial companies, simply because the large firms have more money to spend. For companies that are loaded down with heavy fixed costs or massive sunk investment, redirection becomes much more difficult. Even fabulously well-researched and technically brilliant new products can disappoint in the marketplace.

Stepping-stone options

Stepping-stone options are a series of small investments that lead towards a larger goal one small step at a time. They are consciously staged attempts to sequentially discover new competences to pursue highly promising but very uncertain potential markets or technologies. They are somewhat analogous to compound financial options, in which the value of a portfolio is a function of a sequence of investment choices.[14]

Stepping-stone options are used when the aim is to expose a company to opportunities in which there is high uncertainty both about the final shape of a high-potential market and about the likelihood of being able to develop the necessary competences to serve it. Nevertheless, the potential opportunity is so big that it is irresistible. The company can start with small, exploratory forays into less challenging market niches and use the experiences gained there as stepping-stones to build competences in increasingly challenging and attractive market arenas that it discovers as it goes.

Investments in stepping-stones are thus made as a series of deliberately staged and sequenced options. Staged funding decisions are made only when key milestones are reached and a great many assumptions have been tested. As each milestone is reached, there is the opportunity to continue or stop further development, or even to sell, trade, license or otherwise capture returns on investments in technological and market development to that point. The idea is to keep each successive round of investment to an absolute minimum and to reassess the project frequently.[15]

The primary difference between stepping-stone and scouting options is that scouting options assume that that technology and operations are sufficiently well understood so that only the risk from market uncertainties needs to be proactively managed. Scouting options are designed to explore market demand for a specific product or service. Thus it is possible to make deliberately parsimonious resource allocations designed to pursue carefully selected and increasingly challenging opportunities, with the objective of developing a new competence along an increasingly sophisticated trajectory and deploying it in unfolding markets.

The Kyocera Company in Japan used this approach to pursue the industrial ceramics business in the 1960s. Instead of investing to crack high-level applications like automobile engine cylinders or turbine blades (as did many other smart companies, General Electric included), Kyocera initially invested in low-end applications for known niche markets. For instance, the company developed ceramic scissor blades for the textile industry. Through this initial effort, the company resolved considerable technical uncertainty, such as how to process clays and how to make precise edges with consistent quality. This created an initial technological competence which, as it evolved, took Kyocera along a trajectory of increasing technical sophistication. The firm is now a major global supplier of semiconductor chip substrates and other materials for the digital age, spanning entire industries which were still in their infancy when Kyocera began ceramic development.

The best approach – positioning, scouting or stepping-stone options, or a direct launch with traditional one-shot strategic planning – depends on the precise character of the uncertainty faced. At their simplest, these uncertainties with the development of an innovation (= invention + commercialization) fall into either operational-technological uncertainties or market related uncertainties.[16]

Stepping-stone options are an embodiment of the dictum that it is best to 'take small steps – and fast' which worked so well for the 3M Corporation (see Chapter 3). They are a great strategy for opportunities that present both high technical and high market uncertainty, because the organization has significant opportunities for learning in both dimensions.[17]

WHEN TO USE OPTIONS STRATEGIES

We can summarize the functions for which the available options are useful by mapping the project space according to the level of uncertainty in first, technology and operations, and second, market knowledge, volatility and speed of change (see Figure 8.2).[18]

Positioning options allow the organization to stake out positions in one or more technologies when it is reasonably assured that there will be a market for them, but doesn't know what form, or what competitor, will prevail. Japanese companies such as Yamaha, Mitsubishi and Sony have excelled in staking out positions through patent applications that essentially build a protective wall around a commercializable technology.[19]

Stepping-stone options give the organization small steps to take when technology is still developing (and in a stage of ferment), consumer learning is anticipated to be high in adoption of products and services based on the technology, and there is great uncertainty in how consumers would most like to see the products or services offered. Electronic commerce in the early 1990s was just such a high tech-risk/high market-risk sector. Silicon Graphics founder Jim Clark originally promoted electronic commerce through interactive television, following the French Minitel model. With the rise of the internet from 1993 onwards, interest migrated to an internet platform, but following an 'interactive shopping mall' format (basically an online catalogue). Later shifts in the electronic commerce model abandoned the catalogue format for a stock market model (eBay), social networking mode (Amazon), build-to-order model (Dell) and

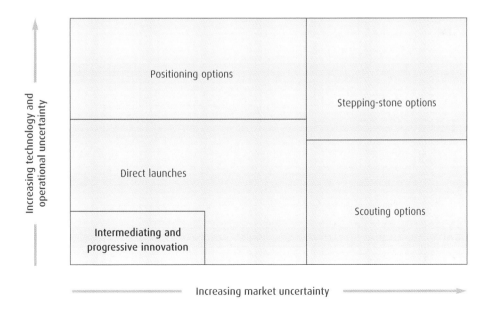

Figure 8.2 Project options in technology – operations and market space

various other successful formats. Few of the initial models did well, but they were important in refining the models that were eventually successful.

Scouting options are primarily vehicles for learning more about consumer needs, or the form and function they may expect from a particular innovation. They are needed because consumers in all areas are notoriously bad in articulating their real desires – particularly with products and services they have never experienced before. Consumers in effect say to the innovator, 'I don't know what I want, but I might let you know if you get it wrong.' Scouting options allow consumers to respond to particular sets of features before the innovator scales up for a full market entry. Since technology risk is low, it is possible to assemble various sets of features cost-effectively and in a short time frame. Microsoft has earned a reputation in the past for presenting what has vindictively been termed 'slideware' or 'vapourware' – software that is announced or is claimed to be in development, but which is in reality introduced to see if demand exists for this feature set.

Where uncertainty is low, the firm is likely to know what customers want and how to meet that need. Thus direct launches of new products and services will be likely to be successful, and can be more timely than those that pre-test the market or technology through options. If the product is not entirely new – if it upgrades an existing product – then it is likely to be the result of intermediating or progressive innovation.

Whether a corporation, venture capitalist, or other source of funding will provide the resources needed for an innovation, there will always be competition with other innovation projects, based on a risk return trade-off which funding sources need to consider. Options strategies provide vehicles for managing risk, thus making funding decisions more palatable. Project risks and market entry strategies can be formally mapped in technology-operations risk and market risk space (see Figure 8.3).

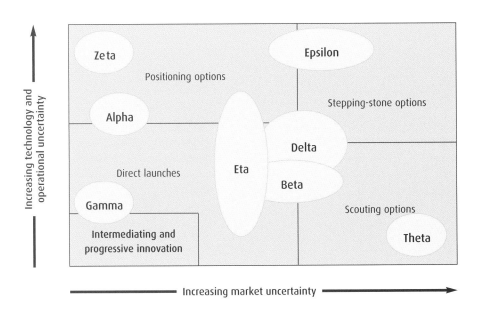

Figure 8.3 Example of projects (alpha, beta, etc.) mapped in technology-operations and market space

Source: McGrath, R. G. and MacMillan, I. (2000) *The Entrepreneurial Mindset*, Boston, Mass.: Harvard Business School Press, Chapter 7,

Technology-operations risk versus market risk mapping addresses one of the greatest challenges that successful companies face – the difficulty in balancing the needs of tomorrow's options (the longer-term growth businesses) with those of businesses that are delivering cash flow today. Where competitive advantage is vested in technological and innovative expertise – both assets that are resident in the employees of the firm – the choice gets even tougher. Decisions about whether to allocate people and resources to speculative projects with payoffs in the distant future, or to invest instead in today's profitable business, present difficult but necessary choices.

The allocation of projects to positioning options, scouting options, stepping-stone options and direct launches can be useful as managers try to sort out these sometimes conflicting demands. The core concept is to let the strategy and available resources guide the choice of how much emphasis to put on each of the categories in Figure 8.3. In general, the company wants a portfolio of projects that suits the environment in which it will have to compete. If it is in a fast-moving, highly uncertain industry, it will want to weight its portfolio more heavily toward options. If it is in a relatively stable or asset- and capital-intensive industry, it should probably be investing more heavily in platform launches.

Action steps

Step 1: Review the organization's list of arena-building and model-transforming opportunities.

Step 2: For each attractive opportunity on the list, assess the market and technical uncertainty. Plot each opportunity to the appropriate option or launch category in a space determined by technology-operations risk and market risk.

Step 3: Decide which projects to allocate to each kind of initiative the organization might want to take: positioning options, scouting options, stepping-stone options, platform launches and enhancement launches.

Step 4: Regularly review capacity, the portfolio of opportunities, and the match of people to projects.

Another factor to consider is that nearly all innovation projects have a life-cycle measured in years. There are both short-range and long-range resource usage issues, as well as short-run and long-run value generation. Though you may have some idea of how you will allocate resources based on these maps, you are still missing a great deal of information needed for proper decisions.

A DISCOVERY-DRIVEN ENTRANCE STRATEGY

Adaptive execution – knowing when to invest as well as how much – adds value because it provides time to gather more information which in turn reduces uncertainty. Positioning, scouting and stepping-stone options are all tools to assist in adaptive execution in entering the market for selling our innovation. They are the tools of a *discovery-driven entrance strategy*.

A discovery-driven entrance strategy incorporates three main activities. First is the decision on a planned entry strategy. This will depend in large part on what the company anticipates the competitive response will be, and the various options provide tools for anticipating competitive behaviour and response. Second is a plan for environmental scanning and intelligence collection. Some intelligence may be provided by the options, but the majority of intelligence will be gathered through scanning media and internet resources, and possibly from surveys and consumer testing. Finally, specific managerial actions will need to be dedicated to assessing and controlling progress as the strategy unfolds. This is where managerial experience and intuition really pay off. Much of the success or failure of an innovation depends on the manager's intuition about unfolding developments and the people that make them happen; it also requires that managers actively intervene in situations that require leadership, motivation of people, and evangelizing for the innovation.[20]

To some extent, the choice of entry strategy helps shape the nature and impact of competitors' reactions. But a discovery-driven strategy can help the organization avoid debilitating competitive interactions by using better intelligence, speed and surprise to outmanoeuvre competitors. It uses imagination and foresight rather than the firm's physical resources, to compete successfully.

THE MOST IMPORTANT SALES ARE
THE FIRST THREE SALES

The first three sales of any particular combination of features that the company envisages for its innovation should be seen as qualitatively different from all other sales. They not only provide the first real feedback on the innovation, they also provide the basis for word-of-mouth and viral marketing, both good and bad. Thus the entry strategy needs to identify the ideal initial customer groups that are needed for product success. Such testing is comparable to a software's 'beta' release, where working software is released to a limited group of users (often current users, or more sophisticated users) in order to create a buzz while the company is attempting to clean up any significant defects.

The initial step in choosing the first three customers relies on tools the company has used previously. It should be able to map a fairly accurate consumption chain, and link attributes of the offering to an attribute map for each segment. The challenge then is to go out there and secure a commitment to purchase from the first few target customers.[21]

Good sales technique plays an important part in the first sales. The innovator needs to possess the ability to get customers to make some kind of commitment to a given set of features – a particular innovation package – that the firm wants to deliver to this group, sometimes even before the product or service had been developed. These innovators see this commitment as affirmation of market acceptance of their new business model. One innovator goes so far as to say that if he does not have some kind of commitment from several key stakeholders, he won't proceed, but will instead go back to his register and select another opportunity.

One note of explanation is needed here on terminology. To keep the guidelines simple, this book uses the term 'customers' as a generic reference, when it really means various key stakeholders that may be critical for the launch: distributors, suppliers, key skilled employees and so on. Obviously, all potential customers are not equally attractive. Nor will an innovation be equally attractive to all of them.

There is a decisive moment in market entry that demands specifics – in company name and individual contact names, reasons for choosing them, and specific features of the innovation that the innovator thinks will be attractive to these customers. Before any further spending it is essential to provide the names of at least three customers with a demonstrated willingness to buy. If the sales person get an order, he or she should be able to get a letter of intent. If he or she can't get a letter of intent, he/she should be able to get a written expression of interest. If the salesperson cannot even get an expression of interest, it is essential to rethink the entire business model.

Where should a firm look for these all-important first few sets of customers? If there is already a business related to the innovation, then the logical place is to look to those the company is already serving well and with whom its sales staff have built a good relationship. If it is a start-up, it should look at potential competitors, and approach their best customers. Companies must stay aware of opportunities to tap into customers who are new to them, either because they are resegmenting a market or because they have achieved a technological or business model breakthrough that will reconfigure the relations between players. In the latter case, the target segment may not even exist yet, and a strategy is needed to bring these new customers on board. If existing customers won't see the value in what the organization is doing, avoid them until the business is off to a good start.

LEAD-STEER CUSTOMERS

This chapter has already mentioned 'beta' releases for software, where working software is released to a limited group of users (often current users, or more sophisticated users) in order to create buzz while the developers are attempting to clean up any significant defects. Every innovation – product or service – has its counterpart in what are called *lead-steer customers*. These are the customers that will set the tone for the market entry, because there is no way to sell thousands of units without having sold three to begin with.[22]

Unilever discovers that its lead-steer customers do not care about health

In one of the greatest advances of the century in food health, Unilever in 1973 filed a British patent application for a hardened, randomized margarine that reportedly contained only 3.2 per cent trans fatty acids. Trans fatty acids were considered a leading health hazard arising from the huge global market for margarine and cooking oil; so serious is the health hazard they pose that New York has banned them completely in foods served in the city after July 2008. Unilever's patent was lauded by European oil chemists as 'the greatest technological advance of recent years'. It permits truly tailor-made fats to be produced, at the same time allowing almost limitless variation in the raw materials used. By 1976 some European margarines with zero trans fatty acid content and high polyunsaturate content were being produced by a modified process.

Despite its importance, the road to 'selling' this improved process was convoluted, and started with a graduate student who licensed a particular catalytic technology from a former professor. Although his innovation made sense in the final market, it didn't offer much in the way of exciter features to his target audience of margarine refiners.

This was because the annual savings for a refinery manager to switch to the new catalyst were modest – perhaps US$15,000 per year per converter. Moreover, the refinery manager wouldn't personally benefit from the savings, which would appear on the plant expense budget and were not part of the criteria on which refinery managers were evaluated. Should a batch of oil be lost, on the other hand, the manager would be held responsible and the cost could exceed $150,000 per batch. This high-risk/low-reward proposition to switch to the new catalyst was a predictably hard sell, and entrepreneurs got nowhere with their 'I'll save you money – trust me' pitch.

Lead-steer customers are opinion leaders in their industry, who are likely to be well regarded by their peers. Corporations like those on the 'most-admired' lists published in magazines such as *Business Week* are prime candidates to become lead-steer customers. Individuals who represent a segment that is highly desirable to the innovator might be more appropriate for a particular innovation. The objective is to use these customers' enthusiasm about the innovation and business model to test the assumptions about attribute maps, and at the same time use their success with the offering to sell to others, to create buzz, to initiate viral, word-of-mouth promotion. Testimonials and actual experiences with real customers are critical if buying the product involves any kind of perceived consumer risk. (Consider, for example, medical innovations such as new drugs or surgical procedures.)

In trying to sell to these customers, bear in mind that the buying decision may be complex. If the organization is trying to market to consumers, a distributor or another channel partner will usually be involved. If it is trying to sell to companies, they invariably have multiple employees who are involved not only in making the purchasing decision but also at many different – and potentially crucial – links in the company's consumption chain.

Unilever gets its lead-steer customers to care about health

(See the box on page 181.) Out of desperation, the entrepreneur who was trying to sell catalytic technology for making margarine called on an old college friend who was running an oil refinery for the Unilever Corporation. The entrepreneur brought with him the professor who had developed the catalyst and who could credibly attest to its safety and quality. He even volunteered to donate the first batch of catalyst at no cost, just so his friend could try it out. His friend was persuaded to make the order. The catalyst worked well, and Unilever made the switch. In this industry at the time, the Unilever plants set the standard for what was considered cutting edge. Once it became known that Unilever had adopted the product, nearly every other plant in the region switched over as well.

The entrepreneur had achieved two critical outcomes. First, for the individual refinery managers, he had removed the risk of switching to his catalyst; in the event something went wrong, they could credibly argue that they were simply following the best practice in their industry. Second, he had increased the downside of their not switching to his product, because a leading manufacturer was using it. This first sale led rapidly to the next few sales required. With momentum well established, the entrepreneur went on to convert the bulk of his target customer segment to the new catalyst within 18 months.

When planning a launch, an innovator needs to know the people involved in making the critical decision on whether to buy from the organization. It is important to get a feel for their needs and interests as far as the offering is concerned. This involves spelling out assumptions about how the sale will be closed, as far as is possible. What will stop the sale? Who will try to stop the sale? Why should they stop the sale? What will clinch the deal? The idea is to be prepared to overcome obstacles to closing the sale before they arise.

The company should be so familiar with these customers' consumption chains that it has a good idea of how risky and difficult it will be for them to buy the innovation. How hard will it be for them to switch to the offering? How much will it cost them? If they need to learn to work with or operate the product or service, what is the training and adjustment burden? The greater the effort they must put into implementing your solution, the more the company must convince them that the effort is worthwhile.

The first step towards choosing the first three sales is to prioritize potential customers according to the extents to which they are thought likely to generate substantial benefits by adopting the offering and to which they perceive it to be a risky, effortful move. Table 8.2 shows the resulting matrix, which can be used to help set priorities.

Table 8.2: *Prospects and strategies for initial sales*

		Risk	
		Low	High
Benefit	Low	Second priority: it is necessary to expend time, effort and money to help manage the potential customers' risk. This may involve new research and technology, especially with innovations in medicine and food.	Not a good prospect for initial sales.
	High	First priority.	Third priority: Warranties and price reductions are needed to convince the customers to buy.

The most important deals, in short, are those that secure the critical first few sales. The front end of the initial marketing plan should focus on how to target customers for these first few sales and how to reduce their risk of purchase.[25]

COMPETITIVE RESPONSE

Generally it should be assumed that the offering is entering a market where there are established competitors. (If it is creating an entirely new market, it is neither necessary nor possible to invest effort in the analysis of past competitive behaviour.) A critical variable is the response of likely competitors, and the success of any new business proposition is critically dependent on the venture's insulation from early, debilitating competitive attack. Unless the organization has overwhelmingly powerful sources of competitive insulation (such as patents in the pharmaceutical industry), the response it gets will be shaped in part by the initial moves it makes.

Two major factors dominate competitive response. The first relates to a competitor's motivation to challenge in that arena, and the second concerns its capacity to make a challenge. Motivation has a lot to do with whether managers in competing organizations will feel threatened by the entry and feel that they must respond urgently. The degree of threat depends on how they view the competitive significance of the arena. If they have a sizable commitment to a competing solution for the customers the organization plans to start selling to, they will have a greater motivation to respond.[24]

Using publicly available information, it is often possible to get a rough estimate of which business areas fall into which category for competitors, at least on a revenue basis. In addition, businesses to which a competitor has made long, accumulated psychological and resource commitments are more likely to be highly valued than new businesses. Another indicator of corporate commitment by competitors is their relative effectiveness in a target arena. This can be gauged by assessing a competitor company's performance on the key drivers for that arena. If the firm regularly outperforms its competitors, it must have a strong position and is more likely to seek to defend it.

Capacity to respond is also critical to a competitor's propensity to react to a move. Even with all the motivation in the world, a competitor without the resources, or without the appropriate skills or technologies, cannot do an innovator much harm. On the other hand, a competitor with cash, high stock valuation, or excess capacity possesses assets that could be mobilized against the company, as could a strong position in distribution, supply or standard-setting. Propensity to respond is a key indicator of the resources the organization will need to expend on market entry.

Competitive tactics

The study of managerial strategy was originally conceived by Peter Drucker in terms that had their basis in military strategy. Although our understanding of management has evolved and expanded to incorporate operations, science and technology, the study of military tactics still has great relevance when planning a market entry. In this case, we can borrow much from study of successful military tactics.

Offensive tactics

Rapid dominance: spectacular displays of power to destroy an adversary's will to fight. A well-known example of dominant manoeuvres occurred when Japanese semiconductor makers advanced on the Intel Corporation's DRAM (dynamic random access memory) business in the mid-1980s. The Japanese firms cut prices on DRAMs for every target customer by 10 per cent until Intel gave up on the customer. The eventual result of these cumulative attacks was Intel's complete withdrawal from the DRAM market.

Planned attack/frontal assault: the direct, hostile movement of forces towards enemy forces in a large number, in an attempt to overwhelm the enemy. This is often referred to as a 'suicide strike', because it is often a commander's last resort when he has run out of strategies.

Flanking manoeuvre/pincer movement (double envelopment): the principle of the flanking manoeuvre is to be sudden and able to catch the enemy by surprise, causing the enemy to overreact or retreat when they are surrounded from a few directions. Usually this type of flanking is concealed in an ambush.

Attrition warfare: this is a strategic concept which states that to win a war, the enemy must be worn down to the point of collapse by continuous losses in personnel and material. The war will usually be won by the side with greater reserves.

Interdiction/control of lines of communication and supply: in business this often involves patent fights and forward contracts to ensure control of scarce resources.

Pre-emptive attack: this aims to gain a strategic advantage in an impending war, the intention being to harm the enemy at a moment of minimal protection, for instance while vulnerable during transport or mobilization.

Divide and conquer: a strategy where small power groups are prevented from linking up and becoming more powerful, since it is difficult to break up existing power structures. Typical elements involve creating or at least not preventing petty feuds among smaller players. Such feuds drain resources and prevent alliances that could challenge the overlords.

Guerrilla warfare: a method of combat by which a smaller group of combatants attempts to use its mobility to defeat a larger, and consequently less mobile, army.

Defensive tactics
Mutual support: an example of the application of this defensive principle is locating weapons in ways that mutually support one another so that it is difficult for an attacker to find a covered approach to any one defensive position.

Scorched earth policy: a military tactic which involves destroying anything that might be useful to the enemy while advancing through or withdrawing from an area.

Trench warfare: a form of war in which both opposing armies have static lines of fortifications dug into the ground, facing each other. Trench warfare arose when there was a revolution in firepower without similar advances in mobility and communications. 'Digging in' can be an useful tactic in other fields too.

Deceptive tactics
Disinformation: this is the spreading of deliberately false information to mislead an enemy as to a position or planned course of action. It also includes the distortion of true information in such a way as to render it useless. Thomas Edison was famous for disinformation campaigns in his war with George Westinghouse for the home electrification market. Edison electrocuted dogs, cats and even an elephant to demonstrate the dangers inherent in Westinghouse's systems.

Feint: a move designed to draw defensive action towards the point under assault. It is usually used as a diversion to force the enemy to concentrate more resources in a given area so that the opposing force in another area is weaker.

Force multiplication: a military tactic that is supposed to visually magnify a force, such as a division or an army, through means of using decoy vehicles or use of terrain to deceivingly create a much larger force than is really present.

FIRST-MOVER ADVANTAGE

Aggressive pursuit of customers makes sense where there are significant network effects and increasing returns to scale. This has been encouraged by the promise of what has been called 'first-mover advantage'.[25] Unfortunately, the first-mover in any market does not always, or even often, hold the competitive advantage.[26] It is better to be a late mover when there are substantial benefits from letting the market leader:

▸ figure out exactly what the customers are willing to pay for and position the product accordingly

▸ develop the underlying technology sufficiently for it to be robust with an easy to use interface

▶ make do with today's technology, when the late-mover can leapfrog with improved technology.

This is a particularly useful tactic if the organization is already a powerful firm in the market, with enough resources to come to the market late.

In contrast to popular myth, first mover advantage is quite rare. It is much more common and widespread for successful competitors to enter a market that is already developed.[27] Table 8.3 provides a brief guide on whether or not to invest in becoming a first mover.

Table 8.3: *When investing to gain first-mover advantage is strategically justified*

	First-mover advantage	Late-mover advantage
Returns to scale	Network effects Learning curve Lack of scale economics	Scale economics (if firm is large) Chance to learn from competitors' mistakes Reverse engineering Leapfrog with superior technology
Switching costs	High switching costs	Low switching costs Scale economics Uniform pricing requirements

Progressive

A classic example of a firm that pursued a guerrilla strategy is Progressive Insurance, which moved into the high-risk niche in automobile insurance. This niche move was actually met with relief on the part of some competitors. This is characteristic of a great guerrilla strategy: if established competitors find a chosen niche difficult to serve or a poor fit with their capabilities, they are unlikely to do anything to stop a rival's progress. For several years, Progressive built its capabilities. Eventually, the company used the competences that evolved from serving its niche base to begin expanding into more attractive niches. Today, fully 15 per cent of Progressive's portfolio of customers are in the standard (that is, low-risk) segment, and the company ultimately hopes to mirror the industry at large, in which only 15–20 per cent of all drivers are in its initial non-standard segment.

Force-field analysis

Peter Drucker's 1964 book *Managing for Results* was originally titled *Business Strategies* – a title that was rejected by the publisher after test marketing. Drucker, with his keen background in European history, borrowed the term 'strategy' from military and political campaigns, with allusions to winning battles. This term was not used widely in business enterprises until the late 1970s, and then only with great resistance from entrenched academics.

A good market entrance strategy is like a good military strategy – it is designed to win, and to do so at a minimum of cost. The original proponent of cost-effective strategy was Sun Tzu, a 6th century BC general in the Chinese state of Wu. The objective of an entrance strategy is to avoid debilitating competitive interaction by using speed, skill and surprise, or by using imagination, innovation and creativity to outmanoeuvre your competitors.

In this vein, we can look for guidance to one of the most lucrative 'wars' in modern history – the weekly battle between the steroid-fuelled goliaths representing competing teams in American football. A good football coach does not say, 'There is one way all great football teams win games, and we must do it the same way.' Rather, he tries to determine which positions on his team are strong and which are weak by testing and observing each individual football player. Then he replaces the weaker players, or teaches them to overcome or disguise their weaknesses. For example, if a defensive end is an ineffective pass rusher, the coach might teach him ways to trick the blocker. Only in this way can the coach bring his team's unique talents into play.

Like a firm or an army, a football team has one goal: to win. To win, the coach will develop a strategy to maximize the team's strengths and minimize its weaknesses. For instance, if a team has a weak defence, the strategy might be to control the ball and keep the defence off the field; if the offence is weak, the coach might teach his team to keep the other team deep in their own territory. By being aware of the positive and negative aspects of his team, the coach most efficiently uses football knowledge to win games.

It is the same with challenges. You must be aware of the positive and negative forces operating in a challenge before you develop a strategy for solving it. Your strategy should allow you to take advantage of the positive factors while eliminating or diminishing the negative ones.

The Japanese martial art of aikido is designed to control an attacker by controlling and redirecting their energy instead of blocking it. It focuses on positive and negative forces, and how to control them to achieve objectives. This is the basic idea underlying *force field analysis*, which was articulated in the West by social psychologist Kurt Lewin. Force-field analysis allows you to see how positive and negative forces push and pull you toward a best case or worst case scenario.

Positive and negative forces won't sit still for a portrait. They are constantly vibrating, pushing and pulling. Force-field analysis is a frame on which you can fasten down these forces and study them. It can help you to:

- better define your challenge
- identify strengths you can maximize
- identify weaknesses you can minimize.

Blueprint
1. Write the challenge you are trying to solve.
2. Describe the best-case scenario and the worst-case scenario; the best that can happen and the worst.
3. List the conditions of the situation. Conditions are anything that modifies or restricts the nature or existence of your subject. They are whatever requirements you perceive to be essential to solving a particular challenge.

Now 'feel the force!' As you list the conditions, you will find the forces pushing you to the best case and those pulling you toward catastrophe. Pit each condition against its opposite on the continuum by specifying its push and pull powers.

In the example in Figure 8.4, assume the centre represents the current situation, while the best- and worst-case scenarios are exerting a force-field over your deliberations, trying to pull you to the left or to the right.

Now let's consider the probability of a certain company getting a major sale. The best-case scenario would be closing the sale, the worst case would be losing the sale entirely. The negative forces are:

- Competitors' products are perceived as superior.
- The price is higher than alternative products.
- The company gave a poor presentation.

The positive forces are:
- The product is better than other comparable products.
- The customer has a real need for the product.
- The customer is able and ready to buy.

The options are:
- Further strengthen the positive forces.
- Reframe the negative forces as challenges to solve. For instance:
  - 'In what ways might our product be perceived as superior?'
  - 'In what ways might we add value to the product to further justify its price?'
  - 'In what ways might we make up for the poor presentation?'
  - 'In what ways might we improve our relationship with the customer?'
- Add more positive forces, such as customer service, packaged financing, bring in support personnel to help obtain the sale, and so on.

In force-field analysis, maximizing strengths is the objective; minimizing weaknesses keeps you out of trouble. Consider how Steven Jobs and Stephen Wozniak created Apple Computers. In 1976, their principal strength was a unique design for a personal computer; their principal weakness was an utter lack of capital. (Between them they had US$1,300.)

- Jobs maximized their principal strength by selling 50 as-yet-unbuilt computers to a string of computer hobby stores, based on their unique design.
- He minimized their weakness by securing credit to buy parts, based on sales of unbuilt computers.
- He added a positive force by using the profits gained from the sale of the first 600 computers to start work on the enormously successful Apple II.

Apple went public at the end of 1980, and after 3 weeks its shares were worth more than Ford Motor Company shares.

Once you identify the forces operating in your challenge, they become as negotiable as a mountain on wheels. You can either learn to live with the negatives by limiting your options and compromising your goals, or you can change their position and neutralize their impact.

Probability of market success				
Best case scenario: top seller	← Positive + force	– Negative → force	Worst case scenario: no sales	
Superior	← Product		Inferior	
None		Competition →	Superior	
Lowest	← Customer need	Price →	High	
Experience	← Customer knowledge		Unaware	
High	← Customer's budget		None	
Good		Advertising →	Unconvincing	

Figure 8.4 A Sample force field analysis

Triumph and Victory enter the market

How does a company enter a market that is dominated by a venerable brand like Harley-Davidson? Harley motorbikes have been a part of American myth and history for a century. This is the challenge that faced John Bloor's revival of the prestigious British Triumph marque, and Polaris, a snowmobile maker that wanted to enter the market with an innovative new marque called Victory.

Motorcycles have grown popular both as recreational vehicles and as alternatives to automotive transportation in warmer climates. There are more than 5.5 million motorcycles registered in the United States; California has roughly 12 per cent of all US-registered motorcycles. Nearly 30 per cent of all motorcycles in operation are located in four states: California, New York, Texas and Illinois. Registrations in both Louisiana and Texas have increased by more than 60 per cent since 1997, which are the highest volume increases in the country. Figure 8.5 shows recent and projected sales of motorbikes (with cruisers such as those sold by Victory and Triumph separated out).

Tastes have generally veered towards more power, as Figure 8.6 shows.

Triumph, though a British marque, perhaps has the upper hand when it comes to its place in American motorcycle history. When Marlon Brando led a group of outlaw bikers in the 1953 film *The Wild One*, he rode a Triumph. It was the obvious choice back then. Britain was the biggest motorbike maker in the world, and Triumph was winning every race in sight. Years of bad management ended the firm in the 1970s, but it was resurrected in 1983 by a coal miner's son and self-made millionaire named John Bloor.

Bloor initially invested US$100 million to revive Triumph, based around three-cylinder engines that he thought would be better able to attract middle-aged men getting back into bikes. Big-bike sales were driven by older people with the money to spend on expensive toys. Many of these born-again bikers hadn't touched a motorbike since their teens, so they were looking for something less demanding than the Japanese sportbikes in the market.

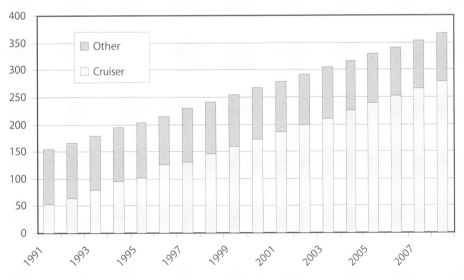

Figure 8.5 Sales of motorcycle of 600cc capacity and above in the United States (000s)

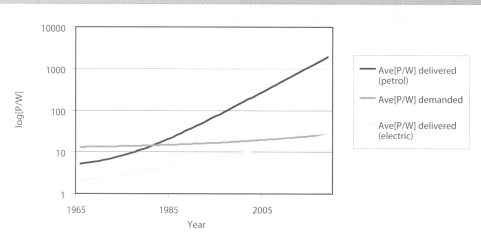

Figure 8.6 Ratio of power (bhp) to weight (kg) for motorcycles of 600cc and above

Triumph's annual sales rose from 2,000 in 1991 to 33,000 in 2006, to an average buyer aged between 35 and 55. American sales (which make up 25 per cent of the total 250,000 big bikes sold in the United States) have soared since Triumph introduced a retro-styled bike called the Bonneville in 2004, and are now rising at an annual rate of 40 per cent. The launch of a Harley-style cruiser style bikes has boosted sales further. Still Triumph sells only a sixth as many bikes as Harley-Davidson.

The new company needed a strong and stable platform from which a range of competitive motorcycles could be developed, thus the concept of the modular range was born. This concept enabled the range to share common components, allowing a number of different types of machine to be constructed from the same base. Crucially, the variants could all be built on one assembly line at the same time.

Design of the new range commenced in 1984, and by 1988 the company was ready to begin building a new factory (the old plant at Meriden had been demolished in the early 1980s). A 10-acre site was purchased in Hinckley, Leicestershire, England, and construction commenced. As soon as the first phase of the site was complete, pre-production began and the first models were launched at the Cologne show of 1990. As production capacity steadily grew, Triumph set about re-establishing a network of export distributors. Two subsidiary companies had been established to prior to production commencing, Triumph Deutschland GmbH and Triumph France SA, and over the next couple of years the network expanded to encompass most of the world's major motorcycle markets, culminating in 1994 with the creation of Triumph Motorcycles America Ltd.

By this time 20,000 new Triumphs had been built, and in January 1995 a Triple Connection clothing range and an accessories range of products were launched to provide the Triumph customer with an all-round package of Triumph apparel and equipment.

Production in 1995 stood at around 12,000 units a year, and as both retail sales and production capacity grew, the company was able to develop more single-minded machines that did not rely on the modular concept. The first of these, the Daytona T595 and the T509 Speed Triple, were launched at the 1996 Cologne Show. The range diversified further with the introduction of the Sprint RS and ST, the Tiger, and more recently with the launch of the TT600 and Hinckley's first twin, the Bonneville.

Triumph has now produced over 140,000 motorcycles and output at the factory was steady at around 140 units per day, which is the maximum that could be achieved at the existing site. In anticipation of this maximum level proving insufficient, planning permission for a new factory had been sought a number of years previously. The construction of Phase one of the new factory was completed in the autumn of 1999, and certain manufacturing processes were subsequently transferred to it. For example all steel spine frames are now being manufactured at the new site and the twin-cylinder engine's crankcase and cylinder head lines are located there.

Victory motorcycles

The Victory Motorcycles division of Polaris (the snowmobile manufacturer) took a different approach to market entry than did Triumph. Rather than going around Harley-Davidson's laid-back cruisers to find a market for middle-aged weekend cowboys, it took aim directly at Harley's customers. Victory entered into the heavyweight-cruiser motorcycle category in the autumn of 1997, when the company's debut V92C cruiser landed on the cover of every major motorcycle magazine and racked up an impressive list of accolades.

Predictably, direct competition with the market leader would not be easy, and Victory got off to a rocky start. Because of what current general manager Mark Blackwell calls 'big-time miscalibration problems', Victory motorcycles didn't arrive in dealerships until more than a year later, in December 1998 – much too late to benefit from any momentum created by the press coup a year before. Uneven quality control and underwhelming performance generated a distinct lack of consumer confidence in the new cruiser manufacturer.

This was the situation that Mark Blackwell found when he took over as general manager of the Victory division of Polaris in September of 2000. Blackwell targeted 2002 as the year that he would relaunch Victory motorcycles, with an aggressive five-year product-development plan, reorganized engineering department and distribution network, and focused market vision.

Mark Blackwell had made his name in motorcycle racing, first in off-road racing in the late 1960s and early 1970s when he became the American Motorcycle Association's first 500cc National MX champion. After an eye injury forced his early retirement from racing, Blackwell earned an MBA and moving on to manage Suzuki's off-road racing team. He later served as vice president of sales and marketing at Husqvarna, doing another term at Suzuki as motorcycle media relations director, then director of its marine division, then as a vice president for sales and marketing for Arctic Cat. Blackwell's knowledge of the powersports industry – and more importantly its customers – was intimate.

Blackwell was honest about Victory's missteps from 1997 to 2000, and instead of apologizing, cited specific steps that he would take to overcome them and avoid repeating them in the future. He was also concerned that Victory might be perceived as just a snowmobile company jumping on the motorcycle bandwagon. Although Victory and Polaris did share staff through a matrix organization structure, the decisions were autonomously made for motorcycle designs, and Blackwell was the final authority. The organization gave Victory more financial clout than a typical start-up, which Blackwell felt was absolutely necessary in competing directly with cruisers from Harley-Davidson, Honda and Yamaha.[28]

By the same token, Blackwell chose not to leverage the Polaris name, simply because of the price differential in products. Polaris management was worried about the reality of selling $15,000 Victory motorcycles, as opposed to $5000 Polaris ATVs. They were concerned that despite consumer acceptance of the Polaris, a $15,000 cruiser would require a different level of prestige.

For an item that would be sold as a middle-aged man's luxury toy (and thus a discretionary expense), such concerns were justified. Nonetheless, the cruiser market was estimated to be worth US$300 to $500 million over the coming decade for Polaris, and it displayed favourable demographics – better than snowmobiles in the same period. Heavy cruisers represented the most vibrant segment in the motorcycle industry; one driven by the demographics of middle-aged men more than product, and one with steady growth every year. Sportbikes, on the other hand, were highly product sensitive. If one year Honda, Yamaha and Kawasaki all came out with new sportbikes, there was a big jump in sales that year; if there were no new models the following year, the market showed smaller growth.

Victory, in fact, picked a better understood market and set of demographics than had John Bloor with Triumph. Cruiser design was conservative, while at the same time expensive. The idea was to recreate the hot-rodded conversions of the Second World War surplus police bikes that were popular in the 1950s. Harleys had gained their immense popularity because since the 1930s they had locked up most US Army and police bike sales, and consequently, by the 1950s, huge numbers were available through war surplus markets. Hot-rodders typically pulled off of these surplus bikes everything that was removable (this was called 'chopping', which led to the vernacular 'chopper' for cruiser-style bikes) in order to make them lighter, and thus faster and more responsive. This and custom paint and chrome work were responsible for the distinctive and unchanging style of the heavyweight cruiser.

The initial segregation of the Polaris and Victory businesses created some tension and inefficiency. Motorcycles and snowmobiles consist mostly of the same parts – a motor, a rigid frame, electronics, steering, seats and so forth. These parts are not interchangeable, but much of the technology can be shared and jointly developed. As a consequence, the plan was to separate operations, but to leverage the engineering expertise of Polaris in building a motorcycle that targeted the planned market, and finally reintegrate the two divisions once the Victory name had been established in the market.

One of the first moves to correct the missteps on Victory's V92C cruiser was to terminate the positions of 15 of Victory's shop technicians (about 20 per cent of the workforce) and add six positions for design engineers with degrees, significantly enriching the skill set of the company. (The net cost impact was about nil given the salary differentials.) Blackwell had found that spending more on the front end with the design saved significantly more on the back end in terms of time and quality. Better design not only meant happier customers, it also meant fewer quality control and production problems.

Polaris has had a profitable history; a US$2 billion corporation that had been around for 47 years. It has been the number one seller of snowmobiles for 16 years. Similar to the Victory venture, it had started an ATV business 20 years earlier that no one had thought could compete, and had grown it to the second largest ATV seller in the world, with many of the same competitors that Victory would face.

Victory had initially entered the heavyweight-cruiser market with a motorcycle that incorporated many typical cruiser design attributes. Those initial Victory bikes seemed lost in a sea of Harley-Davidsons and Harley knock-offs, with styling that was more clone than classic. To make sure it connected with its customer base, Blackwell teamed up with Arlen and Cory Ness (the top designers for American cruisers) on the new Vegas model's overall design. Arlen and Cory Ness's custom touches were very successful in differentiating Victory's motorcycle with enthusiasts. A gentle crease flows down the centre of the bike, creating a split-tail tank that also has recesses in its flanks which hold the Victory badges. The crease ends at the frenched-in teardrop taillight with a clear lens. The detail and dimension drawn

Table 8.4: *Target market for Triumph motorcycles*

Segmentation base	Characteristics	Description of the target customer for Triumph	Strategic rationale/reasoning
Geographic segmentation	Country/ region	UK	Sales are rising by 15 per cent a year, putting Triumph within sight of European rivals such as BMW and Ducati
		Germany + Rest of Europe	
		USA	
Demographic segmentation	Age (range)	Younger genre (25–45)	Triumph should play on its brand equity for racing cars and target the younger strata for the sport bikes. Instead of buying bikes as a second vehicle, it should encourage usage as a primary vehicle. Customers in this segment need to be high earning to be able to afford Triumph bikes and thus the target is a well-placed professional.
	Sex	Males	
	Income	High income	
	Occupation	Professionals, well-to-do	
Psychographic/ lifestyle segmentation	Economy minded	No	Although Triumphs are good value for features offered, they are not inexpensive
	Outdoor enthusiasts	Yes	The target segment includes middle-aged men seeking attention and probably coming back to riding after a while, so seeking a comfortable yet stylish ride.
	Attention seekers		
Use-related segmentation	Purpose	Racing, travelling, hobby	The awareness level of the customer base would be very high. They would be educated bike enthusiasts with high brand loyalty. Therefore, it would be beneficial for Triumph to target this segment as they would be pro this brand and would increase brand awareness by word-of-mouth.
	Usage rate	High	
	Awareness status	Enthusiasts, very high	
	Brand loyalty	High	
Benefits sought	Value for money	Yes	
	Convenience/ handling	Yes	Superbly tight, flicks easily through turns with no handlebar slap
	Power	Yes	The 955cc triple is the best of both worlds, with the powerful torque rumble of v-twins and the high end screaming that inline fours produce; it balances nicely producing a very wide power band in which to use.
	Design/good looks	Yes	Emblazoned on the side of the tank is the original Triumph logo which is a customer magnet

Source: Triumph

into the bodywork of the Vegas are way beyond that of the typical production bike. Fit and finish are top-level, with no exposed sheet-metal seams or plastic covers here.

In addition, Victory's website allows the preordering of up to 300 different customizations on any newly purchased bike. And customers may specify unique paint colours and designs, as well as future customizations. This has allowed to company to connect much more effectively with its customers.

Table 8.5: *Polaris financial statistics as at 31 December 2006 (US$)*

Revenue	$1.70 billion
Gross profit	$359.36 million
EBITDA*	$242.86 million
Net income	$112.79 million
Market capitalization	$1.75 billion
Enterprise value	$1.98 billion
Price/earnings ratio	19.06
Profit margin	6.28%
Operating margin	9.87%
Return on assets	13.85%
Return on equity	41.44%

* Earnings before interest, taxes, depreciation and amortization

Questions and activities for the Triumph and Victory case study

1. Map out a strategy for Triumph for the years 2005–10:
   a. Objectives
   b. Tactics
   c. Information needed to implement strategy
   d. Risk of this strategy.
2. Map out a strategy for Victory for the years 2005–10:
   a. Objectives
   b. Tactics
   c. Information needed to implement strategy
   d. Risk of this strategy.
3. Draw and compare the value maps of Triumph and Victory, and show where each should concentrate its strategy in the future.
   a. If both of these companies are competing in the same (cruiser, big motorbike) market space; why have they evolved such different strategies?
   b. Where is the money made on your value map?
4. Describe where the four types of scaling will manifest themselves in the motorcycle business. (See Chapters 9 and 10.)
5. Define in your strategy how each company should link its R&D and its customer relationship management? Why are these strategies different for the two companies?
6. How does the strategy you defined allow Victory to compete with 'classic' brands like Harley-Davidson?
7. How does the strategy you defined allow Triumph to compete with 'classic' brands?

CHAPTER QUESTIONS FOR REVIEW

1. How do you 'invest' in the capabilities needed to keep up with the changing marketplace? Consider the various types of competences and assets a firm requires – personnel, factory, knowledge and so forth.

2. What decision parameters affect the portfolio of planned products and services that you will introduce in the future?

3. How do you manage risk (of failure or success) in planning to introduce products and services in the future? What types of risks does the company face in new product introduction?

4. Describe the difference between positioning options, scouting options, and stepping-stone options. How is each used in formulating new product strategy?

5. What is the primary source of product design information in a discovery-driven entrance strategy?

CHAPTER 8: KEY POINTS

▷ As markets and technologies change and evolve, organizational capabilities need to evolve to keep up with the changing demand for products and services.

▷ The organization must decide where it will acquire new capabilities (assets and competences) based on an analysis of its existing and planned products/services by growth, profit and revenue size.

▷ Risk (of failure or success) must also be factored into decisions on where capabilities will migrate in the future.

▷ Real options are a variation on the models for analysing options in financial markets.

▷ Three particularly useful options in developing an entrance strategy are positioning options, scouting options and stepping-stone options.

▷ Where risk is low, options do not need to be used, and direct launches are likely to be faster and less expensive.

▷ The key to discovery-driven entrance strategies is early engagement of potential customers.

▷ Identify the first few customers for the new business model.

▷ You cannot sell 100 items before you sell three. The first three customers are the most important in developing an entrance strategy.

▷ Determine the priority to give potential customers, using risk/benefit trade-offs.

▷ Articulate the strategy you will use to persuade customers to begin transacting with the organization by mitigating any risks they anticipate.

▷ The following action steps should be taken to assure the competitiveness of a firm's market entry:
  ○ Identify the first few customers for the new business model (using the 'first three sales' as a guiding principle). Determine the priority to give them, using risk/benefit trade-offs.
  ○ Articulate the strategy to be used to persuade target customers to begin transacting with the organization by mitigating any risks they anticipate. Make sure that all the parties in the client organization who will need to be positively involved in the purchase are clearly identified.
  ○ For each major customer arena the organization intends to pursue, identify the major competitors that will be affected.
  ○ Assess the level of corporate support that each player can expect.
  ○ With their potential corporate support in mind, assess the commitment and capacity of the players to respond aggressively to the organization's potential moves.
  ○ Specify the criteria by which to categorize arena attractiveness. Analyse and map the arena attractiveness of each of the industry's major categories.
  ○ Specify the criteria to be used to decide on the organization's business position, and map competitor positions.
  ○ Map the competitive positions of each player, using one map per player. Use these figures to do a first-cut assessment of the strategic inclinations that the organization and each of its major competitors will have.
  ○ Systematically build a competitive mapping of the organization's business categories versus those of each competitor.

NOTES

1   Chandler's seminal work (Chandler, A. D. (1962) *Strategy and Structure*, Garden City, N.Y.: Doubleday) provides insight into how some aspects of competition and innovation are much the same as they were in the first part of the 20th century.

2   Von Hippel, E. (1988) *The Sources of Innovation*, New York: Oxford University Press.

3   McGrath, R. G. and MacMillan, I. (2000) *The Entrepreneurial Mindset*, Boston, Mass.: Harvard Business School Press, ch. 7; D'Aveni, R. A. (1994) *Hypercompetition: The dynamics of strategic maneuvring*, New York: Free Press.

4   Utterback, J. M. (1994) *Mastering the Dynamics of Innovation: How companies can seize opportunities in the face of technological change*, Boston, Mass.: Harvard Business School Press; Utterback, J. M. and Abernathy, W. J. (1975) 'A dynamic model of process and product innovation', *Omega* 3, pp. 639–56.

5   Chakrabarti, A. (1974) 'The role of champion in product innovation', *California Management Review* 17, pp. 58–62; Chen, M.-J. (1996) 'Competitor analysis and interfirm rivalry: toward a theoretical integration', *Academy of Management Review* 21, pp. 100–34; Dos Santos, B. L. and Peffers, K. (1995) 'Rewards to investors in innovative information technology applications: first movers and early followers in ATMs', *Organization Science* 6, pp. 241–59.

6   Coy, P. (1999) 'Exploiting uncertainty: the real options revolution in decision making', *Business Week*, 7 June, pp. 118–24.

7   Ross, J. and Staw, B. M. (1993) 'Organizational escalation and exit: lessons from the Shoreham nuclear power plant', *Academy of Management Journal* 36, pp. 701–32.

8   Scherer, E M. (1979) *Industrial Market Structure and Economic Performance*, Chicago: Rand McNally; Wageman, R. (1995) 'Interdependence and group effectiveness', *Administrative Science Quarterly* 40, pp. 145–80.

9   Rumelt, R. P. (1987) 'Theory, strategy and entrepreneurship' in D. J. Teece (ed.), *The Competitive Challenge: Strategies for industrial innovation and renewal*, New York: Harper & Row.

10 Source: McNeill, D. (2007) 'Numbers man', *South China Morning Post*, Saturday 12 May, p. C1.

11 Staw, B. M., Sandelands, L. E. and Dutton, J. E. (1981) 'Threat-rigidity effects in organizational behaviour: a multilevel analysis', *Administrative Science Quarterly* 26, pp. 501–24.

12 McGrath, R. G. and MacMillan, I. (2000) *The Entrepreneurial Mindset*, Boston, Mass.: Harvard Business School Press, ch. 7.

13 Weatherford, J. (2004) *Genghis Khan and the Making of the Modern World*, New York: Crown.

14 Cheng, Y. and Van de Ven, A. H. (1996) 'Learning the innovation journey: order out of chaos?' *Organization Science* 7, pp. 593–614.

15 Von Hippel, E. (1978) 'Users as innovators', *Technology Review* 80(3), pp. 30–4.

16 Schmookler, J. (1966) *Invention and Economic Growth*, Cambridge, Mass.: Harvard University Press.

17 Sitkin, S. B. (1992) 'Learning through failure: the strategy of small losses', in B. M. Staw and L. L. Cummings (eds), *Research in Organizational Behaviour*, Vol. 14, pp. 231–66, Greenwich, Conn.: JAI Press; McGrath, R. G. and MacMillan, I. (2000) *The Entrepreneurial Mindset*, Boston, Mass.: Harvard Business School Press, ch. 7.

18 Romanelli, E. and Tushman, M. L. (1994) 'Organizational transformation as punctuated equilibrium: an empirical test', *Academy of Management Journal* 37, pp. 1141–166; Teece, D. J., Pisano, G. and Shuen, A. (1997) 'Dynamic capabilities and strategic management', *Strategic Management Journal* 18, pp. 509–33.

19 Venkataraman, S. and Van de Ven, A. H. (1993) 'Hostile environmental jolts, transaction set, and new business', *Journal of Business Venturing* 13, pp. 231–55.

20 Chen, M-J. and MacMillan, I. C. (1992) 'Nonresponse and delayed response to competitive moves: the roles of competitor dependence and action irreversibility', *Academy of Management Journal* 35, pp. 359–70.

21 Von Hippel, E. (1986) 'Lead users: a source of novel product concepts', *Management Science* 32, pp. 791–805.

22 Vasconcellos, J. A. S. and Hambrick, D. (1989) 'Key success factors: test of a general theory in the mature industrial-product sector', *Strategic Management Journal* 10, pp. 367–82.

23 Van der Heijden, K. (1996) *Scenarios: The art of strategic conversations*, New York: Wiley.

24 Day, G. (1990) *Market Driven Strategy*, New York: Free Press.

25 Eisenmann, T. (2003) 'A note on racing to acquire customers', 15 January, Harvard Business School Press.

26 Golder, P. N. and Tellis, G. J. (1993) 'Pioneer advantage: marketing logic or marketing legend?', *Journal of Marketing Research* 30(2), pp. 158–70.

27 Golder, P. N. and Tellis, G. J. (1993) 'Pioneer advantage: marketing logic or marketing legend?', *Journal of Marketing Research* 30(2), pp. 158–70.; see also Shankar, V., Carpenter, G. S., and Krishnamurthi, L. (1998) 'Late mover advantage: how innovative late entrants outsell pioneers', *Journal of Marketing Research*,

35 (February), pp. 54–70; Chandy, R. K. and Tellis, G. J. (1998) 'Organizing for radical product innovation: the overlooked role of willingness to cannibalize', *Journal of Marketing Research* **35**(4) (November), pp. 474–87; Chandy, R. K. and Tellis, G. J. (2000) 'The incumbent's curse? Incumbency, size, and radical product innovation', *Journal of Marketing* **64**(3) (July), pp. 1–17.

28 Frank, A. (2002) 'An interview with Mark Blackwell', *Motorcyclist Magazine*, October.

TECHNOLOGY AND THE GROWTH OF PRODUCTIVITY

LEARNING OBJECTIVES

After finishing this chapter, you will understand that

▸ every technology has a particular rate of advancement that is stable over long periods of time – this rate of progress is called **technology acceleration**

▸ disruptive innovation and the so-called 'innovator's dilemma' are a consequence of **technology acceleration** greater than the acceleration of consumer demand; when this occurs incumbent firms tend to be locked into existing customers, hampering their ability to adopt better performing technologies

▸ **organizational scaling** results from the substitution or augmentation of labour with better-performing technologies

▸ **geographical scaling** results from the replacement of physical products and transport with information.

After reading the *innovation workout*, you will be able to employ **visualization** to help solve problems.
After reading the Yamaha Piano *case study*, you will be able to understand the **roles of technology acceleration** in the changing landscape of an industry.

Note: Further information, class slides, test questions and other supporting material are available on our companion website at

www.palgrave.com/business/westland

The activities of idea-focused firms, such as innovation, differ in certain respects from other business processes. These differences can alter the cost–benefit considerations and product life-cycles in substantial ways. They also are able to raise nearly insoluble dilemmas in addressing customer needs – ones which systematically plague technology firms, and cause the demise of many.

This chapter addresses several of these unique characteristics of innovation:

- ▶ technology acceleration
- ▶ disruptive innovation
- ▶ labour substitution and organizational scaling
- ▶ geographical substitution and scaling (the 'world is flat' effect)
- ▶ open source alliances.

TECHNOLOGY ACCELERATION

Many, if not most, science and technology advances come through the work of communities of scholars who organize into social networks.[1] As research on a given technology generates more and more revenues, investment in the tools and salaries to conduct the research increase as well. This, in turn, expands the research network. Technologies that cannot generate sufficient income are relegated to universities and other institutions that can support fundamental or non-commercial research. Research in many different arenas has shown that the performance-to-price ratio of commercially viable technologies tends to grow in a constant proportion annually over long periods of time. This growth is called *technology acceleration*, and is the basis of industry rules of thumb such as Moore's law, which predicts a doubling of semiconductor chip performance to price every 18 months.[2]

Moore's law

During a deep-sea fishing trip in 1965 (so the story is told), Gordon Moore, the co-founder of Intel and CEO from 1979 to 1987, was musing on the fact that he had noticed in the four years after the first planar integrated circuit was created that engineers were able to double the transistor density on a manufactured die every year. He thought, 'Hmm, I wonder how long it will take the number of transistors I can get on the chip to double.' And he thought, 'I know; however many fish I catch today; that's how many long it's going to be.' He got 18 fish; it was 18 months.[3]

Technology acceleration in microcomputer hardware

When technologists are asked about the speed at which computer technology is improving, it is common to hear Moore's law cited. But in fact, each component of a computer develops at its own pace. Table 9.1 details the technology acceleration in various microcomputer components.

Whether this story is apocryphal or not, Moore's estimate stuck, and his law has proved surprisingly accurate. If the automotive industry had paralleled the computer's advances in value and efficiency, cars would now cost US$5, and would get 250,000 miles to the gallon.[4]

Table 9.1: *Microcomputer technology acceleration*

Technology	Number of weeks to double	Performance metric
CPU	74 (~1.4 years)	Clock speed (in MHz)
Telecommunications switching	28 (~7 months)	Clock speed (in MHz)
CD-ROM	26 (~0.5 years)	Rotation speed
Printers	21 (~5 months)	Resolution * printing speed (ppm)
Non-volatile RAM	25 (~0.5 years)	Storage amount
Volatile RAM	28 (~7 months)	Storage amount
Monitors	179 (~3.4 years)	Size * resolution * frequency/ point size

Source: Westland, J.C. and See-To, E. W. K. (2007) 'Short-run price performance dynamics in microcomputer technologies', *Research Policy* 36(5) (June), pp. 591–806.

The first formal studies of technology acceleration were done in the late 1950s by economist Zvi Griliches.[5] He studied innovations in agricultural machinery and hybrid crops implemented in the 1930s and 1940s in the United States which had resulted in increasing output per acre of around 2 per cent annually (and incidentally, decreasing farm employment of around 3.3 per cent annually). These trends subsequently continued into the 1990s, by which time most farming in the United States was done by large, integrated corporations and cooperatives.

Griliches' research demonstrated that the adoption of new technologies like hybrid corn was not a single event, but was instead a series of developments that occurred at different rates across geographical space. His study shed light on the numerous individual decisions and economic calculations that drove new hybrid corn technology forward. For example, he found that hybrid corn varieties became available and were adopted by farmers in Iowa by 1934, but spread more slowly into other regions, reaching the Deep South only as late as 1946. Adoption involved many individual decisions where farmers evaluated, for their own land, weather and markets, the potential profitability of making the switch to hybrid corn by calculating the increase in yield per acre due to using hybrid corn minus the cost differences in the seed.

Motorcycle technology acceleration

Table 9.2 provides data on the technology acceleration in the motorcycle industry over the past 50 years, where the performance metric is the ratio of brake horsepower (bhp) to weight in kilograms (kg) for a set of motorcycles that have sold for around US$8000 at year 2000 prices.

Table 9.2: *Technology acceleration in the motorcycle industry, 1950–2001*

Year	Model	bhp/kg
1950	Vincent Black Shadow	0.24
1973	Kawasaki Z1	0.36
1981	Suzuki GSX1100S Katana	0.46
1983	Kawasaki GPZ750 Turbo	0.48
1984	Kawasaki GPZ900R	0.48
1986	Suzuki GSXR1100	0.63
1991	Yamaha FZR1000	0.63
1992	Honda CBR900RR Fireblade	0.66
1998	Yamaha YZF-R1	0.85
2001	Suzuki GSXR1000K	0.94

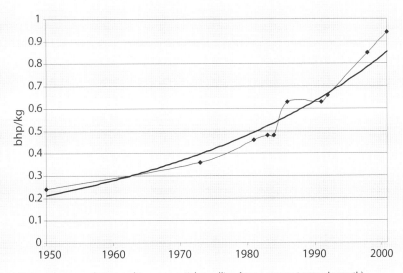

Figure 9.1 Motorcycle power (compared to exponential trendline for 2.1 per cent annual growth)

Labour and light

One of the more influential studies in the exponential performance to price improvements in technology is due to economist William Nordhaus. Nordhaus compiled historical records of the cost of lighting a standard-sized room dating back (incredibly) to the Pleistocene epoch of cavemen and woolly mammoths. Since the starting periods of his dataset predated money, he standardized on a human labour hour of work as a currency unit. The study showed that lighting did indeed show an exponential performance–price improvement over long periods of time. Figure 9.2 details the period from 1800 to the present, covering the technologies of whale and olive oil lights (c.1800), petroleum lights (c.1850), carbon arc (c. 1890), incandescent (c. 1900), gas tube (c. 1930), and most recently light emitting diodes and other forms of 'cool' lighting.[6]

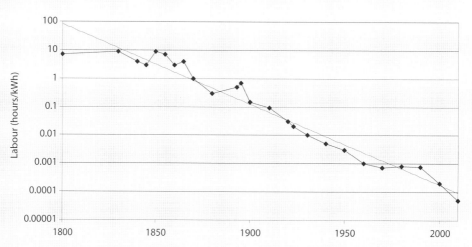

Figure 9.2 The labour cost of lighting, 1800 to the present day

Most technologies may display a constant proportional growth, but underneath this is a steady substitution of technology platforms. For example, computing power has experienced about 60 per cent annual growth since the 1920s, generating exponential performance improvement over time. The platforms evolved from the electromechanical card readers and unit record equipment to the vacuum tube computers of the 1940s, to transistors, then integrated circuits with a variety of chemistries. A new platform is typically not commercialized until it can perform at least as cost-effectively as the existing platform, and thus there is a sequence of platforms, each steadily improving performance to cost at 60 per cent annually. (See Figure 9.3.)

Technology acceleration in the 1980s and 1990s on computer platforms made possible the personal computer, the mobile telephone, digital cameras and numerous other mobile and 'embedded system' platforms. In computers, it has also shortened product life-cycles so dramatically that management now may pay more attention to product development and time to market than any other performance metric for the firm (see the box on Dell Computer on page 206).

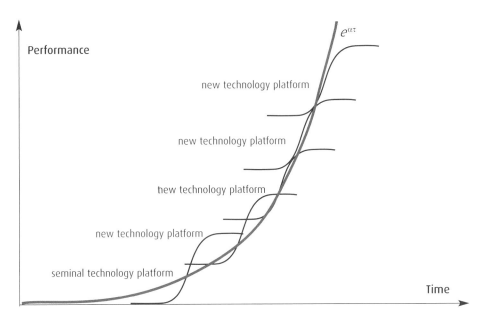

Figure 9.3 Technology acceleration across a series of technology platforms

DISRUPTIVE INNOVATIONS

Disruptive innovations are new products, services or business models that initially target small, seemingly unprofitable customer segments, but eventually evolve to take over the marketplace.[7] The disruptive technologies are usually the next technology platforms in line to be adopted by the industry (see Figure 9.4).[8]

For example, in the hard disk drive industry, the growth of the personal computer was largely ignored in favour of the more expensive mainframe and minicomputer markets which were using 5.25 inch and 8 inch drives.[9] When a group of Quantum Corp. engineers proposed to develop a 3.5 inch drive for the new industry, Quantum helped them to found Plus Development Corp. solely to support the growing PC industry with 3.5 inch drives. Quantum had predicted that its stockholders would not let the company devote significant resources to the low-margin PC market, yet it knew very well the rate of technology acceleration in the hard disk industry, as well as the growth of its customers' market demand. Quantum retained 80 per cent ownership of Plus Development, and when demand for its large hard drives plummeted in the late 1980s, it absorbed Plus Development, placed Plus's management in top slots at Quantum and shifted all of its production to 3.5 inch drives. By 1994, Quantum was the largest drive producer in the world, and it exists to this day as a division of Maxtor.[10]

Quantum's is one of the few success stories during that period in the disk drive industry. Between 1976 and 1995, most drive manufacturers either left or shut down. During the period 129 manufacturers entered the market and 109 manufacturers left it because of disruptive innovation from smaller drives.[11]

The process of disruptive innovation is almost impossible for incumbents to avoid – indeed it should be considered a Darwinian process that is essential to the health of

Dell's war on inventory and property

In less than 20 years, Michael Dell built Dell Computer from a small cluttered University of Texas dorm operation to a US$25 billion a year company. Dell's business model has focused on reengineering its supply chain to minimize the length of time that any inventory needs to be financed by Dell itself. It takes orders and cash upfront from its well-designed and functional online store. It negotiates the best prices from suppliers, and forces many suppliers to hold all inventory until a few hours before Dell assembles the product. (Firms like Sony for monitors will even ship direct to the consumer, using Dell-labelled boxes.) To do all of this, Dell's fundamental supply-chain objective is to replace as much *inventory* as possible in the pipeline with *information* about supplier inventories and production, logistics, customer preferences and anything else that will minimize the inventory the company needs to finance.

Michael Dell realized early – while his competitors were still producing for stock in stores like Best Buy – that material costs consume 75 per cent of a computer manufacturer's revenues. Lowering material costs by 0.1 per cent can have a bigger impact than improving manufacturing productivity by 10 per cent. For most of the 1990s, when competitors carried one to three months of inventory, Dell carried only 5 days' worth. Because of rapid technology acceleration in chips, disk drives and other parts in personal computers, their material costs fall by around 1 per cent per week. Carrying 5 days versus one month of inventory results in savings of around 6 per cent of material cost – an amount that can exceed the computer maker's net income.

Some of Dell's inventory is designed to offset risks and fluctuations in demand – this is the company's safety stock. Safety stocks are both expensive in the volatile computer market, and difficult to reduce. Reduction requires complete and accurate market information and forecasts about production and procurement. The combination of acquiring customer orders in advance of production, with hourly updates of all information from customers to suppliers, allows Dell to run a factory with 5 hours' worth of inventory on hand, including work in progress. This minimizes cycle time at Dell's factories and reduces warehouse space. The warehouse space is replaced with more manufacturing lines. Dell has traded property for information.

The substitution of information at Dell for operations that otherwise would demand substantially more inventory and property – real tangible operating expenses – shows just how important has become the shift to an information-intensive business world. The winners are competitors that control information; the laggards are those with too much property and tangible product.

industry.[12] It starts when incumbent technologies, and producers in pursuit of more profit, deliver a level of technological progress that is far above what customers actually need and can use. This phenomenon of overshooting creates the opportunity for an upstart to come in with something that is cheaper and adequate for a group of customers that sustain the new industry. This new 'disruptive' technology platform may be just adequate for the customers, but the technology is accelerating at a rate faster than customers need.[13] Eventually it meets the needs of even the incumbent's customers, and because it is cheaper, can undersell the incumbent's technology.[14]

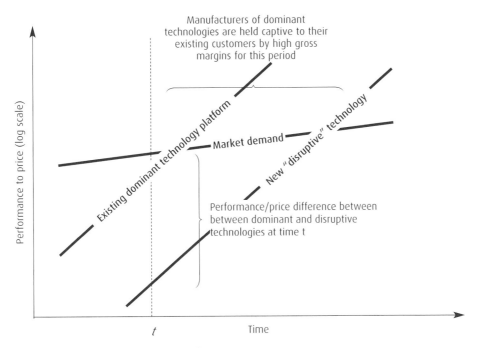

Figure 9.4 How disruptive innovation comes about

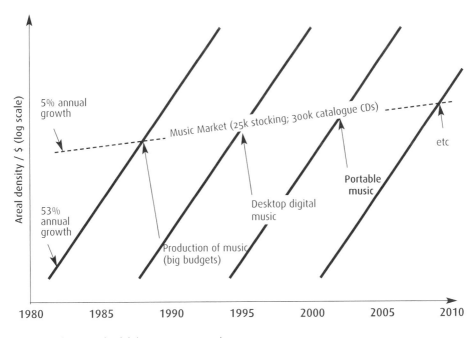

Figure 9.5 Advances in hard disks open up new markets

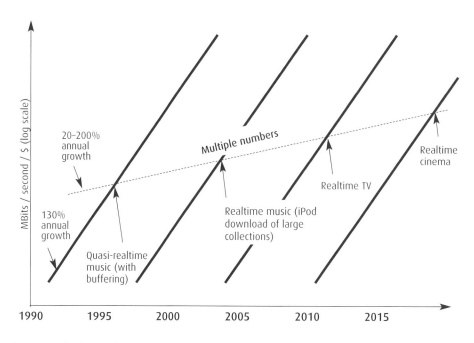

Figure 9.6 Technology acceleration in internet download speed opens up new markets

Disruptive innovations in excavators

Steam shovels (mechanical excavators) were invented in the early 1800s, using cable-operated arms powered by portable steam engines. The first general design change occurred in the 1920s, when the new gasoline engines replaced steam as a power source. For most manufacturers this did not constitute a disruptive innovation, as they could merely replace the steam engine with a gasoline engine, and keep the rest of the mechanics intact. Diesel and electric power followed, again with no disruption of the industry. These machines were huge, and designed for general contracting such as road building, sewer excavation and building site preparation – these required large bucket sizes, and the ability to move huge amounts of soil quickly.

Disruptive change in the excavator came from an unlikely quarter – aircraft technology developed for fighters in the Second World War. Hydraulic activators were developed for both the retraction of landing gear and control of wing shape and attitude. Early hydraulic actuators were not very powerful, limited by the sealing material that was used, but their power increased at a 23 per cent annual rate.

The first hydraulics to the arm and shovel of an excavator were developed in 1947, but the design was too small for commercially viable tasks. Caterpillar (one firm in this market) devised a new business model, and targeted a new market. Its small excavator arm was built as an attachment for the back of small industrial and farm tractors. Caterpillar called it a 'backhoe', and identified the market as a 'residential' one: contractors, farmers and others digging narrow ditches for sewers, cables, flower beds and other jobs that had been done by hand in the past. Limited by the power and strength of available hydraulic pumps' seals, the capacity of Caterpillar's early machines was minuscule and they were of no use in the more lucrative general contracting markets.

Caterpillar developed new metrics to advertise its products. Rather than measuring the quantity of earth that could be moved as the cable-driven manufacturers advertised, it emphasized shovel width (narrow being better for contractors) and the speed and manoeuvrability of the tractor. To bigger companies like Link Belt, Caterpillar was not even a competitor, because it spoke an entirely different language to a different clientele.

Steady acceptance by the residential market sustained and eventually grew Caterpillar's business, and its excavators grew as well. The company introduced steadily larger diesel-tractor excavators, until it reached a level where its machines could handle general contracting jobs as well residential ones. By 1974, the hydraulic excavators had the muscle to lift 10 cubic yards of dirt, a rate of improvement that outstripped demand in any of the excavator markets. In contrast, the largest makers of cable-driven excavators, Bucyrus Erie and Northwest Engineering, concentrated on building better cable-

driven machines for their most profitable customers (to do otherwise was not profit-maximizing) and logged record profits until 1966. But after that, their business plummeted as hydraulic excavators reached competitive capacities.

Much of the shift was driven by labour unions and operators. Hydraulic-powered machines were significantly safer than cable-driven excavators – when a cable snapped because of an overloaded bucket, operators could be killed. And hydraulic excavators were less prone to breakdown. The shift to hydraulic excavators occurred quickly in the early 1970s. Only four of the top 30 excavator manufacturers in the 1950s survived the transition.

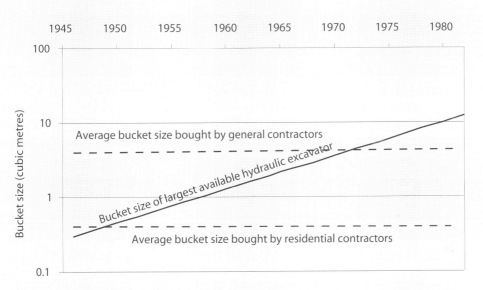

Figure 9.7 Excavator bucket size and markets

ORGANIZATIONAL SCALING

Automation, global transportation and communication networks have brought about fundamental changes in the structure of organizations by substituting existing jobs with machines or outsourced labour. Technology acceleration plays a major role in organizational scaling – technologies that were once too expensive for organizational processes eventually improve their performance, and their price drops sufficiently for them to replace human labour.[15] This influences work in three ways.

First, they have flattened the hierarchy of firms, eliminating vertical 'stovepipes' by enabling communication across and around organizational lines. Firms have become inured to the speed and efficiency of horizontal communications.

Disk drives become too small for human production

Before the early 1980s, most hard disks had 8-inch or 14-inch platters, required an equipment rack and lots of floor space. Large removable-media disks were even referred to as washing machines. Most had a high power requirement, and some required three-phase power hookups because of the large motors they used. Hand labour was extensive in their production – indeed, one reason they were large was that tolerances were not very tight.

The advent of minicomputers and then PCs brought a demand for smaller 3.5 inch disk drives, and at the same time, rising factory costs forced Western firms to move production offshore to lower-cost Asian countries, especially Malaysia and Thailand. In the early 1990s, the Asian disk drive industry employed around 50,000 people assembling these drives. But as technologies advanced, and 2.5 inch, then 1.3 inch drives were introduced, the drives themselves became too small for human hands, and factories were forced to automate, even if the costs of production went up. By 2000 factory employment in the disk drive industry had dropped to around 5000 people, with almost no human hand ever touching a disk drive.

Second, downsizing has culled workers with lower skill levels from organizational ranks. Firms are increasingly composed of a small core of smart, adaptable employees who can learn to use technology to greatly enhance their effectiveness and efficiency.

Finally, global networks provide efficient market alternatives to internal production. Corporations such as Dell and Cisco produce little of their own product. Rather they act as integrators for a global array of suppliers. Many of the emerging economies around the globe owe their growth to the increasing success of internet-enabled value chain integration. In the process, workers around the world become virtual employees of Dell and Cisco; Dell and Cisco conversely are virtual organizations employing many, but with formal employment contracts for only a small professional core of employees.[16]

The hierarchy can be reduced and firms downsized because the speed and volume of information that can automatically be processed and shunted around the firm is several magnitudes greater than in the 1920s when Alfred Sloan implemented the philosophy of command and control through the hierarchical firm, with the exemplar of General Motors. Today competition focuses on time to market, innovation and quality – these are the minimum performance requirements required to survive. Flat firms with a focus on their core competencies can experience sustainable competitive advantage.[17]

The increased availability of efficient market alternatives to formerly internal functions means that the 'make or buy?' question is increasingly answered 'buy'. Organizations are able to develop around individual capabilities and proclivities, making efficient use of individual contributions to organizational goals in a shrinking world. When the communications between negotiating parties are speeded up many of the misunderstandings and dysfunctional behaviours found in group work are eliminated, while this also helps people to avoid decision-making gridlock.

Technology has also transformed the way that work is parcelled into those familiar envelopes we call 'jobs'. We can expect this to accelerate over the next decade as robots and automatons take over more and more industrial tasks. The job is a recent phenomenon, which evolved during the Industrial Revolution to synchronize work that needed doing in the factories of the era. Since power was not portable, factories were set up next to the streams or woods that provided fuel for their production, and people were expected to show up for their jobs when the machines required it.[18]

Competition based increasingly on time to market and the dispersion of necessary skills has created an environment in which work parcelled into 'jobs' in 'offices' is counter-productive. Electricity and small engines have made power (and people) portable. Increasingly the work to be done is intellectual and can be done at home.

Organizational scaling has impelled firms to become more virtual corporations – firms that have no fixed pool of suppliers, workers or processes, but rather continually rewire themselves on-the-fly.

GEOGRAPHICAL SCALING

Each new technology has the potential to remap the 'distances' between people and places; this in turn demands that firms restructure the tasks they perform to remain competitive. 'Distances' should be thought of here as any impediment that makes a particular business model infeasible – it could be cost, geographical distance or risk. In general, the remapping enabled by new information and communications technologies makes the world smaller and flatter. So pronounced has been the effect that it is perhaps more difficult to measure the shrinkage of the world today than it was even a decade ago.

Some of the most dramatic shifts in geographical scaling have taken place in markets, both consumer and vendor. In today's markets, person-to-person selling is far too expensive for many (if not most) products. Still, it is the best way to nurture contacts, obtain sales and negotiate the best price. Communication technologies can pry open previously unavailable markets, and create new opportunities for previously orphaned products. It can do this by lowering the cost of person-to-person selling. The growth of telephone direct selling was only the most recent great communications revolution in sales and distribution channels. The growth of internet selling has fostered a rich, new and exciting way to enter previously unavailable markets.

Marketing channels emerge as a part of the natural evolution of hierarchies and markets in an industry. Although producers may provide many of the channel functions required to stimulate and satisfy demand for their goods and services, economies of scale and access to multiple competing products may make some channel functions better suited to third parties. Channel intermediaries provide value by acting as go-betweens for buyers and sellers. They can lower the costs of transactions and make most goods and services cheaper. They may consolidate particular channel operations from a variety of producers, thus achieving economies of scale. For example, few magazines actually distribute their own products or handle their own subscription services – these services are provided by one or two large subscription processors.

Channel intermediaries smooth the flow of goods and services, helping the producer to better plan and control production, by creating possession, place and time utilities. They do this by representing a large number of producers supplying complementary goods and services. Four benefits are realized by working through intermediaries: *breaking bulk*, *creating assortments*, *reutilization of transactions* and *efficient search*.

New York and Boston get cozy

We take for granted today the ability to pick up a telephone, or send an email to anyplace in the world, and expect the recipient to have that message immediately. But in times past, messages needed physical transport, and their transmission time was restricted by geography. Consider the business dealings between New York and Boston (see Figure 9.8).

In the early 19th century, the only way a New Yorker could manage business in Boston was to send an emissary up by stagecoach. That took a day and a half, and a round trip could consume the better part of a week. Things got better as the roads improved, and even better with railroads. Along came the telegraph service in the 1840s and 1850s, dropping the delay for

pure exchanges of information (which could include monetary transactions) to zero.

On the other hand, materials deliveries, plant inspections and just pressing the flesh are still subject to delays – although as railroads, then cars, enter the scene, these delays become progressively shorter. We can see how, as transportation and communication technologies advance, the world grows flatter and flatter. It doesn't happen all at once, but – one by one – the various delays in doing business fall to zero. A corresponding graph might show that not only are time delays falling to zero, so are costs, providing one more incentive to flatten the landscape of business.

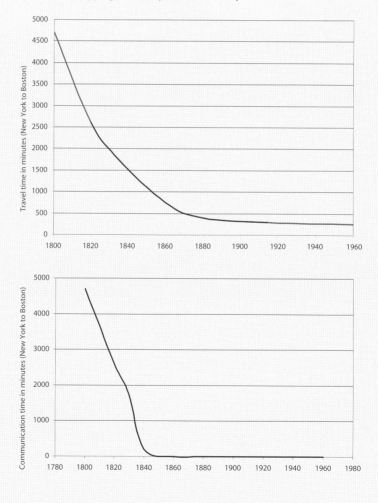

Figure 9.8 Travel (top) and communication (bottom) times from New York to Boston (in minutes)

Consequences of geographical scaling

There are five effects that reflect the technologies that influence geographical scale: *globalization, speed, service orientation, worker dispersion* and *virtual organizations*.

Globalization introduces new competitors for the firm's products at the same time that it offers enormous economies of scale. Firms in global competition tend to compete on market share rather than short-term profit. Transportation and communications technology have created opportunities to compete globally in many additional product markets.

Speed – either in delivering a product or service to customers, or in getting a product designed, built and marketed – has come to define the contemporary age of 'web time'. Most computer technology companies tend to compete globally, and seek market share through first-mover advantage.

Service orientation has grown more important because telephones, email and web chat have put the customer geographically closer to the firm. It has also increased the importance of reputation, since customers can influence other customers through chat rooms. A company's customer base becomes a 'global village' complete with gossip, local heroes and community spirit. Companies do well by treating customers well.

By radically changing the cost of managing people, information and geography, knowledge technology is generating huge leaps in scale economies, creativity and productivity. In the process, work is gradually becoming unstructured and asynchronous, evolving towards a 'jobless' workplace. In the process, we are creating *virtual organizations* where *worker dispersion* has increased dramatically.

ALLIANCES

Relationship enterprises create value by entering into alliances with complementary firms or individuals, and leveraging this complementarity. There are estimated to be about 20,000 such relationship enterprises in the world today. The top 500 multinationals have an average of 60 major strategic alliances each. The largest and most important ones are in the aerospace, airline, telecommunications and automobile industries.[19]

Although their profits are not nearly as great as these multinationals, ostensibly not-for-profit alliances like Linux, the Apache Software Foundation and the Open Source Initiative have had an enormous impact on structure and competition in the computer industry. There has been some speculation that similar open source projects will begin cropping up in other industries, perhaps even undermining the traditional free-market, monetary-based economic system. At least for the immediate future, though, these sorts of voluntary alliances are likely to be in the software sector.

Outside of software, it has been estimated that alliances account for 30 per cent to 40 per cent of revenues for the top European and US companies. Relationship enterprises often extend beyond market or contractual obligations. They share information, knowledge and learning, and attempt to reduce risk and increase profits by collaborating across the supply chain. As a result, competition declines across individual firms and increases up and down the entire supply chains. In recent years, almost half of alliances have failed, primarily, it is conjectured, because of damaged working relationships rather than because the alliance failed to contribute to both businesses' strategic objectives.[20]

Visualization

A significant portion of the human brain is concerned with processing or creating visual information; indeed, more than 30 areas in the brain are dedicated to visual processing. Thus we might suspect that one of the more effective ways to create new patterns of information is through visualization. In the beginning, human communication was primarily visual. Even after language evolved, its tangible storage and representation through writing evolved from pictures. (Indeed, Chinese is still written with highly stylized pictures.)

Sketching provides an alternative way to think out loud; to talk to yourself. It allows you to put your abstract ideas into a tangible form. You start the process of visualization the way you would start the analysis of any problem or design – by articulating your objectives and design components. Except instead of articulating them, you can represent them either as words or pictures. You sketch as many alternative concepts as you think you see. Often the connections between different components will be more important than the components themselves. In fact, that is one of the powerful advantages of sketching – the ability to articulate complex interactions and flows.

Thomas Edison was known to made hundreds of sketches and doodles while formulating his inventions. He would typically hand a stack of his doodles along with written and verbal explanations to his associates, asking them to organize his ideas into workable inventions.

Sketching, doodling, or drawing is complementary to verbal expression – use them together to help create, refine and articulate new ideas.

In Chapter 4, you learned how to sketch business models using a few simple objects – boxes, bubbles and arrows. The boxes represent the competitive environment in which the business model operates and to which it needs to respond. The bubbles represent the owners of processes, and associated strategies and goals. The arrows are the 'value flows' – the particular expenses paid in supporting a process, or the revenues that are generated by the process. For example, you might draw the business model for a typical manufacturing firm as in Figure 9.9.

It is easy to see from the sketch the roles of value flows that underlie the financial accounts of the organization. Dataflow diagrams of this sort have the added advantage that they represent an unequivocal language for describing a business, in the sense that unique business models will have unique dataflow diagrams.

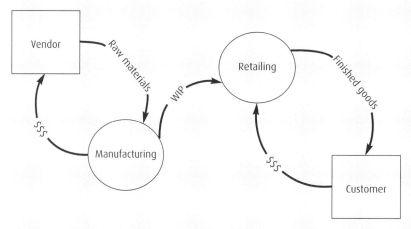

Figure 9.9 Value flows in one company

Blueprint

1. Think about an innovation, problem or goal that you want to work on. Sketch it on paper and reflect on it for a few minutes: What doesn't fit? What is missing? What are the relationships between the items that you have drawn?

2. Initially you should free associate, and not dwell too long on any single part of the drawing. Try to get all of the pertinent goals, components, relationships and other aspects of the problem committed to paper. You have time to reorganize and expand on ideas in the future.

3. Draw a boundary around the particular subset of components that you think are most important to the problem. The purpose is to separate the main features of the problem from its environment and allow you to focus on a smaller problem. A boundary should keep you focused on not much more than seven plus or minus two components of the problem.[21]

4. Focus on the bounded area. Rearrange, redraw, reconnect. When one page becomes too messy, transcribe the drawing to a clean sheet of paper. Make as many drawings as you need.

5. Try to identify each image, symbol, scribble, line, or structure on the page with a single descriptive word – usually a noun or verb.

6. Leave your sketch with descriptions for a few minutes, grab a cup of coffee, then return for a fresh look. Rearrange, redraw, reconnect.

7. Restate the drawing in a paragraph that captures all of the features and descriptions on your sketch. The paragraph should contain three things: first, what you have done, created or solved; second, why it is important; and third, what your solution or invention does. This works for products, services, abstract concepts such as business models, and for many other things in between.

To prepare you for the case study, try this challenge, one which Yamaha is most assuredly thinking about today.

The challenge

You have traditionally made world-class pianos, but two challenges have arisen. First, fewer and fewer people are playing piano today, and thus have less incentive to buy your products. Second, computer technology has made it possible to generate any sound in the universe without having to produce it from a complex half-tonne assemblage of wood and steel. Pianos could conceivably be the size of a wristwatch, if only there were some way to control the music coming out. In fact you suspect that many of the teenagers today would rather hold an instrument that looks like a game controller. Find a better (commercially, aesthetically, musically, or however you define 'better') design for a piano.

Case study: Yamaha Piano

Yamaha was founded in 1887 by Torakusu Yamaha to make pianos. The company built up a reputation for quality (it won prizes at the 1904 World's Fair for its pianos and organs), but suffered with the rest of Japanese industry during the Second World War. When president Genichi Kawakami took over Yamaha in 1950, it only made a few pianos, mouth organs and wind-up gramophones.

Yamaha was always a leader in innovation. It had to be, because the markets were already dominated by European or American names like Steinway. By clever innovation and low pricing, Yamaha could differentiate itself from established brands.

And brand itself was an obsession with Genichi Kawakami. In 1954, to develop a market for pianos as well as the Yamaha brand, he started a music class for young children which evolved into the worldwide chain of Yamaha music schools (as well as showrooms for Yamaha's musical instruments). By the late 1980s, Yamaha had become the world's leading maker of musical instruments of all kinds, not just pianos.

America is Yamaha's largest market, and the one that has thrown up the greatest challenges to the elevation of the Yamaha brand in pianos. The ultimate brand recognition – the sort of prestige that went with, for example, a Steinway piano – seemed to elude Yamaha. Unfortunately for Yamaha, through cultural accident, successful marketing or something truly inherent in Steinway's tone, Steinway pianos produce the sort of tone that has been most sought after in North America for the past hundred years. The 'Steinway sound' is best characterized as having a strong, singing treble and a powerful bass, rich in high harmonics. Asian and European cultural tastes in piano tone incline towards different tonal palettes. Top European brands like Bösendorfer, August Förster and Bechstein emphasize the fundamental tone rather than the harmonics, with a tone that sustains at a lower volume, and a clean, bright and thin treble. This results in a much less powerful sound – one that Steinway aficionados complain is dull. But this tone has been traditional in Europe since before Steinway was founded.

The top Asian brands such as Yamaha and Kawai in contrast have bright, brittle tones that are short on sustain. These are often preferred by jazz pianists for their crispness. It is claimed that the 'Asian tone' was traditionally caused by a difficulty obtaining hardwoods. This led to the widespread substitution of at least some hardwood by softwood in the rim, and this lowers sound reflection back to the soundboard, robbing Asian pianos of power. Still the exclusivity of, say, the Fazioli or Bösendorfer brand (both factories produce only a few hundred pianos per year) has assured the latter brands a mystique that eludes Yamaha. Sometimes as a good becomes rarer or more exclusive, the price of the good rises, which some customers may see as a premium signalling greater quality (although it is difficult to find fault with either Fazioli or Bösendorfer in tone or quality).

There is very little argument about Yamaha's quality control, though, and this has been compared with Steinway's less particular quality control. As one technician commented 'Steinways in general don't come out of the crate as eager to please their prospective owners as Yamahas do. They like to get a thorough working over by very skilled technicians, and then expect to be admired by everyone around them.'[22]

Traditional acoustic pianos

From 1700 to 1750, very few piano sales occurred anywhere. It was just another keyboard novelty. From 1750 to 1800 significant technological improvements were made by the Erards in France, Silberman in Germany, and Zumpe, Clement, Kirkman and especially Broadwood in England. By 1800 Broadwood was selling 400 pianos per year compared with less than 40 by every other manufacturer. In 1850 there were probably less than 50,000 pianos manufactured worldwide. Shops were small and production techniques did not lend well to mass production. Steinway, made by a German family that had set up shop in New York City, was responsible for a steady stream of technological improvements (such as the wing-shaped grand piano) and volume-oriented process improvements which eventually elevated the piano to one of the most technologically advanced consumer products on the market. By 1900 the United States had obtained one half of the world market.

The second half of the 19th century saw widespread interest in the piano as an item for homes in America. This led to an interest in pianos for schools. During the peak period from 1890 to 1928, US sales ranged from 172,000 to 364,000 per year, with the large uprights getting most of the market, selling at $200 to $300 apiece. The market received a boost in 1920 when the player piano (an automated type of keyboard instrument) became widespread, and about 250,000 were made annually up until the depression.

Piano sales slowly recovered after the Second World War, and by the 1970s, Japan (and particularly Yamaha, with an annual output of over 200,000 units) took over as the top producing nation. Throughout the 1970s and 1980s, Japan continued to produce about 400,000 pianos per year. There are nearly one million produced each year now, worldwide. We can imagine that given a life expectancy of 50 and up to 100 years, and the perhaps 50 million pianos sold during the past 100 years, that there must now be many millions either stored or in use.

Computer-based pianos

Piano technology has traditionally been about the quest for more sound. Indeed, the name 'pianoforte' (Italian for soft-loud) was coined by early piano makers who claimed they would fill a much larger room with sound than the contemporary clavichords, while offering dynamics that harpsichords could not.

By the 1950s, there were other ways to create more sound than by changing the design of the piano. Bands were shrinking and vacuum tube amplifiers became popular as these same bands were required to fill larger halls. It was simple economics – larger rooms meant more paying customers; smaller bands meant fewer players to pay.

Wurlitzer electric pianos ruled in the late 1960s and through the 1970s. Pianists looking for the right sound for a song were limited to a few guitar effects boxes. For example, the haunting opening chords of the Beatles' 'I am the walrus' were produced by a Wurlitzer piano heavily processed with guitar effects. On Supertramp's 'The logical song', Roger Hodgson split the Wurlitzer output through a Boss chorus pedal to give it a half-straight and half-modulated chorus sound. Otherwise pianists were stuck with a few 'acoustic' sounds amplified through primitive sound systems.

In 1980 an Australian company, Fairlight Instruments, introduced the first version of the 'Fairlight computer musical instrument'. This was the first keyboard-based digital sampler. It could digitally record any acoustic sound and display it as a visual image on a computer monitor. Users could alter its wave-form with a light-pen. Once they were happy with the new creation, they could play it back using a standard-sized 88-note keyboard and store it on an eight-inch floppy disc.

Once Fairlight showed everyone the possibilities of digital sampling and manipulation, other companies jumped on the bandwagon. Yamaha came out with the analogue Clavinova, an electronic piano, and the DX-7 Digital Synthesizer in 1983. The New England Digital company introduced a Fairlight-like machine called the Synclavier in 1984, costing hundreds of thousands of dollars, but popular for advertising and movie scores.

In 1985 Ensoniq introduced a keyboard synthesizer that came with a built-in sampler. It could hold anywhere from 5 to 40 seconds of material, depending on the memory installed. That made it a powerful machine to use on stage. At the same time, the Japanese company Akai introduced a machine designated the s612. This was a rack-mounted sampler. It had 128 kilobytes of memory (huge for that day), meaning it could hold just 8 seconds of sound at the lowest sampling rate. Users could dump their samples to special 2.8 inch floppy discs, but these things could hold just one sample per side.

Meanwhile, a number of companies had come together to create the MIDI (music instrument digital interface) for communication between instruments and computers. This was an amazing breakthrough. Using MIDI controllers, musicians could hook all their gear together, and create and play unimaginably complex arrangements completely solo.

There was also another technological shift. Up until the middle 1980s, musicians had used analogue synthesizers which built up sounds from oscillators and filters. The tones were purposely artificial. In 1987, keyboards went digital with the introduction of the Roland d50. This meant that sounds could be altered digitally, and the d50 could communicate with other digital devices using the MIDI standard. Roland's keyboard was a huge success.

By the late 1980s all of what today's musicians might consider the basics was on the market: digital keyboards, digital samplers, digital sequencers, computers and specialized music software. The personal computer revolution of the early 1980s had driven up volume, and driven down price to the point where a middle-class teenager could afford to go out and buy digital gear. The doubling of computer performance (under Moore's law) every 18 months quickly put all the power that musicians needed into their hands. Apple's Macintosh was an immediate hit with musicians, thanks to a software program called Protools created by Digidesign. Soon musicians had a thousand times more computing power to make music than the astronauts had when they went to the moon.

Before the early 1980s, most people believed there was no artistic reason to simulate in electronics what could be done by a real musical instrument. For example, if you needed a guitar sound, you found a guitar. But as musicians embraced technology even further, a new set of rules and aesthetics began to emerge.

None of this was lost on Yamaha, which has been leading the market in analogue electronic pianos which were popular with touring bands since its first electric pianos were sold in 1976. These were similar in design to the Fender Rhodes Stage Piano Mark I, but produced a fuller, brighter sound which could cut through louder and more intense rock music. Yamaha was also quick to follow Fairlight into computer-generated piano sounds (so-called digitally modelled pianos) with the DX-7 digital synthesizer (introduced in 1983).

From the brief history of the move from small shop production in the early 20th century, to the proliferation of digital instruments in the early 21st, several technologies – each with their own unique technology trajectories – appeared and were influential in the pianos that Yamaha developed. The market performance – as measured by subjective assessments of tonal quality, touch and various other factors in pianos – grew by around 2 per cent annually (the acoustic piano's rate of technology acceleration in the first half of the 20th century). The endless possibilities of digital instruments raised expectations, and initiated a wide range of requests from customers. Classical and jazz pianists demanded fast actions and rich tonal

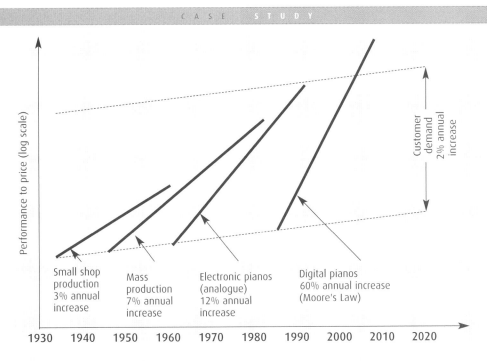

Figure 9.10 Technology acceleration at Yamaha

quality. Still, most of the money and sales volume was at the low-quality end of the scale; but brand reputation, which had an important influence on sales across all quality categories, was developed at the upper end of the scale.

Traditional small-shop production methods, with precise selection of tonewoods and attention to action tolerances, were needed for the best pianos. This is where the high-quality end of the market is satisfied, and Yamaha maintains its own custom shop to this day, making its high-end CFIIIS, S4 and S6 concert grands. Performance to price here is growing at 3 per cent annually. Most traditional acoustic pianos are made with computer-numerical-controlled (CNC) robots in giant factories. Yamaha's R&D and design shops in Japan construct prototypes, and lay out the machining specifications down to the finest detail on computer-aided-design software. These are transferred electronically to robotic factories, where the pianos are actually milled, routed, sawed, assembled and so forth. The technology trajectories of robotics and numerical machine control have allowed organizational scaling to replace people with robots and computers in these megafactories, and through reductions in the cost of production, improved the performance to price of CNC mass-produced pianos by around 7 per cent annually.

From the 1960s on, analogue electric pianos like the Wurlitzer showed a price–performance increase of around 12 per cent annually. In Yamaha's own electric pianos, this was due largely to advances in circuits for FM synthesis. Yamaha's first digital sampling pianos (basically computers with keyboards) were fairly crude affairs. But as these evolved into embedded computer systems with piano-keyboard-style controllers, technology acceleration rapidly rose to around 60 per cent annually, in step with the general advances in core computer technology.[23]

Moving into the future

With fewer people buying traditional pianos and acoustic instruments, Yamaha has been steadily shifting its core business towards electronics, as well as shifting more of its production to low-cost centres such as China and Indonesia. Today there are almost no sounds that cannot be reproduced accurately with computer-based digital signal processing (pianos and violins are the most difficult, and even these have been modelled quite successfully). Producing high-quality musical sound no longer requires artisans – it needs information technology. The 'user interface' often sells the instrument, and that is increasingly used to differentiate Yamaha from its competitors. Customer relationship management is necessary to get the 'user interface' right.

To some extent, there is a reenactment of the player piano boom of the 1920s. A substantial portion (some sources have suggested as much as 40 per cent) of Yamaha's acoustic piano sales are now Disklavier systems, with solenoid key actuators and laser-based velocity and positioning sensors on keys and hammers. Disklavier systems are factory installed on upright and grand pianos, the most expensive system running well over US$300,000. These are not just playback systems (which would have been more important in the 1920 before the advent of broadcast radio) but also intelligent accompaniment systems which are very useful to piano students.

An increasing amount of effort and expense is being put into digital pianos (as well as guitars, double basses and other instruments). Yamaha has developed many of the industry's best instrument models, especially for piano, over the past decade, and embeds these in the hardware of its pianos and digital synthesizers. This market has grown quickly. There are distinct advantages for customers. For city dwellers with small apartments, digital pianos need not be much larger than their keyboards; for those living in very dry, very wet or variable climates, digital pianos do not go out of tune; for touring musicians, they are portable, and many can be tuned with other instruments, or keys can be transposed at the shift of a slider. In all cases the sound (although unfortunately not the key action) can rival that of the company's best grands.

Questions for the Yamaha case study

1. Define Yamaha's business model:
   a. Draw a schematic of Yamaha's business models, identifying major processes at Yamaha, the external parties the company transacts with, and the value flows.
   b. Provide a 'narrative' describing where Yamaha makes its money.
      i. Identify where it should concentrate its strategy in the future.
      ii. Identify where it incurs costs, and estimate the size, given what you know about the price of pianos.
      iii. Identify where it earns revenues, and estimate the size given what you know about the price of pianos.

2. Describe how and where network effects appear in Yamaha's business model.

3. Show how Yamaha has managed and increased the size of its virtual network of piano players (consider the learning curve, and Yamaha's expenditure on learning).

4. How do technology substitutes and the exponential acceleration of performance to price (as predicted by Moore's law) affect Yamaha's business?

a. Describe how Yamaha has managed the growth in demand for 'features' (sometimes called feature creep in software: the demand for the performance of technology trajectory).

b. Describe how the technology performance trajectory for Yamaha has followed Moore's law.

c. Predict past and future times of disruptive technology innovation. (draw the graph yourself). You don't have to be accurate, just make a credible argument for future disruptive innovation.

d. Describe how the innovator's dilemma manifests itself at Yamaha Piano.

5. How should Yamaha link its musical instrument R&D and its customer relationship management (CRM)? R&D needs to design products that customers will want to buy in the future, and CRM serves several functions: making sure that customers are satisfied with existing products, making sure that they know about new and upcoming products, asking them questions to find out what they want in new products, making them aware of new features that they didn't know they wanted.

6. How can Yamaha invest to compete with 'premium' brands like Steinway?

a. Show Steinway's technology trajectory (it builds traditional acoustic pianos, and does not use any computer technology).

b. Will Steinway face a challenge from some sort of disruptive innovation from new information technology by 2015? (Say yes or no, then explain how and why.)

CHAPTER QUESTIONS FOR REVIEW

1	Describe how a growing community of experts on disk drive technology might cause an exponential growth of the storage capacity per dollar.
2	If flash memory were in the near future to replace the disk drive as the primary medium of storage in computers, do you think that the rate of growth of storage capacity per dollar would change substantially? Why or why not?
3	Think of three major technology firms in today's marketplace. Which of these is likely to suffer from some sort of disruptive technology innovation introduced by a competitor over the next decade?
4	Choose a single product or service that you use. How might your experience, or the cost you pay for this in the future, be influenced by ongoing geographical scaling in the industry?

CHAPTER 9: KEY POINTS

▷ Every commercially viable technology has a particular rate of advancement that is stable over long periods of time. This rate of progress is called technology acceleration. It is the source of exponential increases in performance that underlie anecdotal rules such as Moore's law.

▷ Technology acceleration explains how companies come to be held captive by their markets, even though this leads them to destroy their long-term viability. This conundrum of disruptive innovation has been called the 'innovator's dilemma'. The phenomenon was first articulated by Soviet economist Nikolai Kondratieff,[24] and developed throughout the 20th century.

▷ The innovator's dilemma occurs when a firm's most profitable products are in steady (inelastic) demand by customers, effectively locking in the firm to its old technology and customers. If research is developing similar technologies with slightly less performance, but costs that are orders of magnitude lower, then only new markets would buy the new technologies, and they attract producers that operate at smaller scales and larger volumes. Once the new technology's performance overtakes the old, the market entrants grab the old firm's customers, and service them with lower-cost products.

▷ The innovator's dilemma occurs when technology acceleration is greater than the acceleration of consumer demand. When this occurs, incumbent firms tend to be locked into existing customers, hampering their ability to adopt better-performing technologies.

▷ Organizational scaling results from the substitution or augmentation of labour with better-performing technologies. Organization scaling is the reason that technology puts people out of jobs. Typically the replacement of people with machines is not a dramatic one-to-one replacement. Instead, machines can allow one person to improve performance by some amount, leading to a proportional reduction in total employment at the firm. From a business modelling standpoint, organizational scaling represents a reduction in the time and money cost for a given level and quality of output.

▷ Geographical scaling results from the reorganization or replacement of physical products and transport with information. For example, internet download of music occurs nearly instantaneously to any place on the globe; this replaces the need for people to travel to retail stores to purchase CDs, which may take a finite amount of time. In contrast, computer scheduling of postal delivery allows more packages to be delivered to more places in less time. From a business modelling standpoint, both represent a reduction in the time and money cost of product distribution.

NOTES

1 This was recognized long ago in a seminal work: Coase, R. (1960) 'The problem of social cost', *Journal of Law and Economics* 3 (October), pp. 1–44; and in Knight, F. H. (1924) 'Some fallacies in the interpretation of social cost', *Quarterly Journal of Economics* 38 (August), pp. 582–606.

2 Shapiro, C. and Varian, H. R. (1998) *Information Rules: A strategic guide to the network economy*, Boston, Mass.: Harvard Business School Press.

3 Source: Intel chairman emeritus Gordon Moore, 'An update on Moore's law', Intel Developer Forum Keynote Speech, 30 September 1997, San Francisco.

4 Source: Intel chairman emeritus Gordon Moore, 'An update on Moore's law', Intel Developer Forum Keynote Speech, 30 September 1997, San Francisco.

5 Griliches, Z. (1957) 'Hybrid corn: an exploration in the economics of technical change', *Econometrics* 25, pp. 501–22.

6 Sources: Nordhaus, W. D. (1997) 'Do real-output and real-wage measures capture reality? The history of light suggests not', pp. 29-70 in T. F. Bresnahan and R. J. Gordon (eds), *The Economics of New Goods*, Chicago: University of Chicago Press; Nordhaus, W. D. (1998) 'Quality changes in price indices', *Journal of Economic Perspectives* **12**(1) (Winter), pp. 59–68.

7 Schumpeter (in Schumpeter, J. (1950) *Capitalism, Socialism, and Democracy*, 3rd edn, New York: Harper and Row) argued for the importance of disruptive innovations in maintaining a healthy competitive economy; see also Schumpeter, J. A. (1934) *The Theory of Economic Development*, Boston, Mass.: Harvard University Press; Schumpeter, J. A. (1939) *Business Cycles*, New York: McGraw-Hill.

8 Clark, K. B. and Fujimoto, T. (1991) *Product Development Performance: Strategy, organization and management in the world auto industry*, Boston, Mass.: Harvard Business School Press.

9 Christensen, C. (1997) *The Innovator's Dilemma: When new technologies cause great firms to fail*, Boston, Mass.: Harvard Business School Press.

10 D'Aveni, R. A. and MacMillan, I. C. (1990) 'Crisis and the content of managerial communications: a study of the focus of attention of top managers in surviving and failing firms', *Administrative Science Quarterly* 35, pp. 634–57.

11 This may be compared with technologies with less radical jumps in performance such as the VCR: see Klopfenstein, B. C. (1989) 'The diffusion of the VCR in the United States', in M. R. Levy (ed.), *The VCR Age*, Newbury Park, Calif.: Sage.

12 Tushman, M. L. and O'Reilly III, C. A. (1997) *Winning*

Through Innovation: Leading organizational change and renewal, Boston, Mass.: Harvard Business School Press; Tushman, M. L. and Anderson, P. (1986) 'Technological discontinuities and organizational environments', *Administrative Science Quarterly* 31, pp. 439–65.

13 Cowen, T. (ed.) (1988) *The Theory of Market Failure*, Fairfax Virginia: George Mason Press; Fisher, F. M. (1983) *Disequilibrium Foundations of Equilibrium Economics*, Cambridge, UK: Cambridge University Press.

14 Day, D. L. (1994) 'Raising radicals: different processes for championing innovative corporate ventures', *Organization Science* 5, pp. 148–72; Cohen, W. M. and Levinthal, D. A. (1994) 'Fortune favours the prepared firm', *Management Science* 40, pp. 227–51; Farrell, J. and Saloner, G. (1986) 'Installed base and compatibility: innovation, product preannouncements, and predation', *American Economic Review* **76**(5) (December), pp. 940–55.

15 These effects are just one set of examples of systems that evolve when networks appear. For parallels in physics, biology and other fields see Barabasi, A.-L. (2003) *Linked: How everything is connected to everything else and what it means*, New York: Plume.

16 The importance of adopting such standards for successful marketing has been studied at length in Farrell, J. and Saloner, G. (1985) 'Standardization, compatibility, and innovation', *Rand Journal of Economics* **16**(1) (Spring), pp. 70–83; Liebowitz, S. J. and Margolis, S. E. (1990) 'The fable of the keys', *Journal of Law and Economics* **33**(1), pp. 1–26; Liebowitz, S. J. and Margolis, S. E. (1995) 'Are network externalities a new source of market failure?', *Research in Law and Economics* 17, pp. 1–22.

17 Tapscott, D. (1995) *The Digital Economy: Promise and peril in the age of networked intelligence*, New York: McGraw-Hill.

18 Schoemaker, P. (1992) 'How to link strategic vision to core capabilities', *Sloan Management Review* 34, pp. 67–81; Schoemaker, P. and van der Heijden, C. A. J. M. (1992) 'Integrating scenarios into strategic planning at Royal Dutch/Shell', *Planning Review* (May/June), pp. 41–6.

19 Starr, J. A. and MacMillan, I. C. (1990) 'Resource cooptation and social contracting: resource acquisition strategies for new ventures', *Strategic Management Journal* 11, pp. 79–92; Stinchcombe, A. L. (1965) 'Organizations and social structure', in J. G. March (ed.), *Handbook of Organizations*, Chicago: Rand McNally; Tushman, M. L. and Romanelli, E. (1985) 'Organizational evolution: a metamorphosis model

of convergence and reorientation', pp. 171–222 in L. L. Cummings and B. M. Staw (eds), *Research in Organizational Behavior*, Greenwich, Conn.: JAI Press.

20 Ellis, H. S. and Fellner, W. (1943) 'External economies and diseconomies', American Economic Review 33, pp. 493–511; Weick, K. E. and Roberts, K. H. (1993) 'Collective mind in organizations: heedful interrelating on flight decks', *Administrative Science Quarterly* 38, pp. 357–81.

21 The theoretical basis for limiting yourself to seven items was presented in Miller, G. A. (1956) 'The magical number seven, plus or minus two: some limits on our capacity for processing information', *Psychological Review* 63, pp. 81–97.

22 Fine, L. (2000) *The Piano Book,* Jamaica Plain, Mass.: Brookside Press, p. 146.

23 Fine, L. (2000) *The Piano Book,* Jamaica Plain, Mass.: Brookside Press, p. 146.

24 Garvey, G. (1943) 'Kondratieff's theory of long cycles', *Review of Economic Statistics* 35(4), (November).

COMMUNITIES, NETWORKS AND REPUTATION

LEARNING OBJECTIVES

After finishing this chapter, you will understand

- ▶ the action of **network effects** and **industry standards**

- ▶ how **brands and reputation** signal the market concerning minimum quality standards

- ▶ branding as a contracting vehicle for **mutual trust**, and **community responsibility**, however the community and contract are defined.

After reading the *innovation workout*, you will be able to apply **inductive reasoning based on existing successes** to your brand development. After reading the Craigslist *case study*, you will be challenged to define future roles for **community**, the **creative commons**, **principles** and **moral compass** that guide a company, and the mutual effect of **reputation** and **viral network growth** on services such as Craigslist.

Note: Further information, class slides, test questions and other supporting material are available on our companion website at

www.palgrave.com/business/westland

NETWORK EFFECTS

Networks have long been a progenitor of radical change in business. Networks of canals, rails and highways fomented a huge economic shift over a century ago – the shift from an agricultural to industrial economy at the end of the 19th century. Railways accounted for almost 15 per cent of US GDP at the end of the 19th century – similar to IT around the year 2000. With railways, farmers were no longer tethered to the farmers' markets of their local village. They began growing large surpluses of grains for distribution throughout the United States.

Railways made distance irrelevant (or perhaps less relevant). Universal access was important, especially to farmers. For example, the state of Iowa enacted legislation that required railways to provide service to within 6 miles (one day's buggy ride) of any farm in the state. Trustbusters worried about unhealthy synergies between network industries – such as electricity, oil pipelines, telephone and telegraph – which could benefit from the railways' long, uninterrupted rights of way. The Texas Railroad Commissioner grew to be one of that state's power brokers when oil was discovered at Spindletop at the turn of the century – he controlled the flow of oil along the pipelines that followed the rails.

Network industries play a crucial role in modern life. The modern economy would be very much diminished without the transportation, communications, information and rail networks. Most of the major information industries are also either network industries or share many essential economic features with network industries.

The first network bubble

On Black Thursday, 18 September 1873, the New York banking house of Jay Cooke and Company, the financier of the Northern Pacific Railway, collapsed. The enormous cost of the US Civil War, excessive railway building, inflated credit, speculation, over-expansion and capital outlays for new farmland produced a crisis. In a domino effect, railway bankruptcies and bank failures followed. Over 18 per cent of the US railway mileage was put in the hands of receivers, iron and steel works were devastated, and business failures led to massive layoffs. Wages plunged by 25 per cent. Over the next four years, the cost of business failures reached US$775 million ($155 billion in 2002 dollars) and the number of unemployed rose to nearly 3 million (in a country of 45 million).

It didn't end there. Railways burned money on a colossal scale. Textile mills, the country's largest manufacturers, rarely cost more than $1 million ($18 million in 2002 money), whereas the capitalization of the four big east–west trunk lines – Pennsylvania, Erie and Northern Pacific, New York Central, and Baltimore & Ohio – reached $140 million (over $25 billion today). E. H. Harriman, the boldest proponent of the spend money to make money strategy, poured $240 million ($4.8 billion today) into expanding and modernizing the Southern Pacific Railroad. Three months after President Grover Cleveland began his second Democratic term in 1893, railway over-expansion provided a cascading collapse of the economy which, until the 1929 Wall Street Crash, was known as the Great Depression. The 1893 slump brought down the Erie, other debt-ridden railways, and 600 banks. It embittered the already discontented farming regions, and exhausted the silver-mining states.

Conceptually, anything called a network can be described using 'links' that connect 'nodes' (see Figure 10.1).

A phone call from A to B is created by access to the switch of customer A, access to the switch of customer B, and switching services provided by the carrier. Networks where services AB and BA are distinct are named 'two-way' networks. Two-way networks include railways, roads and many telecommunications networks. When one of AB or BA is unfeasible, or does not make economic sense, the network is called a one-way network – for example radio and television broadcasting networks.[1]

The crucial relationship in both one-way and two-way networks is the *complementarity* between the pieces of the network. *Standards* assure that various links and nodes on the network can be mixed and matched at zero marginal cost to produce demanded (and thus valuable) goods.

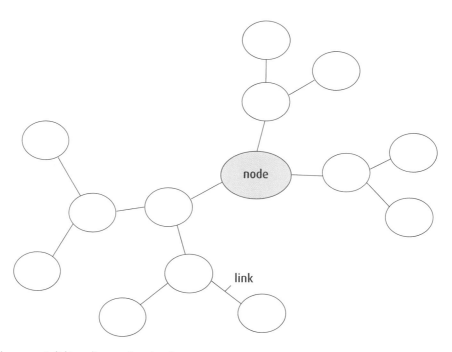

Figure 10.1 Radial tree diagram of a network

Network effects often arise where technologies are used by many people at once, as are those that help establish direct or indirect personal communications – word processors, programming languages, email, telephones, database standards and so forth. It usually takes some time to enable this communication through innovation or standards. Individuals can realize economies of scale when they all adopt the same standard technology in their interactions. The economies of scale are larger where more people adhere to the same standards – they are said to benefit from *network effects* which improve the efficiency of their work.

Electrical standards

Standards are critical, yet often set haphazardly. Nicola Tesla's experiments in the 1860s determined that electric motors ran most efficiently with alternating current at 220 volts and 60 cycles per second. George Westinghouse, the original champion of alternating current, developed his system of generators and transformers to run at 133 cycles per second, but depended on Tesla for motors. For all their efforts, Westinghouse's engineers were unable to adapt his motors to run at 133 cycles per second, and were instead forced to switch all of their generators to 220 volts at 60 cycles per second. And that would have been the end of it except that Westinghouse's competitor, Thomas Edison, had been running his direct current generators on Pearl Street in New York at 110 volts. When Edison switched to generating alternating current, he ran it through the same cables and substations, so kept the voltage at 110 volts but adopted 60 cycles per second.

When the German company AEG built the first European generating facility, its engineers decided to fix the frequency at 50 Hz, because the number 60 didn't fit the metric standard unit sequence (1, 2, 5). At that time AEG had a virtual monopoly, and its standard spread to the rest of the continent. So it adopted Tesla's suggestions for 220 volts, but running at 50 cycles per second.

The system cost of these decisions is enormous. A motor run on current at 50 cycles per second is on average 17 per cent less efficient than one run at 60 cycles per second. This forces Europe to generate perhaps 10 per cent more energy than if it were running its motors at 60 cycles per second. In the United States, Edison's decision to run his system at 110 volts (which ultimately became the US standard) creates problems for the power line going into a house or business. The drop from one end of a typical American house to the other may be as much as 20 volts, forcing distributors of electricity to send 120 volts to the house just to ensure that the voltage will not drop below 100 (which would cause a noticeable dimming in incandescent light bulbs).

Natural monopolies

Theodore Vail, a former director of the US Postal Service, took great advantage of network innovations such as the railway and the telegraph to make the US Post Office the most efficient and profitable in the world. He took control of Bell Telephone (renamed AT&T after J. P. Morgan gained control of the company in 1907). Bell's patents on the telephone had run out in 1894, and since that time the company had faced intense competition from nearly 6000 other phone companies across the United States. Vail believed that Bell Telephone's future would be secure if it could build a national network and function as a national utility before its exclusivity ran out. This was an expensive proposition, but it would be even more expensive for a viable competitor to build a network to challenge Bell Telephone. In AT&T's 1908 annual report Vail argued that:

> A telephone without a connection at the other end of the line is ... one of the most useless things in the world. Its value depends on the connection with other telephones – and increases with the number of connections.

Vail's ideas about the power of network effects were central to arguments he used to justify AT&T's acquisition of smaller competitors throughout the 1920s and 1930s, and to justify its defence of 'universal service' and 'natural monopoly', similar to the post office or railways, up until Bell's break-up in 1982.

Network effects can play an important role in the efficient allocation of resources. In a free-market economy, individuals tend to focus on their own particular welfare, and there may not be proper incentives to build up networks large enough to benefit from network effects. This may be cited as justification for 'natural monopolies' in network industries like power, transportation and telephones, which ostensibly can allow individuals to realize these network benefits.

The networking family

The Vail family played a big part in many of the early network industries in the United States. Lewis Vail, grandfather of Theodore Vail, was a civil engineer who moved to Ohio and made his name building networks of canals and highways, relatively new infrastructures at that point in American history. Theodore's uncle, Stephen Vail, was founder of the Speedwell Iron Works, which built much of the mechanical technology that went into the early steamships that crossed the Atlantic Ocean. Stephen, together with his sons George and Alfred Vail, funded inventor Samuel F. B. Morse to develop his wireless transmitter. Cousin Alfred Vail invented the dot-and-dash alphabet utilized by Morse's telegraph. Theodore Vail's one adopted daughter, Katherine, became one of the founders of Bennington College, and Theodore himself joined the US Post Office, inventing its 'Fast Mail' service, the first mail-only train service, which in 1875 began operations between New York City and Chicago. In 1878 Vail left the Postal Office to become general manager of the recently established American Bell Telephone Company, which was started on 9 July 1877, and he spent many of the subsequent years fending off court challenges from telegraph giant Western Union. Theodore left the company after a decade, but came out of 'retirement' to lead the company in its post-patent days.

Bob Metcalfe,[2] inventor of Ethernet and former CEO of 3Com, developed a characterization of network effects for an Ethernet network in 1980, which suggested that the cost of a computer network increases linearly with the number of nodes, while the value increases by the square of the number of nodes. Metcalfe's idea had great influence during the dot-com boom, where it was used to justify telecommunications investments and standards wars with the idea that network business models have a 'critical mass' beyond which profits and value to adopters grow rapidly, and where higher switching costs tend to lock-in adopters. More recently, Andrew Odlyzko[3] has suggested that Metcalfe over-estimated value and that network value increases logarithmically. In contrast, David Reed[4] suggested that value is scaled exponentially, and that Metcalfe under-estimates value. Though both are widely cited, neither has conducted the empirical work needed to support these claims (and nor has Bob Metcalfe).

The most extensive empirical work on network structure has been conducted by physicist Lazlo Barabási and his colleagues around the world. They have identified three topologies for common networks – random, small-world and scale-free.

Random networks (Erdös–Rényi networks)

Random networks provide a benchmark model used in assessing networks. Though not widely found in the real world, they were the first to be modelled and investigated intensely, by Paul Erdös and Alfréd Rényi in the 1950s. Many important properties of random graphs appear quite suddenly – a phenomenon that corresponds to the 'critical mass' in the economics of networks, and the 'percolation threshold' in many physical phenomena. Random networks are like road networks, where most cities are served by around the same number of major roads (see Figure 10.2), and thus the number of links on the average node tends to cluster around the mean of a normal distribution.

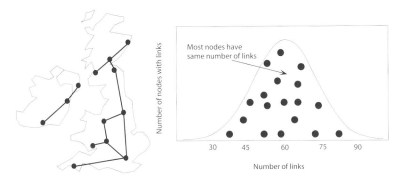

Figure 10.2 Random networks (UK major roads)

Small-world networks

Many real-world networks have relatively short path lengths between nodes – for example, the six degrees of separation between individuals in the world studied by Stanley Milgrom and Manfred Kochen in the 1960s. Duncan Watts and Steven Strogatz have studied such networks, which were inspired by the structures that Milgrom found in his studies (summarized in Watts' book *Six Degrees*[5]). *Small-world networks* add a few extra long-range links to what is otherwise the limited networking of a small local social community. These long-range links drastically shorten the average separation between all nodes, similar to the real world social links that Milgrom discovered.

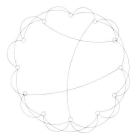

Figure 10.3 Small-world networks

Small-world networks tend to have a few close contacts, and a few nodes that stretch their contacts across the whole network. (In social networks, these will be the most widely 'networked' people in a crowd.)

Scale-free networks

The World Wide Web is a 'scale-free network'. The number of links attached to an arbitrary node tends to follow a power law – in other words, the frequency with which we encounter a node with k links will be determined by x, some fixed number that characterizes the way the scale-free network is connected. Linkages follow a Zipfian distribution (also called Paretian or Yule distribution), a distribution that has been widely studied, and for which several competing models of generation exist. In many real-world networks, $x \approx 2$, possibly giving credence to Metcalfe's law if we assume that value is somehow tied to the number of links to certain nodes. Scale-free networks are like air traffic networks, where a few 'hub' cities have a large amount of the total traffic (see Figure 10.4).

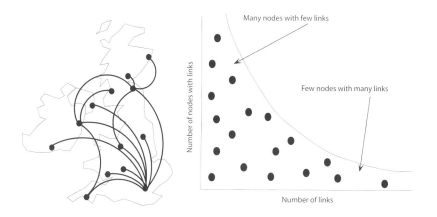

Figure 10.4 UK air traffic (a scale-free network with a power law distribution of links)

In addition to the topology of linkages of a network, we must consider the fact that all links may not be equally strong. This seems to be especially important in social networks (networks of friends, business associates and so forth), because maintaining strong links (such as close friendships) can become prohibitively costly for more than a very few links. Mark Granovetter[6] suggested that most social networks consist of small clusters of tightly connected individuals, with a few individuals maintaining weak ties with a much larger community (see Figure 10.5). This is similar to Watts's small-world network, but with varying strengths of ties. Recent work has reinforced Granovetter's contention that weak ties are more important for the effectiveness and reach of a network (and thus presumably its value to those who use the network) than strong ties.

VALUE DRIVERS IN NETWORK ECONOMICS

If we have some idea of the topology of a particular network which lies at the core of a strategy model (for example, eBay's community of traders is a network that generates

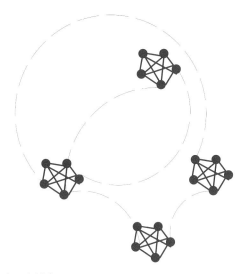

Figure 10.5 Strong and weak social links

all of the value from its business model), then Barabási's research finds that there are three robust measures of network topology, and thus strategy drivers, which may be controlled as well as called upon to forecast value generation. These are:

- *average path length*: the distance between any two nodes
- a *clustering coefficient* (a measure of tendencies of cliques in social and communications networks) which is measured with a standard metric developed by Watts and Strogatz in 1998, who were the first to report that clustering in real world networks tends to significantly exceed that of random networks
- *degree distribution*: the probability distribution giving the probability that there are *k* links attached to an arbitrary node.

Barabási and his colleagues have also shown how these characteristics are generated from particular initial conditions and patterns of growth (adding new links to nodes). There is a dynamic behind the structure, and time implicitly becomes a fundamental value driver in network effects.

STANDARDS, LOCK-IN AND CRITICAL MASS

No discussion of network effects would be complete without mentioning three topics that regularly surface in competitive strategy – first, critical mass; second, customer switching costs and lock-in; and third, competition to set interface, interoperability and other linkage standards. These concepts grew in popularity during the dot-com boom, when many business models made internet networking their centrepiece. The idea is that as networks grow, they reach a 'critical mass' of users, after which network effects are so overpowering that network growth explodes (much like critical mass in a nuclear weapon). Once network effects are this large, customers are locked in to the network, and high switching costs will prevent them from leaving for a competitor. Networks may be real, like the internet, or virtual, like Microsoft's operating systems. Virtual networks depend on 'standards' for interfaces, interoperability and so forth.

So embedded is the received industrial wisdom that it has been graced with its very own supporting mythology (see box on 'Myths about public goods, externalities and lock-in'). Intellectual property rights may indeed accrue to firms that set a standard – for example, Microsoft in operating systems and word processors. And perhaps these are inferior to competitors that do not have the luxury of lock-in and a critical mass of users. But a number of examples cited in support of the concepts of lock-in and critical mass – especially to an inferior standard – have been questioned and found wanting. Thus the verdict is still out on just how important standards, lock-in and critical mass are to competitive strategy.

Myths about public goods, externalities and lock-in

Lighthouses are commonly cited as a natural monopoly that is provided as a pure public good, in order to improve shipping network efficiencies by preventing wrecks. But nearly three decades ago, economist Ronald Coase showed that when lighthouses were first built in Britain they were provided by private enterprise. Tolls to fund them were collected when ships reached port. Another common example, of bees providing a beneficial 'externality' by pollinating flowers for free, was challenged by economist Steven Cheung, who examined beekeeping and apple-growing in the state of Washington. He found that apple-growers paid beekeepers for their bees' pollinating endeavours; those services were not, in fact, an unpriced 'externality'.[7]

But perhaps the most enduring myth was the superiority of the Dvorak typewriter keyboard. The myth goes that early typewriters adopted the QWERTY key arrangement on typewriters (so called because of the top row of keys) to slow down typists who would have jammed their primitive typewriter mechanisms if they repeatedly pressed keys whose printing mechanisms were too close together. By the 1930s, QWERTY standard lock-in was so strong that consumers were unwilling to bear the high switching costs to convert to the vastly superior Dvorak keyboard layout, even though the initial anti-jamming justification for the QWERTY layout was no longer valid. The received wisdom was that users of the QWERTY keyboard were so numerous that they had long since reached critical mass and locked themselves into a vastly inferior standard.

Economists Stan Liebowitz and Stephen Margolis dug deeper into the history of the typewriter[8] to show that the first evidence supporting claims of Dvorak's superiority was extremely thin. The main study was carried out by the US Navy in 1944 (a time when every second counted in the typing pools). The speed of 14 typists retrained on the Dvorak layout was compared with the speed of 18 given supplementary training on QWERTY. The Dvorak typists did better. But it is impossible to say from the official report whether the experiment was properly controlled, as it suffered a variety of oddities – not to mention the curious fact that the experiments were all conducted by one Lieutenant-Commander August Dvorak, the navy's top time-and-motion man, and holder of the patent on the Dvorak layout.

Somewhat later, in 1956, a carefully designed study by the General Services Administration found that QWERTY typists were about as fast as Dvorak typists, and sometimes faster. Ergonomists point out that QWERTY's bad points (such as unbalanced loads on the left and right hand, and excess loading on the top row) are outweighed by other benefits (notably, that alternating hand sequences make for speedier typing). It's interesting, but the point is this: if you have learned to type on a QWERTY keyboard, the pain of retraining for Dvorak, however modest, is not worth suffering. The QWERTY standard is already just as efficient.

Sources: Cheung, Steven N. S. (1973) 'The fable of the bees: an economic investigation,' *Journal of Law and Economics* 16 (April), pp. 11–33.; Coser, L. A. (1956) *The Functions of Social Conflict*, New York: Free Press

SOCIAL NETWORKS
IN THE CITY

Humanity crossed a significant landmark toward the end of 2007, when more than half of the world's population was living in cities. In developed economies, over 70 per cent live in cities; the average proportion of people living in cities in less developed economies is around 40 per cent.[9] Cities impose a much smaller environmental footprint than farming, occupying a mere 0.3 per cent of total land area (and around 3 per cent of the world's total arable land).[10]

Cities provide rich backdrops for numerous sorts of social networking by bringing people close together, where it is easy – in fact unavoidable – for people to bump into each another in the process of going about their daily chores. Physicist Felix Auerback[11] published a study of the distribution of city sizes in 1913, showing an exponential distribution consistent with a scale-free network. Since that time other studies, by Herbert Simon, Xaviar Gabaix and Paul Krugman,[12] have confirmed and expanded our understanding of the way that various factors – including the growth of ideas – are scaled within cities.

Today's cities are larger and more complex than at any time in history, which makes continual demands on the energy and creativity of their inhabitants. Table 10.1 shows how innovation (as measured by patents, inventors, R&D and so forth) grows faster than cities.

City growth is constrained by the availability of resources (which are used both for maintenance and growth) and their rates of consumption. Different social activities exhibit substantially different long-term behaviour depending on whether the exponent β is larger than 1. When the exponent β is less than 1, growth ceases at some time the future as the population of the city reaches some limit in carrying capacity. But where the exponent β is larger than 1, growth is faster than exponential and quickly becomes unbounded. Since this cannot happen in practice – where resources, energy and wealth are limited – major qualitative changes must occur which effectively reset the city's dynamics. It is at these points of collapse in one set of city activities, and the initiation of a new set, that government must proactively manage the direction of change with innovative responses that assure that the next stage of growth continues to create knowledge and wealth.

These successive cycles of superlinear innovation must occur at shorter and shorter intervals as the city grows. Not only does the pace of life increase with city size, but so also must the rate at which new major adaptations and innovations need to be introduced to sustain the city.[13] These predicted successive accelerating cycles of faster than exponential growth are consistent with observations for the population of cities, waves of technological change,[14] and the world population.[15] We shall revisit the scaling of ideas, inventions and innovation in cities, and scaling's economic importance for the future, when we discuss cities in Chapter 13.

Table 10.1: *Social activities as an exponential function of city size*

Measure of social activity	β	95 per cent confidence interval	Adjusted R²	Obs	Country-year of study
New patents	1.27	[1.25,1.29]	0.72	331	USA 2001
Inventors	1.25	[1.22,1.27]	0.76	331	USA 2001
Private R&D employment	1.34	[1.29,1.39]	0.92	266	USA 2002
Supercreative employment	1.15	[1.11,1.18]	0.89	287	USA 2003
R&D establishments	1.19	[1.14,1.22]	0.77	287	USA 1997
R&D employment	1.26	[1.18,1.43]	0.93	295	China 2002
Total wages	1.12	[1.09,1.13]	0.96	361	USA 2002
Total bank deposits	1.08	[1.03,1.11]	0.91	267	USA 1996
GDP	1.15	[1.06,1.23]	0.96	295	China 2002
GDP	1.26	[1.09,1.46]	0.64	196	EU 1999–2003
GDP	1.13	[1.03,1.23]	0.94	37	Germany 2003
Total electrical consumption	1.07	[1.03,1.11]	0.88	392	Germany 2002
New AIDS cases	1.23	[1.18,1.29]	0.76	93	USA 2002–03
Serious crimes	1.16	[1.11, 1.18]	0.89	287	USA 2003
Total housing	1	[0.99,1.01]	0.99	316	USA 1990
Total employment	1.01	[0.99,1.02]	0.98	331	USA 2001
Home electrical consumption	1	[0.94,1.06]	0.88	377	Germany 2002
Home electrical consumption	1.05	[0.89,1.22]	0.91	295	China 2002
Home water consumption	1.01	[0.89,1.11]	0.96	295	China 2002
Petrol stations	0.77	[0.74,0.81]	0.93	318	USA 2001
Petrol sales	0.79	[0.73,0.80]	0.94	318	USA 2001
Length of electrical cables	0.87	[0.82,0.92]	0.75	380	Germany 2002
Road surface	0.83	[0.74,0.92]	0.87	29	Germany 2002
Walking speed (metres/sec)	0.80	[0.74,0.92]	0.80	19	USA 2006

Source: Bettencourt, L. M., Lobo, J., Helbing, D., Kunhert, C., and West, G. B. (2007) 'Growth, innovation, scaling and the pace of life in cities', *Proceedings of the National Academy of Sciences of the USA* **104**(17) (24 April), pp. 7301–6.

BRANDS AND REPUTATION

How much is a brand worth? This is a question that crops up regularly, especially in mergers and acquisitions when negotiating price, to assist with brand management and strategy, and in litigation when one firm accuses another of damaging its brand. Yet there is no pat answer to the question. The problem has less to do with future value than the fact that a brand is a name or a symbol, along with its associated tangible and emotional attributes. Brands identify – in the minds of consumers – the goods or services of one seller in order to differentiate them from their competitors in a positive way.

Patagonia's 'green' credentials

Yvon Chouinard, Patagonia's founder, got his start as a 14-year-old climber in 1953. Not being satisfied with the soft pitons available at the time, he purchased his own coal-fired forge and anvil and began making his pitons out of hard steel. By 1970 he had become the largest supplier of climbing hardware in the United States, and also one of its chief environmental villains because his gear was damaging rock. Climbing had become more popular, and fragile cracks in stone faces had to endure repeated hammering of pitons during both placement and removal. The disfiguring was severe.

Fortunately, there was an alternative: aluminium chocks that could be wedged by hand rather than hammered in and out of cracks, which Chouinard introduced in 1972. Influential Sierra climber Doug Robinson was effusive:

> There is a word for it, and the word is clean. Climbing with only nuts and runners for protection is clean climbing. Clean because the rock is left unaltered by the passing climber. Clean because nothing is hammered into the rock and then hammered back out, leaving the rock scarred and the next climber's experience less natural. Clean because the climber's protection leaves little trace of his ascension. Clean is climbing the rock without changing it; a step closer to organic climbing for the natural man.[16]

This was the first of many environmentally motivated decisions by Patagonia (Chouinard claims that the name, after a region of vast steppe-like plains in southern Argentina, is pronounceable in any language). The company today is a member of several environmental movements and is a major contributor to environmental groups. Patagonia commits 1 per cent of its total sales revenue or 10 per cent of its profit, whichever is more, to environmental groups. Since 1985, when the programme was first started, Patagonia has donated US$25 million to over 1000 organizations. It co-founded the alliance 1% for the Planet. This is an alliance of businesses which, like Patagonia, commit at least 1 per cent of their total sales revenue to the environment.

In 1996, Patagonia converted its entire sportswear line to 100 per cent organically grown cotton, promising never to go back to conventional cotton, regardless of the outcome. Since then the company has become the largest purchaser of organic cotton in the world. Patagonia is a member of the Fair Labor Association. Inspections conducted by the Fair Labor Association rarely finds violations at factories producing Patagonia clothing.

Patagonia's commitment to 'green' causes has made excellent business sense – largely in response to its clientèle who are apt to be much more sensitive than average to the environment, as they are in direct contact with it on their camping trips, and during hiking and other outdoor activities. Although the company is privately held and does not publish financial statistics, the industry press observes that it is one of the fastest growing clothing retailers, and one whose management and product quality set standards for the competition.

The large number of brand acquisitions in the late 1980s alerted investors to the hidden value in highly branded companies and propagated the practice of brand valuation. Some of these acquisitions included Nestlé buying Rowntree, United Biscuits buying and later selling Keebler, Grand Metropolitan buying Pillsbury and Danone buying Nabisco's European businesses. All these acquisitions commanded high price–earnings multiples which were directly attributed to their brand equity by investors.

Interbrand's study of acquisitions in the 1980s showed that, whereas in 1981 net tangible assets represented 82 per cent (on average) of the amount bid for companies, by 1988 this had fallen to just 56 per cent, and companies were being acquired less for their tangible assets and more for their intangible assets.[17] This expansion in the value of intangible assets is also reflected in the ratio of the accounting book value of firms to their market value. The average book-to-market value of the S&P 500 firms dropped from approximately 100 per cent in 1980 to around 50 per cent by 1990.

Procter & Gamble's brand equity

Harley Procter and James Gamble began business in Cincinnati in the 1870s selling candles and soap from a wheelbarrow. James Gamble, an inveterate chemist and tinker, perfected his formula for 'P&G white soap' in 1878. Unsatisfied with this appellation, Harley Procter decided to give the soap a name that people could remember – he named the soap 'Ivory' after the Psalm 45 verse: 'All thy garments smell of myrrh and aloes and cassia, out of the ivory palaces whereby they have made me glad.'

Gamble's floating soap was invented when one of the P&G factory workmen left to go to lunch while the machinery was still running, letting air work its way into the mixture. The product was popular because Cincinnatians often bathed in the Ohio River in those days and the floating soap would never get lost in the Ohio river's murky waters.

A chemical analysis of Ivory soap found that 0.56 per cent of the ingredients did not fall in the 'pure soap' category, so Gamble – being obsessed with truth in advertising – adopted the slogan '99-44/100 per cent Pure'. This was notable because – by accident or not – it was one of the first deliberate exercises in branding, and P&G became one of the first corporations whose main investment was in brand equity.

Successful brands signal to consumers that this firm's product or service is different from those of competitors. The associations consumers make with the brand establish an emotional connection, and an implied contract between the supplier and the consumer – one that is dynamic and ongoing. Consider widely disseminated brands such as McDonald's and Starbucks. The premium that consumers are willing to pay for these brands exists because the brands mitigate risk, by assuring minimum quality. The brand is maintained and defended by its owners simply because this assures security of demand in the future.

Asia's diploma mills (part 1)

Diplomas have always been important in Asia. They determined who would or who would not be able to hold a comfortable lifetime sinecure in the Imperial bureaucracy. Not surprisingly the idea that it might be easier to buy scholarship than to earn it has ancient roots in the region.

The Qing dynasty (1644–1911) Emperor KangXi was clearly frustrated by the education examination system in China when he wrote:

> Even among examiners there are those who are corrupt, those who do not understand basic works …. As to the candidates, not only are there few in the Harlin Academy who can write a proper eulogy, there are many whose calligraphy is bad and who can't punctuate the basic history books. When I had the Chinese Bannermen who'd bought their ranks given a special examination, many either brought in books to copy, or hand in blank sheets. Other candidates hire people to sit the exams for them, or else pretend to be from a province that has a more liberal quota than their own.[18]

Indeed, China boasts the world's oldest continuous systematized programme of national examinations; today it is also arguably the world's most debauched.

In 2006, Chinese police raided the headquarters of the innovatively named Hired Gun Group, established by a 23-year-old university graduate. It provided online services ranging from answers to national exam papers to 'hired guns' – that is, people who would sit the exams for students. The website assured surfers that the activities were legal, thanks to 'friends within the Public Security Bureau', and it 'guaranteed a 95 per cent success rate'. The group took 1.7 million yuan (a little over US$200,000) duping 990 students in 19 provinces and 200 cities.

Even in the capital city of Beijing, the problem is rampant. One examiner at Beijing's Agricultural University was so determined to stop cheating that he invited police officers to check the identity cards of every student sitting his exam. To his relief and surprise, they did not uncover one single 'hired gun'. Only later was it discovered that every student had been an impostor, and because *everyone* had used fake personal ID cards that day, the police thought they were all real.

Professional exam-takers advertise their services on websites and even on university noticeboards. The going rate averages 1500 yuan per exam, with 500 yuan going to the company that makes the deal and the rest to the impostor. For exams required to enter American universities, the rates are closer to 10,000 yuan for each exam, making it a profitable career.

All things must come to an end, though. One company in Tianjin now produces a 6 mm device which, when fitted into a student's ear, can connect him or her to a mobile phone signal. Answers can be read out by a colleague, confronting 'hired guns' with the prospect that, as a result of advances in technology, they may soon become extinct.[19]

Assessment of the 'brand premium' lies at the heart of brand formulations such as those practised by consulting firms like Interbrand. Interbrand began valuing brands in the mid-1990s with a valuation of Rank Hovis McDougal, which was used in its opposition to a hostile takeover bid. With the brand value information, the Rank Hovis McDougal board was able to go back to investors and argue that the bid was too low, and eventually repel it.[20]

Most brand formulations compute brand equity (that is, the market value attributable solely to the brand) based on an 'excess profit' figure by comparing benchmark products or services in the same sector, but without brand recognition, to those of the target firm. Future excess profits are forecast, and then discounted to the present using an industry-specific discount rate.

Asia's diploma mills (part 2)

How would you rate a degree from Britain's Canterbury University, Winchester University or Belford University; Kingston University or Lansbridge University in British Columbia, Canada; or Pacific Western University in the United States? In fact, none of them are recognized as providers of degrees in their home countries: These are 'diploma mills' whose degrees have popped up all over the world alongside degrees from hundreds of other suspect colleges.

Britain's National Recognition Centre (Naric), which vets qualifications for universities in Britain and Australia, and for large companies such as HSBC looking to hire an international workforce, has noticed a steady rise in fake degrees around Asia – especially from Thailand, Malaysia and Singapore. 'We've seen diploma mills in Asia before, but not on the scale we have now', said Allen Ezell, a former FBI agent and author of a book on diploma mills. 'When the job market requires higher levels of education, then credentials become important. With globalization, more and more people are applying for jobs in other countries, it's a problem that knows no boundaries.' Ezell himself has 10 bachelor's degrees, 19 master's, four doctorates and two medical degrees awarded by US 'universities' from his time as a special agent for the FBI's operation DipScam (Diploma Scam), which ran for 11 years in the 1980s and 1990s.

Diploma mills award degrees without requiring students to meet the normal educational standards. They may offer degrees on the basis of 'life experience'. St Regis University in Britain netted revenues of more than US$10 million before it was shut down in 2005. Fake degrees can be picked up on Bangkok's Khao San Road (an estimated 30 per cent of foreign teachers in Thailand have fake qualifications). In one bizarre case in 2006, 120 South Korean musicians were exposed as having bogus music degrees from a Russian 'university' to qualify to play in orchestras or teach music.

Shenzhen is the centre of China's fake degree industry. Operators hand out leaflets or post them on lamp posts. Diplomas are sold over the internet for as little as US$100. Shenzhen's best-known printer, backalleypress.com, advertises 'novelty degrees', claiming to print over 1500 documents in a year. The bulk of the orders come from Chinese, despite the steep cost of US$235 for a bachelor's degree and $475 for a masters.

The Shenzhen operations pale beside the organized providers of unrecognized degrees in Malaysia, Singapore and Cambodia. Many degree mills operate as private colleges and are very well known in Malaysia and Singapore. Private agencies can apply to the Malaysian Quality Assurance Agency for recognition. They operate openly and do big shows and presentations. Irish International University (IIU) has a high-profile presence in Malaysia even though in 2005 the Dublin government asked the Malaysian authorities to shut it down because it was 'neither Irish nor a university'. In 2007, IIU expanded into Cambodia where it formed an alliance with the privately run Build Bright University, which is officially accredited to issue degrees in Cambodia. IIU, in turn, claims to be accredited by 'QAC' located at an unmanned office address in North London, and is now an external examiner for St Clements University, operating out of the Turks and Caicos Islands and Niue, an atoll in the South Pacific. St Clements' actual address in London is the back of a tailor's shop. IIU has apparently set its sights on becoming an 'accreditation mill' to accredit the phoney diplomas of new diploma mills.

The big diploma mills expanding in Asia tend to be from Britain or the United States. Often they have slick websites with 'alumni' statements, graduation pictures, photographs of their vice-chancellors in full regalia; and there are even photo shoots of college sporting victories.[21]

Brand equity calculations can be undermined by unexpected events – and rather quickly. Two brands that in recent history have seen an abrupt reversal of fortune are Firestone and Arthur Andersen. After several Ford SUV rollovers were reported in the press – all caused by blowouts in Firestone tires – the Firestone brand, owned by Bridgestone, went from being an asset to a distinct liability almost overnight. Similarly the Enron debacle brought down Arthur Andersen, once considered the top accounting firm in the world.

Another oddity of brand valuation occurs when good and bad products are mixed in such a way that consumers grow confused. *Adverse selection* occurs in a competitive market where buyer and seller have different information about the quality of a product. The classic example is the 'market for lemons', referring to George Akerlof's example of the used car market.[22] In his example, the demand for used cars vanishes as soon as average quality drops even though there are many good-quality cars. Obviously, the example is extreme. It is meant to make the point that the presence of unidentifiable 'lemons' makes it difficult to sell cars of better quality at a good price, with the implication that the average quality of traded used cars is lower than that of non-traded used cars.

Inductive reasoning in brand development

Your business has a brand whether you manage it or not. One way or another, your customers will form an impression of you. *Branding* is the proactive creation and management of this impression. Implicit in the management of a brand are seven strategic goals:

- to install your brand in the minds of customers and prospective customers
- to identify and enrich customers' perceptions of your business
- to safeguard your product against competing ones
- to appeal to the emotional wants and needs of your customers
- to develop the powerful intangibles that define who you are to your audience
- to create essential elements such as your brand promise, brand logo and brand position
- to maintain these impressions throughout the life-cycle through warranties, quality control and advertising.

Of all the tasks involved in commercializing a new idea, the brand is probably least amenable to creation by checklist. Cookbook formulas for branding are unlikely to capture the creative DNA of a new idea, or to effectively broadcast the promise of your innovation. Every successful brand has been preceded by an overriding element of discovery – of learning from past mistakes.

Instead of formulaic approaches, consider developing a brand by asking people what they believe are good brand names and then attempting to determine what commonalties they possess. Unfortunately, this method tends to be quite time-consuming, and to some extent it depends on people's ability to recall brand names and the images they conjure up.

Consider the task facing the US military in early 2003. Under direction from the US President and his Cabinet, it initiated a highly unpopular offensive against Iraq. To attempt to make this expensive operation more palatable to a sceptical nation, the government searched around for a compelling handle, a 'brand' that would help to sell the war. Initially, the protracted US military build-up in the

Persian Gulf had no handle of its own. Instead, the Pentagon referred to it as simply an extension of 'Operation Enduring Freedom', the name of the US war against terror in Afghanistan and elsewhere. There was a calculated reason for that. From September 2002 – when the Bush administration began trying to compel Iraq to eliminate its alleged stocks of 'weapons of mass destruction' – the White House had tried to cast the secular dictator Saddam Hussein as an Islamic fundamentalist in the employ of the al-Qaida terrorist network. 'Operation Enduring Freedom' helped to simplify the war in the minds of US citizens by casting all of the complex sets of players and relationships opposing US forces as members of a single, monolithic army intent on global domination.

Choosing operation names is serious business to military leaders. The top brass views them as an important part of the public relations battle, where an evocative name can serve as a symbol or 'brand' for the underlying purpose of the military action. The selection of 'Iraqi Freedom' reflects that. The runner-up name – 'Operation Desert Freedom' – was rejected because it didn't send the message that America's intent was to liberate the Iraqi people. Reportedly, the military leadership preferred 'Desert Freedom' because it continued the 'desert' theme begun with 1991's 'Operation Desert Shield', the six-month build-up to the Persian Gulf War, and 'Operation Desert Storm', the air and ground assault that followed. But the President's Office and Cabinet (which has the final word) opted for 'Iraqi Freedom' because it was more explicit.

Even the names of minor items can receive attention. For example, the 'Al-Hussain' missile used in Iraq (a variant of the German V-2 rocket that Iraqi scientists named after Saddam Hussein himself) was invariably referred to in Western press releases by the unflattering 'Scud' moniker, a name used internally by US intelligence agencies for Russian versions of the V-2. Such negative branding helped belittle the enemy.

The current era of military operation nomenclature began with the 1989 US incursion into Panama to capture Manuel Noriega. Until that invasion was imminent, it was being called 'Operation Blue Spoon', a nonsense combination generated with a computer's help. At the last minute, however, 'Blue Spoon' was replaced with 'Operation Just Cause', after top officials answered the rhetorical question posed by one general: Do you want your grandchildren to say you served in 'Blue Spoon?'

A compromise inductive reasoning approach to choosing a brand name – and for brainstorming elements such as your brand promise, brand logo and brand position – is to work from a list of actual brands. To get you started, Table 10.2 lists the 20 most valuable brands in the world, and the dollar value of these brands as computed by Interbrand.

Split into discussion break-out groups of between three and four individuals for approximately 15 minutes of brainstorming. The task for each group is to identify any rules or guidelines that they believe are at work in the branding decisions made by these companies. Do the brand names suggest what is being sold, a particular life-style choice, an industry or technology sector? See whether you can figure out what makes the most valuable brands tick.

Going from the specific cases – an inductive approach – helps to develop your inductive reasoning skills, while the group aspect fosters teamwork and friendly competition amongst groups.

Table 10.2: *The 20 most valuable brands in the world*

Ranking	Firm	Brand value (US$ billion)
1	Coca-Cola	67.5
2	Microsoft	60.0
3	IBM	53.3
4	GE	47.0
5	Intel	35.5
6	Nokia	26.4
7	Disney	26.4
8	McDonald's	26.0
9	Toyota	24.8
10	Marlboro	21.1
11	Mercedes-Benz	20.0
12	Citi	19.9
13	Hewlett-Packard	18.8
14	American Express	18.5
15	Gillette	17.5
16	BMW	17.1
17	Cisco	16.6
18	Louis Vuitton	16.0
19	Honda	15.8
20	Samsung	15.0

Source: *BusinessWeek* (2005) 'The 100 top brands', 1 August 2005; valuation by Interbrand.

The Craigslist network

Having observed people on other websites helping one another in a friendly, social and trusting community way, and feeling a bit isolated as a relative newcomer to San Francisco, Craig Newmark decided in 1995 to create something similar for local events. He called it Craigslist. The soul of the site is expressed by the simple populist formulation that Craig Newmark states over and over again when he is asked about his purpose: 'We are just trying to give people a break.' Users throng the site not only because it is free, fast and stripped-down, but because of the communitarian values flowing from the founder. Newmark started with an email distribution list marketed solely through word of mouth, to tell friends about upcoming tech or art events in San Francisco. Once the number of people on the list grew too large, Craigslist became a formal website, which friends encouraged him to call 'Craig's list' since that was how recipients had referred to the email list. The content expanded from events to classifieds, to the full range of categories offered on the site today. Craigslist will add a new city to the site when there are enough requests from users. It did not specifically target 'social influencers', nor does it conduct any pre-launch marketing in any new market it enters. Even in 1998, Newmark still viewed his career as software engineer – Craigslist was a cool hobby that was getting him invited to the best parties for geeks and nerds.

Ultimately, that changed. Craigslist became incorporated in 1999, and in 2007 it operated with a staff of 24 people serving 450 cities around the world. Its sole source of revenue is paid job ads in selected cities (it currently charges US$75 per ad for the San Francisco Bay area; $25 per ad for New York, Los Angeles, San Diego, Boston, Seattle and Washington DC), and paid broker apartment listings in New York City ($10 per ad). Although the company does not disclose financial information, journalists have speculated that its annual revenue approached $10 million in 2004. It serves over 5 billion page views per month, to 10 million unique visitors. With over 10 million new classified ads each month, Craigslist is the leading classifieds service in any medium. The site receives over 500,000 new job listings each month, making it one of the top job boards in the world. It is the number 7 ranked site in the United States (and 25th globally).[23]

Craigslist offers a centralized network of online urban communities – a network of community networks. It offers free classified advertisements (with jobs, internships/work experience, housing, personals, for sale/barter/wanted, services, community, gigs and resumé/CV categories) and forums sorted by various topics. Newmark says that Craigslist works because it gives people a voice, a sense of community, trust and even intimacy. Other factors he cites are consistency of down-to-earth values, customer service and simplicity. After first being approached about running banner ads, Newmark decided to keep Craigslist non-commercial.

Yet the commercial impact of Craigslist is huge: a business study in the Bay area showed that local newspapers were losing as much as $50 million a year in revenue to Craigslist. The awareness of the trend has since avalanched. Classifieds make up as much as 50 per cent of big-city newspaper ad revenues; at a time when the newspaper industry is in crisis with circulations going down by as much as 2.6 per cent a year as readers die off and the young go elsewhere for their information, Craigslist has gained a reputation as the newspaper killer.

CEO Jim Buckmaster has told investment analysts, much to their dismay, that Craigslist has little interest in maximizing profit from the website but instead prefers only to help users find cars, apartments, jobs and dates. Craigslist fashions itself as more of a public service than a for-profit entity, ignoring the numerous opportunities to monetize its user base. However,

Craigslist has clearly established itself as one of the leading online brands and the dominant presence in the US online classifieds market.[24]

Craigslist is unusual in that it develops products and strategy by following particular guiding principles. At the core of these principles are three objectives:

▸ *Create a culture of trust*: Craig and the Craigslist staff actively respond to user emails, and do not make any major changes to the site without first announcing and testing the response from users. Its lack of banner advertising and pop-ups contributes to the perception that Craigslist is 'not in it for the money'.

▸ *Social contributions from the site take precedence over commercial aspects*: free classifieds under the rubrics 'Casual encounters', 'Rants and raves', and 'Missed connections' generate no revenue, but clearly arouse considerable interest in readers and posters. They provide forums for visitors to air their thoughts, giving users a voice in their community. This creates a pattern of usage that is more frequent than buying or selling an item. Newmark argues that the ability to make such postings fosters the sense of community and trust that give consumers greater confidence in the commercial-oriented classifieds.

▸ *Site ease of use*: The site is clean, almost clinical in its sparseness, and allows anonymous posting and browsing. The user self-service site publishing tools are also intuitive and core to the site.

Much of Craigslist's growth has to be attributed to an amazing amount of positive mainstream PR and word of mouth. Newmark is happy to make a good living for the employees of Craigslist without the need to make an extravagant profit. He has turned down many acquisition offers for Craigslist which would by any measure make him a very rich man. Craigslist's CEO Jim Buckmaster has stated that Craigslist could probably make ten times the revenue it makes today if it tried.

So what is Craigslist worth? Assuming it could make $200 million in revenue at a 40 per cent net margin, and applying an eBay-type EBITDA multiple, that would place the value of the company at around US$2.5 billion. Auction giant eBay would be the most logical acquirer, given that it already owns a 25 per cent stake through a rather dubious stock sale by a former trusted employee of Craigslist.[25]

Questions for the Craigslist case study

1. Everyone from the big boys (eBay, Google, MSN) to start-ups (LiveDeal, Edgeio, Oodle) has an online classifieds offering. Many of these new offerings are employing Web 2.0 technologies and strategies, while Craigslist has continued to maintain its relatively spare text-based webpage. Should Craigslist be afraid of this competition? How should it respond to it: what strategies, changes to the website, and new offerings should it consider?

2. Craigslist doesn't advertise, yet it has posed the greatest threat to classified advertising that newspapers have ever seen, threatening to bankrupt many of them. Is advertising dead? If you answered 'No', then what is Craigslist's success secret? If you answered 'Yes', then what will replace advertising?

3. Discuss the concept of 'viral marketing' in the context of the case study. Viral marketing is clearly cheap (indeed free), but is it as effective as paid advertising? Is it as controllable?

4. What are the advantages of the spare, text-based user interface of Craigslist compared with the more complex Web 2.0 interfaces of competitors?

5. Craigslist might be rightly called an 'information commons' or 'commune' (recall the Paris Commune which challenged the rights of French royalty and clergy). The theme of social revolution pervades Craig Newmark's offerings. Is this a new business model, or is it just hype?

6. Discuss the benefits and costs (including opportunity costs) of the community element that lies at the core of Craigslist's strategy. This community will be hard for competitors to replicate. It is not just a more robust classified post or search feature that makes for a more compelling user experience. The consumer loyalty that Craigslist has developed over the last 10 years is highly defensible.

7. If you were a competitor seeking to enter Craigslist's market, which of the following four strategies to differentiate your site from Craigslist would be most likely to succeed, and which would be least likely to succeed:

   a. incorporate user reputation and feedback into the classifieds?

   b. make it easier for users to submit classified listings (especially power users)?

   c. adjust the business model away from a straight listing fee per classified?

   d. offer a larger selection of items/postings?

8. Do you think that the incorporation of user reputation into a classifieds site might be a possible winning strategy (just as the authorship of a book may be more important than topic and content)?

9. Is reputation/feedback of higher value than user anonymity? For which categories?

CHAPTER QUESTIONS FOR REVIEW

1	Think about the relationship between networks, communities and reputation. What role does each play in a successful business? Start by considering the role of 'trust' enabled by a good reputation, and how this can enable (or the lack of it can disable) communication or contracting between any two individuals. Communities are predicated on trust; networks are more active and less costly with trust, because there doesn't have to be as much policing and security.
2	How might network businesses differ if the network is random, small-world or scale-free? What differences would you expect in business models, cost structures and profitability with scale?
3	Are network businesses inherently unstable, like the railroads in the 19th century or the dot-coms in the 20th century? Explain why or why not.
4	Many of the important network cost and revenue relationships follow power-law rather than linear models. How should business models be constructed to take advantage of this?
5	How large a problem is presented by fake diplomas? What sorts of problems might fake diplomas create? How would you feel if your next surgeon held a degree from Pacific Western University? What is the appropriate legal action against diploma mills?

CHAPTER 10: KEY POINTS

▷ Conceptually, anything called a network can be described using 'links' that connect 'nodes':
  - Two-way networks include railroad, road, and many telecommunications networks.
  - One-way networks include radio or television broadcasting networks.

▷ The crucial relationship in both one-way and two-way networks is the *complementarity* between the pieces of the network.

▷ *Standards* assure that various links and nodes on the network can be mixed and matched at zero marginal cost to produce demanded (and thus valuable) goods.

▷ *Network effects* are a net benefit that arises to all users of the network, that increases (perhaps at a non-linear and increasing rate) as the number of network 'nodes' increases.

▷ *Lock-in* of a user to a network occurs because the size of the network effect makes it costly to switch to competing networks. Critical mass is the size at which (purportedly) the lock-in effect becomes significant.

▷ There are three models that have been used to describe real-world networks; each has its own functional form of network effect:
  - *Random networks* where the number of links on the average node tends to cluster around the mean of a normal distribution.
  - *Small world networks* which add a few extra long-range links to what is otherwise the limited networking of a small local social community. These long-range links drastically shorten the average separation between all nodes.
  - *Scale-free networks* where the number of links attached to an arbitrary node tends to follow a power law – i.e., the frequency with which we encounter a node with k links will be k^{-x} where x is some fixed number that characterizes the way the scale free network is connected. The World Wide Web is a scale-free network.

▷ The value drivers defined by these models, as they contribute to network economics are:
  - *Average path length:* the distance between any two nodes.
  - *Clustering coefficient:* a measure of tendencies of clusters to occur; and
  - *Degree distribution:* the probability that there are k links attached to an arbitrary node.

NOTES

1   Tushman, M. L. (1978) 'Task characteristics and technical communication in research and development', *Academy of Management Review* 21 ,pp. 624–45; Tushman, M. L. and Moore, W.L. (eds) (1988) *Readings in the Management of Innovation*, New York: HarperCollins.

2   Interviewed in *Forbes ASAP*, 21 February 2000, p. 97.

3   Briscoe B., Odlyzko, A., and Tilly, B. (2006) 'Metcalfe's law is wrong', July 2006 IEEE Spectrum.

4   http://www.reed.com/Papers/GFN/reedslaw.html

5   Watts, D. J. (2004) *Six Degrees: The science of a connected age*, New York: Norton.

6   Granovetter, M. (1973) 'The strength of weak ties', *American Journal of Sociology* 78 (May), pp. 1360–80.

7   Buchanan, J. and Stubblebine, W., 'Externality' (1962) *Economica* (November), pp. 371–84.

8   Leibowitz, S. and Margolis, S. (1990) 'The fable of the keys', *Journal of Law and Economics* 33, pp. 1–25.

9   *South China Morning Post*, 28 June 2007, p. A11; Crane, P. and Kinzig, A. (2005) 'Nature in the metropolis', *Science* 308, p. 1225.

10 Henderson, J. V. (1977) *Economic Theory and the Cities*, New York: Academic Press.

11 Auerbach, F. (1913) 'The distribution of population concentrations', *Peterman's Letters* vol. 59, pp. 74–6.

12 Simon, H. (1995) 'On a class of skew distributions', *Biometrika* 44, pp. 425–40; Gabaix, X (1999) 'Zipf's law and the growth of cities', *American Economic Review* 89, pp. 129–32; Krugman, P. (1991) 'Increasing returns and economic geography', *Journal of Political Economy* 99, pp. 483–99.

13 Watts, D. J. (2004) *Six Degrees: The science of a connected age*, New York: Norton.

14 Westland, J. C. and See-to, E. (2007) 'The short-run price-performance dynamics of microcomputer technologies', *Research Policy* 36, pp. 591–604.

15 Cohen, J. E. (1995) 'Population growth and Earth's human carrying capacity', *Science* 269, pp. 341–6; Dremer, M. (1993) 'Population growth and technological change: One million B.C. to 1990', *Quarterly Journal of Economics* 108, pp. 681–716.

16 Source: Patagonia website, www.patagonia.com

17 De Chernatony, L. and McDonald, M. H. B. (1998) *Creating Powerful Brands in Consumer, Service and Industrial Markets*, 2nd edn, New York: Butterworth-Heinemann.

18 Source: Brahm, L. (2006) 'Cheating, Chinese style', *South China Morning Post*, 21 February, p. A14.

19 Source: Brahm, L. J. (2001) *China's Century*, New York: Wiley, pp. 89–96.

20 Stobart, P. and Perrier, R. (1997) *Brand Valuation*, New York: Premier Books.

21 Source: 'Making the grade', *South China Morning Post*, 14 June 2007, p. A16.

22 Akerlof, G. A. (1970) 'The market for "lemons": quality uncertainty and the market mechanism', *Quarterly Journal of Economics* 84, pp. 488–500.

23 Source: http://en.wikipedia.org/wiki/Craigslist (accessed 18 June 2007).

24 Nisan Gabbay, http://www.startup-review.com/blog/authors/ (accessed 18 June 2007).

25 Sources: Weiss, P. (2005) 'A guy named Craig', *New York Times* Online, http://nymag.com/nymetro/news/media/internet/15500/ (accessed 18 June 2007); *San Francisco Chronicle*, 'On the record: Craig Newmark', 15 August 2004, http://sfgate.com/cgi-bin/article.cgi?file=/c/a/2004/08/15/NEWMARK.TMP (accessed 18 June 2007).

FINANCING INNOVATIONS

LEARNING OBJECTIVES

After finishing this chapter, you will understand

- ▶ that innovators need strategies to manage both the **consumer market** for their product and the **capital markets** that fund their operations

- ▶ **figures of merit**, and which are most appropriate for their innovations and businesses

- ▶ the function of the **behavioural model** and the **strategy model** in forecasting the value of an innovation and its associated business model

- ▶ how a **value cone** displays risk and return

- ▶ the **choice of discount factor** to compute present value.

After reading the *innovation workout*, you will understand
and be able to conduct a scenario analysis.
After reading the eBay *case study*, you will be able to
identify the roles of **behavioural models**, **strategy drivers**
and **value metrics** in forecasting business value.

Note: Further information, class slides, test questions and other
supporting material are available on our companion website at

www.palgrave.com/business/westland

TWO MARKETS

Innovation pays. By one measure[1] innovators realized a median profit margin growth of 3.4 per cent a year between 1995 and 2007, compared with 0.4 per cent for the median Standard & Poor's Global 1200 company. That's a huge achievement, thanks in large part to innovation. And the group's median annual stock return of 14.3 per cent was a full three points better than the S&P 1200 median over the decade.

To realize the innovation payoff, though, aspiring innovators must prepare to compete in not just one, but two markets – first in the consumer market for their new product or service, and second in the capital market to finance their innovation. Too often, though, inventors trust that if you build it, consumers will come, and someone else will underwrite the bill. More realistically, incomplete market strategy is likely to render their innovation stillborn.

Financial markets for funding innovation are as challenging as consumer markets, but in different ways. Traditionally financial analysts have looked to the past, for precedents for a particular business, in the process of trying to predict future returns. Innovation denies them that opportunity. A truly novel innovation will not have been tested before in the market, depriving the analyst of historical insight into the prospects for the innovators' new business.

Great strides have been made over the past two decades in the valuation and financing of ventures. Financial markets offer a growing and increasingly complex array of investments, sold automatically with trading latencies measured in milli-seconds. The complexity of methods required for valuation of investments has grown even more rapidly. The time when ventures could be calculated on computer spreadsheets using published information and linear extrapolation is long since past, replaced by ever more mathematically sophisticated and computer-intensive approaches. One chapter is – unfortunately – insufficient for more than a very superficial review of these methods. Consequently, this chapter limits itself to much more modest objectives of:

- describing what decisions need to be made in valuation of projects for commercializing an innovation
- identifying the data that must be collected
- defining the objectives and outcomes that should be expected of financial analysis for innovative ventures.

Let's start by reviewing the role of the analyst, and the move to assessing tools and techniques that are available to make the case for funding – which could be through either external loans and venture capital, or internal funding with its implicit opportunity costs. The chapter references analysis techniques from finance and econometrics that are used to assess the financial viability of an innovation. The details of the techniques will fill a course of its own (or two), and thus we direct you to appropriate resources that you will need to effectively complete the financial analysis of your business plan.

THE ROLE OF FINANCIAL
ANALYSIS AND THE MARKET

Financial analysis and reporting play an essential role in a business' 'reporting–control' cycle. A firm's or project's performance is realized on many dimensions – profit, competitive positioning, strength of workforce and so forth. But only a few of these dimensions will capture the ongoing attention of management, and on even fewer of these dimensions does any particular stakeholder group possess levers of control.

For example, common stockholders of publicly traded firms are provided with audited financial reports each year, and quarterly unaudited financial reports. These are intended to provide them with the information they need for decisions about whether to buy, hold or dispose of their inventory of the firm's stock. Stock sales and purchases are the only decisions shareholders can make unless they own enough shares to influence management. The specific financial 'statistic' that fixates shareholder attention is the stock price, which is presumed to be correlated with earnings, assets and other reported measures (although during the dot-com boom, curiously this correlation was often negative). Time plays an important role, because shareholders' objectives are directed towards maximizing future returns – the percentage stock price increase per year.

All of this should suggest that, in practice, identifying the relevant financial

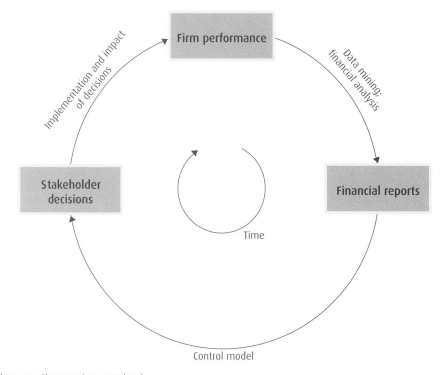

Figure 11.1 The reporting–control cycle

information that will satisfy stakeholders' decision making is not a simple task. Financial reporting directed just toward the simple task of buying and selling stock is extensive and costly. The more complex and nuanced decisions involved in managing a firm's operations require the sophistication of advanced managerial and budgetary accounting models – and ample quantities of subjective managerial 'judgement'.

Financial reporting is complex in a going concern; it grows even more complex in a new venture, because there are no ongoing operations, market outlets or precedents to guide decision makers. The need for financial information is even greater for innovations than for existing products and services.

FINANCIAL ANALYSIS FOR INNOVATIONS

Perhaps the most difficult task in selling any innovation is providing a convincing story of what the innovation is worth. Unfortunately, this task is not optional – if you expect someone to invest in your idea, they need to know where they will make their money; what will be their return on investment.

The analysis of business and asset value is an extensively researched and well-developed field of study. Economics, finance and accounting all boast sizeable groups of scholars and practitioners who research the assessment of corporate value. Nonetheless, most of them would readily admit the shortcomings of existing knowledge. We need look no further than the dot-com crash which began in mid-2000, and destroyed 80 per cent of the value of NASDAQ (the stock exchange on which most of these companies were quoted), and perhaps as much as US$9 trillion in wealth. The crash was driven by flawed financial analysis which inflated stock prices of unsustainable business models; it was inevitable after companies started to fail. More recently, a sharp decline in profits at several large firms that had previously announced moves to become more innovative raised alarm bells concerning the 'fad' of innovation.[2] Both of these situations are the result of flawed financial analyses that set unreasonable expectations, often for the wrong product or business model.

Several factors complicate an assessment of an innovation's value. First, by definition, an innovation is new, and thus there is no history of production or marketing to guide analysis; or if there is some, it will be incomplete and with very few datapoints.

Second, innovation business can be several orders of magnitude riskier than traditional business; the returns can commensurately be several orders of magnitude higher as well (see Table 11.1). Standard financial analysis methods tend to report a single 'value' figure for a business or asset – for example, saying that the business is worth $10 million. But when ideas and businesses have never been tried before, the high risk necessitates computing specific values for each potential outcome scenario – best case, worst case, case if test marketing fails, and so forth.

Finally, the actual drivers of an innovation and its business model are too often things that never appear in the financial statements – such as the size of the network externality, the rapidity with which the technology's performance improves, or the appeal of the brand. For that reason alone, forward-thinking firms like eBay now dedicate significant portions of their financial statements to the non-financial measures that dictate their firm's performance.

Rocket science and the reachability of goals[3]

In the summer of 1975 two Viking spacecraft were launched from Cape Canaveral. Their intended destination was Mars. On 20 July 1976 the Viking 1 Lander touched down at its predetermined destination, Chryse Planitia, while the Viking 2 Lander touched down at Utopia Planitia on the opposite side of the planet on 3 September 1976.

Mechanical and scientific challenges aside, the essential problem faced by the Viking engineers was getting these landers from Cape Canaveral to their Martian destinations. Engineers need to answer the question, 'Can you get there from here?' This is called the problem of reachability. Obviously if there were no way to reach Mars with existing technology, any other engineering problems would be irrelevant.

Even if the answer to the reachability question is 'yes' there is no guarantee that the trip can be made. The vehicle must be built with the proper controls in order to allow the chosen trajectory to be followed. It also needs systems to observe whether those controls have actually done what they are expected to do. The latter observability problem needs to be solved in order to keep the rocket ship on its proper trajectory by adjusting its controls in what engineers call a 'closed loop' system.

Fortunately, there is a tool called the Kalman filter that allows engineers to determine the optimal trajectory out of all trajectories possible, identifying the one that incurs some minimum combination of time, fuel and other scarce resources.

Well, it's not rocket science, but just about every country in the world is faced with trying to juggle two economic objectives: first, to achieve full employment without inflation, and second, to maintain a positive balance of international payments. These objectives need to be attained by manipulating controls such as interest rates and budget expenditures. It turns out that problems of reachability, observability and correct trajectories crop up in economics as well as in industry. To solve them, managers and planners turn to the Kalman filter.

Table 11.1: *The success rate in selected technology-intensive industries*

Industry	Innovation success rate %
Toys	1.0
Groceries	2.0
Music	2.0
Airlines	2.0
Mobile telephony	3.0
Financial services	3.0
Computer hardware	4.0
Computer software	4.0
Pharmaceuticals	7.5
Venture capital firms	31.0

Source: Doblin Group, quoted in 'The world's most innovative companies', *Business Week Special Report*, 26 April 2006.

Assessment of an innovation's value requires relevant data along with accurate models for assessing value. Since innovation strategies are often driven by non-financial factors – time to market, design quality, and so forth – the acquisition of data that is not in the public domain (as, for example, the data in audited financial statements) can be costly and error prone. Because, by definition, the business models of 'innovations' are somehow new, they cannot rely on past relationships and dynamics in forecasting future earnings flows.

Assessing the value of an innovation and its business model requires new sources of *business intelligence*, and *data mining* to acquire relevant data. Assessment also requires *forecasting methodologies* with a level of sophistication not previously seen in the valuation of traditional investments. The next sections of this chapter briefly survey how to identify and acquire relevant data for innovation value assessments. They briefly cover the objectives and reporting requirements of forecasting methods required to support the innovator's competition for venture funding. Finally, we discuss how the valuations demanded of innovation compare with existing valuation approaches, and with non-standard approaches such as brand-equity valuation and intangibles accounting.

STRATEGY DRIVERS AND FIGURES OF MERIT

Strategy drivers are the 'levers of control' that management uses to direct operations. Since the actual strategy drivers may not be directly observable (for instance, customer satisfaction can be observed only indirectly), they are measured through figures of merit – observable, sometimes synthetic, measures that move in tandem with the strategy drivers. For example, when you buy a computer, you can seldom be assured that it will perform well for your particular computing tasks; but a synthetic workload figure of merit like SPEC CPU2006, measuring the combined performance of the CPU, memory and compiler, can help you choose an appropriate price/performance package.

Our definition of innovation is 'invention that is commercialized' – an invention (or brand, or any other intangible asset) has no value until it is a component of some business model. Chapter 4 delineated the concepts and development of business models – these underlie the valuations placed on a particular invention. In practice, inventions are integrated into as many different business models as make sense, in the same way that organizations might try to sell a product to as many customer groups, for as many purposes as they can – that way it can justify longer production runs and economies of scale. Similarly an innovative software engine or video mechanism will be put into every marketable device it is suitable for.

Corporate figures of merit

When corporate executives are asked what the most important goal of their decision making should be, they seldom say profits. Markets may demand fast product cycles; technological leadership requires new patents; stockholders are concerned about the share price. Figure 11.2 reflects the priorities of one survey of executives. This alone should warn that value of a business model is not just about profits.

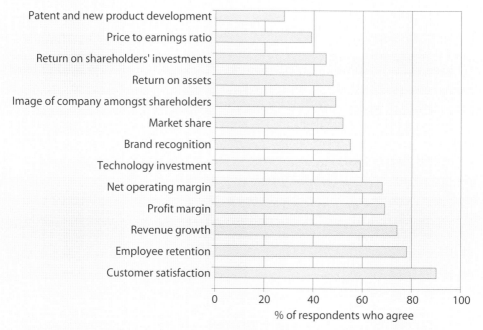

Figure 11.2 What is most important in firm decisions

Source: Results of a survey of 250 executives across industry on essential performance measures: Andrew Osterland, 'CFO's third annual Knowledge Capital Scorecard', *CFO Magazine*, 1 April 2001, p. 19.

The business model – and there may be several of them for any given innovation – is the basic unit of value analysis. One business model is given one set of valuations. For purposes of value assessment, we can ignore the larger strategic intricacies that motivate the choice of this particular business model, and consider only the value generation, and the strategy drivers – the specific features that are actively managed in the business model – that are responsible for creating value. The business value generated is a function of the values taken on by the strategy drivers over time. These drivers, in turn, are influenced by managerial strategy, by the intensity of competition, and by external factors in the competitive market such as advances in technology.

Both consumer markets and capital markets have their own distinct figures of merit that are used to assess the desirability and value of a particular investment proposition. You cannot manage what you cannot measure – and the success of a particular business model is ultimately measured by its performance on some figure of merit. In the current context, this is the metric we use to measure $Value_t$. The chosen figure of merit will reflect the objectives that got the organization into a particular business, and which motivated the R&D for the innovation to begin with. For example, the value of online auction software is likely to be judged on the size of the online community that it is able to develop; the value of a mail-order distribution channel might be measured on the percentage of the market that it is able to capture. Both of these measures of $Value_t$ are non-financial measures, but they ultimately have financial implications based on the cost–benefit structure of the business model. Management often considers such non-financial measures to be the primary objective of their investments (see the box on page 258).

THE ROI FIGURE OF MERIT

Certain financial figures of merit are widely encountered, and we shall review them here. The primary financial figure of merit is the annualized return on investment (ROI):

$$ROI = \frac{V_{t+1} - V_t}{V_t}$$

where V_t is the net value of an investment at time and V_{t+1} is the value one year later. Several factors influence investors' assessment of the *hurdle rate* – that is, the minimum ROI required for them to be willing to invest money. Investors are a type of consumer, but rather than paying a price p for something of value v received immediately (the product or service), they pay a price p for a promise to return $p+i$ next year. If v is not high enough, the consumer doesn't contract to trade; if i isn't high enough (that is, higher than the hurdle rate) then the investor will not contract to invest. One significant difference between investors and consumers is *risk*. The consumer's transaction is over instantly, but many things can happen to the investor's money in a year. For this reason, at any $p \leq v$ the consumer will trade; but the hurdle rate has to be strictly less than i to accommodate the risk of something happening in the coming year.

In addition to risk, the investor needs to consider exactly what is meant by 'value' and how to measure V_t and V_{t+1}. Not only are there several alternative definitions of value, but V_{t+1} is also a future value, and can only be guessed. It will be influenced by inflation, the risk that investors will not receive all of the proceeds from the investment, and the liquidity of the investment. Analysis of all of these issues is beyond the scope of this book, but you need to be aware that such issues are the reason that investment analysis, especially in speculative innovations, can become so complex.

Figures of merit: Shigeru Miyamoto's Wife-o-meter

One path to great innovation is to challenge the industry's figure of merit. Shigeru Miyamoto – master designer behind Nintendo's innovative and highly successful Wii console, and games like *Donkey Kong, Super Mario World* and *Goldeneye* – wanted in early 2006 to look beyond the traditional gaming market which was mainly competing on graphics speed and resolution. Rather than following the same old, but true, gaming conventions, Miyamoto started to think about games for the non-gamer – a class exemplified by his wife. To do this, he needed a new figures of merit for game and console performance, one that would measure how appealing a game is to someone who is normally a non-gamer. He called this the 'Wife-o-meter' – a whimsical measure of the strength of his wife's attraction or aversion to a particular game.

His first experiment with this new figure of merit revolved around the game *Nintendogs*. Observing the interaction between dogs and his wife, Miyamoto figured that a game about animal interaction could expand the gamer base. 'When I eventually showed *Nintendogs* to my wife, she finally started to look at video games in a different way', Miyamoto said. *Nintendogs* moved the Wife-o-meter up significantly, but Miyamoto knew he could do even better. The next major innovation for non-gamers was *Brain Age*, the brain training game originally marketed to the older

Japanese market as a way to stave off senility. 'Brain Age ... this is the game that turned my wife into a true gamer.'

Eventually, Mrs Miyamoto played *Wii Sports* and participated in the voting channel on her own, which Miyamoto said surprised him no end. 'This is a big event in my house, it would have been more expected for me to come home and find Donkey Kong eating at our table,' he said.

Miyamoto points out that Nintendo, unlike its competitors, is a company that is solely focused on the gaming experience and nothing else. The Wii, a risky proposition, was the combined effort from the entire company, and Miyamoto is extremely proud of the freedom given to designers thanks to the Wii Remote. For him, creative vision is paramount in creating a fun experience for the player. Miyamoto also hopes for games to promote communication. With Wii, people are playing together and exchanging ideas. Miyamoto has even created a Mii (pronounced 'me') channel to create custom avatars for players (called Miis) by selecting from a group of facial and bodily features based on Kokeshi, a form of Japanese doll used as souvenir gifts in Japan.

Miyamoto encourages the industry to 'always remember the human touch' when designing games. 'After all, if we can convert my wife, we can convert anyone.'[4]

Information assets

Microsoft founder Bill Gates once quipped that 'Our primary assets, which are our software and our software-development skills, do not show up on the balance sheet at all. This is probably not very enlightening from a pure accounting point of view.'[5] His point was that traditional financial accounting measures fail to capture the corporate wealth embodied in ideas, innovation and the potential for competition. Accounting concentrates on measuring the past. This is a far cry from the days when Vladimir Lenin assured his followers that 'Accounting and control have been simplified by capitalism to the utmost and reduced to extraordinarily simple operations – which any literate person can perform

– of supervising and recording, knowledge of the four rules of arithmetic, and issuing appropriate receipts.'[6]

Increasingly the assets of importance to industry – ideas, innovations and technology – are not accounted for. This is shown in Figure 11.3, which tracks the ratio of the book value of the firm that is computed on the financial statements, divided by the value that investors (who pay real money to own a portion of the firm) think that the firm is worth.

Up until the late 1970s, the total balance sheet valuation of the S&P 500 firms (which as the name suggests, are more heavy industry than high-tech start-up) hovered around their stock market

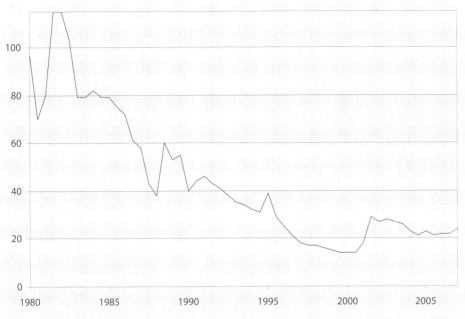

Figure 11.3 Book value against stock market capitalization of S&P 500 firms

Source: Compustat database.

valuation. But by the early 1980s, something unusual happened – the ratio of balance sheet assets to stock market value began to decline. By 1990 book value had declined to around 40 per cent of the market value; by 2000 it was at less than 20 per cent of the market value.

Since the market value is the value at which investors are willing to exchange cash for the real economic assets of the company, this must imply that book value is not measuring a substantial portion of the assets of the firm. These 'unmeasured' assets are the ideas, patents, skills and other intangibles of a modern enterprise. As intangible assets have become a larger and larger part of all business, and as non-linear effects such as technology acceleration and network effects influence markets, the value of a successful company is more and more dependent on its constant innovation. These innovations and the firm's ability to continually innovate are priced in the market valuation of the firm. Figure 11.4 shows how the importance of intangible assets varies in different industries.

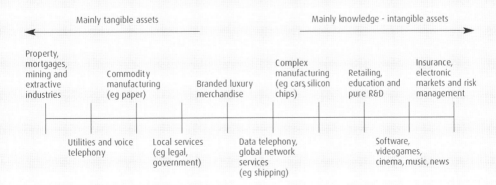

Figure 11.4 The role of intangibles and knowledge in various industries

THE PROFIT FIGURE OF MERIT

Central to ROI is the measurement of profit, defined as $V_{t+1} - V_t$. Profit serves a crucial function in a free-enterprise economy, where firms are presumed to behave in a profit-maximizing fashion. High profits are the signal that consumers want more of the output of the industry. High profits provide the incentive for firms to expand output and for more firms to enter the industry in the long run. For a firm of above-average efficiency, profits represent the reward for greater efficiency. On the other hand, lower profits or losses are a signal that consumers want less of the commodity and/or that production methods are not efficient. Profits provide the crucial signals for the reallo-cation of society's resources to reflect changes in technology, liquidity and customers' tastes over time.

Accounting profit refers to the revenue of the firm minus the explicit or accounting costs of the firm. *Explicit costs* are the actual out-of-pocket expenditures of the firm to purchase or hire the inputs it requires in production. These expenditures include the wages to hire labour, interest on borrowed capital, rent on land and buildings, and expenditure on raw materials. Economists extend this concept to define an *economic profit*, which equals the revenue of the firm minus its explicit costs and implicit costs. *Implicit costs* – including *opportunity costs* – refer to the value of the inputs owned and used by the firm in its own production processes.

Research metrics

Academics are required to publish as a central part of their job, but not all publication outlets are created equal. Publications are considered 'better' or 'worse' in loosely defined ways. Scholars have tried repeatedly to generate an unequivocal 'quality' metric for journals and their papers, so that their research output can be computed in terms of quantity x quality.

Over the past decade, the most important of these research metrics has been the ISI's Journal Impact Factor from publisher Thomson Scientific (which purchased ISI from founder Eugene Garfield in 1995). ISI's Impact Factor and accompanying citation counts have been arguably the most influential metrics for the hiring and firing of academics and researchers. Interestingly, like most metrics they can be 'gamed', and apparently are.

To get an idea of the benchmark for the Impact Factor, consider that the widely read and influential *Harvard Business Review* scored 1.148 in 2006; most business journals score around 0.500, and an Impact Factor of 1 is comparatively good. These benchmarks seem to be accurate for a broad swath

of academic journals. But several clusters of business and information science journals, for example, seem to be garnering Impact Factors in the range of 3 to 4 – several times higher than the *Harvard Business Review*. It turns out that editorial policy at these journals tends to strictly limit a paper's publication in the journal to a narrow group of topics, and to require their authors to extend their lists of citations with suggestions from the editorial board (lists of 90 citations for a single 20-page paper are not uncommon). Such editorial policies artificially inflate their own journal Impact Factor metrics, as well as the citation counts of individual papers in the journals for a small group of researchers.

Academics have recently seized on an alternative to Impact Factor and ISI citation counts in their use of citations counts from Google Scholar. Google Scholar's citation metrics are considered less prone to abuse because Google's counts represent actual lookups (which are difficult to manipulate) as opposed to gratuitous additions to lists, which can be influenced by journal editorial policy.

Opportunity costs include the salary that the entrepreneur could earn from working for someone else in a similar capacity (say, as the manager of another firm) and the return that the firm could earn from investing its capital and renting its land and other inputs to other firms. The inputs owned and used by the firm in its own production processes are not free to the firm, even though the firm can use them without any actual or explicit expenditures. Economic profit rather than accounting profit must be used in order to reach correct investment decisions.

Accounting measures V_t and V_{t+1} in terms of their book value; the difference $V_{t+1} - V_t$ is variously called net income, profit or accounting profit. But book value and accounting profit are increasingly seen as irrelevant to the valuation of assets – especially information assets. In 2007, for example, as we have seen, the average stock market value of an S&P 500 industrial company was over five times its accounting value. For that reason, analysts have adopted a varied set of alternatives. Often there is little agreement on which is best, and analysts are called upon to defend their particular figures of merit vis-à-vis those of the accounting profession, or those of other analysts.

Additionally, the natural rate of profitability differs significantly between industries. Indeed, the greatest draw of innovation, despite its myriad headaches, is profit that is significantly higher than average. Across industries, profit from innovations overall is about 1.5 to 3 times normal profit. But in certain industries such as electronics and software, radical innovations can be hundreds of times more profitable than incremental innovations or traditional products and services. In addition, they may be the only way for a firm to survive and thrive in the coming years. Firms in such industries as steel, textiles and rail transport generally earn very low profits both absolutely and in relation to the profits of firms in pharmaceutical, office equipment and other high-technology industries. Several theories attempt to explain these differences.

Firms will vary in their assessment of an appropriate measure of profit for various reasons. Firms require above-normal returns from economic profits to enter and remain in such fields as petroleum exploration with above-average risks. Similarly, the expected return on stocks has to be higher than on bonds because of the greater risk of the former.

Another economic theory suggests that profits arise as a result of friction or disturbances from long-run equilibrium. That is, in long-run, perfectly competitive equilibrium, firms tend to earn only a normal return (adjusted for risk) or zero (economic) profit on their investment. At any time, however, firms are not likely to be in long-run equilibrium and may earn a profit or incur a loss. For example, at the time of the energy crisis in the early 1970s, firms producing insulating materials enjoyed a sharp increase in demand, which led to large profits. With the sharp decline in petroleum prices in the mid-1980s, many of these firms began to incur losses. When profits are made in an industry in the short run, more firms are attracted to the industry in the long run, and this tends to drive profits down to zero, and leads to firms earning only a normal return on investment.

In other cases, monopoly firms can restrict output and charge higher prices than under perfect competition, thereby earning a profit. Because of restricted entry into the industry, these firms can continue to earn profits even in the long run. Monopoly power may arise from the firm's owning and controlling the entire supply of a raw material required for the production of the commodity, from economies of large-scale production, from ownership of patents, or from government restrictions that prohibit competition.

The innovation theory of profit postulates that (economic) profit is the reward for the introduction of a successful innovation. The US patent system is in fact designed to protect the profits of a successful innovator – at least temporarily – in order to encourage the flow of innovations. Inevitably, as other firms imitate the innovation, the profit of the innovator is reduced and eventually eliminated.

The *managerial efficiency theory of profit* relies on the observation that if the average firm (by definition) earns only a normal return on its investment in the long run, firms that are more efficient than the average would earn above-normal economic profits.

Rather than seeing these as competing economic theories of how to measure profit, the analyst should see them as differing models of how (and how much) value is generated in specific industries or by specific products and services. The point is that the measurement of V_t, V_{t+1}, and profit $V_{t+1} - V_t$, is complex, and at least partly a matter of informed judgement, industry and firm context, and macroeconomic influences.

Profits in the personal computer industry

In 1976, Steven Jobs and his friend Steve Wozniak developed a personal computer directed towards the hobbyist market. Initially advertised through word of mouth, sales of Apple computers grew rapidly from US$3 million in 1977 to more than $1.9 billion in 1986, with profits exceeding $150 million. Apple's success was not lost on potential competitors; more than 75 companies jumped into the personal computer market within a decade. Intense competition reduced profits from an average of 11.5 per cent of sales in to 1985 to around 6.5 percent in 1990. Since that time, PC prices have been falling by 20 to 40 per cent per year, and the PC has now become practically a commodity.

In 1985, Jobs was ousted from Apple's management after a power struggle with John Scully, who was president at the time. Jobs competed by introducing the innovative NeXT computer in 1986, while Apple, under Scully, went from one failed product to the next. Apple Computer purchased NeXT in 1997 for approximately US$400 million in cash (returned to the initial NeXT investors) and 1.5 million Apple shares (which went to Steve Jobs, giving him significant power over Apple's strategic direction). Jobs returned to Apple as a consultant in 1997, and by 2000 was CEO.

Jobs revived Apple by simplifying its confusing product line to a few basic models, by integrating technology developed at NeXT, and by introducing a succession of path-breaking designs and business models, including the iPod and the iTunes Music Store in 2003, which merged computing and entertainment.

Jobs's reward from the setting-up of Apple resulted from correctly anticipating, promoting and satisfying an important type of market demand. Competitors, attracted by the huge early profits, were quick to follow, thereby causing profits in the industry to fall sharply. In the process, however, more and more of society's resources were attracted to the computer industry, which supplied consumers with more functional, higher-quality personal computers at sharply declining prices.[7]

THE SALES REVENUE FIGURE OF MERIT

Economist William Baumol suggested that, to satisfy stockholders, managers of modern corporations seek to maximize sales after an adequate rate of return has been earned.[8] Baumol argued that a larger firm may feel more secure, may be able to get better deals in the purchase of inputs and lower rates in borrowing money, and may have a better image with consumers, employees and suppliers than its smaller rivals. He also noted that some studies have shown a strong correlation between executives' salaries and sales, but not between sales and profits (this point is contentious, as other studies have found the opposite). As a consequence, he has suggested that at least some companies – notably those in oligopolistic markets – would seek sales growth over profitability.

Figure 11.5 shows total revenue and cost curves for a hypothetical firm. The profit-maximizing firm would produce quantity 30; but a sales maximizing firm would operate at quantity of 50, where profit was approaching zero. The kink in the total cost curve reflects potential additional costs of extra shifts, quality problems, or perhaps outsourcing that can arise when the firm operates beyond its 'normal' levels.

STRATEGY MODELS

The value of an innovation lies in the future, and in the plans that management have for commercializing that innovation. Consequently, the valuation of that innovation demanded by potential investors and creditors must be based on a plausible case for its ability to generate future value.

The *strategy model* is the econometric forecasting counterpart to the *business model* presented in Chapter 4. As with the business model, the strategy model has two parts – a compelling *narrative story line* about how, why and when cash will be generated from the innovation, and a *forecasting model* that ties this out to the numbers. The strategy model is an extension of the business model; it is focused only on the main drivers of value generation (whereas the business model is likely to be more complex and nuanced, dwelling on technological, social and market issues as well).

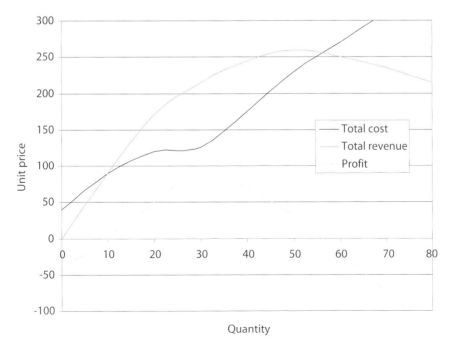

Figure 11.5 Sales maximization versus profit maximization

IBM and modern accounting

One of the most radical financial innovations in history was introduced on 7 April 1964. IBM revolutionized the industry with its S/360 line of computers, which became the mainstays of corporate accounting. IBM's S/360 had been up to that time the largest private venture in American history, with US$5 billion spent on five new plants and an additional 60,000 employees. The subsequent decade was marked by a sea change in the structure of corporate accounting departments. Within a decade, corporate accounting departments at Sears, Ford, GM, DuPont and other giants dwindled from huge 'bullpens' accommodating hundreds of clerks, to warrens of cubicles housing only 10 per cent to 20 per cent of their original number. Those who remained were dedicated to the care and feeding of IBM's computerized accounting systems.

In many ways, IBM's accounting revolution in the 1960s paralleled a similar gamble from 1930 to 1932, at the start of the Great Depression, when the company chose to continue producing at full capacity, and to spend $1 million on one of the first corporate research labs. In those days, IBM estimated that only 5 per cent of business accounting functions were mechanized. IBM quickly introduced the Type 405 Alphabetic Accounting Machine, the 600 series punch card machines, and a system of machines designed for the banking industry. Continued production during the Depression ensured that only IBM was capable of handling the massive volumes required of Social Security accounting, which arose in the mid-1930s.

Figure 11.6 shows that a given innovation's strategy model consists of three submodels:

▸ a behavioural model based on what is known about the firm's prior behaviour (or some similar firm's prior behaviour)
▸ a forecast model which lays out the future project scenario on a real options format for the innovation project
▸ a discounting model which articulates an attitude to the time value of money.

In this structure, the forecast model sets out the firm's plans for innovation R&D and market entry, the behavioural model assures that it makes realistic assumptions about demand and costs, and the discounting model describes how aggressive it will be in demanding repayment of investments.

The last part – the discounting model – is often glossed over in traditional cash flow analysis; the rule of thumb is to use a risk-free rate. In venture capital, though, both risk and impatience may be embedded in the discount, and it is common to see hurdle rates of 40 per cent to 70 per cent in venture capital investments. There is also evidence that in practice, managers act as if they demand substantially higher discounts than the risk-free rate. Thus it should be required that assumptions concerning discounting be made explicit upfront when dealing with risky and uncertain high-technology and innovation ventures.[9]

THE BEHAVIOURAL MODEL

Any pitch for funding of a new and innovative product or service will revolve around a single question – 'Where do the investors make their money?' Venture capitalists, banks,

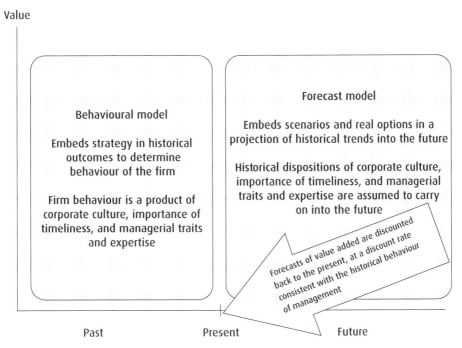

Figure 11.6 Components of the strategy model

shareholders, family, or whoever else is asked to put money into a new business are concerned about how money is to be generated in the future, and how much of it they will receive from their investment. The forecast model tells the story that ties the salient operating and business characteristics of an innovation to the generation of money in the future. If this linkage cannot be articulated clearly, it is unlikely that the innovation will be of interest to investors. Advances in technology, and especially the phenomenal expansion of the internet over the past decade, have made possible a vastly expanded set of available strategies for new business. (These are discussed at greater length in Chapter 13.) Just as important is the fact that 'ideas' have become more important than 'things' in driving value.

The behavioural model describes the 'behaviour' of the firm in generating value, given particular 'stimuli' by management. Management has only limited control over firm performance. For example, it can influence the product mix and level of output from its assembly lines; but it generally cannot influence exchange rates, the price of raw materials or the global economy. Yet the corporation's success depends on both controllable and uncontrollable 'drivers' of value.

Management's formula for generating future value is likely to differ from its plans in the past. Future strategies will also change depending on contingent events in the future. Thus at best the past can tell us how the firm will react to specific management inputs. This reflects what might be characterized as the corporate 'culture'.

MySpace's market entry

MySpace has arguably been one of the great business successes based on Web 2.0 (social networking and data mash-up) technologies. MySpace was launched by the former ResponseBase team within Intermix, a group with a strong background in direct email marketing and CPA tactics. Their entry used both traditional and cost per acquisition (CPA) campaigns through established online brands. In less than three years, MySpace leapfrogged early social networking leader, Friendster, to become one of the top five most visited sites in the United States, with 48 million unique visitors and 27 billion page views in June 2006. While it will probably never come close to the profitability of Google, eBay or Yahoo, it has become a very profitable provider of internet platform technology.

Chris DeWolfe and Tom Anderson came to Intermix – the developer of MySpace –through the acquisition of ResponseBase. Much of the ResponseBase team had formerly come from X-drive as well, so they had a background in both online consumer services and direct marketing. After witnessing the initial success of Friendster and having the ResponseBase/Intermix resources at their disposal, they thought they could create a strong competitor. ResponseBase had a database of around 100 million email addresses, and Intermix had a number of internet sites directed at teenagers, the MySpace target market.

MySpace took three months to build a site with similar features to Friendster, launching at the end of 2003. DeWolfe and Anderson started promoting MySpace by running a cash prize contest for Intermix's 250 employees, asking them to invite friends to use the site. This had some success, but was limited to reaching only a certain size. MySpace then began promoting the site offline, sponsoring parties in Los Angeles with clubs, bands and party promoters. This began to build the buzz around the site, but more importantly attracted offline groups of people to use the site together.

DeWolfe and Anderson were not only clever in market entry, but adept at responding to teenagers' needs, and adaptively executing their entrance strategy. When small community groups of 100 to 1000 people started creating group profile pages around interests and associations, MySpace accepted this behaviour where Friendster did not. MySpace listened to user feedback and quickly iterated the product with rapid development cycles. MySpace added blogs, comment boards, message boards and IM, long before Friendster was able to upgrade its product given scalability issues. It was also much better at addressing poor site performance (a normal problem in scaling up) whereas Friendster was not.

Small community groups were critical for the viral marketing that propelled MySpace to success. Once this initial audience had been established, they leveraged Intermix's media buying and channel relationships, propelling it to number one status. It is unlikely that MySpace would have grown as fast as it did without employing this more traditional marketing tactic. Once MySpace reached its current scale of operations, its continued success could almost be guaranteed, as existing users drew in their friends through viral marketing based on photos, chat and 'my spaces'.

How much information is in a dataset?

In the mid-1930s Claude Shannon established the field of information theory, counting among his many contributions some of the more successful early algorithms for casino gambling and computer chess as well as a formalization of the quantity of information in any collection of data.[10]

In a business context, Shannon's view of information can be described in terms of implementing a strategy and observing the consequent outcome (see Figure 11.7).

Assume that a strategy B is chosen with probability P(B), and outcome A occurs with probability P(A). Then the information that management has about the outcome of control strategy B is P(A|B). Conversely, if we observe outcome A, the probability that management had implemented B is P(B|A). According to Shannon, the information about B that is contained in the dataset, message or observation A is

$$I(A,B) \equiv \log_b \frac{P(B|A)}{P(B)}$$

The logarithmic base b is arbitrary and serves to define a unit for I. If $b = 2$ is used, the unit for I is the 'bit' (by far the most common unit used). If base 10 is used in definition of information I then the unit for I is the 'hartley', in honour of Ralph Hartley who first proposed a logarithmic measure of information.[11]

Shannon information measures the 'distance' between two probability densities P(B|A) and P(B). If the two are the same, the 'distance' is zero, implying that A provides no information about B.

There are other measures of the distance between two densities, and these are also called 'information' measures: there are the Fisher, Wooters, Renyi, Tsallis, Hellinger and Kullback-Leibler information measures, to name a few.

Most financial information is highly multi-colinear, meaning that the data contained in additional balance sheet or income statement accounts generally does not provide much new information about the business. This problem arises first because of the double entry system, which replicates exactly the same journal information in two different accounts, one debit and one credit. Second, it arises because different account entries will reflect the same transaction at different times in the transaction cycle. For example, a purchase will create journal entries for accounts payable, cash disbursements and inventory increment and decrement – all of them for the same transaction but at different times in its life-cycle. Thus the actual information content of a fixed-sized set of data items from a corporate financial dataset may vary widely between firms or even between time periods. Being able to measure the actual amount of information in the data collected for forecasting provides guidance in collecting additional data needed for risk reduction, as well as assurance that existing datasets are adequate for the financial analysis at hand.

In building the behavioural model, our problem is to figure out how much our historical outcomes A from manipulating particular controllable strategy drivers can tell us about the potential for a given strategy B to generate value in the future. The strategy itself will be a given configuration of values

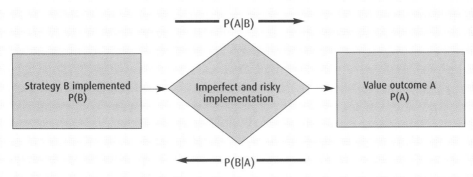

Figure 11.7 Shannon's model of information

of controllable strategy drivers, based on predictions of the exogenous strategy drivers. So assuming that these strategy drivers have yielded specific outcomes in the past, we can set particular values of the drivers *in order to* predict the future generation of value. This prediction will only be as good as the information in the historical observations A. This is where Shannon information comes in; it can predict how good is our dataset of historical observations (typically a set of financial statements augmented with a collection of non-financial data).

Shannon information measures the amount of information provided by the behavioural model about value generated by the strategy model. This provides a general measure of the effectiveness of a strategy.

The effectiveness that is ultimately 'achievable' will vary between industries, contingent on the riskiness of those industries.

In general, measures of minimum achievable risk and information measures are inversely correlated. For example the inverse of Fisher information gives the Cramer–Rao lower bound on variance.

In practice, distributional information about B is unknown, and cannot be discovered from a finite dataset. Thus probability densities P(B|A) and P(B) are unknown, and I(A,B) must be computed indirectly. This is done by computing the *average* of information I(A,B) over all possible values. Further information on these calculations can be found in the readings at the end of this chapter.

Such behaviour can be characterized in a simple and inherently limited, but formal linear equation:

$$V_t = Value_t = f_t(\{strategy\ drivers\}) = f_t(\{controllable\ SD;\ exogenous\ SD\})$$

where *Value*$_t$ is a set of historical values of the figure of merit, and {*strategy drivers*} (SD) are historical values of a set of strategy drivers that is partitioned into those that can be controlled by management decisions (such as factory output) and those that are out of management's control, and thus are usually predicted when making decisions (such as foreign currency exchange rates). This is the firm's behavioural model.

It is desirable that the behavioural model be as simple as possible, yet predict as much of the variation in value as possible. The model is also constrained by the data available. For example, published financial data on public firms is quite easy to obtain from databases such as the US Securities and Exchange Commission's EDGAR. It is also constrained by paucity of data. For traditional firms, it is often hard to justify forecasts based on more than 10 years of historical data, because of changes in the business environment and competition. With innovations and firm start-ups, there is often no historical data; you may be lucky enough to find a similar firm that can serve as a benchmark for the start-up or innovation project. But the risk of building models based on someone else's experience is substantially larger than the risk with basing the model on historical data.

Given a set of historical values for a single figure of merit *V* and *n* corresponding strategy drivers s_i from the firm (or a benchmark firm if this is a start-up), the initial strategy model is the linear formula:

$$V = \beta_0 + \beta_1 s_1 + \ldots + \beta_n s_n$$

The most useful strategy models will be comprised of between one to five strategy drivers. Some of the strategy drivers will be controllable, and for the forecast model, will be set by management's plan. The rest will be exogenous, and must be predicted.

A detailed exploration of the statistical methods available to simplify the strategy model is beyond the scope of this book, but exploratory and data reduction approaches such as stepwise regression provide useful tools for developing an optimal behavioural model from historical data. In addition, techniques to identify and characterize autocorrelation in historical behaviour (for example, how much last year's changes in output affected value generated this year) can profoundly lower risk in forecast models. The error in calculation can be assessed by the coefficient of determination R^2 of the behavioural model. R^2 – the proportion of variability (that is, the variance, or equivalently, sum of squares) in the data that is accounted for by the behavioural model – indicates the potential risk in building a forecast model based on this behavioural model.

The MySpace strategy model

What drives MySpace's success? The short answer is teenagers – the site's target audience. The longer answer tells us how they use the site: for communicating with friends, creating their best possible personal 'image' ('my space') on the web, and sharing pictures (MySpace allowed users to add more pictures to their pages than other sites, through third party services like PhotoBucket and ImageShack).

Thus for financial analysis, we might conclude that:

Value generated = f(social networking)

or

Value generated = f(unique visitors, page views)

But these are not directly controllable by managerial decisions, nor are they particularly easy to measure.

Instead, we would like to compute value as something that can be controlled by management strategy – a true strategy model.

Value generated = f(features for communication; 'image' creation features; picture-sharing features)

And we would look for metrics to measure the quantity and quality of features for communication, 'image' creation features and picture-sharing features. This model also benefits from a network effect that could conceivably be incorporated into the model. This will give us a 'steady state' strategy model, but will fail to capture all the uncertainty of start-up. Thus we could use such a formula to estimate the revenues that could be generated say one or two years after start-up, when the MySpace community had reached a critical mass.

THE FORECAST MODEL

Real options

Some investment decisions give the manager an unprecedented level of 'flexibility' in contracting. This 'flexibility' can take different forms – the ability to change the rate of production, defer development or abandon a project. Traditional project valuation approaches, such as discounted cash flow (DCF), are biased towards binary choice – invest *now*, or forever hold your peace. *Options contracts*, introduced in Chapter 8, in contrast will allow that choice to be taken up to some specified time in the future.

An important form of flexibility is the ability to make 'follow-on' investments. For example, start-ups are often required to prove a technology concept and market in stages, funded by multiple rounds of financing. Venture capitalists may use this to encourage value creation, ensure good management, and protect themselves against downside risk. The first right of refusal for a later stage of financing is often written into the investment contract. This is management's equivalent to the securities market 'call option' – which is a contractual right, but not an obligation, to purchase some number of shares at a price and time in the future at an agreed price.[12]

Real options are about modelling both decisions and uncertainties related to investments. In real options the focus is on options, decisions that are made after some uncertainties have been resolved, but this time the options involve 'real' assets as opposed to financial ones. For example, in wildcat oil drilling, an option would allow a company to gather information about a prospective oil field before deciding whether to 'exercise its option' and drill the prospect.

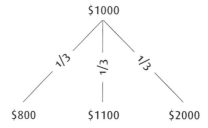

Figure 11.8 Option with three possibilities

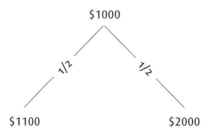

Figure 11.9 Option with two possibilities

Management typically invests in assets that will be used to generate a profit. Sometimes, though, management will invest in an opportunity to do business, without putting money into assets in place. Such opportunities might arise from a one-time opportunity to enter a foreign market, enter into a strategic alliance or acquire a one-of-a-kind asset. Management may have no firm intention of using these opportunities at the time of purchase, but want to retain the option to profit from them in the future. In these situations, discounted cash flow analyses are too simplistic to produce accurate valuations.[13]

Consider the following example comparing a DCF valuation to a real options valuation of the same project (see Figures 11.8 and 11.9). Say that the investment decision extends over two periods – today (period 1) and a year from today (period 2). Assume a $1000 investment today will generate cash inflows next year that discounted to today's dollars are either $800, $1100 or $2000 with equal probability. This gives expected return of $300 = ($800 + $1100 + $2000)/3 – $1000. But what if the manager can delay the investment until next year, and avoid investing if cash inflows turn out to only be $800? If the manager waits and gathers information (that is, what is only being forecast in the DCF model), he or she might discover that the expected return is $550= ($1100 + $2000)/2 – $1000. This 'real option' to defer the decision until next year is worth $250 = $550 – $300 (that is, the difference between the two expected returns) today.

Real options pricing has received mixed appraisals for two reasons. First, it requires the collection and forecasting of more parameters than alternative approaches; and second, it has usually been prescribed as an all-in-one alternative to DCF. The first objection is unavoidable, but really only involves estimation of one additional parameter – project option risk. Since there will be no history of accounting data for most investments that fit the 'flexible' real options criteria, it will be difficult to provide any objective basis for the estimation of risk.

The second objection arises in practice because option pricing does not fit naturally into most companies' existing capital budgeting systems. Decision-tree analysis, simulation and scenario analysis are typically offered as alternatives to real options approaches, but tend to suffer from similar problems. In general, real options approaches must be run in parallel with DCF approaches.

Real options approaches start by assuming that most investment opportunities have embedded in them a series of managerial options. For example, in an imaginary oil company, management may believe that they have found an oil field, but know neither how much oil it contains nor what the price of oil will be once they are ready to pump. A prudent hedge would simply put enough money down to buy or lease the land and explore. If no oil is found, they can cap their outlays at the costs already sunk. If they do strike oil, however, they might invest a bit more and put the drilling gear in place. But suppose the oil price then plummets. Management could put the project on hold and let the field lie fallow. Perhaps they could also switch to producing gas instead of oil. Or they could drop the project and sell the land, perhaps as farmland. If, on the other hand, the oil price goes up, the firm is ready to pump. Since oil prices and other factors are uncertain, in other words, the mere option to produce has value.

Real options analyses tend to draw heavily on analogies with financial options, which apply the Black–Scholes formula for valuing a European call option – specifically an option to buy an asset at a specific date in the future. Where management is not constrained to exercising the option at specific times, other formulas exist – formulas for American options, compound options and 'rainbow' options can be used in more complicated situations. A common theme in these models is the use of continuous-time stochastic processes and frequent decision making. The models are often formulated using the language of stochastic differential equations, and solved using binomial trees or lattices, which are, in essence, recombining decision trees or dynamic programs. Because of the difficulties in solving these models, real options analyses usually focus on the evolution of a few (one or two) stochastic factors that determine the value of the investment over time, and the cash flows are usually simple functions of these factors. The models thus tend to focus on 'dynamic complexity' at the expense of 'detail complexity'.

This is in contrast to more direct and simple corporate decision analysis models which tend to consider great detail the cash flow and many uncertainties, but include relatively little in the way of dynamic decision making or downstream decisions. Although downstream decisions are something decision analysts know about, they are frequently overlooked or over-simplified in the analyses. Too often, decision models consider only a single decision made up front – such as what strategy to choose – without considering the opportunities for later adjustments or changes in the strategy.

SCENARIO ANALYSIS AND DECISION TREES

The real options approach assumes that pivotal managerial decisions are made, and that an uncertain world subsequently unfolds, either rewarding or punishing that decision. The real options decision tree assumes that the manager makes a decision, then finds out what happens. This fails when the manager finds out what happens (or at least guesses what might happen) prior to making a decision. In this case, scenario analysis and decision trees are better suited for the task of dealing with uncertainty. There are a number of easy-to-use programs that support scenario analysis and decision tree approaches to valuation.

MONTE CARLO SIMULATIONS

Where decision trees become especially complex, perhaps growing into involved networks of options and decisions, simple decision tree software may meet its limits. The mathematics of mixing random variables in any degree approaching the real structure and transaction flows in business is daunting, if not impossible to implement in practice. For this reason, analysts may choose to use Monte Carlo simulations to compute complex forecasts involving the interplay of multiple random variables. Unfortunately, each of these individual components can become a major source of error. Their combined effect can easily swamp the entire simulation.

There exists extensive empirical evidence on the statistical behaviour of account balances, accounting errors and accounting transactions that have showed that these are both right-skewed and highly kurtotic. Sums and differences of accounting errors are neither stationary nor well behaved. Interactions between skewed and kurtotic errors and accounts tend to multiply any uncertainties. Even though Monte Carlo simulation may in theory allow the solution of forecasting problems that are not mathematically tractable, it fails in practice because errors swamp out any valid forecasts. The forecast error of a simulation is often orders of magnitude larger than the cash or income flows forecast, rendering these forecasts useless for valuation. In such situations, valuations become hyper-sensitive to new data, changing several hundreds of per cent with even small changes in income or investment transactions.

REAL OPTIONS IN INNOVATION STRATEGY

Real options assume that future performance will not be the result of a series of smooth future cash flows, as with, say, a traditional investment such as a bank's mortgage contract. Rather cash flows will be contingent on future events or management decisions which may or may not occur and are uncertain in timing and amount. When properly constructed, real options models can help us make informed decisions about how much to invest, when to invest, and expected returns or losses on projects as a whole.

Innovations distinguish themselves from more conventional investments in three ways:

▸ Technology development and marketing both need intense, adaptive management.
▸ There is no history of investment performance which might yield insights in the value of the innovation.
▸ The potential value of the innovation depends on future events and managerial decisions which cannot be foreseen.

This sets up impediments to commercializing an innovation which can make resource planning and investment extremely difficult. Innovations are inherently riskier, with added risk compensated for by high returns – research suggests on average about three to four times as great as traditional products and services, but significantly higher for 'blockbusters'.

Successful innovators minimize their expenditures as they adapt their execution towards a successful launch of their product or service, in much the same way that investors manage risk and expense via stock options. Options allow the acquirer to write a contract to execute a sale or purchase at a specific price within some future time frame. If the contract is profitable at a future date then the option is executed; if not, it is not, and the investor bears a small out of pocket cost for writing the option contract.

Similarly, successful innovators rarely spend money when expenditures can be delayed or avoided. The problems facing innovators both inside and outside the firm are similar – they are expected to maximize return on a highly risky investment, and tend to accomplish this by being stingy with cash. Corporations worry about the opportunity costs (the lost revenue from other more profitable uses of the investment money); banks, venture capitalists and stock investors worry about the returns on their out-of-pocket investments.

With real options, both groups can realize the upside potential of an innovation, while protecting themselves from the inherent higher risk of loss that innovations entail. Often the real options approach is imposed by corporations and investors themselves through tranches (portions of the total investment) that are made available after specific milestones – such as proof of concept – are reached. If an investment yields information that demonstrates the viability of the opportunity, the investor can proceed with further investments with more confidence than if the earlier investment had not been made. Because the insight and experience gained by investing in an option is captured only if the initial investment is made, learning from options investments can give an edge over competitors, who won't be privy to the knowledge because they have not experienced the same learning.

The behavioural model establishes the 'levers of control' that are available to management to influence future corporate value generation. But the future will be most strongly impelled by the actual plans that management implements, and the contingencies on which they pivot. In nearly every new product or change initiated by the innovation, management is confronted with an array of scenarios, each demanding a unique response in structuring the business model.

Fortunately situations such as these are amenable to the real options approach. From a standpoint of financial analysis, such an array of scenarios and the managerial responses they elicit or demand can most simply be shown as a decision tree (see Figure 11.10).

Figure 11.10 shows a decision tree with branches occurring upon particular events. In practice the decisions might take place at a fixed time, upon completion of some milestone event (perhaps completion of some task), or on the occurrence of some contingent event (such as whether the price of oil hits $60 a barrel). Whatever the case, between consecutive points in time, the value-generating business model that management implements can be expected to remain unchanged. After the event, one of two possible business models will reflect management's response to the outcome of the event.

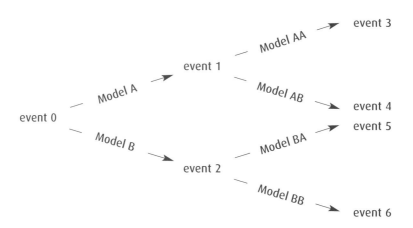

Figure 11.10 Hypothetical decision tree with milestones at t=1 and t=2

We wind up with a sequence of discounted value flow analyses (similar to DCF, but with the added latitude to define a unique value metric appropriate for the innovation and its business model).

The models on each individual branch will be made up of planned levels of controllable strategy drivers; and predicted levels of those that management cannot control. These planned or predicted values will be determined in response to the event at the beginning of the branch.[14]

Forecasts

Physicist Nils Bohr once quipped that 'prediction is very difficult, especially if it's about the future'. Nearly all attempts at valuation need to rely on some guessing about the future – and because of that, it *is* very difficult. Even financial accounting which is primarily concerned with tracking historical transactions needs to make forecasts of the future life of assets in order to compute depreciation. Whether or not a valuation method is or is not a forecast method is one of degree. Figure 11.11 compares various valuation methods and the degree to which they are involved in future (forecast) or historical valuation; and the degree to which they are appropriate for valuing tangible physical assets, versus intangible assets (such as ideas, innovations or abilities).

Good forecasting involves making educated guesses. Good forecasts satisfy four criteria:

▸ *Non-arbitrary*: Forecasting methodology defines a clear role for data, model drivers, assumptions and hypotheses, which will be applied consistently from analysis to analysis. We can minimize these biases by using a standard formal methodology which encourages four traits of good research:
 – explains observed phenomena
 – is consistent with previously established knowledge
 – is verifiable by other parties with access to the same data
 – stimulates further discussion, investigation, and revision as data become available.
▸ *Collective*: Forecasts should be easily understood by others, and their assumptions stated clearly enough to assure that others can replicate their conclusions.
▸ *Reliable*: Forecasts can be relied upon to make decisions. Reliability implies not only a specified degree of accuracy in financial reporting, but a clear idea of how accurate the reported numbers are through reporting of a dispersion statistic – for example, variance or standard deviation – to measure the reliability of the reported value.
▸ *Consistent and robust*: Forecasts will not change in the absence of fundamental information. Robust methods limit variability and ensure that different analysts using similar data produce similar valuations, or where they are different, can clearly explain the assumptions that account for that difference.

This sort of valuation analysis is common in financial analysis – the representation is called a binomial variance lattice representation of a real options problem – and the problem is that of finding the value of management's real option. In financial options analysis, there are multiple methodologies and approaches used to calculate an option's value, including closed-form equations like the Black–Scholes model and its modifications, Monte Carlo path-dependent simulation methods, lattices, variance reduction and other numerical techniques, and partial-differential equations (of which the Black–Scholes model is but one solution). Binomial lattices are easy to implement and easy to explain. In the limit, results obtained through the use of binomial lattices tend to approach those derived from closed-form solutions.[15] Furthermore, the process of graphing management's options in a binomial lattice adds clarity to the planned sequence of market positioning, entry and performance evaluation tasks that were outlined in Chapter 8.

The path through the real options in Figure 11.12 generates value over time, and that value can be graphed. Additionally, recall from the behavioural model that we defined not only the impact of the strategy drivers on value creation, but also the variability. The greater this variability, the more imprecise the forecast will be, and the more risky investment in the innovation will be. So if we graph the value generated by management's decisions, we would define the value generated by the innovation and its business model as an area that lies between its upper and lower statistical confidence bounds. Furthermore, we can discount these future bounds back to the present, and say that the expected present value of the innovation and its business model lies between two numbers. The further apart the numbers are, the riskier the project is.

Consider two possible outcomes of the real options analysis (see Figure 11.13). The first graph shows a business model with modest value generation, but where the confidence bounds are close together, so there is some assurance of what value might be generated. The second graph shows a much riskier, but potentially higher return investment.

The expanding range of possible values between the confidence limits (the two lines extending into the future) is called a 'value cone', and describes the risk profile of the particular business model that management designs to promote the innovation. The value cone reflects the projection of the variability in the behavioural model into the future. It is in general expanding because forecasting errors are compounded as we move further into the future. Any misestimation of value generation next year will incorrectly forecast the path of development of the business model, and that misforecast will in turn create even greater forecast errors in the subsequent years. Forecast errors result because, first, we have incomplete control over the drivers of value creation, and second, we have imperfect knowledge about exogenous events that influence the success of the business.[16]

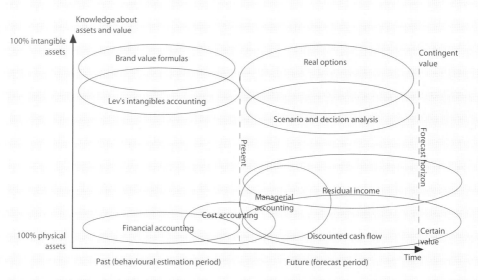

Figure 11.11 Various methods of valuation

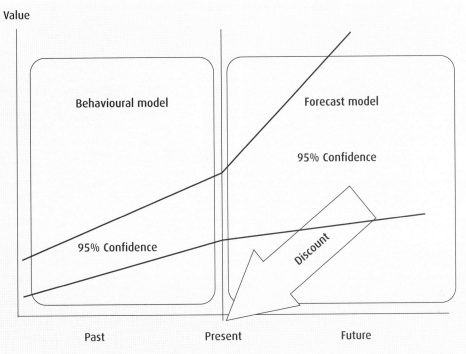

Figure 11.12 Value cone of the business model

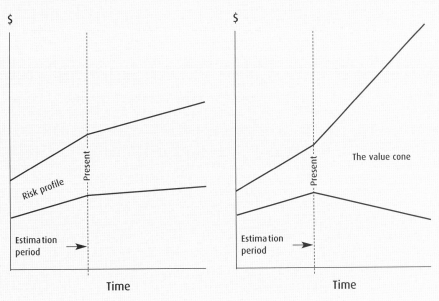

Figure 11.13 A 'safe' low-return investment versus a 'risky' higher-return investment

DISCOUNT MODEL

The forecast models just discussed generate estimates and confidence bounds for value flows that will be generated from the business surrounding the innovation over a series of future time periods. In order to obtain a present value for the business (or more correctly, a pair of confidence limits for the present value), it is necessary to discount the future values back to the current value (see Figure 11.12). This is done by summing all the future values generated in future periods t by a discount factor $1/(1 - r)^t$, where r is the discount rate for each period. The discount rate r can be viewed as either a measure of management's impatience – how quickly they want to get their investment back – or an opportunity cost – a measure of potential return from other investment opportunities which were foregone in order to fund this innovation business. From either perspective, deciding on the appropriate discount rate can be difficult. There is an extensive literature in finance that addresses the selection of discount rates. A detailed review is beyond the scope of this text, but we shall briefly look at some of the more important considerations here.

Because debt and equity financing may involve different levels of risk and return (among other things, the two are treated differently in taxation), it is typical to find that one or the other is more appropriate for a firm's particular business model. DCF methods often recommend a weighted average cost of capital (WACC) discount rate which considers the tax advantage from debt financing:

$$r_{WACC} = \frac{D}{D + E} r_D (1 - \tau) + \frac{E}{D + E} r_E$$

where D is the amount of corporate debt, E is the amount of corporate equity, and τ is the tax rate (estimated or target rate for future earnings). The cost of debt r_D and the cost of equity r_E are both opportunity costs (since they are being applied to future value flows), each with its own time value and risk premium. This general form can be extended to more complex capital structures by adding more summation terms, multiplying yields by 'weights' $x/D + E + \dots$ and tax adjustments.

Historical values for r_D may be found in the company's financial reports, or external benchmarks may be derived from treasury bill rates or other government debt. The historical discount rates simply provide a baseline for choice of a discount rate or managerial target for the particular business model at hand. Discount rates for equity financing are a bit harder to assess, but convention uses the capital asset pricing model or its variant, the arbitrage pricing model, to compute yield based on historical correlation with the market.

Other approaches tend to try to quantify management's 'impatience' and possibly also some measures of risk aversion, and then implant them into the discount rate applied to valuing a business model. Venture capitalists, for example, may apply an arbitrary rate, perhaps as high as 40 per cent to 60 per cent annually for new start-ups. This high rate reflects both a desire for quick repayment on their investment, and the high risk of failure of start-ups. Evidence exists that managers may use similarly high rates for internal company investments, although the reasons are different. In internal investment, it is common to periodically rank proposed projects (for instance, annually during budget setting), and determine how much out of a fixed size fund might be allocated to each project. All projects considered need to offer returns on investment greater than some 'hurdle rate' (often set as the return offered by external investments). But since only the highest return projects will be selected because of the fixed size of the budget, the return on projects actually implemented may be very high – again, above 40 per cent.

Another bias derives from upwardly mobile managers who may see themselves holding a particular divisional position for only a short period of time, and are looking for the maximum project payback in that short period. Thus they will be biased towards selecting projects that can generate a lot of near-term cash flow, as opposed to projects that have long-term strategic importance. In all of these cases, where innovations are developed into new businesses, it is likely that management will assign relatively high discount rates to assessing their present value – discount rates that are often above 40 per cent annually.[17]

TERMINAL DIVIDEND

Anyone used to traditional DCF analysis is familiar with the 'terminal dividend' in that analysis set-up. DCF analysis usually assumes a forecasting horizon – a time after which forecasting is considered to be too error-prone or speculative to be useful. So speculation beyond this horizon is halted, and replaced with a terminal dividend that reflects not a cash payment as such, rather an estimate of the market value. The terminal dividend is either the value of an annuity payable into perpetuity, or some price/earnings multiple. However it is computed, the horizon is typically far enough in the future that the terminal value presents only a small portion of total present value (although this assumption was widely abused during the dot-com boom). The approach was promoted in a popular finance text back in the 1960s, and called the Gordon growth model after the text's author.[18]

The assumption of a terminal dividend is typically irrelevant in analysis of innovations because of high risk, short product cycles and demands for quick payback. All of these tend to raise managerial 'impatience' and thus the required hurdle rate for investments in innovation-based business models. High discount rates reduce any value generated past the forecast horizon to negligible amounts. Consequently there is no need to calculate a terminal dividend for most innovation-based businesses.[19]

FURTHER STUDY

The preceding has merely sketched out the approach that must be taken to construct credible valuations of any business model that might be proposed to commercialize an innovation. Only the simplest calculations have been touched upon. The finance literature is extensive, well developed and mathematically complex. All of the approaches presented in this chapter can be extended and made much more accurate by the application of available techniques. The study of these techniques (and new ones appear in the academic journals every day) is a topic for a degree in itself, and is far beyond the scope of the current text. But the fundamental approaches that are tailored to the character and availability of information useful for commercializing innovations are fundamentally as outlined in this chapter.

Scenario analysis

All human experience is expansive and omnidirectional, including the future. Because the future is not linear, you cannot prepare for it with one single plan. To harvest profits in the future, you should have several alternative plans based on improbable as well as probable future events. Think of future profits as future fruit. Having only one scenario is like planting one strawberry instead of a whole field of possible strawberries. Scenarios, like strawberries, may spoil. If you have only one scenario and it spoils, you have a problem.

The year 2005 was strangely reminiscent of 1973. In that earlier time, Henry Kissinger suggested to the Shah of Iran that Iran could pay for its expensive US-made military equipment by rationing production and increasing the price of its oil. In short order the world was hit by an oil shortage and a sudden quadrupling of prices. Oil companies were caught by surprise, except for one: Royal Dutch Shell. It had realized that improbable events can take place without warning, and that such events demand swift and sure management, ideas and decisions. Its staff had prepared several different future scenarios, from 'boom or bust' to 'constrained growth', to address any economic eventuality. A period of constrained growth did in fact follow the oil shortage, and its 'constrained growth' scenario positioned Royal Dutch Shell to exploit the shortage. Royal Dutch Shell grew from eighth largest to second largest petroleum company in the world during the 1970s by taking quick advantage of unexpected opportunities.

Royal Dutch Shell had listened to oil consultant – and subsequently Pulitzer Prize-winning author – Daniel Yergin, who suggested that it adopt scenario planning as a part of its strategy analysis. Yergin, in turn, had adapted scenario analysis to business planning from its original use in US military strategy planning addressing thermonuclear war and its aftermath (where it had been popularized by Hermann Kahn).

Blueprint
The procedures for preparing for the future are:

- *Identify a particular problem* in your business.
- *State a particular decision* that has to be made.
- *Identify the forces* (economic, technological, product lines, competition and so on) that have an impact on the decision.
- *Build four or five future scenarios* based on the principal forces. Use all the available information, and develop scenarios that will give you as many different and plausible possibilities as a pinball in play.
- *Develop the scenarios into stories or narratives* by varying the forces that impact the decision. Change the forces (interest rates escalate, a key performer quits, need for your product or service disappears and so on) and combine them into different patterns to describe the possible consequences of your decision over the next five years.
- *Search for business opportunities* within each scenario. Then explore the links between opportunities across the range of your scenarios, and actively search for new ideas.

Suppose you are worried about future competitive trends in your business – in particular the pricing of your product. A number of forces have an impact on pricing: profits, return on investment, cash flow, capitalization structure, the competition's pricing and so on. You can build four or five different, plausible scenarios around the forces you have identified (see Figure 11.14).

Scenario 1. Nothing changes. Everything remains the way it is today (*ceteris paribus*).

Scenario 2. Your major competitor reduces prices by 25 per cent (*price war and commoditization*).

Scenario 3. A major technological breakthrough prices out your major product line (*disruptive innovation*).

Scenario 4. The country is hit by a deep recession and customers postpone purchasing indefinitely (*economy-wide deflation*).

Scenario 5. The economy heats up and inflation drives interest rates up to 15 per cent. (*economy-wide inflation*).

Each of these scenarios points to different actions you might take, and different business opportunities.

What future scenarios might a petrol service

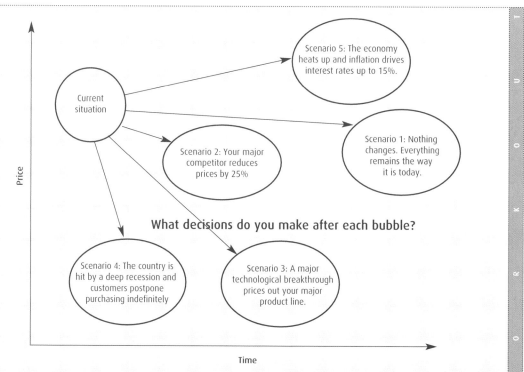

Figure 11.14 Five different scenarios

station develop? One might be: a major technological breakthrough makes petrol obsolete.

Two very real possibilities are methanol and natural gas. Methanol is getting good PR as clean fuel, but its corrosive and toxic qualities require special handling. What if the handling problem is solved and methanol replaces petrol? Or, consider natural gas, which is clean, plentiful, and politically popular and is being used in the Netherlands. So far, compressing natural gas is a cumbersome process, but what if someone solves this problem?

How can the service station position itself now to take advantage of the new opportunities that alternative fuels will bring? One thing it could do today is install a few methanol pumps for motorists who are willing to handle it and to make more frequent fill-ups.

Methanol will probably require larger automobile fuel tanks. Another probable future opportunity will be in the design of the new tanks. The company might consider getting involved in the design and manufacture of methanol tanks for automobiles.

Another service station scenario could be predicated on new technology that makes petrol more clean-burning and cheap. The problems with a cheap, clean-burning form of petrol become pricing,

competition and service. To position itself now to exploit future opportunities in this scenario, the service station could:

▸ Stress service. Install a car wash and provide free washes with fill-ups. Once they are built, car washes cost operators about 15 cents per car. Experts say washes can pump up petrol sales by 25 per cent.
▸ Provide an unusual service, such as haircuts.
▸ Turn the station into a 'pit stop'. This would appeal to harried commuters. Staff might service the car and bring them their coffee, juice, cigarettes, and morning paper while they wait.
▸ The station could also have a drive-by window where people who don't need petrol can drive up and get coffee, a paper, or whatever.

Creating future scenarios pushes you to think about possible futures which, in turn, push you to generate ideas that will work now and give the company the edge over its competition. It is thinking about getting into alternative fuels or the automobile design business, adding car washes, hairdressing and pit stops, while a competitor is still pondering whether to use air dryers or paper towels in the washroom.

Behavioural and strategy models for valuing eBay's business

By 2002, over 50 of the more than 200 Web companies that survived the dot-com bust of the previous two years were making money, and more of them did so in 2003–05. But eBay never missed a step – it has been profitable each year since its founding. The interesting thing about internet companies is that once they have built their website and set up their basic operations, it is very cheap for them to process additional orders, and profits can grow then much faster than revenues. For example, eBay's revenues in the first quarter of 2002 jumped 59 per cent to US$245 million, while costs rose only by 39 per cent to $197 million, so that profits more than doubled from $21 million a year before to nearly $48 million. Market capitalization was $44 billion in 2007 and its registered users exceed 150 million in 15 countries around the world, with 60 million active users (those that have bid for or listed items within the last year).

A look through the 10-K and 10-Q filings online at the US SEC's EDGAR database (http://www.sec.gov/edgar.shtml) shows eBay is keen to detail the processes, progress and risks of its business model. There are extensive lists including business risks and strategies for addressing them, a clear value proposition, and historical value drivers for estimating future performance.

Ebay's value proposition is clear from its annual reports:

> Our mission is to build the world's most efficient and abundant marketplace in which anyone, anywhere, can buy or sell practically anything … and through our PayPal service, we enable any business or consumer with email to send and receive online payments securely, conveniently and cost-effectively. Our marketplace exists as an online trading platform that enables a global community of buyers and sellers to interact and trade with one another. Our role is to create, maintain, and expand the technological functionality, safety, ease-of-use, and reliability of the trading platform while at the same time, supporting the growth and success of our community of users.

The objectives of eBay are not substantially different from stock markets – to expand the number of traders and their volume of trades by making trading easy, accessible and cheap, and by streamlining payment and clearing.

Figure 11.15 plots various figures of merit for eBay since its listing in 1997, and projects revenues and associated costs into the future using a quadratic function (note that both R^2 values are above 0.99).

During the same period we can look at listings and active users (see Figure 11.16). Again there is a very good fit ($R^2 \sim 0.99$) to a quadratic growth, which would lead us to two conclusions. First, listings, revenues and cost of sales can be represented as linear functions of the number of active users (only about half of registered users are active in any year according to eBay's annual reports). And second, the number of active users grows by the square of the time that the market has been active.

The second characteristic is reflective of what Laszlo Barabási[20] calls a scale-free network in which the number of connections (such as contacts, transactions, friends) to any individual user follows a power law. Such networks are 'scale-free' because the appearance and operation of the network for any individual user is independent of their position on the network, or the size of the network – conditions that accurately describe the service eBay tries to provide its users. Such networks are not static structures, but are the result of particular patterns of growth. Thus *time* implicitly becomes a driver of desirability of being on such a network of traders.

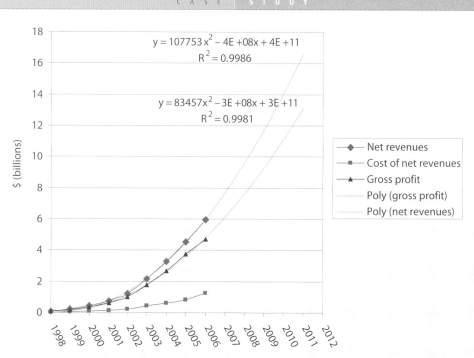

Figure 11.15 eBay's figures of merit, with future projections

Source: eBay website

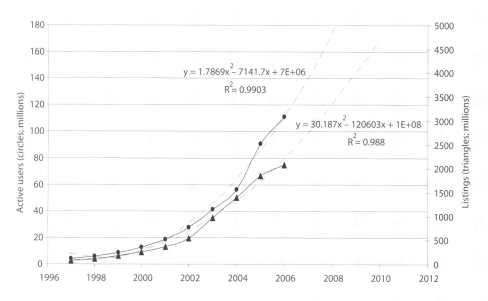

Figure 11.16 eBay users and listings per year

Source: eBay website

Using this logic, we can build a very simple model of value generation by eBay's business model which is nonetheless quite good at predicting the future:

$$V_t = \beta_0 + \beta_1 t^2$$

If we choose V_t to be net revenue, and t to be the age of eBay (1997, the year it went public, being
$t = 0$), then our strategy model is:

$$V_t \cong 74{,}401 t^2 - 282{,}290$$

i.e. $\beta_0 \cong -282{,}290$ and $\beta_1 \cong 74{,}401$ with an $R^2 \cong .99$

If we adopt a 40 per cent discount rate to compute present value (ignoring the value cone limits in this example for simplicity), the present value of eBay's revenues is about US$3.2 billion.

This in fact is eBay management's strategy model, assuming it does nothing but support its existing set of services. In fact eBay has proactively worked to improve the attractiveness of its network – for example by purchasing PayPal and Skype, and working to integrate these into their auction services. A closer look at historical results would show that the integration of PayPal into eBay's system in 2003 both pushed up the number of users, and more importantly, significantly boosted revenue per user. More accurate forecasts become possible when these additional activities are worked into the strategy model for the auction.

Questions for the eBay case study

1. Where is eBay generating its money? Does free cash flow tell the entire story?
2. How does eBay measure success in its management and operations?
3. eBay clearly is benefiting from network externalities, judging from the growth of both its auctions and revenues. How does this influence its cash flow and future profitability?
4. eBay is able to increase its revenue per customer by acquiring new complementary businesses (for example, the purchase of PayPal, which substantially increased income per customer transaction from under $1 to around $2.15). Could eBay leverage its name to continue adding complementary business like PayPal? If your answer is yes, name several new businesses in addition to the recently added Skype that eBay might add in the next five years.

CHAPTER QUESTIONS FOR REVIEW

1	During the dot-com boom, there were numerous financial analyses that justified the exceptionally high stock valuations of internet companies (for example, Yahoo traded at a price earnings multiple over 1000). Were these valuations valid? If they were, why did the stock value drop? If they were not, what were the flaws in their mechanics?
2	How would you incorporate non-linear network effects and technology acceleration into traditional discounted cash flow analyses?
3	How would you incorporate risk into discounted cash flow analyses? Is this the normal method of assessing risk in stock shares?
4	Risk is often characterized as the variance of either stock price or some other metric of firm performance. What are the strengths and weaknesses of a variance 'metric' for risk?

CHAPTER 11: KEY POINTS

▷ The value of an innovation lies in the future, and in the plans that management have for commercializing that innovation.

▷ To realize the innovation payoff, innovators must prepare to compete in not just one, but two markets – first in the consumer market for their new product or service, and second in the capital market to finance their innovation.

▷ Financial analysis and reporting play an essential role in a business's 'reporting–control' cycle.

▷ A firm's or project's performance is realized on many dimensions – profit, competitive positioning, strength of workforce and so forth.

▷ Three factors complicate an assessment of an innovation's value:
- by definition, an innovation is new, and thus there is no history of production or marketing to guide analysis; of if there is it will be incomplete and with very few datapoints
- innovation business can be several orders of magnitude riskier than traditional business; the returns can commensurately be several orders of magnitude higher as well
- the actual drivers of an innovation and its business model are too often things that never appear in the financial statement – such as the size of the network externality, the rapidity with which the technology's performance improves, and the appeal of the brand – and which are measured through *figures of merit* – observable, sometimes synthetic, measures that move in tandem with the strategy drivers.

▷ Up until the late 1970s, the total balance sheet valuation of the S&P 500 firms hovered around that of the stock market. But by the early 1980s, the ratio of balance sheet assets to stock market value began to decline. By 1990 book value had declined to around 40 per cent of the market value; by 2000 it was at less than 20 per cent of the market value. The majority of firm value today is contained in 'unmeasured' assets such as ideas, patents and skills.

▷ The *strategy model* is the econometric forecasting counterpart to the *business model*. As with the business model, the *strategy model* has two parts – a compelling narrative story line about how, why and when cash will be generated from the innovation, and a forecasting model that ties this to the numbers that can generate future forecasts and present values.

▷ Real options assume that future performance will not be the result of a series of smooth future cash flows, as with, say, a traditional investment such as a bank's mortgage contract. Rather cash flows will be contingent on future events or management decisions which may or may not occur and are uncertain in timing and amount.

▷ Forecasts should be non-arbitrary, collective, reliable and consistent.

NOTES

1 'Creativity pays', *Business Week*, 24 April 2006, reporting a study done for *Business Week* by the Boston Consulting Group using data from Standard & Poor's Compustat database.

2 'The innovation backlash', *Business Week*, 12 February 2007.

3 Stengel, R. F. (1994) *Optimal Control and Estimation*, New York: Dover.

4 Source: Huang, E. (2007) 'Nintendo legend discusses Wiis and Miis', GamePro.com, 9 March 2007.

5 Gates, B. (1999) 'Microsoft', London Business School *Business Strategy Review*, 2, pp. 11–18

6 Lenin, V. (1918) *The State and Revolution*, available at www.marxists.org.

7 Sources: 'Steve Jobs vision was on target at Apple, now is falling short', *Wall Street Journal*, 25 May 1993, p. A1; 'The second coming', *Fortune*, November 1998, pp. 86–100; 'Apple and PC given for dead are rising anew', *New York Times*, 6 April 1999, p. C1; 'Apple', *Business Week*, 31 July 2000, pp. 102–13; 'The new iMac', *Fortune*, 10 June 2002, p. 2; 'How low can a PC go?' *U.S. News & World Report*, 4 November 2002, p. 62; 'I.B.M. division headed to China has made no profit in 31/2 years', *New York Times*, 31 December 2004, p. C4; 'Notebooks without wide margins', *Business Week*, 5 September 2005, p. 38.

8 Baumol, W. J. (2004) *The Free-Market Innovation Machine: Analyzing the growth miracle of capitalism*, Princeton, N.J.: Princeton University Press, p. 42.

9 Conner, K. and Prahalad, C. K. (1996) 'A resource-based theory of the firm: knowledge versus opportunism', *Organizational Science* 7, pp. 477–501; Diamond, D. W. (1991) 'Monitoring and reputation: the choice between bank loans and directly placed debt', *Journal of Political Economy* 99, pp. 689–721.

10 Shannon, C. E. (1948) 'A mathematical theory of communication', parts I and II, *Bell Systems Technology Journal* 27, pp. 379–423, 623–56.

11 Hartley, R. V. L. (1928) 'Transmission of information', *Bell Systems Technology Journal* 7, p. 535.

12 Porter, M. E. (1991) 'Towards a dynamic theory of strategy', *Strategic Management Journal* 12 (Winter), pp. 95–117.

13 Faulkner, T. W. (1996) 'Applying "options thinking" to R&D valuation', *Research Technology Management* 39(3), pp. 50–6.

14 Luehrman, T. A. (1998) 'Strategy as a portfolio of real options', *Harvard Business Review* **76**(5) (Sept–Oct), pp. 87–99; Luehrman, T. A. (1998) 'Investment opportunities as real options: getting started on the numbers', *Harvard Business Review* **76**(4) (July–Aug), pp. 51–67.

15 Mun, J. (2005) *Real Options Analysis: Tools and techniques for valuing strategic investment and decisions*, 2nd edn, New York: Wiley.

16 Fenn, G. W., Liang, N. and Prowse, S. (1995) 'The economics of private equity', Board of Governors of the Federal Reserve System, Washington, DC, December; Jensen, M. C. (1976) 'Theory of the firm: managerial behaviour, agency costs, and ownership structure', *Journal of Financial Economics* 3, p. 305; Morris, P., Teisberg, E. and Kolbe, A. L. (1991) 'When choosing R&D projects, go with long shots', *Research Technology Management* (Jan–Feb), p. 3540; Taylor, A. III and Davis, J. E. (1994) 'Iacocca's minivan: how Chrysler succeeded in creating the most profitable products of the decade', *Fortune*, 30 May.

17 Brealey, R. A. and Myers, S. C. (1995) *Principles of Corporate Finance*, New York: McGraw-Hill; Dixit, A. K. and Pindyck, R. S. (1994) *Investment under Uncertainty*, Princeton, NJ: Princeton University Press.

18 Gordon, M. (1962) *The Investment, Financing and Valuation of the Corporation*, Homewood, Ill.: Irwin.

19 Leland, H. and Pyle, D. (1997) 'Information asymmetries, financial structure, and financial inter-mediation', *Journal of Finance* 32, pp. 863–78; Ross, S. A. (1977) 'The determination of financial structure: the incentive signalling approach', *Bell Journal of Economics* 8, pp. 23–40.

20 Barabási, L. (2003) *Linked: How everything is connected to everything else and what it means*, New York: Plume.

UNDERSTANDING AND MANAGING CREATIVE PEOPLE

After reading the *innovation workout*, you will be able to conduct **group brainstorming sessions** appropriate for a wide **variety of cultural settings** to enable a group of experts to innovate in products, markets and services. After reading the *case study* interview with jazz vibraphonist Gary Burton you will better understand how **leadership, strategy and management of creative endeavours** differ from that of traditional products and services.

Note: Further information, class slides, test questions and other supporting material are available on our companion website at

www.palgrave.com/business/westland

TYPES OF CREATIVE PEOPLE

The topic of creativity invites many differing opinions and perspectives. One reason is that there are many different sorts of individuals, playing different roles, all of whom must communicate and contribute in successful innovation. Creativity requires at least five types of people for success[1] – the invention is just the beginning of the process (and some might say the easiest part). These five types are:

▶ *idea generators*: individuals who can sift through large quantities of technological and market data to identify potentially successful innovations, filling the opportunity register of the firm
▶ *gatekeepers and boundary spanners*: individuals who communicate ideas from one department, company or industry, to another
▶ *champions*: entrepreneurs, evangelists and other promoters of new ideas, who see the market value even though they may not have very great technical knowledge
▶ *sponsors*: coaches and mentors who can clear the way politically for an idea or invention.
▶ *project managers*: administrators who can attend to the details required of a high-quality, timely product introduction.

It is important to note that each of these types of people work best if they exhibit a unique personality suited for the role. Gatekeepers and boundary spanners are social and gregarious, whereas idea generators may tend towards introversion. It is probably best that champions be politically savvy and independent from the inventor. Individuals may share roles, but often in practice, the various individuals that make a firm creative may not get along with each other all that well. This adds a considerable challenge to management's task of team building.

There is literally a cottage industry in methods for 'team building'. Suffice it to say that methods vary – what may be good for one company or industry is likely to fail elsewhere. Management needs to tailor its approach to team building to the individual personalities and corporate culture. There are several caveats that should be heeded:

▶ Recognize that team building takes time, occurs through pairwise collaborations, and that each of these pairs will be unstable at times.
▶ Teamwork cannot be forced, it has to be encouraged, often with rewards and (used sparingly) threats.
▶ Start early with team-building efforts, and with a compelling and well-articulated project description, including milestones and deliverables.
▶ Consider using a formal 'team-building' method, but benchmark its performance at other firms to assess whether it is appropriate for your project.
▶ Reiterate and reinforce the project description throughout the project.

HOW SUCCESSFUL TECHNOLOGY COMPANIES
MANAGE CREATIVE TEAMS[2]

Google believes that successful technology businesses need to follow Peter Drucker's advice and 'strip away everything that gets in their knowledge workers' way'.[3] Both

Google[4] and Microsoft[5] have drawn on decades of managerial wisdom, beginning with the seminal work of Drucker, through ongoing studies of how their best technology competitors contend. Here are some of the management lessons that have worked for successful technology firms to help them keep innovating, They can be applied in many differing sectors.

Peter Drucker's 'knowledge workers'

Peter Drucker observed that 'knowledge workers do not respond to financial incentives, orders or negative sanctions the way blue-collar workers are expected to'. Drucker contends that knowledge workers are best treated as 'de facto volunteers' tied to the firm by commitment to its aims and purposes and often expecting to participate in its administration and its governance. We know from surveys of knowledge workers that Drucker is right (and prescient as well, given that he made these comments a quarter of a century ago): creative workers value four aspects (in decreasing order of importance) of their jobs:[6]

- ▸ **Challenge and responsibility**; but employees expect to have a hand in choosing their challenges.
- ▸ **Peer recognition**; with peers who they respect, and who are interested in the same challenges.
- ▸ **Job security**; not the old contract for life of the 1950s Organization Man, but one that balances flexibility, reward and security to allow the creative worker to focus first and foremost on the challenge at hand.
- ▸ **Salary**; money is important, but not as important as the first three items. Because creative workers do not expect a job for life, they want to collect their income now, rather than being rewarded at retirement for a lifetime of loyalty.

- ▸ **Hire by committee**. Virtually every person who interviews at Google talks to at least half a dozen interviewers, drawn from both management and potential colleagues. When you hire good people and involve them intensively in the hiring process, you build a positive feedback loop.
- ▸ **Hire smart problem solvers.** Microsoft gives its applicants problem-solving tests. Google has been known to place difficult problems on highway billboards, not allowing applicants to the next stage of application unless they can solve the problem shown.
- ▸ **Cater to their every need.** On top of the standard package of fringe benefits, include first-class dining facilities, gyms, laundry rooms, massage rooms, haircuts, carwashes, dry cleaning, commuting buses – just about anything a hard-working engineer might want. Programmers want to programme, they don't want to do their laundry, so make it easy for them to do both. Make the office feel like home. Give everyone their own office (even if it is small); don't impose dress codes; make it a place that employees would like to stay.
- ▸ **Pack them in.** Almost every project at Google is a team project, and teams have to communicate. The best way to make communication easy is to put team members within a few feet of each other – nearly everyone at Google shares an office.
- ▸ **Make coordination easy.** Each employee emails a snippet once a week to his or her work group describing what he/she has done in the last week. This gives everyone

an easy way to track what everyone else is up to, making it much easier to monitor progress and synchronize work flow.

▶ **Communicate effectively and frequently.** Every Friday Google holds an all-hands assembly with announcements, introductions and questions and answers. Google has remarkably broad dissemination of information within the organization and remarkably few serious leaks. It believes that it is the first fact that causes the second: a trusted work force is a loyal work force. Google's challenge is to scale this communication as the company grows internationally.

▶ **Use your own products and services wherever you can.** One of the reasons for Gmail's success is that it was beta tested within Google for many months. The use of email is critical within the organization, so Gmail had to be tuned to satisfy the needs of some of the most demanding customers – Google's knowledge workers. Conversely, avoid the 'not invented here' syndrome. Good engineers are always convinced they can build a better system than the existing ones, and they may be right, but not necessarily at a competitive cost or delivery time. Labour spent developing a product internally that already exists on the market is labour not spent on innovations that can give a competitive advantage.

▶ **Put a management focus on consensus.** The role of the manager is that of an aggregator of viewpoints, not a dictator of decisions. Building a consensus sometimes takes longer, but always produces a more committed team and better decisions.

▶ **Don't be evil.** No matter how passionate people are about their views, they need to be presented in an atmosphere of tolerance and respect. Engineers are competitive by nature and they have low tolerance for those who aren't as driven or as knowledgeable as they are. But almost all engineering projects are team projects; having a smart but inflexible person on a team can be deadly. When management sees a recommendation that says 'smartest person I've ever known' combined with 'I wouldn't ever want to work with them again', they decline to make them an offer. One reason for extensive peer interviews is to make sure that teams are enthused about the new team member.

▶ **Base decisions on empirical analysis.** Every decision should be based on quantitative analysis with real data. Google builds systems to manage information, not only on the internet at large, but also internally. Google keeps a multitude of online 'dashboards' that provide up-to-the-minute snapshots of business position.

▶ **Expect employees to fail.** Failure is an essential part of the creative process. Google's CEO Eric Schmidt has said, 'Please fail very quickly, so that you can try again.'[7] Make sure the cost of failure is small (by taking small steps) and that the repercussions of failure are not career threatening.

▶ **Encourage an 'us' versus 'them' mentality.** Constantly remind employees that their competition is other companies, not their colleagues. Product cycles are now so short, and markets so volatile, that failure to stay competitive can quickly put the company at risk.

▶ **Sustain a start-up mentality.** Not just Google and Microsoft, but Dell, Amazon and other successful companies fight complacency by maintaining an ever-present sense of urgency that the business must succeed. Watch costs, keep project teams small and delivery times short. Keep the office environment comfortable but frugal.

Unitech Networks, Hong Kong

Alex Chan, the CEO of Unitech Networks in Hong Kong, encourages his 150 consulting and network engineering employees to constantly seek new business opportunities. In his market, opportunities arise only if demand exists for a product or service, and if his people have the needed technical expertise. Because an employee's education in a particular piece of software or hardware may require a lead time of several months, Alex likes to anticipate markets for new switches, routers, software such as WAP 2.0 for phones, and so forth by buying the software or hardware and making it freely available to all of his engineers (often by sticking it in the centre of his office space or making it available from their network).

Employees are allowed from 10 to 20 per cent of their time to 'play around' with new equipment or software that Alex feels might ultimately become a future business. In addition, employees are encouraged to bring their toys in from home (often robots and remote-controlled cars, planes and helicopters) and play with them during off-hours in the workplace. The idea is to, first, keep his employees minds active, but not chain them to a rigid set of problems, and second, keep employees around the workplace at all hours, so it becomes a second home and social club. The approach has proven very successful for Unitech, which has experienced low turnover and a profitable, expanding business throughout its 15 years of existence.

▶ **Management is responsible for maintaining focus.** Engineers and programmers love to figure out how to solve problems, but once they've done the hard part, they often get bored and want to move on to something else. It is management's responsibility to insist on deliverables, and to reinforce the idea that the job is not complete until they are satisfied with the deliverable.

▶ **Recruit for diversity, hire for philosophy.** In addition to problem solving, workers should satisfy two other goals. First, their philosophy and character should be aligned with the firm. Cisco actively seeks out firms for acquisition, but the acquisition goes ahead, or is halted, based on whether the two cultures fit. A poor cultural match provides a quick path to disappointment. But, a great creative culture allows latitude for diversity – of ideas, backgrounds, knowledge and so forth. Diversity drives creativity by forcing different ideas together. Part of the creative firm's culture has to be one that embraces a wide range of ideas and people.

▶ **Recognize their limitations.** Creative workers can be brilliant at what they do best – and remarkably naïve about the world outside their area of expertise. Because creativity is solitary and mentally intensive, it tends to attract introverts. The more the firm can connect them to the real world, the more they're likely to understand some of the decisions that management, customers and clients make. Firms can benefit from regular applications of inspiration: outside speakers, art and photo exhibits, and social events. But keep it fun.[8]

▶ **Develop people's speaking skills.** The same introversion and focus that make creative workers brilliant can trip them up when presenting their ideas to others. Engineers and programmers benefit greatly from learning a bit of the language of accountants and financial types, or of the marketing staff. Public speaking and regular presentation of ideas should be encouraged even if individuals are not that good at it, because it will change the way they think about their own work.

- ▶ **Allow 10 to 20 per cent of employees' time for their own projects.** This is a source of new insights and products for the firm, and a way for knowledge workers to actively recharge their enthusiasm. Disseminate these ideas widely through a mailing list – a company-wide suggestion box where people can post ideas on anything, which are then commented on and rated.
- ▶ **Protect creative workers from creativity killers.** Creative individuals are often more emotionally exposed, and tied to their ideas, than other workers, and consequently more vulnerable to criticism. It is important to explain to them why some ideas don't pass muster, and to keep an open communication channel if they have questions.
- ▶ **Add liberal doses of fun.** Being creative on demand is hard work. It is intellectually taxing and emotionally exhausting. There needs to be latitude for workers to break away from their problem, shift gears, and do something else for a while until they regain their enthusiasm. If you have hired well, creative employees will be too busy solving problems to disappoint you by taking advantage of the last suggestion.

CREATIVE MINDS

Perhaps best known in the field of business are the ideas of Edward de Bono, who has made a high-profile business of 'teaching' creativity. To de Bono, creativity happens through numerous cognitive tricks that enable people to break old habits and preconceptions, and visualize a problem from a new angle.[9] Even without discussing the merits of de Bono's approach, it is still worthwhile to study whether this is indeed how people who are agreed to be truly 'creative' manage to act so creatively.

The creative impulse is inherent in the human mind, and as economist Paul Romer observed, 'an ant will go through its life without ever coming up with even a slightly different idea about how to gather food. But people are almost incapable of this kind of rote adherence to instruction. We are incurable experimenters and problem solvers'.[13]

The abode of creativity is the human brain – a still poorly understood collection of function-specific regions. We have yet to identify a physical 'organ of creativity' in the brain (and indeed, there may not be one). Our brain is a very expensive organ in terms of energy consumption, drawing up to 25 per cent of an adult's energy (and 60 per cent of an infant's). Since it is 70 per cent fat, feeding the brain is one of the primary motivations behind the modern addiction to fatty foods (and perhaps the 'geek' proclivity for that sugar and fat-laden junk food rush). As a percentage of body weight, the human brain is 15–20 times larger than those of other mammals. By inference, much of that added tissue weight is not dedicated to mammalian tasks such as muscle coordination and autonomic control of metabolism. Rather it arose, as economist Paul Seabright[14] details it, to deal with a society of 'murder, reciprocity, trust, hoarding and stealing', which occurred when early man was forced out of the forest and into the more brutal environment of the savanna.

Creative paradigm shifts

Exceptional innovators possess something that sets them apart – exceptional 'creativity'. For example, history since Pythagoras has seen many talented musicians advance the art – but very few, if any, who could match the creative impact of Miles Davis. Miles Davis's *Kind of Blue* kicked bebop into the modern era, with its expanded modal palette, inventive form and harmony. Extraordinary innovators like Miles Davis can bring about extraordinary cultural impact: innovations, ideas and acts so compelling that they bring about a paradigm shift. Other examples include Sigmund Freud's founding of psychoanalysis and Newton's formulation of the laws of motion.

Yet the quality called creativity is elusive, and is perceived differently depending on how it is approached. George Kneller observed that 'creativity consists largely of re-arranging what we know in order to find out what we do not know'. Creativity by individuals and teams is a starting point for innovation; it is a necessary but not sufficient condition for innovation.[10] Margaret Bodin observed that:

a person needs time, and enormous effort to amass mental structures and to explore their potential. It is not always easy (it was not easy for Beethoven). Even when it is, life has many other attractions. Only a strong, commitment to the domain – music, maths, medicine – can prevent someone from dissipating their energies on other things.[11]

Joel Mokyr notes that technological creativity is highly sensitive to culture, and has risen, then faded dramatically when social and economic institutions turn rigid and act against it, as was the case in late medieval Islamic and Chinese societies. Both societies had been leaders in mathematics, mechanics, art and many other fields, only to fall far behind the emergent West. He comments:

Technological progress is like a fragile and vulnerable plant, whose flourishing is not only dependent on the appropriate surroundings and climate, but whose life is almost always short. It is highly sensitive to the social and economic environment and can easily be arrested.[12]

Our brain evolved to handle specific challenges in our evolutionary environment. Most of the distinctly human aspects of our bearing evolved early in our lineage – our large brains did not. Our *australopithecines afarensis* forbears living 3 to 4 million years ago had brains about 450–500 cm³ in volume, not much larger than that of a chimpanzee. There appear to have been two bursts in absolute brain size – one 1.8 million years ago when our brains jumped to about 850 cm³ in volume and another about 150,000 years ago when our brains reached the modern 1400 cm³ in volume. The bursts appear to have been associated with climate changes in Africa.

Creativity is just one aspect of humans' unique capability for abstract thought. But creativity underlies the process of invention; indeed a useful definition is that inventions are the end product of the creative process. As innovations are commercialized inventions, the whole process of innovation is more or less predicated on the activities of creative individuals.[15]

Creativity is not just something that happens inside someone's head. To be able to declare something as 'creative', it has to be compared to a standard. For instance, we could say that Einstein's theory of general relativity is truly creative when compared with previous theories of the operation of mechanics and the cosmos. Creativity involves relations between three domains: the creative person, the domain in which the creative act occurs (such as mathematics, music, literature), and the field of practitioners that set the 'standard' (such as other mathematicians, museum curators, literature readers and critics).[20]

Einstein's brain[16]

Albert Einstein died on 18 April 1955 at Princeton Hospital in New Jersey. Thomas S. Harvey, the pathologist who performed the autopsy, removed the physicist's brain, dissected it into 240 pieces, and embedded the pieces in a plastic-like substance called celoidin.

For more than two decades, no one, not even Einstein's family, knew that Einstein's brain was being kept in jars at Harvey's home. In 1978 Steven Levy, then a reporter for the *New Jersey Monthly*, tracked Harvey down at his home in Wichita, Kansas. After a long conversation with the reporter, Harvey admitted that he had the brain. Out of a box labelled 'Costa Cider', he pulled the two Mason jars that contained the brain that had brought about a revolution in science.[17]

Since then, Harvey has allowed three teams to examine parts of the brain. University of California, Berkeley anatomist Marian Diamond and her colleagues published a paper on Einstein's brain in 1985. They found that the ratio of neurons to glial cells (the cells that support and protect neurons) in one part of Einstein's brain was smaller than the ratios in 11 normal brains. While the authors concluded that the larger number of glial cells per neuron might indicate that Einstein's neurons worked harder – needed more energy – than normal, this interpretation was later questioned by other researchers. A second paper,

by Britt Anderson of the University of Alabama at Birmingham, was published in 1996. Anderson and Harvey showed that while Einstein's brain weighed less than the average (2 lb 11.4 oz (1230 g) compared with 3 lb 1.4 oz (1400 g) for the average) it packed more neurons in a given area.[18]

Finally, in 1999, McMaster University neuropsychologist Sandra Witelson and her colleagues discovered what was hailed as a potential key to Einstein's genius. The inferior parietal region, which is thought to be used for mathematical reasoning, was found to be 15 per cent wider than normal. In addition, a groove (sulcus) was found to be partially missing in that area. The researchers argued that the absence of that fissure could have resulted in more effective communication among neurons. Although interesting, all of this research could not be regarded as conclusive. After all, even though Witelson's study used 35 brains as a control group, it had only one brain in the experimental group – Einstein's.[19]

The remaining pieces of Einstein's brain were eventually brought by Harvey to their final resting place, the Pathology Department at Princeton Hospital. When asked why he took the brain in the first place (Einstein's body was cremated), Harvey explained that he felt obligated to salvage the precious grey matter for posterity.

Another story

The story of discoverers could be told in simple chronological order, since the latest science replaces what went before. But the arts are another story – a story of infinite addition...creators in all the arts

have enlarged, embellished, fantasized and filigreed our experience...in the random flexings of the imagination.

Daniel Boorstin, *The Creators* (Vintage, 1993)

TRAITS OF CREATIVE PEOPLE

Metrics

Many attempts have been made to develop a *creativity quotient* for individuals. However these have been unsuccessful, as the measure of creativity is too personal and subjective to submit to standardized measurement. One of the earliest formal attempts arose from work by mathematician George David Birkhoff (best known for his contributions in ergodic theory and geometry), who developed an Aesthetic Index to measure the quality of creative output. The best-known recent measure is J. P. Guilford's Torrance Tests of Creative Thinking.[21] These present subjects with a bank of tests which measure:

- **fluency**: the total number of interpretable, meaningful, and relevant ideas generated in response to the stimulus
- **flexibility**: the number of different categories of relevant responses
- **originality**: the statistical rarity of the responses among the test subjects
- **elaboration**: the amount of detail in the responses.

But psychometric measures of creativity have always been controversial; many researchers recommend measures that are more qualitative and situational.[22] Bringing about a paradigm shift in a field of invention does not necessarily require genius. Studies have shown that beyond a certain level of IQ (around 120), there is no clear correlation between intelligence and creativity. True creativity probably requires some degree of intelligence, but there is absolutely no guarantee that a person with an IQ of 170 will be any more creative than one with an IQ of 120. This is possibly because the field of practitioners and consumers of innovation set a de facto standard for creativity. In the 1930s, Lewis Terman's tests of gifted children discovered a cognitive disconnect between individuals with more than 30 points of IQ differential. If consumer intelligence tends to hover around an 'average' IQ of 100, then perhaps a slightly above average intelligence, but below 130 IQ, may yield the best innovations simply because innovators can communicate them to practitioners and consumers.

Creative qualities

Psychologist Ellen Winner has noted about gifted children:

> for those who do make it into the roster of creators, a certain set of personality traits proves far more important than having a high general IQ, or a high domain-specific ability, even one at the level of prodigy. Creators are hard-driving, focused, dominant, independent risk-takers.[23]

While researchers have not been able to discern with any certainty whether personal characteristics can indeed be the direct causes of creativity, there is little doubt that some qualities are intimately involved in the creative process. So what are these traits?

Psychologists John Dacey and Kathleen Lennon[24] emphasize tolerance of ambiguity: the ability to think, operate and remain open-minded in situations where the rules are unclear, where there are no guidelines, or where the usual support systems (family, school, society) have collapsed. Indeed, without the competence to function where there are no rules, painter Pablo Picasso would have never invented cubism and mathematician Evariste Galois would not have come up with group theory. Tolerance of ambiguity is a necessary condition for creativity.

Complexity, another qualitative measure, reflects an individual's ability to harbour tendencies that normally appear to be at opposite extremes.[25] For instance, most people are somewhere in the middle of the continuum between being rebellious or highly disciplined. Very creative individuals can alternate between the two extremes almost at the drop of a hat. Michael Csikszentmihalyi interviewed many dozens of creative people from a wide range of domains, stretching from the arts, humanities and sciences to business and politics. Based on these interviews, he compiled a list of ten dimensions of complexity – ten pairs of apparently antithetical characteristics that are often both present in the creative minds. The list includes:

▸ bursts of impulsiveness that punctuate periods of quiet and rest
▸ being smart yet extremely naive
▸ large amplitude swings between extreme responsibility and irresponsibility
▸ a rooted sense of reality together with a hefty dose of fantasy and imagination
▸ alternating periods of introversion and extroversion
▸ being simultaneously humble and proud
▸ psychological androgyny – no clear adherence to gender role stereotyping
▸ being rebellious and iconoclastic yet respectful to the domain of expertise and its history
▸ being on one hand passionate but on the other objective about one's own work
▸ experiencing suffering and pain mingled with exhilaration and enjoyment.

Interestingly, psychologist Ellen Winner[26] finds that child prodigies usually exhibit only one extreme of the spectrum of characteristics – they tend to be intense, driven and introverted. We should remember, however, that gifted children are still in the soaking-up knowledge mode, rather than in the creative mode. The reality that most prodigies do not become particularly creative in their adult life may reflect, among other things, the fact that only a small fraction of gifted children actually possess the capacity for creativity.

Dacey and Lennon identify a few additional traits that in their opinion contribute to tolerance of ambiguity and to its role in promoting creativity. One of these – stimulus freedom – is what we might call the ability to think outside the box. To a large extent, the very essence of creativity is the capacity to break out of common assumptions and to escape any pre-existing mind-sets.

From an administrative standpoint, we can see how the sum of these traits can quickly place a huge burden on managers. Leadership of creative types is not easy.

There are in addition to these abstract qualities behind creative minds, three tangible traits commonly associated with creative minds: loss of a father, youth, and psychosis. We shall look at each of these in turn.

Loss of a father

A particular characteristic that appears to be shared by many creative individuals is the loss of a father early in life. Among nearly 100 creative interviewees, Csikszentmihalyi actually found that no fewer than three out of ten men and two out of ten women were orphaned by the time they reached their teens.[27] Orphans avoid the huge psychological burden of having to live up to the perceived expectations of their missing father, while gaining opportunities to reinvent themselves. The French philosopher Jean-Paul Sartre observed that:

> the death of [Sartre's father] Jean Baptiste was the big event of my life: it sent my mother back to her chains and gave me freedom .... Had my father lived, he would have lain on me full length and would have crushed me. As luck had it, he died young.[28]

Forty lives in bebop

Psychiatrist Geoffrey Wills studied the lives of 40 of the great jazz innovators in the period 1945–60 (six trumpeters, three trombonists, four alto saxophonists, one alto doubling tenor saxophonist, five tenor saxophonists, three baritone saxophonists, five pianists, five bassists, four drummers, one guitarist, one vibraphonist and two arrangers).[29] Some of the jazz musicians suffered from self-medication: for example Miles Davis developed sickle-cell anaemia and used excessive amounts of cocaine and barbiturates to control the arthritic pain. As a result, he developed paranoid delusions and auditory hallucinations, searching in his house for imaginary people whose voices he thought he heard. Among Wills' sample there was a high rate (52.5 per cent) of addiction to heroin at some time during the musicians' lives. This usage was very likely anomalous, as heroin use was widespread and in fashion among jazz musicians after the Second World War, but as jazz gradually became more accepted, and as younger musicians saw the harm caused to their older colleagues, usage began to fall off. In other psychological parameters, jazz musicians fared similarly to their classical brethren:

- 28.5 per cent of jazz musicians suffered mood disorders compared with 41 per cent and 34.6 per cent for classical composers in prior studies.
- 7.5 per cent of jazz musicians suffered psychotic illness compared with 10 per cent and 1 per cent of classical composers in prior studies.
- 27.5 per cent of jazz musicians had alcohol problems, compared with 40 per cent and 21.2 per cent of classical composers.

Youth

Some of the most creative mathematicians, lyric poets, and composers of music were extraordinarily young when they produced their best work. Most painters, novelists and philosophers, on the other hand, continue to create and are often at their peak well into old age. Disciplines that are intense and analytic tend to require youth; reflective and artistic disciplines may be pursued well into old age. At the extreme is polymath Thomas Young, who exhibited one of the most creative minds of the 18th century. By his mid-30s he had estimated the size of the atom within an order of magnitude, introduced the term 'Indo-European language' after comparing some 400 different languages, posited the tri-colour theory of human light perception, figured out how to translate the hieroglyphics of the Rosetta stone, and provided numerous other insights in physics and medicine.[30]

It is important to note here a decisive difference from creation in the sciences or mathematics. Individuals in these latter areas begin to be productive at an early age and may make numerous innovations during their early years. But the speed of change in the sciences tends to favour the energies of youth. In either case, Howard Gardner has proposed a 'ten-year' rule, which suggests that creative individuals contribute their most important work only after ten years of effort in their domain.

Psychosis

The most enduring (and perverse) speculations about creativity involve its correlation with madness. Such prejudices are fuelled by popular films such as *A Beautiful Mind*, which chronicles the madness of Nobel laureate John Nash, and *Proof*, in which Gwyneth Paltrow is the brilliant and troubled daughter of a mathematician (Anthony Hopkins) whose descent from mathematical ingenuity into insanity keeps the audience guessing whether Paltrow will follow in her father's footsteps. *Proof* itself plays on three recurring themes, each with a basis in reality: creativity and the loss of a father, creativity and youth, and creativity and madness.

Prejudices about psychosis and creativity have ancient roots, dating at least to the speculations of Roman philosopher Seneca. The 19th-century psychiatrist W. L. Babcock published an article entitled 'On the morbid heredity and predisposition to insanity of the man of genius', in which he claimed that like proneness to early death, creativity and genius was a characteristic of inferior genetic makeup.[31] On a more solid footing is recent research that supports the general association of creativity with psychopathology, at least in some creative domains. One study of creative individuals found that 28 per cent of prominent scientists experienced at least some sort of mental disturbance; this increased to 87 per cent among outstanding poets.[32] Psychometric evaluation of many creative mathematicians, architects and writers has revealed that creative individuals consistently scored higher on dimensions that are indicative of various affective disorders such as schizophrenia, depression and paranoia,[33] thus providing evidence for associating creativity with psychosis.[34] Creative individuals tend to exhibit 'complexity' – in other words, very creative individuals can alternate between the two extremes of being rebellious or highly disciplined – which is consistent with the sorts of psychoses associated with creativity.

TRAITS OF CREATIVE SOCIETIES

Some societies have a reputation for creativity, and this has led some political scientists and economists to look for characteristic indicators of governance in promoting societal creativity. For example, Italy has a well-deserved reputation for cutting-edge innovation in cars, motorcycles, furniture and fashion, and Japan is known for innovation in products and industrial processes. What is it about the social or governmental systems of these countries that inspires innovation? Can it be duplicated at the country, firm or group level?

Economist Paul Seabright argues that the major social stimuli for creativity are:

▶ enough wealth to give those with ideas some hope of finding patrons or jobs
▶ a substantial immigrant population eager to challenge the established order
▶ a total population large enough to contain a critical mass of talent, but with enough focus in its geography to allow for effective networking.[35]

Historian David Landes provides evidence that creativity has thrived in societies that:

▶ operate, manage and build instruments of production
▶ create, adapt and master new technologies
▶ impart expertise and knowledge to the young
▶ choose people for jobs by competence and relative merit
▶ promote and demote on basis of performance
▶ encourage initiative, competition and emulation
▶ let people enjoy and employ the fruits of their labour, enterprise and creativity.[36]

Landes describes the government's role in promoting creativity, arguing that innovation has flourished in the past when governments:

▶ encourage saving and investment
▶ enforce rights of contract
▶ secure rights of personal liberty against tyranny and crime
▶ are stable, though not necessarily democratic
▶ are responsive
▶ provide no rents or favours for government position
▶ are moderate, efficient and non-greedy.

Landes also argues against government behaviour that is likely to squelch creativity. For example, he says that direct government involvement in innovation tends to favour the creation and maintenance of powerful, conservative, expensive scientific bureaucracies which rob would-be innovators of scarce talent. Landes's lists effectively explain why we see huge populations of creative people centred in clusters of innovative companies around Silicon Valley and Santa Monica, despite the high cost of living in California. Where governments have tried to build such environments, they have often failed. The most obvious examples are the 50-odd 'Science Parks' constructed around the world in the past two decades, which with only a few exceptions either lie dormant or provide low-rent homes for government-favoured national champions.

Open source software

Open source software, such as the Linux operating system or the Apache netserver, provides guides to how the alignment of objectives, an open horizontal structure and voluntary membership can develop innovative, high-quality commercial products. Open source software is based on the voluntary cooperation of developers in many different locations, with a shared 'culture' across a diffuse community of practice. There are minimal reporting relationships, assignments or clear lines of responsibility. But underneath there is a society based on performance, capability and peer review. There is a distinct division of labour: the software itself is modular, and programmers tend to specialize on particular functional modules. In addition there are diffuse organizations that impose order, like the Apache Software Foundation which manages the Apache netserver, a meritocracy where membership is granted only to core volunteers who have actively contributed to Apache projects.

Although there are over 13,000 open source developers contributing to Linux, Apache and other code, less than 0.1 per cent contribute around three-quarters of the code to these projects.[37] Within this diverse community, subtle codes of conduct arise which in many ways fill the same roles as corporate management, policy and procedure. Members exert strong peer pressure against non-compliance with rules or standards, through flaming, spamming and refusal to acknowledge contributions. This is reminiscent of a tribal society where active monitoring of community members' behaviour fosters order and productivity.

Brainstorming

Alex Faickney Osborn was the 'O' in the name of advertising giant BBDO. In 1948, Osborn condensed his years of decision-making experience at BBDO in the bestseller *Your Creative Power*. Among others, he presented his technique of brainstorming, which had been in use at BBDO since the late 1930s. Osborne's brainstorming was designed to encourage a group to express various ideas and to defer critical judgement until later. Everyone offers ideas that are listed, combined, improved, and changed into various other ideas. In the end, the group agrees on a final resolution.

The practice of brainstorming is a distinctively American practice, mirroring that environment of the town hall meetings that played a formative role in developing the American culture. Of course, not all cultures share this outspoken tradition. Asian cultures in particular tend to respect a culture of 'groupthink', defined by Irving Janis as 'a mode of thinking that people engage in when they are deeply involved in a cohesive in-group, when the members' strivings for unanimity override their motivation to realistically appraise alternative courses of action'.[38] Curiously, what is seen as desirable in most Asian cultures is generally viewed in a derogatory manner by Americans, being generally attached to *poor* decisions and not to collective successes. Implementers need to be sensitive to such cultural differences in both setting expectations, and in the practice of brainstorming. Toward the end of this workout, several suggestions are provided that modify the approach to be useful in less outspoken cultures.

Successful brainstorming creates an environment that encourages imaginative ideas to flow. The usual method is to have a small group (from 6 to 12 people) discuss a specific problem. One member records the remarks and suggestions. All withhold judgement on all suggestions. After the session, the various ideas and suggestions are reviewed and evaluated.

The two basic principles of brainstorming are:

▸ **Quantity breeds quality.** You should never attempt to solve a challenge with only a single idea. The more ideas you come up with, the more likely you are to arrive at the best solution.

▸ **Defer judgement.** Groups instinctively tend to anchor on the first idea thrown out (this is an inherent fault known as 'groupthink' studied extensively by Irving Janis in the 1950s). We naturally defer judgement when shopping for clothes; it is similarly the right way to shop for ideas.

Blueprint

A chain is only as strong as its weakest link, and a negative thinker can derail a proposal by focusing on only a fraction of it. Showing that one part of the whole is absurd, he or she implies that the whole is equally absurd. By destroying a part, a person can destroy the whole and feel a sense of achievement without taking the time or making the effort to create anything.

When we collaborate and align and attune ourselves to a common purpose, our energies must be channelled in constructive directions. The success of any brainstorming session depends upon all members understanding the importance of creating a positive environment. To encourage this, avoid making negative judgemental statements about ideas such as:

▸ Let's shelve that for the time being.
▸ Who is going to do it?
▸ I have something better.
▸ We tried that before.
▸ It won't fit our operation.
▸ It's against all our combined logic.
▸ Not enough return on investment.
▸ It's great, but . . .
▸ Someone must have already tried it.
▸ I thought of that a long time ago.
▸ We can't afford that.
▸ You'll never get approval.
▸ You're on the wrong track.
▸ Don't rock the boat.
▸ The market is not ready yet.
▸ It's not a new concept.

Group brainstorming helps re-educate people to think positively about ideas. The procedures are:

1. Select your problem. Write the problem as a definite question, as specifically as possible.

2. Choose the participants. The ideal number is between 6 and 12. Participants should have a positive mental attitude and be fluent and flexible thinkers. They should be strong, independent personalities who are excited about participating and feel a genuine need to improve goods and services. Someone who has the power to make and implement decisions should also be present (although it is extremely important for the group leader to control and put in perspective the decision-implementer's comments, as nothing subdues a subordinate faster than the strong opinion of authority).

3. Choose the environment. The preferred location is a comfortable room off-site. The meeting leader should communicate a strong sense of urgency and a hunger for innovative ideas, but should allow for frequent breaks.

4. Select a group leader. The group leader should have strong interpersonal skills and be able to paraphrase and find analogies for suggestions. The group leader should:

   ▸ **Prepare in advance as much as possible.** Ask each participant to become as familiar as they can with creativity exercises. Plan the meeting carefully.

   ▸ **Invite people from diverse areas: non-experts as well as experts on the situation, and people who can make decisions about ideas generated by the group.** Discourage observers, onlookers and guests. Every attendee should be a participant.

   ▸ **Write an agenda and send it to all invitees.**

   ▸ **Employ a variety of creativity techniques to get ideas flowing.** Use humour and bizarre examples to loosen people up.

   ▸ **Focus on the challenge.** Be specific about what decisions have to be made, and continuously summarize the group's progress throughout the meeting.

   ▸ **Encourage any and all ideas, the more bizarre the better.** Pay attention to the ideas, and avoid identifying specific ideas with the person who suggested them.

   ▸ **Be prepared to go back and manipulate ideas.** Creativity always involves manipulation. Use questions that are designed to manipulate the subject in some way so as to change its position, rearrange its components, exaggerate some part, or alter the attributes to produce a series of ideas in a short time.

   ▸ **Emphasize everyone's unique contribution to the meeting.**

   ▸ **Select a recorder.** Assign someone to record all ideas the group suggests. If the ideas are not recorded, they will vanish completely.

After brainstorming, the group leader or the group as a whole should arrange the ideas into related groups to prioritize and evaluate them. In the evaluation stage, some will be discarded, some will stand out as worthwhile, and others will lend themselves to further modification and manipulation.

Try using generative graphics such as large wall-mounted scrolls of paper to facilitate group problem solving. Record the ideas with a cartoon, diagram or written phrase using large coloured felt markers. The idea is to stimulate full and energetic participation, and to find colourful, stimulating, and graphic ways to portray ideas and illustrate the group's thinking. For many of us, this method of sketching ideas is closer to how our thoughts naturally grow. Later, your generative graphics can be translated and recorded.

5. Follow up. Directly after the meeting, have a lunch, dinner or drinks party to celebrate the group's achievements. Write letters to the supervisors of participants acknowledging each individual's contribution to the session.

   ▸ It's a good idea to send each person a categorized list of the ideas that the group generated so that they can continue working on those ideas and keep the momentum of the brainstorming session going.

   ▸ Another good follow-up is to ask each participant to report back on at least one idea he or she thinks is worthy of action, and four or five recommendations for implementing the idea.

6. Evaluate the ideas. If you try to get hot and cold water out of a faucet at the same time, all you get is lukewarm water. If you try to evaluate ideas as they are being generated, you will not

get the ideas hot enough or the criticism cold enough. Do not evaluate ideas until the end of the session.

At the end of a brainstorming session, make three lists: ideas of immediate usefulness, areas for further exploration, and new approaches to the problem. The leader can categorize the ideas alone, or he or she can have the group evaluate the ideas by voting on the most useful.

Strive for quantity. List all ideas as they pop up no matter how similar they may seem.

Variations

Variations on the basic process of brainstorming have been designed to overcome resistance or dysfunction which may occur in cultures that encourage reticence, deference to hierarchy and power, or which may be instinctively critical. These variations may allow participants more anonymity, or a greater chance to ponder and record their thoughts before commitment.

Brainwriting

The term 'brainwriting' was coined by scientists at the Batelle Institute in Frankfurt, Germany. This is a brainstorming approach in which a group generates ideas silently in writing. Each person writes their ideas on a sheet of paper and then exchanges it for another member's sheet. The ideas on the new sheet will stimulate more ideas, which are added to the list. The process continues for a specified time period, usually 15 minutes. The rules for brainstorming also apply to brainwriting: strive for quantity, defer judgement, encourage freewheeling, and seek combinations and improvements.

Brainstorming bulletin board

Use a bulletin board to brainstorm creative ideas at your office. Place the bulletin board in a central location, write the problem to be solved on a piece of coloured paper, and place it in the centre of the board for all interested parties to see. Anyone with an idea or suggestion about the problem writes it on a white piece of paper and places it under the problem on the board.

The advantages of this technique are:

▸ **The problem is visible, and thus will be on the minds of all interested people.**
▸ **It spurs ideas by association.** As a person reads the problem and ideas already posted on the board, he or she is likely to think of a new idea.
▸ **You can leave the problem up as long as you like.** This gives people sufficient time to consider it.
▸ **If few or no people offer ideas, you might consider ways to encourage workers to become more creative.**

Solo brainstorming

If you are doing a solo brainstorm, write your ideas on index cards. Jot down one idea per card until you run dry. Write the ideas as they come to you – good ones, bad ones, absurd ones – without regard to logic or value. You end up with a pack of ideas that you can then sort, re-sort, and add to as you shuffle them around to decide the best ones to pursue for your purposes.

Assume your challenge is to come up with ways to differentiate your bank from other banks. The first idea that occurs to you is: 'Why not make the bank comfortable and homey?'. Rather than rejecting this idea as impractical, you could come up with a new way of handling banking transactions. For example, you could create a bank where customers hand their money and forms to a receptionist who passes them to a row of clerks for processing. Instead of waiting in line, you could sit in a 'homey' atmosphere in a comfortable chair, watch television, read magazines and sip coffee. The clerk would call your name when your transaction was complete.

The key is to write down every thought, regardless of its appropriateness to the challenge. It doesn't matter what the thought is. If you think it, write it.

Visual brainstorming

Brainstorming can also take other forms: a golfer can brainstorm different shots while playing, a composer can brainstorm with music, actors and actresses can brainstorm expressions while acting, and a visual thinker can brainstorm by sketching ideas as they occur.

Ideas usually appear in rapid succession, and spontaneous sketching can create a momentum in which expression keeps pace with thinking. In addition, drawing an idea helps prevent you from making judgements about it before it is fully developed and evaluated.

The basic principles of visual brainstorming are:

▸ **Fluency and flexibility of thinking.** Fluent thinking means coming up with a large number of ideas; flexible thinking demonstrates diversity and variety.

▸ **Deferred judgement.**

▸ **Quick response.** If you fail to draw the idea at once, you may lose it.

However it may be conducted, brainstorming when well run can generate the insights and innovative power of quizzing and stream of consciousness idea generation, but fuelled by all of the experience and wisdom of the group. The secret is to avoid groupthink and encourage everyone to exercise their imagination through these short bursts of creative fecundity.

Q&A with jazz vibraphonist Gary Burton
who talks about managing creative people

Vibraphonist Gary Burton is well known in jazz circles. He was *Down Beat* magazine's 1968 Jazzman of the Year, is a member of the Percussion Hall of Fame, and is currently Dean of Curriculum of the Berklee College of Music in Boston. He is known worldwide as a musical innovator and master improviser. In a career that has spanned three decades, he's recorded with jazz legends like Chick Corea, Stan Getz, George Shearing and Quincy Jones, pop and rock stars like k.d. lang and Eric Clapton, and led the Burton Quartet.

Conventional wisdom says that jazz combos are free and spontaneous, and symphony orchestras are dominated by autocratic conductor/CEOs. Do those images correspond to reality?

Unless you've been inside a jazz combo or an orchestra you can't know how they really work. For example, there's a very strong leader in the jazz group. For all the talk of openness and spontaneity, a jazz group can't adopt a communistic attitude: 'We're all equals here.' There's a need for vision and concept, and only one person can effectively establish and define a vision. Once you have this vision, your job as leader is to bring out the best in the people who're working with you. I want my piano player to have as much input as I can stand – as long as it doesn't bump into the vision. I need to communicate to him what my vision is, so the stuff he contributes fits it.

Just how collaborative are jazz combos really?

If it's my group my judgement is ultimate. I'll talk with my musicians about how I see the song. Each song is like a little play that we've been given. Usually it's about 30 seconds of information – a chord sequence, a tempo, a mood and a concept. We're going to take that and spin it into a story for the next 8 or 9 minutes.

I'll say to the group, 'Here's the script. It's set in Argentina, and it's got a melancholy feel to it, and this is what I see happening.' I describe this to the group in two ways: I play it for them myself and say, 'I hear it at this tempo, and I hear a crescendo in this section, and then it tapers off in this section.' So I'm showing them how I feel the tune should be played, and I'm also describing it in words as much as possible.

Within the context of that vision, individual players start to contribute their ideas. Occasionally, I have to say, 'What you're doing there doesn't really work. Could you try something else?' Everybody makes suggestions, we discuss them, eventually we work it out. If we have a standoff, the leader makes the decision and everyone goes along with it.

The jazz leader I most admired was Miles Davis. That may come as a surprise, because he had a reputation as an eccentric. The way he looked was absolutely intimidating, and he was mesmerizing to watch and hear in action. But he was also the most creative and daring musician. The best jazz musicians wanted to play with Miles because they knew that he could get them to go places musically that otherwise they wouldn't be able to go. He would sign up the biggest stars to play with him, encourage them to do their best work, and be strong enough himself to bring them all together and meld them into a cohesive group. As demanding and intimidating as he was, it was worth it.

That's more like what you hear about conductors of symphony orchestras. Is a conductor more like a CEO who defines a vision and then makes sure everybody executes it appropriately?

That's certainly the general image. But there's a dark side of orchestras that most people don't know about – a strange political battle between orchestra members and conductors. The members of the orchestra are constantly harassing and challenging the conductor, doing anything they can to try to mess him up, including very childish things. It's almost like they defy the conductor to make them tow the line. It's very common.

Is that the musical equivalent of corporate alienation?
One of my classical friends, a violin soloist, experienced this when she was guesting at Lincoln Center, with the New York Philharmonic.

She went to rehearsal and there was Zubin Mehta conducting and the players were being incredibly disrespectful. They weren't paying attention, they were talking to each other, listening to the ballgame on the radio. She turned to one of her friends and said, 'I had no idea things were this bad.' He said, 'We're all on good behaviour tonight because you're here.'

Gamesmanship like that is fairly familiar in corporations. What accounts for it in orchestras?
I guess it's a psychological thing: because the conductor literally has all the control, the players then abdicate. They've been disempowered, as they say in the business world. I know it sounds exactly like the corporate environment: 'I just type whatever they give me. It's none of my business whether it's all wrong or not, or whether I could make a suggestion. Every time I make a suggestion, nobody cares anyway, so let them stew in their own juice.' It turns out the same thing applies to a large corporate structure or a symphony orchestra.

Businesses say they want their traditional management teams to become as spontaneous and improvizational as a good jazz combo. How hard is it to teach a classical musician to feel comfortable improvizing?
It's a very difficult transition for someone who has been a typical classical musician for decades. A lot of my classical music friends say to me, 'I'd love to be able to improvize. Tell me how to do it. You're a teacher – help me out.'

It's not out of the question. But I have to tell them, 'You'll learn a process, you'll understand it, but you'll have to unlearn or replace a lot of ingrained habits.'

It turns out that classically trained musicians are the toughest ones to teach. It's easier to teach somebody who's a beginning musician. Performing music – or managing in a company, for that matter – is all about developing habits and ways of doing things that your unconscious mind controls. A very modest example of this would be the way people learn to play the piano. You don't start out for the first year saying, 'This year we're going to start using just these two fingers and get good at that, and then next year go to four fingers.' You don't work your way up to ten because that would mean relearning your concept of how to function on the instrument all over again. You learn one way of doing it and that becomes your natural, spontaneous physical connection to the process.

One of the paradoxes of improvization is that it's a mixture of two opposites – tremendous discipline and regimen balanced by spontaneity, listening and playing in the moment. We spend countless hours going over and over things, trying to learn parts, trying to get our playing perfected. We practise exercises, we play the passage repeatedly until we can get it right, and then as soon as we get that one right we move on to another one and start doing it over and over again. Every musician puts in anywhere from an hour to several hours a day for years just to get their basic craft organized. Now that kind of experience is highly regimented – it's totally lacking in spontaneity.

At the same time, musicians have a highly developed instinct to be spontaneous. When something in us says, 'Do it!' we're able to just go ahead and do it. As a musician you have to be able to live by those spontaneous instincts or you simply become nonfunctional. One of the things I suspect about the colourful behaviour of musicians, whether classical, jazz, or rock, is that it's a way to shake off all that regimen and get back in touch with the raw emotion of music.

Are there techniques you use with students to try to teach them to be spontaneous?
I tell them to use their ears instead of their brains. If I'm working with a student, I'll play something and tell them to play something back to me. Respond to it. React to it. Don't stop and study it. Answer it. Make musical conversation happen.

Gradually what happens is that you let your unconscious mind make the decisions. This is the essential element for the jazz musician. When I'm playing, my mind has to make thousands of little decisions incredibly quickly. I couldn't possibly think about each one, consider each one, and make the decision. My unconscious mind can weigh all these alternative possibilities, pick the right one, time it exactly, coordinate the muscles, and make it happen.

As I start to play a song, in those first few moments of playing I step back from the process mentally, and the playing starts going on its own. I start watching it as if I'm an observer. The unconscious mind is now doing it. It's very natural for me now, after doing it for years. It wasn't so natural in my early days when I was much more conscious about my playing. But you learn to trust your unconscious mind.[39]

Gary Burton interview – questions for review

1. What are the distinctive characteristics of the most creative people that you know?
2. What habits or behavioural traits do you like about these people?
3. What habits or behavioural traits do you dislike about these people? How would you ask them to change? What impact might this have on their creativity?
4. What sort of business environment can you envisage that would maximize the amount of innovation contributed by these creative individuals?

CHAPTER QUESTIONS FOR REVIEW

1. Alan Afuah defines five types of people that are needed for successful innovation: idea generators, boundary spanners, evangelists, coaches and project managers. What role does creativity play in the execution of each of these functions?

2. Creative people need to be managed differently than do workers whose jobs are more structured and routine. What suggestions could you give managers for getting the most out of their creative staff?

3. What personality traits tend to be shared by creative people? Do you think that any or all of these would create significant challenges for the managers of creative workers?

4. What are the social and governmental characteristics of countries that are highly creative?

CHAPTER 12: KEY POINTS

▷ Understanding creative people
- No one knows exactly what triggered the increases in brain size that differentiate human beings from apes, and presumably the concurrent rise in human creativity. But can you, in a Darwinian context of random genetic mutations, and aggressive natural selection, outline a scenario in which creativity becomes as much of a human necessity as hunger or sex?
- Beyond a certain level of IQ, probably around 120, there is no clear correlation between intelligence and creativity.
- Creators are hard-driving, focused, dominant, independent risk-takers.
- Complexity is the ability to harbour tendencies that normally appear to be at opposite extremes. Very creative individuals can alternate between the two extremes of being rebellious or highly disciplined almost at the drop of a hat.
- Psychological androgyny – being on one hand very sensitive and more 'feminine' and on the other aggressive and offensive – is another creative trait.
- Child prodigies usually exhibit only one extreme of the spectrum of characteristics – they tend to be intense, driven and introverted.
- Creative people exhibit stimulus freedom – what we might call the ability to think outside the box.

▷ Managing creative people
- Recruit for diversity, hire for philosophy.
- Rehab the neighbourhood.
- Within limits, let them make the rules.
- Keep their eyes on the prize.
- Feed their heads.
- Teach them a new language.
- Allow time for blue-sky thinking.
- Protect your team from creativity killers.
- Add liberal doses of fun.

NOTES

1 Afuah, A. (2003) *Innovation Management*, Oxford: Oxford University Press, pp. 37–9.

2 Schmidt, E. and Varian, H. (2005) 'Google: ten golden rules', *Newsweek*, 2 December.

3 Drucker, P. F. (2000) 'Managing knowledge means managing oneself', *Leader to Leader* 16 (Spring).

4 Vise, D. and Malseed, M. (2006) *The Google Story*, New York: Delta.

5 Selby, R. and Cusumano, M. (1999) *Microsoft Secrets*, New York: Free Press.

6 Florida, R. (2003) *The Rise of the Creative Class*, New York: Basic Books, pp. 132–7.

7 Source: 'The rise and fall of corporate R&D', *Economist*, 3 March 2007, pp. 69–71.

8 Tischler, L. (2004) 'The care and feeding of the creative class', *FastCompany* 89 (December), p. 93.

9 Rothenberg, A. and Hausman, C. R. K (eds) (1976) *The Creativity Question*, Durham, N.C.: Duke University Press; Sternberg, R. J. (ed.) (1998) *Handbook of Creativity*, Cambridge, UK: Cambridge University Press.

10 Amabile, T. M., Collins, M. A., Conti, R., Phillips, E., Picariello, M., Ruscio, J., and Whitney, D. (1996) *Creativity in Context: Update to the psychology of creativity*, Boulder, Colo.: Westview.

11 Bodin, M. (1990) *The Creative Mind: Myths and mechanisms*, New York: Basic Books, pp. 254–5.

12 Mokyr, J. (1991) *The Leaver of Riches*, Oxford, Oxford University Press.

13 Romer, P. (1993) 'Ideas and things', *Economist*, 11 September 1993.

14 Seabright, P. (2004) *The Company of Strangers*, Princeton, N.J.: Princeton University Press, pp. 110–15.

15 Bloom, H. (2002) *Genius*, New York: Warner; Brockman, J. (ed.) (1993) *Creativity*, New York: Touchstone; Florida, R. (2002) *The Rise of the Creative Class*, New York: Basic Books.

16 Abraham, C. (2002) *Possessing Genius: The bizarre odyssey of Einstein's brain*, New York: St. Martin's Press.

17 Witelson, S. F., Kigal, D. L., and Harvey, T. (1999). 'The Exceptional brain of Albert Einstein', *The Lancet* 353, p. 2149.

18 Diamond, M. C., Scheibel, S., Murphy, G. J. M. Jr. and Harvey, T. (1985) 'On the brain of a scientist: Albert Einstein', *Experimental Neurology* 88, p. 198.

19 Anderson, B. and Harvey, T. (1996) 'Alterations in cortical thickness and neuronal density in the frontal cortex of Albert Einstein', *Neuroscience Letters* 210, p. 161.

20 Csikszentmihalyi, M. (1996) *Creativity*, New York: Harper Collins.

21 Guilford, J. P. (1967) *The Nature of Human Intelligence*, New York: McGraw-Hill.

22 See e.g. for citations Sternberg, R. J. and O'Hara, L. (1999) 'Creativity and intelligence', pp. 251–72 in R. J. Sternberg (ed.), *Handbook of Creativity*, New York: Cambridge University Press.

23 Winner, E. (1997) *Gifted Children: Myths and realities*, New York, Basic Books.

24 Dacey, J. S. and Lennon, K. H. (1998) *Understanding Creativity*, San Francisco, Calif.: Jossey-Bass.

25 Csikszentmihalyi, M. (1996) *Creativity*, New York: Harper Collins.

26 Winner, E. (1997) *Gifted Children: Myths and realities*, New York, Basic Books.

27 Csikszentmihalyi, M. (1996) *Creativity*, New York: Harper Collins.

28 Sartre, J.-P. (1964) *The Words*, trans. B, Frechtman. New York: George Braziller.

29 Wills, G. I. (2003). 'Forty lives in the bebop business: mental health in a group of eminent jazz musicians', *British Journal of Psychiatry* 183, pp. 255–9.

30 Gardner, H. (1993) *Creating Minds*, New York: Basic Books.

31 Lombroso, C. (1895) *The Man of Genius*, London: Scribner's; Ludwig, A. M. (1995) *The Price of Greatness: Resolving the creativity and madness controversy*, New York: Guilford; Post, F. (1994) 'Creativity and psychopathology: a study of 291 world-famous men', *British Journal of Psychiatry* 165, pp. 22–34.

32 Ludwig, A. M. (1995) *The Price of Greatness: Resolving the creativity and madness controversy*, New York: Guilford.

33 MacKinnon, D. W. (1975) 'IPAR's contribution to the conceptualization and study of creativity', in I. Taylor and J. W. Getxels (eds), *Perspectives on Creativity*, Chicago, Ill.: Aldine.

34 Simonton, D. K. (1999) *Origins of Genius*, Oxford: Oxford University Press.

35 Seabright, P. (2004) *The Company of Strangers*, Princeton, N.J.: Princeton University Press, pp. 110–15.

36 Landes, D. S. (1998) *The Wealth and Poverty of Nations: Why some are so rich and some so poor*, New York: W. W. Norton, chs 27–29.

37 Lerner, J and Triole, J. (2000) 'The simple economics of open source software', NBER Working Paper 7600 (December).

38 Janis, Irving L. (1982) *Groupthink: Psychological studies of policy decisions and fiascoes*, 2nd edn, New York: Houghton Mifflin.

39 Source: Schrage, M. (2006) 'The Gary Burton Trio: Lessons on business from a jazz legend', *Fast Company* 6, pp. 110.

SOCIETY AND INNOVATION

LEARNING OBJECTIVES

After finishing this chapter, you will understand

► the changes being impelled by **rapid innovation** in economies and societies around the world

► the role of **tolerance**, **diversity** and **creativity** in economic wealth

► what **governments can and cannot do** to promote an innovation-based economy.

After reading the *innovation workout*, you will be challenged to **put together everything** you have learned about innovating in the prior chapters. After reading the Meade Instruments *case study*, you will understand why **creative passion** is important in technology industries.

Note: Further information, class slides, test questions and other supporting material are available on our companion website at

www.palgrave.com/business/westland

THE INNOVATION SOCIETY

Why are some societies more innovative than others? The answer to this question matters greatly, because the world – though flat from a manufacturing and services perspective – has increasingly clustered around creative centres. And at these centres are cultures and lifestyles that foster innovation. These centres are also where most of the world's wealth is being created.

The rise of the innovators

Figure 13.1 shows graphically how innovation has steadily risen to become the most important generator of both jobs and wealth in the United States. Agriculture has steadily been consolidated and automated, while automation and global outsourcing have flattened the demand and income of industrial jobs.[1] All of the growth since the 1960s has been in information-intensive jobs for innovators, and the low-paid service jobs through which new innovations are implemented.

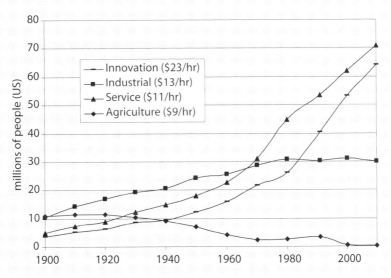

Figure 13.1 Historical structure of the US job market

Source: Florida, R. (2003) *The Rise of the Creative Class*, New York: Basic Books.

T. M. Amabile observes that 'creativity by individuals and teams is a starting point for innovation; the first is a necessary but not sufficient condition for the second'.[2] There is widespread agreement on this – you can't innovate if you don't first fill your opportunity register with new ideas. And the corollary to this observation is that a critical mass of creative people will not guarantee successful innovation, but lack of creative people will assure that there will not be innovation.

INNOVATION'S ROLE
IN ECONOMICS

Adam Smith incorporated the political constituencies of land, labour and capital into his distinct world view. Smith wrote *An Inquiry into the Nature and Causes of the Wealth of Nations*[3] with a view to explaining England's rise to global prominence and wealth in the 18th century. In England's case it was not the climate and soil, or the extent of its territory, or industriousness (many people in England didn't work at all) that made England wealthy. Smith concluded that it was *specialization* (the division of labour) that made England uniquely productive.

Specialization created the opportunity for increasing returns to scale. But increasing returns could only be realized through innovations – the division of the job into ever more specialized categories, which simplified production and deskilled jobs so that even the simplest of workers could perform them well. Adam Smith could easily have been describing the process by which modern jobs are deskilled and outsourced today.

Other observers of the Industrial Revolution were more strongly influenced by France's class struggles. David Ricardo was less concerned with operations, and more with class conflict between land, labour and capital; he argued for equitable *distribution* of wealth among social classes.[4] Karl Marx took this further, incorporating the social impact of rapid innovation and the marriage of machine and man.[5] Marx referred to the *ratio of labour to machines* as the '*organic composition of capital*'. In Marx's mind, machinery could not produce value itself, but was necessary in order to gain a temporary price advantage over competitors. His reasoning was that machines are a tool of man, and essentially an amplifier of their labour. Both men foresaw the rising conflict between the scientists, designers and innovators that created machines and defined the character of work, and the industrial and service workers at the business end of these designs.[6]

Marx saw how the Industrial Revolution was altering the landscape of power in the early 19th century. Materials, labour and capital were the new powers in Europe – materials from mines and farms of the landowning nobles (about 3 per cent of the population); capital from the savings and investment of bankers, merchants and entrepreneurs (about 10 per cent of the population); and labour from the working classes, often poor, displaced serfs or sharecroppers (the remainder).[7] The particular claims and contributions of these political groups were legitimized in the account classifications which to this day provide much of the basis for financial reporting and economic analysis.[8]

The increasing returns of Adam Smith's pin factory (see the box) tended to be less influential in economics in the subsequent two centuries, where there was an implicit assumption that any rise in production would be subject to the same decreasing returns on investment that had always been true for traditional extractive or agricultural businesses. For example, the more you mine a vein of gold, the less return you can expect from each hour of effort; the first few barrels of fertilizer spurs greater crop production, but more will burn the crops.[9]

Adam Smith's pin factory

To take an example, therefore, from a very trifling manufacture; but one in which the division of labour has been very often taken notice of, the trade of the pin-maker; a workman not educated to this business (which the division of labour has rendered a distinct trade), nor acquainted with the use of the machinery employed in it (to the invention of which the same division of labour has probably given occasion), could scarce, perhaps, with his utmost industry, make one pin in a day, and certainly could not make twenty. But in the way in which this business is now carried on, not only the whole work is a peculiar trade, but it is divided into a number of branches, of which the greater part are likewise peculiar trades. One man draws out the wire, another straights it, a third cuts it, a fourth points it, a fifth grinds it at the top for receiving the head; to make the head requires two or three distinct operations; to put it on, is a peculiar business, to whiten the pins is another; it is even a trade by itself to put them into the paper; and the important business of making a pin is, in this manner, divided into about eighteen distinct operations, which, in some manufactories, are all performed by distinct hands, though in others the same man will sometimes perform two or three of them. I have seen a small manufactory of this kind where ten men only were employed, and where some of them consequently performed two or three distinct operations. But though they were very poor, and therefore but indifferently accommodated with the necessary machinery, they could, when they exerted themselves, make among them about twelve pounds of pins in a day. There are in a pound upwards of four thousand pins of a middling size. Those ten persons, therefore, could make among them upwards of forty-eight thousand pins in a day. Each person, therefore, making a tenth part of forty-eight thousand pins, might be considered as making four thousand eight hundred pins in a day. But if they had all wrought separately and independently, and without any of them having been educated to this peculiar business, they certainly could not each of them have made twenty, perhaps not one pin in a day; that is, certainly, not the two hundred and fortieth, perhaps not the four thousand eight hundredth part of what they are at present capable of performing, in consequence of a proper division and combination of their different operations.

Source: extract from *An Inquiry into the Nature and Causes of the Wealth of Nations*.[10]

Economists saw increasing returns, where costs fall and profits increase with more output, as being associated mainly with machine output, which allocated the fixed cost of machinery over longer and longer production runs. In the 19th century, another source of increasing returns was found to come from the growth of networks, such as rail, telegraph, telephone and oil pipelines.[11] Theodore Vale, the first president of Bell Telephone after Bell's patents ran out, argued persuasively that the increasing returns in industries like the telephone were because they were 'natural monopolies' that should be regulated by government, rather than let free to dominate their industries, a view that prevailed throughout much of the 20th century.[12]

By the turn of the 20th century, many industries with increasing returns to scale populated the economic landscape. Alfred Marshall characterized these as benefiting from 'external increasing returns' economies, a term which was quickly shortened to 'externality'.[13] Marshall went on to put economics on a firm algebraic footing with his marginal productivity theory (ironically, economist Francis Edgeworth complained that Marshall's system left no room for innovation and entrepreneurs), and the view that technological innovations were somehow external to the functioning of the economy prevailed through most of the 20th century.[14]

Virtual economies

In March 1999, a small number of Californians discovered a new world called Norrath, populated by an exotic but industrious people. About 12,000 people call this place their permanent home, although some 60,000 are present there at any given time. The nominal hourly wage is about USD 3.42 per hour, and the labors of the people produce a GNP per capita somewhere between that of Russia and Bulgaria. A unit of Norrath's currency is traded on exchange markets at USD 0.0107, higher than the Yen and the Lira. The economy is characterized by extreme inequality, yet life there is quite attractive to many. The population is growing rapidly, swollen each day by hundreds of emigres from various places around the globe, but especially the United States. Perhaps the most interesting thing about the new world is its location. Norrath is a virtual world that exists entirely on 40 computers in San Diego.

So began a report by Edward Castronova on the state of multi-player game economies in 2001.[15] Since that time, virtual economies residing entirely on network servers, but connecting with real-world economies through real money transactions (RMT), have grown explosively, comprising a US$3 billion economy in 2006. Many of the transactions take place on public auction sites like eBay, but virtual items residing only on game servers are increasingly getting their own search-auction sites. Eye On MOGS, GamerPrice, MMOFX, Gold Price Watcher and GameUSD all provide virtual economy specific search and sales for real money. In addition, game developers such as Sony are considering their own foreign exchange markets for virtual currency. For example, the game *There* has therebucks that sell for US dollars. The currency in *Entropia Universe*, Project Entropia Dollars (PED), could be bought and redeemed for real-world money at a rate of 10 PED for US$1. An island in *Project Entropia* sold for US$26,500. One gamer also purchased a virtual space station for US$100,000 and plans to use it as a virtual nightclub.[16]

Marshall suggested that there are two kinds of 'increasing returns'. The first were due to allocating fixed costs over larger and larger production runs; the second were external and the result of general development in the industry (like greater connectivity offered as rail or telephone networks expand). In his analyses, Marshall recognized the importance of innovation, technology and knowledge as both factors and engines of production, but characterized them under his second type of externality. Innovation was characterized as a 'gift' somehow uncontrollable by human decisions or activity.

Around the 1970s, economists started giving more thought to identifying the distinguishing feature of an innovation, as either an input or output of production. Innovations are special sorts of goods; they are neither a conventional good, nor a pure public good (one shared by all, and owned by none). Rather, an innovation is a non-rival good (that is, you and I can both enjoy the good at the same time without influencing the other's consumption or enjoyment of it) and a partially excludable good (that is, 'owners' may limit access to it).[17] Rival goods are objects; non-rival goods are ideas – atoms versus bits. Such features of innovation show up in a variety of packages: the pattern for a pair of Calvin Klein jeans, a personal computer operating system, an operatic performance, a logic chip design, an encrypted message, a map of the *E. Coli* genome, the formula for a new drug, a genetically modified rice seed and the process that created it, a Calder sculpture, the text on this page. All of these are non-rival goods because they can be copied or shared and used by many people at the same time. Most are partially excludable as well. Access to them can be controlled to some degree, in the manner of access by members of a club.[18]

The economics of alternative realities

Entertainment – consisting of motion pictures, music, television, video games and so forth – is globally around a US$200 billion annual business. Traditionally, motion pictures and music provided the most profitable sectors. But as the 1990s wore on, internet technologies made it difficult to control property rights on music, and the industry dwindled. By 2006 the motion picture industry generated around $30 billion annually; video games were estimated to generate 150 per cent to 200 per cent of that amount.[19] The two genres were linked by the tendency to release blockbuster movies as video games, and vice versa. The youth market comprises the largest share of the motion picture market, and 17 of the top 20 films were PG or PG-13 rated.[20]

The fanciful realities of children's entertainment constitute a huge industry – an industry with some of the most innovative and forward-thinking artists in the world. The advent of ever more powerful computers has steadily increased the 'animation' content of films, though these may be called something else, like special effects or post-production work. But Hollywood sees a day not far off when photorealistic animation will completely replace expensive, capricious actors, complex sets and location visits, providing a far greater range of artistic control than is possible with physical sets and actors.

Such whimsy always been the domain of some. In the early days of American film, cartoonists such as Walt Disney, Paul Terry and Max Fleischer created imaginary characters and worlds with simple pen and ink tools. The medium steadily evolved, becoming technically more sophisticated, as well as providing ideas and technologies for motion pictures and games.

Some modern giants of animation still opt for the creative control and low costs of pen and ink. Foremost is Hayao Miyazaki of Studio Ghibli in Tokyo. Miyazaki's films *Princess Mononoke* and *Spirited Away* were the highest-grossing films of all time in Japan, displaying his recurring themes of humanity's relationship to nature and technology.

Better indicators of trends in modern computer animation are the movies *Sin City* and *300*, both based on graphic novels (which also served as story boards) by Frank Miller. Both were primarily shot on sound stages with blue and green screen backdrops. Sets, stunts and even actors were supplemented using computer animation techniques. The resulting films were both critical and commercial successes, enjoying an aesthetic and dramatic impact that it would have been difficult to achieve with either location settings or pen and ink cartoons.

CATEGORIES OF RESEARCH EXPENDITURE

David Stokes divided research expenditures into three categories – *basic, use-inspired basic* and *applied*. In many countries, including the United States, these three categories mainly occur in their own unique institutional structures. Universities tend to focus on basic research; industrial laboratories concentrate on products, and thus pure applied research; government laboratories such as the US Center for Disease Control concentrate on use-inspired basic research such as vaccines and cures for cancer. Figure 13.2 shows the level of spending in the United States on these three classes of research.

Stokes distinguished between the motivation for particular innovations and scientific pursuits in terms of practical applicability and utility versus fundamental understanding of the character of nature (see Table 13.1).[21]

Stokes and others realized that scientists, firms and inventors actually made decisions about where they wanted their innovations to take them, and these decisions had different economic implications. Economist Robert Solow wove this into economic theory by assuming two types of factors of production – first, conventional economic

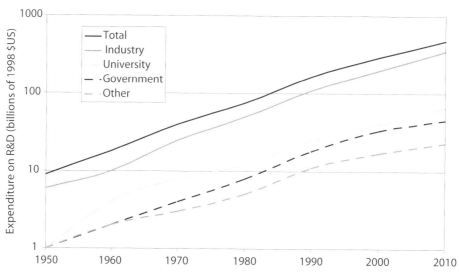

Figure 13.2 R&D spending in the United States (1950-2010 est.)

Source: National Science Foundation, Division of Science Resource Studies.

Table 13.1: *David Stokes's taxonomy of research*

		Considerations of use	
		No	Yes
Quest for fundamental understanding?	Yes	Pure basic (Bohr)	Use-inspired basic (Pasteur)
	No		Pure applied (Edison)

Source: Stokes, D. E. (1997) *Pasteur's Quadrant: Basic science and technological innovation*, Washington, DC: Brookings Institution Press.

inputs, and second, exogenous technology, improving at a steady rate outside this system of production.[22] From this perspective, technology is a universally available, pure public good, available to anyone who wants it, provided by governments through universities and other government-funded institutions.[23] Solow's model was incomplete in that it left no defined role for private R&D or for patents, and indeed in his framework, corporate R&D seems a bit irrational.

A role for firm-specific innovation was introduced by Paul Romer, in an approach that is now called the New Growth Theory.[24] Romer built a model of economic growth driven by innovation (he called it 'technological change'). In New Growth Theory, technological change is driven by intentional investment decisions made by profit-maximizing agents. The distinguishing feature of innovation-driven processes is that knowledge – the primary input factor to production – is neither a conventional good nor a public good. Rather it is non-rival and partially excludable, and standard free-market assumptions of price-taking competition cannot be supported. Instead, the equilibrium is one with monopolistic competition. New Growth Theory's main conclusions are that:

- ▶ The stock of human capital (the source of new knowledge) determines the rate of growth of an economy or business.
- ▶ Too little human capital is devoted to research in equilibrium.
- ▶ Integration into world markets will increase growth rates.
- ▶ Having a large population is not sufficient to generate growth.

TECHNOLOGY, TALENT AND TOLERANCE

Economists can be seen to approach the role of innovation in economics and business by going from theory to data, while sociologists approach the question by going from data to theory. In the latter class are the detailed case studies and demographic data evaluations by Richard Florida, presented in his book *The Rise of the Creative Class*.[25] Florida crunched demographic data from around the world in search of the correct recipe for cities to generate future wealth – a question similar to that asked by Adam Smith two centuries earlier. The key institution, found Florida, was the university.

The university plays three roles in the modern economy – contributing *technology*, *talent* and *tolerance*. The best and most influential academics are employed in universities – and this attracts both technology and talent. Their students are likely to be corporate leaders, and particularly the fresh graduates are going to be doing the most cutting-edge work with new ideas. As a result, technology centres around the world tend to be associated geographically and demographically with world-class universities.

The university's role in engendering tolerance is perhaps a bit more difficult to articulate. In part, tolerance is required because the high energy level, mental intensity, the unique backgrounds and the deep insights that are the domain of the most talented academics also tend to emphasize any social or personal eccentricities that these individuals may hold. And these may be on display to classrooms of impressionable students or other audiences. But it is also needed because universities house not only the natural and applied sciences – engineering, physics, biology and so on – but also the social science faculties – philosophy, sociology, political science. These latter faculties may build their academic careers around challenging existing cultural and political norms. They generate ideas, solve problems and enrich a culture of creativity – but they cannot survive in a climate of intolerance.

Innovations and the steady rise in complexity of products and services have shifted value away from purely physical assets in more recent years. Various authors have used different names to described society's shift away from productivity and wealth based on 'things', and towards 'idea'-based wealth. Daniel Bell, in his book *The Coming of Post-Industrial Society*,[26] marked the year 1971 as the start of the 'post-industrial society', following two years that saw a four-fold increase in world oil prices. Peter Drucker used several terms to describe the restructuring of work, starting with the 'post-capitalist society', but which he eventually ended up calling the 'knowledge based society', or 'knowledge economy'.[27] Richard Florida is more specific, calling it the creative economy.[28] Like Ricardo and Marx, Florida predicts a new class struggle in the creative economy altering the landscape of power throughout the 21st century. His studies focus on the United States, but are likely to accurately depict the new divisions in Europe, Japan, and other OECD countries.

The most and least creative cities in the United States

Internationally, regions like Vancouver and Toronto already have concentrations of immigrants and bohemians that surpass all US regions, and are building dynamic creative climates and turning out creative products. Sydney and Melbourne would rank sixth and seventh among US regions on the Creativity Index. European regions from Dublin and London to Helsinki, Amsterdam and Copenhagen are moving up quickly as well. New creative centres can emerge and surpass established players very quickly. Austin and Seattle rose

quickly in the United States, fuelled by the proclivity of creative Americans to quickly pull up stakes and head to new centres of opportunity. Clearly the same forces are at work for the Chinese, Japanese, Israeli and Lebanese diaspora, despite their loss of a clearly definable geographical region. The creative and economic leaders of the future will not necessarily be emerging giants like India and China. They certainly won't be countries that focus on being cost-effective centres for manufacturing and basic business processing.

Table 13.2: *US regions with the highest Creativity Index scores*

Creativity Index rank	Region	Technology rank	Talent rank	Diversity rank	Creativity rank (out of 276 regions)
1	Austin	1	3	7	1
2	San Francisco	3	5	6	2
3	Seattle	6	6	1	3
4	Boston	12	4	3	5
5	Raleigh-Durham	2	2	20	6
6	Portland OR	4	19	2	7
7	Minneapolis	16	9	4	10
8	Washington-Baltimore	15	1	16	11
9	Sacramento	5	11	17	13
10	Denver	22	8	8	14

Source: Florida, R. (2002) *The Rise of the Creative Class*, New York: Basic Books. Compiled by Kevin Stolarick for 49 metropolitan regions over 1 million population.

Table 13.3: *US regions with the lowest Creativity Index scores*

Creativity Index rank	Region	Technology rank	Talent rank	Diversity rank	Creativity rank (out of 276 regions)
39	Detroit	48	22	37	113
39	Norfolk	37	30	46	113
41	Cleveland	40	32	43	118
42	Milwaukee	43	40	41	124
43	Grand Rapids	33	48	32	131
44	Memphis	27	43	48	132
45	Jacksonville	49	39	33	143
46	Greensboro	41	46	39	145
47	New Orleans	47	35	39	147
48	Buffalo	41	37	47	150
49	Louisville	45	47	44	171

Source: Florida, R. (2002) *The Rise of the Creative Class*, New York: Basic Books. Compiled by Kevin Stolarick for 49 metropolitan regions over 1 million population.

Tolerance, diversity and creativity

Creative cities are diverse, with a high tolerance for divergent life styles, new immigrants and artistic inclinations.

Growing a creative ecosystem is an organic process. Each place has unique assets to do this, and there is no cookie-cutter strategy which can be reenacted anywhere. Science parks are a non-starter, and the idea that 'creative' types can be lured to relocate like a sports franchise is deeply misguided. Jane Jacobs liked to say that the 'key to attracting creative citizens is to "squelch the squelchers" – the controlling leaders, micromanagers, and broader structures of social control and vertical power – that quash and derail creative energy.'[29]

Table 13.4: *US regions with the highest diversity*

| Tolerance rank* | Region | Concentration of: | | | |
		Foreign born rank*	Gays rank*	Artist, musicians, etc. rank*	Racial diversity rank
1	Seattle	18	4	6	5
2	Portland OR	19	10	13	1
3	Boston	14	5	9	8
4	Minneapolis	27	25	10	4
5	Providence	16	19	15	7
6	San Francisco	3	1		39
7	Austin	15	3	7	29
8	Denver	20	13	11	17
9	Orlando	17	14	8	27
10	Los Angeles	2	11	1	44

Source: Florida, R. (2002) *The Rise of the Creative Class*, New York: Basic Books. Compiled by Kevin Stolarick for 49 metropolitan regions over 1 million population.

Table 13.5: *US regions with the lowest diversity*

| Tolerance rank* | Region | Concentration of: | | | |
		Foreign born rank*	Gays rank*	Artist, musicians, etc. rank*	Racial diversity rank
39	Greensboro	31	37	43	30
39	New Orleans	37	6	46	45
41	Milwaukee	35	41	21	35
42	Cincinnati	49	46	24	9
43	Cleveland	40	42	29	33
44	Louisville	47	36	48	11
45	Pittsburgh	48	48	38	3
46	Norfolk	42	42	41	25
47	Buffalo	43	49	40	19
48	Memphis	45	27	49	46
49	St. Louis	46	44	42	32

Source: Florida, R. (2002) *The Rise of the Creative Class*, New York: Basic Books. Compiled by Kevin Stolarick for 49 metropolitan regions over 1 million population.

Florida sees three groups comprising the new landscape:

▶ the Creative Class (currently around 30 per cent of the US working population, of which around 12 per cent is what Florida calls the Creative Core)
▶ the Industrial Class (around 25 per cent of the US working population)
▶ the Service Class (around 45 per cent of the US working population).

Florida dismisses farmers as no longer a power; much of US farming is done by corporations, and less than 0.1 per cent of employees make their living as full-time farmers.

Dublin: building the high-tech mecca

In the 1980s, Ireland suffered from double-digit unemployment, stagnant incomes and a steady exodus of talent. Today the Irish economy is the fastest growing in the OECD; at the centre of its renaissance is a dynamic technology sector offering productivity levels among the highest in Europe. It is the largest exporter of packaged software in the world, having outpaced the United States in 2001. It boasts high-tech companies that are rapidly becoming global players. For example, Realtime Technologies assembles as many as 25 to 30 white-box servers a week for Google, Rackable Systems sells data centre servers in the European market; Cicero Networks is an emerging player in the VoIP business, and Shenick makes diversifEye test equipment used by Qwest, Alcatel, Cisco and BellSouth. Ireland's rate of export growth has outpaced world trade growth by a factor of three. The country's per capita exports were seven times those of the United States and six times those of Japan. Seven of the top 10 IT companies in the world – IBM, Intel, HP, Dell, Oracle, Lotus and Microsoft – have more than 45,000 employees in Ireland. Ireland's government-backed Enterprise Ireland has spawned Vordel, Iona Technologies, Dajeil and PolarLake and other global players, with many new firms starting up each year.

This is clearly the sort of success story that other regions are trying to promote through their science parks and government-backed research labs. Yet Ireland has succeeded in its quest to transform into a high-tech mecca, while the science park countries still see virtually all of their technology developed in the private sector, often against significant commercial and political odds.

How did they do it? Through technology, talent and tolerance. Two decades ago, Ireland's Industrial Development Authority actively recruited US technology companies through financial and tax-related incentives. IBM, Lotus, Intel, Microsoft, Dell, Gateway and Oracle had already been attracted by the many talented graduates emerging from the country's world-class universities. The idea was to bring these companies closer so that citizens could see how successful companies worked. It also helped that Irish spoke English, and the multinationals investing were American. (A similar linguistic tie has helped India, where most college graduates speak excellent English.)

The country wanted to make sure that exposure to multinationals spurred local entrepreneurship, and subsequently set up Enterprise Ireland to support entrepreneurship and venture capital and foster an indigenous high-tech industry. Today the Irish software industry is made up of some 900 firms, employing over 30,000 people. Many of these employees boasted an apprenticeship with one of the multinationals.[30]

Part of the draw for multinationals was talent. Ireland's educational system both generates and attracts world-class talent. Since the 1960s, the Irish government has heavily funded technical skills in electronics and computer-related disciplines through a system of regional technical colleges. Today, 60 per cent of Ireland's university students major in engineering, science or business studies. Again, there are strong parallels with the growth of India's economy, which is now benefiting from the educational and caste reforms initiated by Jawaharlal Nehru in the 1950s.

The final ingredient in Dublin's recipe for success was tolerance and diversity; what has set Dublin apart is its attempt to refashion itself as a lifestyle community. Ireland has a legacy of culture, art and music which resonates with English speakers around the world. The distinguishing feature of communities of writers, musicians, artists and other bohemians is a sense of diversity – of ideas, of cultures and of lifestyles – and a sense that new ideas will be tolerated.[31] It was easy to build on this, as well as Dublin's picturesque downtown, to create a trendy, vibrant, interesting lifestyle centre attractive to dynamic creative people and those who want to be around such amenities. The 30 and 40-something professional crowd are less influenced by alcohol-centric pubs, and instead seek art houses, music venues, coffee shops, bookstores and boutique shopping. Because they may work odd hours, they like these to be available from the morning into the evening. Up into the 1990s, downtown Dublin still tended to close up at 5 pm. Since then the city has been obsessive in building on its history by restoring its Temple Bar district, restoring the same pubs where James Joyce, Bram Stoker and Samuel Beckett might have once downed a Guinness. Dublin spent US$25 million in European Union tourism funds to emphasize Temple Bar's rich history, trying 'not to turn the neighbourhood into a Euro-Disney of faux-Georgian architecture, but to encourage innovative design.'[32]

Today Temple Bar is hip and energetic, with cobblestones and small, eclectic bars and restaurants located along its winding roads. Dublin is now extending this approach to other districts throughout the city. Today, some 53 per cent of new immigrants are returning Irish, and 40 per cent of the country's population is now under 30 years old.

Some of the trends that Florida finds are reminiscent of earlier revolutions in power. Creative workers and service workers are entwined in the same manner as were capitalists (bankers and entrepreneurs) and labourers in the 19th century. Creative workers define as well as streamline, outsource and modify the jobs that are held by service workers; service workers are their new proletariat. Today's industrial workers are fated with a bleak future similar to that which vexed the landed nobility in the 19th century. Comfortable factory positions protected by union contracts will be whittled away over time as the Creative Class figures out new ways to outsource and automate, just as the bankers and entrepreneurs whittled away the privilege of nobility in the 19th century.

Asia's Dublin?

Dublin's recipe for success has resonated throughout the world. For example, Singapore has long been considered one of the economic successes of Asia, but it has had difficulty spurring a competitive technology sector. Despite being home to the Asian operations of a large number of multinationals, its investments in technologies such as consumer electronics have not kept pace with Japan, Korea or China, and until recently, biotechnology investments have generated losses. This has worried Singapore's leaders, who can boast good universities, an educated populace, great infrastructure, and continued investment in science parks and other property projects intended to spur technology entrepreneurship.

In short, Singapore was a country with technology and talent, but historically without tolerance. In fact, it touted just the opposite – a reputation distinguished by brutal intolerance for even the small indiscretion of chewing gum, administered by an oppressive no-nonsense bureaucracy. After decades of trying to jump-start high-tech entrepreneurial business through science parks and handouts, around 2005, senior government officials realized that they would have an easier time attracting talent if they just became more tolerant of diverse ideas.

The Singapore government changed direction quickly, tackling one of the most controversial topics. In 2000, the government committed itself to make Singaporeans more sensitive to aesthetics by having art programmes in schools, encourage art festivals and building cultural infrastructure. Taking action on Richard Florida's research conclusions that a city's attitudes towards the gay community was a fundamental barometer of its 'tolerance', in 2001 the Singapore government not only revealed that there were gays in the senior levels of government, but even announced promotion of 'pink dollar' tourism to attract gays to the city, promoting the city's openness to gay culture and other previously discouraged lifestyles. It dedicated money towards remaking Chinatown and Clarke Quay, a pretty nightlife district on the river, into trendy areas like Temple Bar. Time magazine has even gone so far as to call Singapore a 'funky town'.

Putting it all together (with a digression on 'the blues')

The 6th-century BC mathematician Pythagoras is known best for his theorem relating the length of the sides of a right-angled triangle, but he also invented the blues scale. Pythagoras and his followers built a religion full of rituals, and believed in immortality and this transmigration of souls. At the heart of this was a universe based on numbers. Every aspect of life was expressible in numbers. Marriage for example was the number 5, as the union of a man = 3 and a woman = 2. Musical harmony was similarly expressible in numbers – the length of string determined the note produced, and that note was then related exactly to other notes by fixed ratios of string length. The heavens were ruled by a pentatonic harmony, with each of the five known planets of Pythagoras's day occupying a sphere whose radius allowed it to vibrate harmonically with the others – what came to be known as 'the music of the spheres.' Pythagoras' pentatonic harmonies of planetary motion have their modern scientific restatement in Bode's law.

Pythagorean tuning is based on geometric note relationships; the pentatonic scale was devised with the use of only the octave, fifth and fourth (that is, a fifth down). It produces three intervals with the ratio 9/8 and two larger intervals. Think of this as a minor blues scale (sans 5b) on the piano – in C it would be C, Eb, F, G, Bb (this is also called the 'rock' scale). Think of building a scale only with 5ths and octaves: from C you go up a 5th for the G, down a 5th for the F, down another 5th for the Bb, and down another 5th for the Eb. These are 'just' intonations (there are no beats or dissonances in the notes in the scale) so that scale is, from a human hearing standpoint, an ideal scale. Unfortunately, this neat Pythagorean number system breaks down for intervals other than the octave, fourth and fifth (Pythagorian thirds just don't cut it), which was the reason that other tunings were invented. Modern equal temperament, for example, keeps the fourths and fifths within 5 cents of the Pythagorean tuning, and spreads the dissonance across all the notes of a diatonic or chromatic scale.

The intervals of the pentatonic scale are integral to the psychology of music and to human

hearing. It somehow resonates with us at a very fundamental level. It is found in the tuning of the Ethiopian krar and the Indonesian gamelan, the melodies of Chinese folk music, African-American spirituals, Celtic folk music, Polish highlanders from the Tatra Mountains and the music of French composer Claude Debussy. It is the musical counterpart to Noam Chomsky's 'deep structures', a universal grammar underlying all languages and corresponding to an innate capacity of the human brain.

In the Middle Ages, the church outlawed the secular pentatonic melodies along with major-minor (Ionian, Aeolian modes) and substituted the church modal systems for religious music. The medieval church wanted people to pull away from the sensual and secular; to get people to stop dancing and tapping feet. Later the church introduced the pipe organ into services to accompany the choir, and along with it the first incarnations of the modern keyboard. Originally these keys were large levers which were operated by a whole hand. Keyboards until the 15th century had seven naturals to each octave –in other words, they had only 'white keys' playing in the key of C. Church modes would simply start on a note higher or lower than C. As there were no accidentals ('black keys') it was impossible to play a pentatonic scale, even if anyone dared to do so in a church.

The pentatonic came back into use in the Renaissance with the spread of secular music. Instruments such as the clavichord were small, designed for private dwellings, and added 'black keys' to their distinctly smaller keyboards in order to enable the player to play in other keys and accompany other instruments.

The modern jazz blues scale grew out of impromptu pentatonic harmonies in the folk music of the rural South. At the turn of the 20th century, W.C. ('Father of the Blues') Handy composed a campaign song for E.H. Crump, the candidate for mayor of Memphis, Tennessee, using harmonies that he first heard from a banjo player while waiting at a train station in Mississippi. The song, 'Mr Crump', was later retitled 'Memphis blues' and became very popular, to be followed by 'St Louis blues', and so forth. Handy's 'blues scale' added the flat 5th (in C this is C, Eb, F, Gb, G, Bb) which arose from the country music technique that took a flat 5 'bent' note and would slide it into the dominant.[33] On the piano for which Handy's music was published, with its tempered, enharmonic tunings, the blues scale became something else, a scale that could fit with a diverse array of harmonies.

All this brings us to the following list of problems with the modern piano keyboard:

► Tuning: The organ keyboard (which preceded the stringed keyboard instruments by several centuries) predates any agreement on the best way to tune the instrument. It was designed to simplify the execution of one scale (C major) and a number of other church modes which are not common today. In so doing, it complicated the remaining scales. Tuning in the early days of the keyboard was a topic of heated debate. Johann Sebastian Bach in particular was a proponent of equal temperament (although one that is different than we use today). The major builders of pianos and organs, such as Bach's contemporary and colleague Gottfried Silbermann, preferred simpler tunings, given that they had to tune on organs with thousands of pipes. Bach disagreed with Silbermann's organ tuning so vehemently that he called a third of it 'barbaric' and once launched into a piece in A-flat major on purpose – the worst key in Silbermann's tuning – just to pique Silbermann in public. Silbermann, it is said, retaliated by grabbing Bach's wig and throwing it off the choir loft.

► Ergonomics of the keyboard's physical configuration: Mastering the correct division of function between the thumbs (which need to tuck under the other fingers) and the remaining fingers necessitates a high level of training. Interestingly, it was J. S. Bach who originated the widespread use of the thumb undertuck. Prior to Bach, pianists were even more hobbled by technique that considered the thumb to be an ungainly stub, and didn't use it at all.

► Ergonomics of chord and scale shapes: The keyboard was designed originally to play in one key – C. But today, most music is played in any key but C, and typically shifts keys at least once per song. Chord and scale shapes are different in all 12 keys because of the configuration of raised black keys. This requires substantially more memorization of shapes than is required for other instruments.

► Ergonomics of the physical interface: Physical interface problems arise from weighting, relative keyboard and hand dimensions, and responsiveness of the mechanism. Because the keys are elongated rectangles, the hand attacks the very high or low notes at substantially different angles from the keys in the centre of the keyboard.

Thinking about the problem: a potential innovation

Although there are many competing ways to tune modern stringed instruments such as violins, guitars and harps, the 'oriental tuning' (that is, tuning in fourths, E-A-D-G) which is standard for the bass guitar offers some distinct advantages. It removes the irregularity of the interval of a third between the second and third strings. With oriental tuning, chords can simply be moved down or across the fretboard, dramatically reducing the number of different finger positions that need to be memorized. Could this structure be carried over to the piano keyboard without creating other problems?

Fleshing out the innovation

Here is one potential solution to the prior problems: a keyboard with round (typewriter-style) keys in a tiered arrangement of four rows (see Figure 13.3).

Consider how this eases the process of transposing chords and key centres. On the tiered keyboard, the shape of the C, C# and F# scales (and corresponding chords) are all the same; on a traditional keyboard they change, increasing complexity, memorization problems and ergonomic problems.

Where would we look for markets? Essentially, anyplace where these problems repeatedly assert themselves, and where there may not be much resistance to learning a new technique. Traditional classical performers would probably be unwilling to adopt, but adopters might be found in:

Figure 13.3 Redesign of piano keyboard for easy transposition and greater reach (5½ octaves)

- vocal accompaniment, where the ability to learn in one scale and transpose without problem is a valuable asset
- rock and jazz keyboardists, where innovation is embraced, and transposition is central to the music
- improvisatory music, orchestral transcriptions (where large intervals need to be spanned), or where other complex, flashy music not specifically designed for the traditional piano is to be played.

Innovation workout activity

1. (Vision) What would a company selling this keyboard innovation look like in:
   a. two years?
   b. five years?
   c. ten years?
2. (Business model) Draw a value map for a business model for selling this keyboard innovation.
   a. Identify where the company should concentrate its strategy in the future.
   b. Identify where it will incur costs, and estimate them given what you know about the price of computer chips.
   c. Identify where it will earn revenue, and estimate it given what you know about the price and volume of sales of computer chips.
   d. Describe how and where network effects appear.
3. (Industry dynamics) Describe how exponential growth in technology performance over time manifests itself in this business.
   a. Predict past and future times of disruptive technology innovation.
   b. Describe how and when the innovator's dilemma will manifest itself in the future decades.
4. (R&D-CRM) How would the company. link its product development R&D and its customer relationship management (CRM) functions? R&D needs to design products that customers will want to buy in the future, and CRM serves several functions: making sure customers are satisfied with existing products, making sure they know about new and upcoming products, asking them questions to find out what they want in new products, making them aware of new features that they didn't know they wanted.
5. (Investment) How can the company. invest to compete with 'traditional' keyboard instruments? Your answer to this question is important, because outside investors will provide the money for these investments, and in answering this question, you will need to let them know 'where they will make their money'.
6. (People) What sort of people should the firm hire to develop a commercially successful product, and what should these people do? Consider:
   a. idea generators (those who can sift through large quantities of technological and market data to identify 'innovations')
   b. gatekeepers and boundary spanners (who bring ideas from one department, company or industry, to another)
   c. champions (entrepreneurs, evangelists and other promoters of new ideas, even though they may not have very great technical knowledge)
   d. sponsors (coaches and mentors who can clear the way politically for an innovation)
   e. project managers.
7. (Milestones) How will you translate your innovation development and market entry strategy into specific milestones (in other words, deliverables)? Define three milestones for the business. Each milestone must trigger a test of one of your underlying assumptions about the

business and product. Specify an assumption test for each milestone you list.

8. (First customers) Identify your best choice for the first three customers, and explain why. These should be specific company or individual names, or at least defined precisely enough to be specifically identifiable.

9. (Combatants) Identify your major combatants. You may make references to generic categories of products or generic names of industries.

10. (Entry tactic) Choose and elaborate upon a single 'best' entry tactic that is based on your answers to the questions above. Your objective should be to avoid debilitating competitive interaction by using speed, skill and surprise, rather than scarce start-up resources. Explain in detail how your choice of entrance strategy achieves these objectives better than any other possible entrance tactic. You want to use your imagination, innovation and creativity to outmanoeuvre your competitors, not resources.

Meade reaches for the stars

'I was miserable. I'd never held a job before, and I hated working for someone else,' recalls John Diebel about his first job as an engineer at Hughes Aircraft Company in Los Angeles. Shortly after starting at Hughes, he began browsing the periodicals at the Los Angeles Public Library for other business opportunities, and sent out letters to companies that interested him. After several months of no responses, Diebel was finally contacted by Japan's Towa Optical Manufacturing Company with an invitation to distribute its optical products in the United States.[34]

In 1972, armed with his agreement with Towa, the 29-year-old entrepreneur started with a loan of US$2500 from the Hughes Aircraft credit union (after other banks had flatly refused him any credit). He ordered $2000 worth of Towa telescopes, got a post office box, and set up business in the kitchen of his small apartment. Following a vacation trip to Lake Mead in Nevada, he decided to call his company Meade Instruments, adding the 'e' because he thought it looked nice. He took out an advertisement in the July 1972 issue of *Sky & Telescope* (at that time the only mass magazine targeted at amateur astronomers) offering Towa's line of refracting telescopes. By the end of his first year in business, he had netted $8000 in sales, quit Hughes, moved the company to a warehouse in Costa Mesa, California, and hired his father, a retired furniture store owner, to help with the rapidly expanding sales. 'I didn't know anything about running a business. My father taught me everything, from preparing financial statements to talking to the bank.' Business expanded rapidly, and Diebel realized that he had accidentally tapped into a potentially huge market.

The Meade-Towa products were attractive to amateur astronomers in the 1970s because of Towa's unheralded innovations, which were not offered by US competitors, such as spring-loaded gearboxes for smooth focusing, and viewfinder eyepieces with wider fields. By 1975, the firm was making a net profit of $55,000 on $259,000 sales.

In those days, Japanese firms were still struggling to enter US markets and gain recognition for their rapidly improving quality. Towa's managers were thrilled with John Diebel's success, and their corporate and personal relationships grew close. In the late 1970s, Diebel married the daughter of Towa's founder.

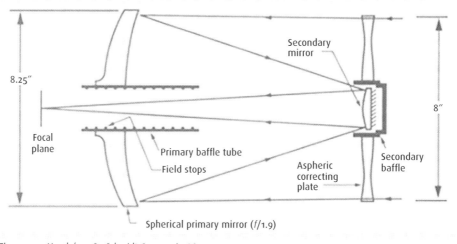

Figure 13.4 Meade's 2080 Schmidt-Cassegrain AQ

By 1976 demand for tube assemblies for reflecting telescopes exploded, and Diebel began manufacturing the assemblies in Costa Mesa to meet demand. The first telescopes of its own production (the model 628 and 826 6-inch and 8-inch reflecting telescopes) were so good that Meade quickly gained a large share of the market. By 1978, its sales had topped $2 million.

By the late 1970s, amateur astronomy was a rising fad. Another southern California telescope maker named Tom Johnson – founder of Meade's perennial rival Celestron – had pioneered the amateur (read affordable) Schmidt-Cassegrain telescope (SCT).[35] Johnson's design utilized two mirrors and a corrector plate to produce wide-field, high resolution images. Ready to take on the challenge, Meade directed all of its resources into the development of a Schmidt-Cassegrain to compete with Celestron's, which had been on sale since the 1960s. By September 1980, Meade was ready to sell its first Schmidt-Cassegrain model, the 8-inch 2080.

The company continued to release new models and new accessories, and by 1985, it had surpassed competitor Celestron as the largest telescope manufacturer in the world. The news came the same year that the famous Halley's comet was about to return, an event which unleashed an unprecedented wave of interest in amateur astronomy among the general public and boosted sales substantially.[36]

By 1986 Meade employed a staff of about 100 people, generating $13 million in sales. Still profits were small, and Diebel was forced to personally guarantee all of the company's loans. Seeking more personal security he sold Meade for $6.5 million to the Harbor Group, a holding company based in St Louis Missouri,[37] while remaining as the company president.[38]

This however was not a happy marriage. Harbor Group was the archetypal finance-MBA-driven venture capital firm, interested primarily in pumping up the financial statements of its acquisitions in pursuit of an initial public stock offering. While Diebel was customer and product driven, Harbor was focused on profits and (ultimately) the potential to take the firm public. Meade's R & D suffered under Harbor's bureaucratic management style; Diebel found himself saddled with paperwork, meetings and marketing studies; and any new product development soon ceased almost entirely.

After two years, Diebel had had enough. He quit, moved to Hawaii, played golf, consulted for a diminished Meade one day a week, and watched as Meade's sales plummeted.[39] Harbor Group tried to resolve this problem the only way it knew – not by improving the product, but by looking for a merger or acquisition target. In July 1990, it announced that Meade would merge with its main competitor Celestron International to create (on paper at least) a firm with $21 million in annual sales. The US Federal Trade Commission, though, blocked the merger. By the end of 1990, Meade was nearly bankrupt, running a loss of $2 million on $10 million annual sales.[40]

By February 1991, Harbor Group's 'value-building' had driven Meade's net worth to a negative $2 million, and Meade's creditors called in their loans. Diebel quickly returned from Hawaii to loan Meade $65,000 of his own money to meet the weekly payroll while he negotiated a buyout of the company with three partners. In the end, Harbor sold all of Meade's stock along with all its assets and liabilities to the group of partners for a nominal $1000, of which $510 came from John Diebel's own pocket, and Diebel once again regained majority ownership of Meade.

Accepting an annual salary of only $1, Diebel put up $1.8 million of his proceeds from the earlier sale to Harbor. His three partners, all Meade employees, mortgaged their homes and came up with $250,000 in cash.[41] That money was put toward revitalizing Meade's R&D

programme, beginning with the ETX a small (90–125 mm) telescope modelled on Questar's 3.5 inch Maksutov-Cassegrain telescopes. Questar's founder, Lawrence Braymer, had been a commercial artist by trade, and his artistic talents had created an expensive but visually stunning telescope with intuitive controls. The ETX provided all the same features at one-quarter the price of the Questar.[42]

Meade's other blockbuster product – the LX200 – relied on John Diebel's background in electrical engineering. (Diebel had an undergraduate electrical engineering degree from CalTech, and his PhD from the University of Southern California.) It was to be a $2000 SCT and mount equipped with computer controls to automatically slew the scope to 64,000 celestial objects.[43] Diebel put over $1 million into R&D for the LX200, but even so, by 1993 the company was profitable, and by 1995, Meade telescopes were outselling all competitors combined throughout the world. In 1996, Meade's sales rose to $29.8 million. Sales would again double by 1998, and yet again by the end of the 2000 fiscal year.[44] By the end of 1999, Meade boasted a 70 per cent share of the high-end telescope market[45] and 40 per cent share of the low-end market.[46]

Meade became peripherally involved in some of the dot-com madness when it was engaged by TeraBeam to manufacture optical components for TeraBeam's fibre optic networks.[47] Meade, which had gone public, saw its stock rise on the association (because fibre optics are a key component of the internet) and in early May of 2000 made public a two-for-one stock split.[48]

The subsequent financial news was disappointing, as the retail chain of Natural Wonder stores merged with World of Science stores, and then stopped carrying Meade's products. The 2000 Christmas season saw retail sales plummet, and by the end of the first quarter of 2001, the company had reported a loss of $4.7 million.[49] The dot-com-fuelled stockmarket crash claimed Meade's rival, Celestron, which went bankrupt when its owner Tasco Worldwide began the process of liquidating after failing to service debts to its secured lenders.[50] The US Federal Trade Commission once again prevented Meade from purchasing Celestron's assets, and to this day, Celestron remains a separate enterprise.[51]

John Diebel turned 64 in 2006, and still spends 40 per cent of his time with Meade, which in fiscal 2006 had sales of $120 million (but unfortunately a $14 million net loss). Meade's 530 employees hold about 40 per cent of the company, with John Diebel now controlling about 16 per cent of the 19.8 million outstanding shares.[52] The shares peaked in value in April 2000 at about $39.50 per share, and in 2007 trade at about $2.50 per share.[53]

Telescope sales now account for about 85 per cent of Meade Instruments' business. Of those, sales to amateur astronomers represent 60 per cent, with the entry level refracting and reflecting telescopes making up 60 per cent of sales and 98 per cent of shipped telescope units. These inexpensive 60 mm to 114 mm telescopes are distributed by retailers such as Discovery Channel Stores, Wal-Mart, Sam's Club and Costco. Wal-Mart (including Sam's Club) alone accounts for 13 per cent of net Meade sales. The more advanced telescopes account for only 2 per cent of shipped telescope units, and 16 per cent of sales.

Diebel recently commented to astronomer David Levy:

> I love my job; I wouldn't trade it for any other – when I wake up each morning I can't wait to get to work. I am still an amateur astronomer at heart. Whenever we think of a new product, I imagine myself using it and try to put myself in the customer's position. We never forget who our customers are; the amateur astronomer is the ultimate arbiter of our performance as a company.

Questions for the Meade case study

1. Why did Harbor Group's 'value-building' drive Meade's net worth to a negative $2 million?
2. Why was Diebel able to successfully turn Meade's business around after his group repurchased it from Harbor Group?
3. Why did Diebel choose to come back to a very troubled business, one that was consuming huge amounts of his personal wealth, when he could have stayed in Hawaii and played golf?
4. What single characteristic of Meade's business model was most responsible for its success?

CHAPTER QUESTIONS FOR REVIEW

1	Which countries will be the wealthiest economically in 2020?
2	Which countries will decline in wealth over the next decade?
3	What can a city do to ensure a healthy economy in the next decade?
4	What shouldn't a city do if it is to survive?
5	Many countries espouse nationalistic objectives, and make it very difficult for immigrants to obtain visas or citizenship. Will these countries have an economic role to play in the future? What kind of role? Why would it be beneficial to limit immigration into a country?
6	Do you believe that we are moving into a non-egalitarian world where social classes are differentiated by learning and creativity? Explain what news events or insights contribute to your view.
7	From a personal perspective, how do you go about assuring that you can be a part of the creative class, as opposed to the lower-paid working or service classes?

CHAPTER 13: KEY POINTS

▷	Some societies are more innovative than others, which is important because wealth has increasingly clustered around creative centres.
▷	The distinguishing feature of innovation driven processes is that knowledge is the primary input factor to production. ○ Knowledge is neither a conventional good, nor is it a public good. ○ Knowledge is non-rival and partially excludable. Standard free market assumptions of price-taking competition cannot be supported, and equilibrium in a knowledge economy is one with monopolistic competition.
▷	New Growth Theory concludes that government intervention may be necessary for optimal levels of innovation, because: ○ the stock of human capital determines the rate of growth of an economy or business ○ too little human capital is devoted to research in equilibrium ○ integration into world markets will increase growth rates ○ having a large population is not sufficient to generate growth.
▷	Creative cities are diverse, with a high tolerance for divergent life styles, new immigrants and artistic inclinations.
▷	Creative nations tend to set insure a stable, reasonably fair system of government for the activities of creative people.

NOTES

1 The rise of innovation was commented on repeatedly throughout the 20th century, notably in Chandler, A. D. (1962) *Strategy and Structure*, Garden City, N.Y.: Doubleday. This provides insight in how some aspects of competition and innovation are much the same as they were even in the first part of the 20th century. See also Kelly, P. and Kranzberg, M. (eds) (1978) *Technological Innovation: A critical review of current knowledge*, San Francisco, Calif.: San Francisco University Press; Cyert, R. M. and March, J. G. (1963) *A Behavioural Theory of the Firm*, Englewood Cliffs, N.J.: Prentice-Hall.

2 Amabile, T. M., Conti, R., Coon, H. et al. (1996) 'Assessing the work environment for creativity', *Academy of Management Review* **39**(5), pp. 1154–84.

3 Smith, A. (1776/1977) *An Inquiry into the Nature and Causes of the Wealth of Nations*, facsimile edn, Chicago, Ill.: University Of Chicago Press.

4 Ricardo, D. (1817/2004) *The Principles of Political Economy and Taxation*, New York: Dover.

5 Marx, K. (1859/1993) *Capital: A critique of political economy*, New York: Penguin Classics.

6 Freeman, C. (1982) *The Economics of Industrial Innovation*, 2nd edn, London: Frances Pinter; Galbraith, J. R. (1982) 'Designing the innovative organization', *Organizational Dynamics* (Winter), pp. 3–24.

7 Nonaka, I. (1991) 'The knowledge creating company', *Harvard Business Review* (Nov–Dec), pp. 96–104.

8 These influences come less from Marx than his contemporary Physiocrats, who strongly influenced early accounting. The perspective of the Physiocrats is still promulgated in the stewardship orientation of accounting that dominates thinking at the US Financial Accounting Standards Board.

9 Chandler, A. D. (1962) *Strategy and Structure: Chapters in the History of American industrial enterprise*, Cambridge, Mass.: MIT Press.

10 Smith, A. (1776/1977) *An Inquiry into the Nature and Causes of the Wealth of Nations*, facsimile edn, Chicago, Ill.: University Of Chicago Press.

11 Nelson, R. R. and Winter, S. (1982) *An Evolutionary Theory of Economic Change*, Boston, Mass.: Harvard University Press.

12 Kondratieff, N. D. (1935) 'The long waves in economic life', *Review of Economic Statistics* 17, pp. 6–105, reprinted in *Readings in Business Cycle Theory*, Homewood, Ill.: Richard D. Irwin (1951).

13 Marshall, A. (1890/2006) *Principles of Economics*, ? place: Cosimo Classics.

14 Patel, P. and Pavitt, K. (2000) ''How technological competencies help define the core (not the boundaries) of the firm', pp. 313–33 in G. Dosi, R. Nelson and S. G. Winter (eds), *The Nature and Dynamics of Organizational Capabilities*, Oxford: Oxford University Press.

15 Castronova, E. (2001) 'Virtual worlds: a first-hand account of market and society on the cyberian frontier', CESifo Working Paper 618 (December); Castronova, E. (2005) Synthetic Worlds: The business and culture of online games, Chicago, Ill.: University of Chicago Press; Castronova, E. (2005) 'Real products in imaginary worlds', *Harvard Business Review* (May), pp. 19–20.

16 Virtual Economy Research Network, http://virtual-economy.org/

17 Cohen, W. M. and Levinthal, D. A. (1990) 'A new perspective on learning and innovation', *Administrative Science Quarterly* **35**(1), pp. 128–52.

18 Rothwell, R. and Zegveld, W. (1985) *Reindustrialization and Technology*, London: Longman; Rothwell, R. (1992) 'Successful industrial innovation: critical factors for the 1990s', *R&D Management* **22**(3), pp. 221–39.

19 These two genres have protected themselves against piracy by locking their content into particular platforms. Video games are tied to game consoles by unique identifiers in both machine and programme which can be verified through the internet. Motion pictures have resisted the transition to digital film (essentially high-resolution digital television) by distributing on film.

20 Motion Picture Association of America: http://www.mpaa.org/index.asp

21 Abernathy, W. J. and Utterback, J. (1978) 'Patterns of industrial innovation', p. 97–108 in M. L. Tushman, and W. L. Moore, *Readings in the Management of Innovation*, New York: HarperCollins.

22 Solow, R. M. (1999) *Growth Theory: An exposition*, 2nd edn, Oxford: Oxford University Press.

23 Pavitt, K. (1990) 'What we know about the strategic management of technology', *California Management Review* **32**(3), pp. 17–26; Parkin, M., Powell, M. and Matthews, K. (1997) *Economics*, 3rd edn, Harlow: Addison-Wesley.

24 Romer, P. (1990) 'Endogenous technological change', *Journal of Political Economy* **98**(5) (October), pp. S71–102; Romer, P. (1986) 'Increasing returns and long run growth', *Journal of Political Economy* **94**(5) (October), p. 1002–37.

25 Florida, R. (2003) *The Rise of the Creative Class: And how it's transforming work, leisure, community and everyday life*, New York: Basic Books. Florida has followed up with three more analyses: Florida, R.(2005) *The Flight of the Creative Class: The new*

global competition for talent, London: HarperBusiness; Florida, R. (2005) *Cities and the Creative Class,* London: Routledge; Florida, R. (2008) *Who's Your City?* (in development).

26 Bell, D. (1999) *The Coming of the Post-Industrial Society,* reissue edn, New York: Basic Books.

27 Drucker, P. F. (2003) *The Essential Drucker: The best of sixty years of Peter Drucker's essential writings on management,* New York: Collins.

28 Florida, R. (2003) *The Rise of the Creative Class: And how it's transforming work, leisure, community and everyday life,* New York: Basic Books.

29 (Jane Jacobs quote)

30 Allen, T. J. (1977) *Managing the Flow of Technology,* Cambridge, Mass.: MIT Press; Burns, T. and Stalker, G. M. (1961) *The Management of Innovation,* London: Tavistock.

31 Woodward, J. (1965) *Industrial Organization: Theory and practice,* 2nd edn, Oxford: Oxford University Press.

32 Williams, F. (2000) 'Dublin: now fair and worldly', *New York Times,* 12 October.

33 The 'blues' scale is more formally called a hemitonic relative minor pentatonic scale in classical theory, but anyone using the term should rightly be considered an insufferable pedant.

34 Levy, D. L. (2000) 'The man behind Meade', *Sky and Telescope* **100**(1) (July), p. 80.

35 Laurent Cassegrain was a 17th-century Catholic priest who allegedly offered a competitor design to Newton's reflecting telescope; Bernhard Schmidt was the one-armed Estonian telescope maker of the Schmidt wide-field telescope at Palomar, as well as other influential designs. When he was aged 14 Schmidt blew his arm off in a chemistry experiment that went awry while his parents were at Sunday church. He continued to grind complex mirrors single-handedly (literally) throughout his life, despite his disability. It is said that Schmidt often demanded to be paid in cigars and cognac. Tom Johnson helped refine the Schmidt-Cassegrain design in the 1950s.

36 Berkman, L. (1990) 'FTC has eyes on telescope firm merger monopoly', *Los Angeles Times,* 10 October.

37 'Missouri holding company acquires Meade Instruments', *Los Angeles Times,* 9 January 1987, p. D3.

38 'Telescope firm focuses on stock sale', *Orange County Register,* 6 February 1997.

39 'FTC opposes telescope merger', *Los Angeles Times,* 9 October 1990, p. P3.

40 'Federal Trade Commission moves to block telescope venture', *Dow Jones News Service-Ticker,* 9 October 1990.

41 Levy, D. L. (2000) 'The man behind Meade', *Sky and Telescope* **100**(1) (July), p. 80.

42 Stevens, T. (2001) 'Master of his universe', *Industry Week,* 15 January, p. 76.

43 Yu, R. (1998) 'Telescope maker seeks to expand its small universe', *Orange County Business Journal,* 4 May.

44 Lindquist, D. (1998) 'Irvine telescope firm looks to Tijuana', *San Diego Union-Tribune,* 28 November, p. C1.

45 Berry, K. (1999) 'Meade's telescope sales make it an industry star', *Orange County Register,* 17 October.

46 Hirsch, J. (1997) 'Irvine telescope builder proved to be farsighted', *Orange County Register,* 14 September; Johnson, G. (1997) 'Irvine telescope manufacturer Meade plans IPO', *Los Angeles Times,* 6 February, p. D5.

47 'Meade Instruments shares soar on word of alliance with TeraBeam', *Dow Jones Business News,* 15 March 2000; 'Meade stock will split 2-for-1', *Los Angeles Times,* 6 May 2000, p. C2.

48 Fields, R. (2000) 'Meade shares soar 77 per cent on Terabeam deal', *Los Angeles Times,* 16 March, p. C8.

49 Kafka, P. (1999) 'In focus', *Forbes,* 15 November, p. 210; Kelleher, J. B. (2000) 'Meade Instruments is soaring', *Orange County Register,* 13 March.

50 Grover, R. (2000) 'Back from a black hole', *Business Week,* 29 May.

51 'Meade shares fall back a bit', *Orange County Register,* 17 March 2000.

52 O'Dell, J. (1996) 'Workers acquire a stake in Meade', *Los Angeles Times,* 20 July, p. D4.

53 'Meade Instruments CEO says R&D investment paying off', *Dow Jones Business News,* 30 December 1999; Meade Instruments Corp. (2000) 'Comments on OEM agreement', *Business Wire,* 29 March; 'Meade Instruments posts earnings well below analysts' reduced estimates', *Dow Jones Business News,* 19 December 2000.

FURTHER READING

Abernathy, W. and. Clark, K. B. (1985) 'Mapping the winds of creative destruction', *Research Policy* 14, pp. 3–22.

Afuah, A. (2003) *Innovation Management*, Oxford: Oxford University Press.

Barabási, L. (2003) *Linked: How everything is connected to everything else and what it means*, New York: Plume.

Barney, B. (2001) 'Is the resource-based "view" a useful perspective for strategic management research? Yes,' *Academy of Management Review* 26, pp. 41–57.

Barney, J. B. (1997) *Gaining and Sustaining Competitive Advantage*, Reading, Mass.: Addison-Wesley.

Baumol, W. J. (2004) *The Free-Market Innovation Machine: Analyzing the growth miracle of capitalism*, Princeton, N.J.: Princeton University Press.

Bell, D. (1999) *The Coming of the Post-Industrial Society*, rev. edn, New York: Basic Books.

Bloom, H. (2002) *Genius*, New York: Warner Books.

Brockman, J. (ed.) (1993) *Creativity*, New York: Touchstone.

Bodin, M (1990) *The Creative Mind: Myths and mechanisms*, New York: Basic Books,

Castronova, Edward (2005) 'Real products in imaginary worlds', *Harvard Business Review*, May, pp. 19–20.

Castronova, Edward (2005) *Synthetic Worlds: The business and culture of online games*, Chicago, Ill.: University of Chicago Press.

Chandler, A. D. (1962) *Strategy and Structure: Chapters in the history of the industrial enterprise*, Cambridge, Mass.: MIT Press.

Cheung, Steven N. S. (1973) 'The fable of the bees: an economic investigation', *Journal of Law and Economics* 16 (April), pp. 11–33.

Christensen, C. (1997) *The Innovator's Dilemma: When new technologies cause great firms to fail*, Boston, Mass.: Harvard Business School Press.

Christensen, C. M. and Bower, J. L. (1996) 'Customer power, strategic investment and failure of leading firms', *Strategic Management Journal* 17, pp. 197–218.

Clark, K. B. and Wheelwright, S. C. (1994) *Managing New Product and Process Development*, New York: Free Press.

Conner, K., and Prahalad, C. K. (1995) 'A resource-based theory of the firm: knowledge versus opportunism', *Organization Science* 7(5), pp. 477–501.

Critser, Greg (2005) *Generation Rx: How prescription drugs are altering American lives, minds, and bodies*, New York: Houghton Mifflin.

Csikszentmihalyi, M. (1996) *Creativity*, New York: Harper Collins.

Cyert, R. M. and March, J. G. (1963) *A Behavioural Theory of the Firm*, Englewood Cliffs, N.J.: Prentice-Hall.

D'Aveni, R. A. (1994) *Hypercompetition: The dynamics of strategic maneuvering*, New York: Free Press.

Drucker, Peter F. (2000) 'Managing knowledge means managing oneself', *Leader to Leader* 16 (Spring).

Eisenmann, T. R. (2002) *Internet Business Models and Strategies: Text and cases*, New York: McGraw-Hill.

Florida, R. (2003) *The Rise of the Creative Class: And how it's transforming work, leisure, community and everyday life*, New York: Basic Books.
Florida, R. (2005) *Cities and the Creative Class*, London: Routledge.
Florida, R. (2005) *The Flight of the Creative Class. The new global competition for talent*, New York: HarperBusiness/HarperCollins.
Freeman, Chris and Soete, Luc (1997) *The Economics of Industrial Innovation*, 3rd edn, Cambridge, Mass.: MIT Press.
Friedman, T. L. (2005) *The World is Flat*, New York: Farrar, Straus and Giroux.

Granovetter, Mark (1973) 'The strength of weak ties', *American Journal of Sociology* 78 (May), pp. 1360–80.
Grant, R. M. (2002) *Contemporary Strategy Analysis: Concepts, techniques, applications*, Oxford: Blackwell.
Griliches, Z. (1957) 'Hybrid corn: an exploration in the economics of technical change', *Econometrics* 25, pp. 501–22.
Gulati, R. (1998) 'Alliances and networks', *Strategic Management Journal* 19, pp. 293–317.

Hatch, Mary Jo (1997) *Organization Theory*, Oxford: Oxford University Press.
Henderson, R. and Clark, K. B. (1990) 'Architectural innovation: the reconfiguration of existing product technologies and the failure of established firms', *Administrative Science Quarterly* 36, pp. 9–30.
Henry, J. and Walker, D. (eds) (1991) *Managing Innovation*, London: Sage/Open University Press.
Hill, C. W. L. and Jones, G. R. (1995) *Strategic Management: An integrated approach*, Boston, Mass.: Houghton Mifflin.

Kelly, P. and Kranzberg, M. (eds) (1978) *Technological Innovation: A critical review of current knowledge*, San Francisco, Calif.: San Francisco University Press.

Landes, David S. (1998) *The Wealth and Poverty of Nations: Why some are so rich and some so poor*, New York: W. W. Norton

Madsen, A. (1999) *The Deal Maker*, New York: Wiley
Magretta, Joan (2002) *What Management Is: How it works, and why it's everyone's business*, New York: Free Press.
March, J. G. and Simon, H. (1958) *Organizations*, New York: Wiley.
Mayer, N. Zald (1970) *Power in Organizations*, Nashville, Tenn.: Vanderbilt University Press.
McGrath, R. G. and MacMillan, I. (2000) *The Entrepreneurial Mindset*, Cambridge, Mass.: Harvard Business School Press.
Mokyr, J. (1991) *The Leaver of Riches*, Oxford: Oxford University Press.

Mun, J. (2005) *Real Options Analysis: Tools and techniques for valuing strategic investment and decisions*, 2nd edn, New York: Wiley.

Nordhaus, William D. (1997) 'Do real-output and real-wage measures capture reality? The history of light suggests not', in T. F. Bresnahan and R. J. Gordon (eds), *The Economics of New Goods*, Chicago: University of Chicago Press.

Nordhaus, William D. (1998) 'Quality changes in price indices', *Journal of Economic Perspectives* 12(1) (Winter), pp. 59–68.

Oster, S. (1999) *Modern Competitive Analysis*, New York: Oxford University Press.

Porter, M. E. (1990) *The Competitive Advantage of Nations,* New York: Free Press.

Prahalad, C. K. and Hamel, G. (1990) 'The core competence of the corporation', *Harvard Business Review* 68(3), pp. 79–91.

Priern, R. and Butler, J. E. (2001) 'Is the resource-based "view" a useful perspective for strategic management research?' *Academy of Management Review* 26, pp. 22–41.

Rybczynski, Witold (2001) *One Good Turn: A natural history of the screwdriver and the screw*, New York: Scribner/First Touchstone.

Saloner, G., Shepard, A. and Podolny, J. (2001) *Strategic Management*, New York: Wiley.

Schmidt, Eric and Varian, Hal (2005) 'Google: ten golden rules', *Newsweek*, 2 December.

Schon, D. A. (1963) 'Champions for radical new inventions', *Harvard Business Review* 41, pp. 77–86.

Schrage, M. (1999) *Serious Play: How the world's best companies simulate to innovate*, New York: Random House

Schrage, M. (1996) 'The Gary Burton Trio: lessons on business from a jazz legend', *Fast Company*, December 1996, issue 6, p. 110.

Schumpeter, J. A. (1934) *The Theory of Economic Development*, Boston, Mass.: Harvard University Press.

Schumpeter, J. A. (1939) *Business Cycles*, New York: McGraw-Hill.

Schumpeter, J. A. (1950) *Capitalism, Socialism, and Democracy*, 3rd edn, New York: Harper and Row.

Seabright, P. (2004) *The Company of Strangers*, Princeton, N.J.: Princeton University Press.

Shapiro, C. and Varian, H. R. (1998) I*nformation Rules: A strategic guide to the network economy*, Boston, Mass.: Harvard Business School Press.

Stabell, C. B. and Fjeldstadm, O. D. (1998) 'Configuring value for competitive advantage: on chains, shops, and networks', *Strategic Management Journal* 19, pp. 413–37.

Taylor, F. (1947) *Scientific Management*, New York: Harper & Row.

Teece, D. J. (1986) 'Profiting from technological innovation: implications for integration, collaboration, licensing and public policy', *Research Policy* 15, pp. 285–306.

Vise, D. and Malseed, M. (2006) *The Google Story*, New York: Delta.
Von Hippel, E. (1988) *The Sources of Innovation*, Oxford: Oxford University Press.
Von Hippel, E. (2005) *Democratizing Innovation*, Cambridge, Mass.: MIT Press.

Watts, D. J. (2004) *Six Degrees: The science of a connected age*, New York: Norton.
Westland, J. C. (with Clark, E.) (2000) *Global Electronic Commerce: Theory and case studies*, Cambridge, Mass.: MIT Press.
Westland, J. C. (2002) *Valuing Technology: The new science of wealth in the knowledge economy*, New York: Wiley.
Westland, J. C. (2003) *Financial Dynamics: A system for valuing technology companies*, New York: Wiley.
Westland, J. C. and See-to, E. (2007) 'The short-run price–performance dynamics of microcomputer technologies', *Research Policy* 36, pp. 591–604.
Whittington, Richard (2000) *What Is Strategy and Does It Matter?* London: Thomson Business Press.
Wilford, J. N. (2001) *The Mapmakers*, London: Pimlico.

BIBLIOGRAPHY

Abernathy, W. and. Clark, K. B. (1985) 'Mapping the winds of creative destruction', *Research Policy* 14, pp. 3–22.

Abernathy, W. J. and Utterback, J. (1978) 'Patterns of industrial innovation', p. 97–108 in M. L. Tushman and W. L. Moore, *Readings in the Management of Innovation*, New York: HarperCollins.

Abraham, C. (2002) *Possessing Genius: The bizarre odyssey of Einstein's brain*, New York: St. Martin's Press.

Adler, M. (1988) 'An algebra for data flow diagram process decomposition', *IEEE Trans. Software Engineering,* February.

Afuah, A. (2003) *Innovation Management*, Oxford: Oxford University Press.

Akerlof, G. A. (1970) 'The market for "lemons": quality uncertainty and the market mechanism', *Quarterly Journal of Economics* 84, pp. 488–500.

Allen, T. J. (1977/1984) *Managing the Flow of Technology*, Cambridge, Mass.: MIT Press.

Alpert, E. (1993) 'Breadth of coverage for intellectual property law: encouraging product innovation by broadening protection', *Journal of Product and Brand Management* 2, p. 2.

Amabile, T. M., Collins, M. A., Conti, R., Phillips, E., Picariello, M., Ruscio, J. and Whitney, D. (1996) *Creativity in Context: Update to the psychology of creativity*, Boulder, Colo.: Westview.

Amabile, T. M., Conti, R., Coon, H. et al. (1996) 'Assessing the work environment for creativity, *Academy of Management Review* **39**(5), pp. 1154–84.

Anderson, B. and Harvey, T. (1996) 'Alterations in cortical thickness and neuronal density in the frontal cortex of Albert Einstein', *Neuroscience Letters* 210, p. 161.

Anderson, C. (2006) *The Long Tail: Why the future of business is selling less of more*, New York: Hyperion.

Arias, J. T. G. (1995) 'Do networks really foster innovation?' *Management Decision* **52**(5), 15 December, pp. 33, 9.

Arthur, W. B. (1989) 'Competing technologies, increasing returns, and lock-in by historical events', *Economic Journal* 99 (March), pp. 116–31

Arthur, W. B. (1990) 'Positive feedbacks in the economy', *Scientific American* 262 (February), pp. 92–9.

Auerbach, F. (1913) 'The distribution of population concentrations', *Peterman's Letters* vol. 59, pp. 74–6.

Badden-Fuller, C. and Pitt, M. (eds) (1996) *Strategic Innovation*, London: Routledge.

Badenhausen, K. (1995) 'Brands: the management factor', *Financial World*, 1 August, pp. 50–69.

Bainbridge, D. I. (1996) *Intellectual Property*, 3rd edn, London: Pitman.

Baldwin, N. (1995) *Edison*, Chicago, Ill.: Chicago University Press.

Barabasi, A.-L. (2003) *Linked: How everything is connected to everything else and what it means*, New York: Plume.

Barney, B. (2001) 'Is the resource-based "view" a useful perspective for strategic management research? Yes', *Academy of Management Review* 26, pp. 41–57.

Barney, J. B. (1997/2002) *Gaining and Sustaining Competitive Advantage*, Reading, Mass.: Addison-Wesley.

Barney, J. B. and Arikan, A. M. (2001) 'The resource-based view: origins and implications,' working paper, Fisher College of Business, Ohio State University.

Baumol, W. J. (2004) *The Free-Market Innovation Machine: Analyzing the growth miracle of capitalism*, Princeton, N.J.: Princeton University Press.

Bell, D. (1960) *The End of Ideology*, Glencoe, Ill.: Free Press

Bell, D. (1973) *The Coming of Post-Industrial Society*, New York: Basic Books.

Bell, D. (1976) *The Cultural Contradictions of Capitalism*, New York: HarperCollins.

Bell, D. (1999) *The Coming of the Post-Industrial Society*, reissue edn, New York: Basic Books.

Berkman, L. (1990) 'FTC has eyes on telescope firm merger monopoly', *Los Angeles Times,* 10 October.

Berry, K. (1999) 'Meade's telescope sales make it an industry star', *Orange County Register,* 17 October.

Bettis, R. A and Prahalad, C. K. (1995) 'The dominant logic: retrospective and extension', *Strategic Management Journal* 16, pp. 5–14.

Bloom, H. (2002) *Genius*, New York: Warner.

Bodin, M. (1990) *The Creative Mind: Myths and mechanisms*, New York: Basic Books.

Borg, E. A. (2001) 'Knowledge, information and intellectual property: implications for marketing relationships', *Technovation* 21, pp. 515–24.

Bowman, E. H. and Helfat, C. E. (2001) 'Does corporate strategy matter?' *Strategic Management Journal* 22, pp. 1–23.

Boyd, J. (2002) 'In community we trust: online security communication at eBay', *Journal of Computer Mediated Communication* 7(3) (April).

Brahm, L. J. (2001) *China's Century*, New York: Wiley.

Brahm, L. (2006) 'Cheating, Chinese style', *South China Morning Post*, 21 February, p. A14.

Brealey, R. A. and Myers, S. C. (1995) *Principles of Corporate Finance*, New York: McGraw-Hill.

Briscoe B., Odlyzko, A. and Tilly, B. (2006) 'Metcalfe's law is wrong', *IEEE Spectrum*, July.

Brockman, J. (ed.) (1993) *Creativity*, New York: Touchstone.

Buchanan, J. and Stubblebine, W. (1962) 'Externality', *Economica* (November), pp. 371–84.

Burgelman, R. A. (1983) 'A process model of internal corporate venturing in the diversified major firm', *Administrative Science Quarterly* 28, pp. 225–44.

Burns, T. and Stalker, G. M. (1961) *The Management of Innovation*, London: Tavistock.

Burrows, P. and Khar, O. (2005) 'Cisco's consuming ambitions', *Business Week*, 5 August, p. 13.

Business Week (1973) 'The rebuilding job at National Cash Register: how Singer got the jump on the industry's top supplier', 26 May.

Business Week (2000) 'Apple', 31 July, pp. 102–13.

Business Week (2005) 'Notebooks without wide margins', 5 September, p. 38.

Business Week (2006) 'Creativity pays', 24 April.

Business Week (2007) 'The innovation backlash', 12 February.

Business Wire (2000) Meade Instruments Corp. 'Comments on OEM agreement', 29 March.

Buzan, T. (1991) *The Mind Map Book*, New York: Penguin.

Byron, K. (1998) 'Invention and innovation', *Science and Public Affairs*, Summer, Royal Society.

Castronova, E. (2001) 'Virtual worlds: a first-hand account of market and society on the cyberian frontier', CESifo Working Paper 618 (December).

Castronova, E. (2005) 'Real products in imaginary worlds', *Harvard Business Review* (May), pp. 19–20.

Castronova, E. (2005) *Synthetic Worlds: The business and culture of online games*, Chicago, Ill.: University of Chicago Press.

Chakrabarti, A. (1974) 'The role of champion in product innovation', *California Management Review* 17, pp. 58–62.

Chandler, A. D. (1962) *Strategy and Structure: Chapters in the history of the industrial enterprise*, Cambridge, Mass.: MIT Press.

Chandy, R. K. and Tellis, G. J. (1998) 'Organizing for radical product innovation: the overlooked role of willingness to cannibalize', *Journal of Marketing Research* 35(4) (November), pp. 474–87.

Chandy, R. K. and Tellis, G. J. (2000) 'The incumbent's curse? Incumbency, size, and radical product innovation', *Journal of Marketing* 64(3) (July), pp. 1–17.

Chen, M.-J. (1996) 'Competitor analysis and interfirm rivalry: toward a theoretical integration', *Academy of Management Review* 21, pp. 100–34.

Chen, M-J. and MacMillan, I. C. (1992) 'Nonresponse and delayed response to competitive moves: the roles of competitor dependence and action irreversibility', *Academy of Management Journal* 35, pp. 359–70.

Cheng, Y. and Van de Ven, A. H. (1996) 'Learning the innovation journey: order out of chaos?' *Organization Science* 7, pp. 593–614.

Chesbrough, H. W. and Teece, D. (1996) 'When is virtual virtuous? Organizing for innovation', *Harvard Business Review* 11 (Jan–Feb), pp. 65–73.

Christensen, C. (1997) *The Innovator's Dilemma: When new technologies cause great firms to fail*, Boston, Mass.: Harvard Business School Press.

Christensen, C. M. and Bower, J. L. (1996) 'Customer power, strategic investment and failure of leading firms', *Strategic Management Journal* 17, pp. 197–218.

Church, J. and Gandal, N. (1992) 'Network effects, software provision, and standardization', *Journal of Industrial Economics* (March), pp. 85–104.

Clark, D. and Strecker, W. D. (1980) 'Comments on the case for the reduced instruction set computer', *Computer Architecture News* 8(6), pp. 34–8.

Clark, K. B. and Fujimoto, T. (1991) *Product Development Performance: Strategy, organization and management in the world auto industry*, Boston, Mass.: Harvard Business School Press.

Clark, K. B. and Wheelwright, S. C. (1994) *Managing New Product and Process Development*, New York: Free Press.

Clark, P. and Rutter, M. (1979) 'Task difficulty and task performance in autistic children', *Journal of Child Psychology and Psychiatry* 20, pp. 271–85.

Clark, P. and Staunton, N. (1993) *Innovation in Technology and Organization*, London: Routledge.

Coase, R. (1960) 'The problem of social cost', *Journal of Law and Economics* 3 (October), pp. 1–44.

Cohen, J. E. (1995) 'Population growth and Earth's human carrying capacity', *Science* 269, pp. 341–6.

Cohen, W. M. and Levinthal, D. A. (1989) 'Innovation and learning: the two faces of R&D', *Economic Journal* 99, pp. 569–96.

Cohen, W. M. and Levinthal, D. A. (1990) 'A new perspective on learning and innovation', *Administrative Science Quarterly* 35(1), pp. 128–52.

Cohen, W. M. and Levinthal, D. A. (1994) 'Fortune favours the prepared firm', *Management Science* 40, pp. 227–51.

Collins, J. C. and Porras, J. I. (1994) *Built to Last: Successful habits of visionary companies*, New York: HarperBusiness.

Collis, D. J. and Montgomery, C. A. (1995) 'Competing on resources: strategies for the 1990s', *Harvard Business Review* (July–Aug), pp. 118–28.

Conner, K. and Prahalad, C. K. (1996) 'A resource-based theory of the firm: knowledge versus opportunism', *Organizational Science* 7(5), pp. 477–501.

Cowen, T. (ed.) (1988) *The Theory of Market Failure*, Fairfax, Va.: George Mason Press.

Coy, P. (1999) 'Exploiting uncertainty: the real options revolution in decision making', *Business Week*, 7 June, pp. 118–24.

Crane, P. and Kinzig, A. (2005) 'Nature in the metropolis', *Science* 308, p. 1225.

Critser, G. (2005) *Generation Rx: How prescription drugs are altering American lives, minds, and bodies*, New York: Houghton Mifflin.

Csikszentmihalyi , M. (1996) *Creativity*, New York: Harper Collins.

Cyert, R. M. and March, J. G. (1963) *A Behavioural Theory of the Firm*, Englewood Cliffs, N.J.: Prentice-Hall.

D'Aveni, R. A. (1994) *Hypercompetition: The dynamics of strategic maneuvring*, New York: Free Press.

D'Aveni, R. A. and MacMillan, I. C. (1990) 'Crisis and the content of managerial communications: a study of the focus of attention of top managers in surviving and failing firms', *Administrative Science Quarterly* 35, pp. 634–57.

Dacey, J. S. and Lennon, K. H. (1998) *Understanding Creativity*, San Francisco, Calif.: Jossey-Bass.

Das Gupta, S. (2002) 'Building a call centre', *Network Magazine*, December.

David, P. A. 'Clio and the economics of QWERTY', *American Economic Review* 75 (May), pp. 332–7.

Dawkins, R. (1986) *The Blind Watchmaker*, New York: Norton.

Day, D. L. (1994) 'Raising radicals: different processes for championing innovative corporate ventures', *Organization Science* 5, pp. 148–72.

Day, G. (1990) *Market Driven Strategy*, New York: Free Press.

De Chernatony, L. and McDonald, M. H. B. (1998) *Creating Powerful Brands in Consumer, Service and Industrial Markets*, 2nd edn, New York: Butterworth-Heinemann.

Demery, P. (2003) 'Getting personal', *Internet Retailer*, October, p. 416.

Demery, P. (2004) 'The new Wal-Mart?' *Internet Retailer*, May, p. 2.

Derwent (1998) *Derwent World Patents Index*, Derwent Scientific and Patent Information (online) www.Derwent.com.

Diamond, D. W. (1991) 'Monitoring and reputation: the choice between bank loans and directly placed debt', *Journal of Political Economy* 99, pp. 689–721.

Diamond, M. C., Scheibel, S., Murphy, G. J. M. Jr., and Harvey, T. (1985) 'On the brain of a scientist: Albert Einstein', *Experimental Neurology* 88, p. 198.

Dixit, A. K. and Pindyck, R. S. (1994) *Investment under Uncertainty*, Princeton, N.J.: Princeton University Press.

Dos Santos, B. L. and Peffers, K. (1995) 'Rewards to investors in innovative information technology applications: first movers and early followers in ATMs', *Organization Science* 6, pp. 241–59.

Dow Jones Business News (1999) 'Meade Instruments CEO says R&D investment paying off', 30 December.

Dow Jones Business News (2000a) 'Meade Instruments shares soar on word of alliance with TeraBeam', 15 March.

Dow Jones Business News (2000b) 'Meade Instruments posts earnings well below analysts' reduced estimates', 19 December.

Dow Jones News Service-Ticker (1990) 'Federal Trade Commission moves to block telescope venture', 9 October.

Doyle, P. (2001) 'AIDS and the pharmaceutical industry', *Guardian*, 10 March.

Dremer, M. (1993) 'Population growth and technological change: One million B.C. to 1990', *Quarterly Journal of Economics* 108, pp. 681–716.

Drucker, P. (1994) 'The theory of strategy', *Harvard Business Review* (Sept–Oct), pp. 95–105.

Drucker, P. F. (1964/1993) *Managing for Results,* New York: Collins.

Drucker, P. F. (2000) 'Managing knowledge means managing oneself', *Leader to Leader* 16 (Spring).

Drucker, P. F. (2003) *The Essential Drucker: The best of sixty years of Peter Drucker's essential writings on management*, New York: Collins.

Dyer, J. H. (1996) 'Specialized supplier networks as a source of competitive advantage: evidence from the auto industry', *Strategic Management Journal* 17, pp. 271–92.

Dyer, J. H. and Nobeoka, K. (2000) 'Creating and managing a high performance knowledge-sharing network: the Toyota case', *Strategic Management Journal* 21, pp. 345–67.

Economist (1994) 'International banking survey', 30 April, pp. 1–42.

Economist (2000) 'The knowledge monopolies: patent wars', 8 April, pp. 95–9.

Economist (2005) An overdose of bad news,' 15 March, pp. 73–5.

Economist (2007a) 'Maxing out', 1 March.

Economist (2007b) 'The rise and fall of corporate R&D', 3 March, pp. 69–71.

Economist (2007c) Obituary: Alfred Chandler, 10 May, p. 87.

Economist (2007d) 'Apple: the third act' and leader, 7 June, pp. 63–7.

Eisenmann, T. (2003) 'A note on racing to acquire customers', 15 January, Harvard Business School Press.

Eisenmann, T. R. (2002) *Internet Business Models and Strategies: Text and cases*, New York: McGraw-Hill.

Ellis, H. S. and Fellner, W. (1943) 'External economies and diseconomies', *American Economic Review* 33, pp. 493–511.

Farrand, P., Hussain, F. and Hennessy, E. (2002) 'The efficacy of the "mind map" study technique', *Medical Education* **36**(5), pp. 426–31.

Farrell, J. and Saloner, G. (1985) 'Standardization, compatibility, and innovation', *Rand Journal of Economics* **16**(1) (Spring), pp. 70–83.

Farrell, J. and Saloner, G. (1986) 'Installed base and compatibility: innovation, product preannouncements, and predation', *American Economic Review* **76**(5) (December), pp. 940–55.

Faulkner, T. W. (1996) 'Applying "options thinking" to R&D valuation', *Research Technology Management* **39**(3), pp. 50–6.

Federal Aviation Administration (1995) *Business Process Improvement* v.1.0, FAI Office of Information Technology (AIT), Washington, DC, 30 November.

Fenn, G. W., Liang, N. and Prowse, S. (1995) 'The economics of private equity', Board of Governors of the Federal Reserve System, Washington DC, December.

Fields, R. (2000) 'Meade shares soar 77 per cent on Terabeam deal', *Los Angeles Times*, 16 March, p. C8.

Financial Times (1997) 'Gene is out of the bottle', 30 October, p. 15.

Financial Times (2005) 'Merck to pay $253 million after losing Vioxx suit,' 21 August, p. 1.

Fine, L. (2000) *The Piano Book,* Jamaica Plain, Mass.: Brookside Press.

Fisher, F. M. (1983) *Disequilibrium Foundations of Equilibrium Economics*, Cambridge, UK: Cambridge University Press.

Fiske, S. T. and Taylor, S. E. (1991) *Social Cognition*, New York: McGraw-Hill.

Florida, R. (2003) *The Rise of the Creative Class: And how it's transforming work, leisure, community and everyday life*, New York: Basic Books.

Florida, R. (2005a) *Cities and the Creative Class*, London: Routledge.

Florida, R. (2005b) *The Flight of the Creative Class: The new global competition for talent,* London: HarperBusiness.

Florida, R. (2008) *Who's Your City?* (in development).

Forbes ASAP (2000) Interview with Bob Metcalfe, 21 February, p. 97.

Fortune (1998) 'The second coming', November, pp. 86–100.

Fortune (2002) 'The new iMac', 10 June, p. 2.

Frank, A. (2002) 'An interview with Mark Blackwell', *Motorcyclist Magazine*, October.

Free Republic (2006) 'The world's biggest bank opens in Japan', 3 January, p. 1.

Freeman, C. (1982) *The Economics of Industrial Innovation*, 2nd edn, London: Frances Pinter.

Freeman, C. and Soete, L. (1997) *The Economics of Industrial Innovation*, 3rd edn, Cambridge, Mass. MIT Press.

Friedman, T. L. (2005) *The World is Flat*, New York: Farrar, Straus and Giroux.

Gabaix, X (1999) 'Zipf's law and the growth of cities', *American Economic Review* 89, pp. 129–32.

Galbraith, J. R. (1974) 'Organization design: an information process view', *Inter-faces* 4, May, pp. 28–36.

Galbraith, J. R. (1982) 'Designing the innovating organization', *Organizational Dynamics* 10 (Winter), pp. 5–25.

Gardner, H. (1993) *Creating Minds*, New York: Basic Books.

Garvey, G. (1943) 'Kondratieff's theory of long cycles', *Review of Economic Statistics* **35**(4), (November).

Gates, B. (1999) 'Microsoft', London Business School *Business Strategy Review*, 2, pp. 11–18.

Ghemawat, P. (1991) *Commitment: The dynamics of strategy*, New York: Free Press.

Golder, P. N. and Tellis, G. J. (1993) 'Pioneer advantage: marketing logic or marketing legend?', *Journal of Marketing Research* **30**(2), pp. 158–70.

Gordon, M. (1962) *The Investment, Financing and Valuation of the Corporation*, Homewood, Ill.: Irwin.

Graham, N. (1998) 'Inventor cleans up with profits', *Sunday Times*, 1 March, pp. 4, 16.

Granovetter, M. (1973) 'The strength of weak ties', *American Journal of Sociology* **78**(6) (May), pp. 1360–80.

Grant, R. M. (2002) *Contemporary Strategy Analysis: Concepts, techniques, applications*, Oxford, UK: Blackwell.

Griffiths, T. L. and Tenenbaum, J. B. (2006) 'Optimal predictions in everyday cognition', *Psychological Science* **45**, pp. 56–63.

Griliches, Z. (1957) 'Hybrid corn: an exploration in the economics of technical change', *Econometrics* 25, pp. 501–22.

Gross, N., Coy, P. and Port, O. (1995) 'The technology paradox', *Business Week*, 6 March, p. 78.

Grover, R. (2000) 'Back from a black hole', *Business Week*, 29 May.

Grover, R. (2004) 'A spotlight on Gemstar and Pixar', *Business Week*, 4 August.

Grover, R., Palmeri, C. and Elstrom, P. (2002) 'Qwest: the issues go beyond accounting', *Business Week*, 25 March, pp. 66–8.

Guilford, J. P. (1967) *The Nature of Human Intelligence*, New York: McGraw-Hill.

Gulati, R. (1998) 'Alliances and networks', *Strategic Management Journal* 19, pp. 293–317.

Gulati, R., Nohria, N. and Zaheer, A. (2000) 'Strategic networks', *Strategic Management Journal* 21, pp. 203–15.

Gundling, E. (2000) *The 3M Way to Innovation: Balancing people and profit*, New York: Kodansha International.

Hambrick, D. C., Geletkanycz, M. A. and Fredrickson, J. W. (1993) 'Top executive commitment to the status quo: some tests of its determinants', *Strategic Management Journal* 14, pp. 401–18.

Hamel, G. M. and Prahalad, C. K. (1994) *Competing for the Future*, Boston, Mass.: Harvard Business School Press.

Hamm, R. O. (1972) 'Tubes versus transistors: "is there an audible difference?"' *Journal of the Audio Engineering Society*, 14 September.

Hammer, M. and Champy, J. (1993) *Reengineering the Corporation. A manifesto for business revolution*, New York: HarperBusiness.

Hartley, R. V. L. (1928) 'Transmission of information', *Bell Systems Technology Journal* 7, p. 535.

Heilemann, J. (2000) 'The truth, the whole truth, and nothing but the truth', *Wired*, November, pp. 68–127.

Heller, M. A. and Eisenberg, R. S. (1998) 'Can patents deter innovation? The anti-commons in biomedical research', *Science* 280(1 May), pp. 698–701.

Henderson, J. V. (1977) *Economic Theory and the Cities*, New York: Academic Press.

Henderson, R and Clark, K. B. (1990) 'Architectural innovation: the reconfiguration of existing product technologies and the failure of established firms', *Administrative Science Quarterly* 35, pp. 9–30.

Henry, J. and Walker, D. (eds) (1991) *Managing Innovation*, London: Sage/OU Press.

Hill, C. W. L. and Jones, G. R. (1995) *Strategic Management: An integrated approach*, Boston, Mass.: Houghton Mifflin.

Hirsch, J. (1997) 'Irvine telescope builder proved to be farsighted', *Orange County Register*, 14 September.

Hovanesian, M. D. (2006) 'Nightmare mortgages', *Business Week,* 11 September.

Howell J. M. and Higgins, C. A. (1990) 'Champions of technological innovation', *Administrative Science Quarterly* 35, pp. 317–41.

Huang, E. (2007) 'Nintendo legend discusses Wiis and Miis', *GamePro.com,* 9 March.

Iansiti, M. (1993) 'Real-world R&D, jumping the product generation gap', *Harvard Business Review* (May–June), pp. 138–47.

International Labour Office (2007) *Global Employment Trends*, January.

Jana, R. (2007) 'Service innovation: the next big thing', *Business Week*, 29 March.

Janis, Irving L. (1982) *Groupthink: Psychological studies of policy decisions and fiascoes*, 2nd edn, New York: Houghton Mifflin.

Jensen, M. C. (1976) 'Theory of the firm: managerial behaviour, agency costs, and ownership structure', *Journal of Financial Economics* 3, p. 305.

Johne, A. and Storey, C. (1998) 'New service development: a review of the literature and annotated bibliography', *European Journal of Marketing* **32**(3/4), pp. 84–251.

Johnson, G. (1997) 'Irvine telescope manufacturer Meade plans IPO', *Los Angeles Times*, 6 February, p. D5.

Johnston, R. and Clark, G.. (2001) *Service Operations Management,* London: Financial Times Prentice Hall.

Jones, O. (1992) 'Postgraduate scientists and R&D: the role of reputation in organizational choice', *R&D Management* 22, p. 4.

Kafka, P. (1999) 'In focus', *Forbes*, 15 November, p. 210.

Kahn, A.E. (1988) *The Economics of Regulation: Principles and institutions*, Cambridge, Mass.: MIT Press.

Katz, D. and Kahn, R. L. (1966) *The Social Psychology of Organizations*, New York: Wiley.

Katz, M. L. and Shapiro, C. (1985) 'Network externalities, competition, and compatibility', *American Economic Review* **75**(3) (June), pp. 424–40.

Kelleher, J. B. (2000) 'Meade Instruments is soaring', *Orange County Register*, 13 March.

Kelly, P. and Kranzberg, M. (eds) (1978) *Technological Innovation: A critical review of current knowledge*, San Francisco, Calif.: San Francisco University Press.

Klopfenstein, B. C. (1989) 'The diffusion of the VCR in the United States', in M. R. Levy (ed.), *The VCR Age*, Newbury Park, Calif.: Sage.

Knight, F. H. (1924) 'Some fallacies in the interpretation of social cost', *Quarterly Journal of Economics* 38 (August), pp. 582–606.

Kondratieff, N. D. (1935) 'The long waves in economic life', *Review of Economic Statistics* 17, pp. 6–105, reprinted in *Readings in Business Cycle Theory*, Homewood, Ill.: Richard D. Irwin (1951).

Krugman, P. (1991) 'Increasing returns and economic geography', *Journal of Political Economy* 99, pp. 483–99.

Lague, D. (2006) 'Next step for counterfeiters: faking the whole company', *New York Times*, 1 May, p. B6.

Landes, D. S. (1998) *The Wealth and Poverty of Nations: Why some are so rich and some so poor*, New York: W. W. Norton.

Langrish, J., Gibbons, M., Evans, W. G. and Jevons, F. R. (1972) *Wealth from Knowledge*, Macmillan, London.

Lardner, J. (1987) *Fast Forward: Hollywood, the Japanese, and the onslaught of the VCR*, New York: W. W. Norton.

Lawrence, P. R. and Lorsch, J. W. (1967) *Organization and Environments: Managing differentiation and integration*, Homewood, Ill.: Irwin.

Leland, H. and Pyle, D. (1997) 'Information asymmetries, financial structure, and financial inter-mediation', *Journal of Finance* 32, pp. 863–78.

Lenin, V. (1918) *The State and Revolution* (online) http://www.marxists.org/archive/lenin/works/1917/staterev/index.htm (accessed 11 December 2007).

Lerner, J. and Triole, J. (2000) 'The simple economics of open source software', NBER Working Paper 7600 (December).

Levy, D. L. (2000) 'The man behind Meade', *Sky and Telescope* **100**(1) (July), p. 80.

Liebowitz, S. J. and Margolis, S. E. (1990) 'The fable of the keys', *Journal of Law and Economics* **33**(1), pp. 1–26.

Liebowitz, S. J. and Margolis, S. E. (1995) 'Are network externalities a new source of market failure?', *Research in Law and Economics* 17, pp. 1–22.

Lindquist, D. (1998) 'Irvine telescope firm looks to Tijuana', *San Diego Union-Tribune*, 28 November, p. C1.

Lombroso, C. (1895) *The Man of Genius*, London: Scribner's.

Los Angeles Times (1987) 'Missouri holding company acquires Meade Instruments', 9 January, p. D3.

Los Angeles Times (1990) 'FTC opposes telescope merger', 9 October, p. P3.

Los Angeles Times (2000) 'Meade stock will split 2-for-1', 6 May, p. C2.

Ludwig, A. M. (1995) *The Price of Greatness: Resolving the creativity and madness controversy*, New York: Guilford.

Luehrman, T. A. (1998) 'Investment opportunities as real options: getting started on the numbers', *Harvard Business Review* **76**(4) (July–Aug), pp. 51–67.

Luehrman, T. A. (1998) 'Strategy as a portfolio of real options', *Harvard Business Review* **76**(5) (Sept–Oct), pp. 87–99.

MacKinnon, D. W. (1975) 'IPAR's contribution to the conceptualization and study of creativity', in I. Taylor and J. W. Getxels (eds), *Perspectives on Creativity*, Chicago, Ill.: Aldine.

Madsen, A. (1999) *The Deal Maker*, New York: Wiley.

Magretta, J. (2002) *What Management Is: How it works, and why it's everyone's business*, New York: Free Press.

March, J. G. and Simon, H. (1958) *Organizations*, New York: Wiley.

Marcus, J. (2004) *Amazonia. Five years at the epicentre of the dot-com juggernaut*, New York: New Press.

Marshall, A. (1890/2006) *Principles of Economics*, New York: Cosimo Classics.

Marx, K. (1859/1993) *Capital: A critique of political economy*, New York: Penguin Classics.

Mayer, N. Zald (ed.) *Power in Organizations*, Nashville, Tenn.: Vanderbilt University Press.

McGahan, A. M. (2004). *How Industries Evolve: Principles for achieving and sustaining superior performance*, Cambridge, Mass.: Harvard Business School Press.

McGahan, A. M. and Porter, M. E. (1997) 'How much does industry matter? Really?' *Strategic Management Journal* 18 (summer special issue), pp. 15–30.

McGrath, R.G. and Ian MacMillan, I. (2000) *The Entrepreneurial Mindset*, Cambridge, Mass.: Harvard Business School Press.

McNeill, D. (2007) 'Numbers man', *South China Morning Post*, Saturday 12 May, p. C1.

Miller, G. A. (1956) 'The magical number seven, plus or minus two: some limits on our capacity for processing information', *Psychological Review* 63, pp. 81–97.

Mintzberg, H. (1978) 'Patterns in strategy formulation', *Management Science* 24, pp. 934–48.

Mokyr, J. (1991) *The Leaver of Riches*, Oxford, Oxford University Press.

Moore, G. (1997) 'An update on Moore's law', Intel Developer Forum Keynote Speech, 30 September, San Francisco.

Morris, P., Teisberg, E. and Kolbe, A. L. (1991) 'When choosing R&D projects, go with long shots', *Research Technology Management* (Jan–Feb), p. 3540.

Motion Picture Association of America (online) http://www.mpaa.org/index.asp

Mun, J. (2005) *Real Options Analysis: Tools and techniques for valuing strategic investment and decisions*, 2nd edn, New York: Wiley.

Nelson, R. R. and Winter, S. (1982) *An Evolutionary Theory of Economic Change*, Boston, Mass.: Harvard University Press.

New York Times (1999) 'Apple and PC given for dead are rising anew', 6 April, p. C1.

New York Times (1999) 'Congress passes wide-ranging bill easing bank laws', 5 November, p. 1.

New York Times (2004a) 'Delicate balance needed in uniting of drug companies,' 27 April, p. C1.

New York Times (2004b) 'I.B.M. division headed to China has made no profit in 31/2 years', 31 December, p. C4.

Nonaka, I. (1991) 'The knowledge creating company', *Harvard Business Review* (Nov–Dec), pp. 96–104.

Nonaka, I. and Kenney, M. (1991) 'Towards a new theory of innovation management: a case study comparing Canon, Inc. and Apple Computer, Inc.', *Journal of Engineering and Technology Management*, 8, pp. 67–83.

Nonaka, I., Takeuchi, H. and Umemoto, K. (1996) 'A theory of organizational knowledge creation', *Internal Journal of Technology Management* 11, pp 833–45.

Nordhaus, W. D. (1997) 'Do real-output and real-wage measures capture reality? The history of light suggests not', pp. 29-70 in T. F. Bresnahan and R. J. Gordon (eds), *The Economics of New Goods*, Chicago: University of Chicago Press

Nordhaus, W. D. (1998) 'Quality changes in price indices', *Journal of Economic Perspectives* **12**(1) (Winter), pp. 59–68.

O'Dell, J. (1996) 'Workers acquire a stake in Meade', *Los Angeles Times*, 20 July, p. D4.

Orange County Register (1997) 'Telescope firm focuses on stock sale', 6 February.

Orange County Register (2000) 'Meade shares fall back a bit', 17 March.

Oster, S. (1999) *Modern Competitive Analysis*, New York: Oxford University Press.

Overholt, A. (2002) 'Technorecovery?' *FastCompany* 60 (June), p. 61.

Pagès, H. (1999) 'A note on the Gordon growth model with nonstationary dividend growth', Bank for International Settlements Working Paper no. 75, Basle, Switzerland.

Parkin, M., Powell, M. and Matthews, K. (1997) *Economics*, 3rd edn, Harlow: Addison-Wesley.

Patel, P. and Pavitt, K. (2000) ''How technological competencies help define the core (not the boundaries) of the firm', pp. 313–33 in G. Dosi, R. Nelson and S. G. Winter (eds), *The Nature and Dynamics of Organizational Capabilities*, Oxford: Oxford University Press.

Pavitt, K. (1990) 'What we know about the strategic management of technology', *California Management Review* **32**(3), pp. 17–26

Pavitt, K. (1994) 'Sectoral patterns of technological change: towards a taxonomy and theory', *Research Policy* 13, pp. 343–73.

Pear Sheene, M. R. (1991) 'The boundness of technical knowledge within a company: barriers to external knowledge acquisition', paper presented at R&D Management Conference on the Acquisition of External Knowledge, Kiel, Germany.

Perrow, C. (1970) *Organizational Analysis: A sociological view*, London: Tavistock.

Peteraf, M. A. (1993) 'The cornerstones of competitive advantage: a resource-based view', *Strategic Management Journal* **14**(3), pp. 179–91.

Porphyry the Philosopher to Marcella, Kathleen (1987) trans. W. O'Brien, Society of Biblical Literature.

Porter, M. E. (1979) 'How competitive forces shape strategy', *Harvard Business Review*, March–April, pp. 137–56.

Porter, M. E. (1980) *Competitive Strategy: Techniques for analysing industries and competitors*, New York: Free Press

Porter, M. E. (1985) *Competitive Advantage: Creating and sustaining superior performance*, New York: Free Press

Porter, M. E. (1990) *The Competitive Advantage of Nations*, New York: Free Press.

Porter, M. E. (1991) 'Towards a dynamic theory of strategy', *Strategic Management Journal* 12 (Winter), pp. 95–117.

Porter, M. E. (1996) 'What is strategy?' *Harvard Business Review* (Nov–Dec), pp. 61–78.

Porter, M. E. (1998) *On Competition*, Boston, Mass.: Harvard Business School Press.

Porter, M. E. and Stern, S. (1999) *The New Challenge to America's Prosperity: Findings from the Innovation Index*, Washington, DC: Council on Competitiveness.

Porter, M. E. and van Opstal, D. (2001) 'U.S. Competitiveness 2001: strengths, vulnerabilities and long-term priorities', Washington, DC: Council on Competitiveness.

Post, F. (1994) 'Creativity and psychopathology: a study of 291 world-famous men', *British Journal of Psychiatry* 165, pp. 22–34.

Prahalad, C.K. and Hamel, G. (1990) 'The core competence of the corporation', *Harvard Business Review* **68**(3), pp. 79–91.

Priem, R. and Butler, J. E. (2001) 'Is the resource-based "view" a useful perspective for strategic management research?' *Academy of Management Review* 26, pp. 22–41.

Priem, R. and Butler, J. E. (2001) 'Tautology in the resource-based view and the implications of externally deter-mined resource value: further comments', *Academy of Management Review* 26, pp. 57–67.

Rae, J. M. (2007) *Innovating Services in the Post-Six Sigma Era*, Peer Insight, Keynote speech at 2007 BMA annual conference.

Rankin, I (2006) *The Naming of the Dead*, London: Orion.

Ricardo, D. (1817/2004) *The Principles of Political Economy and Taxation*, New York: Dover.

Roberts, E. B. and Fushfield, A. R. (1981) 'Staffing the innovative technology-based organization', *Sloan Management Review* (Spring), pp. 19–34.

Romanelli, E. and Tushman, M. L. (1994) 'Organizational transformation as punctuated equilibrium: an empirical test', *Academy of Management Journal* 37, pp. 1141–166.

Romer, P. (1986) 'Increasing returns and long run growth', *Journal of Political Economy* **94**(5) (October), pp. 1002–37.

Romer, P. (1990) 'Endogenous technological change', *Journal of Political Economy* **98**(5) (October), pp. S71–102

Romer, P. (1993) 'Ideas and things', *Economist*, 11 September.

Ross, J. and Staw, B. M. (1993) 'Organizational escalation and exit: lessons from the Shoreham nuclear power plant', *Academy of Management Journal* 36, pp. 701–32.

Ross, S. A. (1977) 'The determination of financial structure: the incentive signalling approach', *Bell Journal of Economics* 8, pp. 23–40.

Rothenberg, A. and Hausman, C. R. K (eds) (1976) *The Creativity Question*, Durham, N.C.: Duke University Press.

Rothwell, R. (1976) 'Innovation in the UK textile industry: some significant factors in success and failure', Science Policy Research Unit, Occasional paper series 2, June.

Rothwell, R. (1992) 'Successful industrial innovation: critical factors for the 1990s', *R&D Management* **22**(3), pp. 221–39.

Rothwell, R. and Zegveld, W. (1985) *Reindustrialization and Technology*, London: Longman.

Rowan, D. (1997) 'Signing up to a patent on life', *Guardian*, 27 November, p. 19.

Rumelt, R. (1991) 'How much does industry matter?' *Strategic Management Journal* 12, pp. 167–85.

Rumelt, R. P. (1987) 'Theory, strategy and entrepreneurship' in D. J. Teece (ed.), *The Competitive Challenge: Strategies for industrial innovation and renewal*, New York: Harper & Row.

Rutkowski, E. J. (2005) '3GSM World Congress 2005 coverage: Microsoft and Flextronics announce Peabody', (online) msmobiles.com, 14 February (accessed 10 October 2007).

Rybczynski, W. (2001) *One Good Turn: A natural history of the screwdriver and the screw,* New York: Scribner/First Touchstone.

Saloner, G., Shepard, A. and Podolny, J. (2001) *Strategic Management*, New York: Wiley.

San Francisco Chronicle (2004) 'On the record: Craig Newmark', 15 August, http://sfgate.com/cgi-bin/article.cgi?file=/c/a/2004/08/15/NEWMARK.TMP(accessed 18 June 2007).

Sartre, J.-P. (1964) *The Words*, trans. B, Frechtman. New York: George Braziller.

Scherer, E. M. (1979) *Industrial Market Structure and Economic Performance*, Chicago: Rand McNally.

Schmidt, E. and Varian, E. (2005) 'Google: ten golden rules', *Newsweek*, 2 December.

Schmookler, J. (1966) *Invention and Economic Growth*, Cambridge, Mass.: Harvard University Press.

Schoemaker, P. (1992) 'How to link strategic vision to core capabilities', *Sloan Management Review* 34, pp. 67–81.

Schoemaker, P. and van der Heijden, C. A. J. M. (1992) 'Integrating scenarios into strategic planning at Royal Dutch/Shell', *Planning Review* (May/June), pp. 41–6.

Schon, D. A. (1963) 'Champions for radical new inventions', *Harvard Business Review* 41, pp. 77–86.

Schrage, M. (2006) 'The Gary Burton Trio: Lessons on business from a jazz legend', *Fast Company*, pp. 6, 110.

Schumpeter, J. A. (1934) *The Theory of Economic Development*, Boston, Mass.: Harvard University Press.

Schumpeter, J. A. (1939) *Business Cycles*, New York: McGraw-Hill.

Schumpeter, J. A. (1950) *Capitalism, Socialism, and Democracy*, 3rd edn, New York: Harper and Row.

Seabright, P. (2004) *The Company of Strangers*, Princeton, N.J.: Princeton University Press.

Selby, R. and Cusumano, M. (1999) *Microsoft Secrets*, New York: Free Press.

Shankar, V., Carpenter, G. S. and Krishnamurthi, L. (1998) 'Late mover advantage: how innovative late entrants outsell pioneers', *Journal of Marketing Research*, **35**(11) (February), pp. 54–70.

Shannon, C. E. (1948) 'A mathematical theory of communication', parts I and II, *Bell Systems Technology Journal* 27, pp. 379–423, 623–56.

Shapiro, C. and Varian, H. R. (1998) *Information Rules: A strategic guide to the network economy*, Boston, Mass.: Harvard Business School Press.

Sheene, M. R. (1991) 'The boundness of technical knowledge within a company: barriers to external knowledge acquisition', paper presented at R&D Management Conference on the Acquisition of External Knowledge, Kiel, Germany.

Simon, H. (1995) 'On a class of skew distributions', *Biometrika* 44, pp. 425–40.

Simonton, D. K. (1999) *Origins of Genius,* Oxford: Oxford University Press.

Sitkin, S. B. (1992) 'Learning through failure: the strategy of small losses', in B. M. Staw and L. L. Cummings (eds), *Research in Organizational Behaviour*, Vol. 14, pp. 231–66, Greenwich, Conn.: JAI Press.

Slevin, D. P. and Covin, J. G. (1990) 'Juggling entrepreneurial style and organizational structure: how to get your act together', *Sloan Management Review*, Winter, pp. 43–53.

Smith, A. (1776/1977) *An Inquiry into the Nature and Causes of the Wealth of Nations*, facsimile edn, Chicago, Ill.: University of Chicago Press.

Smith, C. M. and Alexander, P. L. (1988) *Fumbling the Future*, New York: William Morrow.

Solow, R. M. (1999) *Growth Theory: An exposition*, 2nd edn, Oxford: Oxford University Press.

South China Morning Post (2007) 'Making the grade', 14 June, p. A16.

Stabell, C. B. and Fjeldstad, O. D. (1998) 'Configuring value for competitive advantage: on chains, shops, and networks', *Strategic Management Journal* 19, pp. 413–37.

Starr, J. A. and MacMillan, I. C. (1990) 'Resource cooptation and social contracting: resource acquisition strategies for new ventures', *Strategic Management Journal* 11, pp. 79–92

Staw, B. M., Sandelands, L. E. and Dutton, J. E. (1981) 'Threat-rigidity effects in organizational behaviour: a multilevel analysis', *Administrative Science Quarterly* 26, pp. 501–24.

Stengel, R. F. (1994) *Optimal Control and Estimation*, New York: Dover.

Sternberg, R. J. (ed.) (1998) *Handbook of Creativity*, Cambridge, UK: Cambridge University Press.

Sternberg, R. J. and O'Hara, L. (1999) 'Creativity and intelligence', pp. 251–72 in R. J. Sternberg (ed.), *Handbook of Creativity*, New York: Cambridge University Press.

Stevens, T. (2001) 'Master of his universe', *Industry Week*, 15 January, p. 76.

Stinchcombe, A. L. (1965) 'Organizations and social structure', in J. G. March (ed.), *Handbook of Organizations,* Chicago: Rand McNally.

Stobart, P. and Perrier, R. (1997) *Brand Valuation*, New York: Premier Books.

Stuart, T., Hoang, H., and Hybels, R. C. (1999) 'Interorganizational endorsements and the performance of entrepreneurial ventures', *Administrative Science Quarterly* 44, pp. 315–49.

Tapscott, D. (1995) *The Digital Economy: Promise and peril in the age of networked intelligence*, New York: McGraw-Hill.

Taylor, A. III and Davis, J. E. (1994) 'Iacocca's minivan: how Chrysler succeeded in creating the most profitable products of the decade', *Fortune*, 30 May.

Taylor, F. (1947) *Scientific Management*, New York: Harper & Row.

Teece, D. J. (1986) 'Profiting from technological innovation: implications for integration, collaboration, licensing and public policy', *Research Policy* 15, pp. 285–306.

Teece, D. J., Pisano, G. and Shuen, A. (1997) 'Dynamic capabilities and strategic management', *Strategic Management Journal* 18, pp. 509–33.

Thompson, A. A. and Strickland, A. J. (2003) *Strategic Management: Concepts and cases*, New York: McGraw-Hill.

Tiberius, R. (2002) 'Educational abstracts', *Academic Psychiatry* 26 (June), pp. 128–30.

Tidd, J. (2000) *From Knowledge Management to Strategic Competence: Measuring technological, market and organizational innovation*, Imperial College Press, London.

Tidd, J. (2001) 'Innovation management in context, organization and performance', *International Journal of Management Reviews*, **3**(3).

Tidd, J. and Hull, F. M. (eds) (2003) *Service Innovation: Organizational responses to technological opportunities and market imperatives*, London: Imperial College Press.

Tidd, J., Bessant, J. and Pavitt, K. (2001) *Managing Innovation*, 2nd edn, Wiley, Chichester.

Tischler, L. (2004) 'The care and feeding of the creative class', *FastCompany* 89 (December), p. 93.

Tushman, M. L. (1977) 'Communication across organizational boundaries: special boundary roles in the innovation process', *Administrative Science Quarterly* 22, pp. 587–605.

Tushman, M. L. (1978) 'Task characteristics and technical communication in research and development', *Academy of Management Review* 21 ,pp. 624–45.

Tushman, M. L. and Anderson, P. (1986) 'Technological discontinuities and organizational environments', *Administrative Science Quarterly* 31, pp. 439–65.

Tushman, M. L. and Moore, W.L. (eds) (1988) *Readings in the Management of Innovation*, New York: HarperCollins.

Tushman, M. L. and Nadler, D. (1978) 'An information processing approach to organizational design', *Academy of Management Review* 3, pp. 613–24.

Tushman, M. L. and O'Reilly III, C. A. (1997) *Winning Through Innovation: Leading organizational change and renewal*, Boston, Mass.: Harvard Business School Press.

Tushman, M. L. and Romanelli, E. (1985) 'Organizational evolution: a metamorphosis model of convergence and reorientation', pp. 171–222 in L. L. Cummings and B. M. Staw (eds), *Research in Organizational Behavior*, Greenwich, Conn.: JAI Press.

U.S. News & World Report (2002) 'How low can a PC go?' 4 November, p. 62.

Utterback, J. M. (1975) 'The process of technological innovation within the firm', *Academy of Management Review*, 12, pp. 75–88.

Utterback, J. M. (1994) *Mastering the Dynamics of Innovation: How companies can seize opportunities in the face of technological change*, Boston, Mass.: Harvard Business School Press.

Utterback, J. M. and Abernathy, W. J. (1975) 'A dynamic model of process and product innovation', *Omega* 3, pp. 639–56.

van de Ven, A. H. (1986) 'Central problems: the management of innovation', *Management Science* **32**(5), pp. 590–607.

Van der Heijden, K. (1996) *Scenarios: The art of strategic conversations*, New York: Wiley.

Vasconcellos, J. A. S. and Hambrick, D. (1989) 'Key success factors: test of a general theory in the mature industrial-product sector', *Strategic Management Journal* 10, pp. 367–82.

Venkataraman, S. and Van de Ven, A. H. (1993) 'Hostile environmental jolts, transaction set, and new business', *Journal of Business Venturing* 13, pp. 231–55.

Vise, D. and Malseed, M. (2006) *The Google Story*, New York: Delta.

Von Hippel, E. (1978) 'Users as innovators', *Technology Review* **80**(3), pp. 30–4.

Von Hippel, E. (1986) 'Lead users: a source of novel product concepts', *Management Science* 32, pp. 791–805.

Von Hippel, E. (1988) *The Sources of Innovation*, Oxford: Oxford University Press.

Von Hippel, E. (1994) '"Sticky information" and the locus of problem solving: implications for innovation', *Management Science* **40**(4), pp. 429–39.

Von Hippel, E. (2005) *Democratizing Innovation*, Boston, Mass.: MIT Press.

Wageman, R. (1995) 'Interdependence and group effectiveness', *Administrative Science Quarterly* 40, pp. 145–80.

Wall Street Journal (1991) 'Competition rises in global banking', 25 March, p. Al.

Wall Street Journal (1993) 'Steve Jobs vision was on target at Apple, now is falling short', 25 May, p. Al.

Wall Street Journal (2003) 'Drug makers see "branded generics" eating into profits', 18 April.

Wall Street Journal (2004) 'In face of growing U.S. Rivals, Europe's banks balk at talk that consolidation is needed', 29 June, p. CI.

Ward, M. and Dranove, D. (1991) 'The vertical chain of research and development in the pharmaceutical industry', mimeo, Northwestern University.

Watts, D. J. (2004) *Six Degrees: The science of a connected age*, New York: Norton.

Weatherford, J. (2004) *Genghis Khan and the Making of the Modern World*, New York: Crown.

Weick, K. E. (1979) *The Social Psychology of Organizing*, Reading, Mass.: Addison-Wesley.

Weick, K. E. and Roberts, K. H. (1993) 'Collective mind in organizations: heedful interrelating on flight decks', *Administrative Science Quarterly* 38, pp. 357–81.

Weiss, P. (2005) 'A guy named Craig', New York Times Online, (online) http://nymag.com/nymetro/news/media/internet/15500/ (accessed 18 June 2007).

Westland, J. C. and Lang, K. (2002) 'Electronic delivery of convenience: a service innovation at the 7-Eleven retail chain in Hong Kong', *Journal of Information Technology Cases and Applications* (JITCA) **2**(3), pp. 77–86.

Westland, J. C. and See-to, E. (2007) 'The short-run price-performance dynamics of microcomputer technologies', *Research Policy* 36, pp. 591–604.

Whittington, R. (2000) *What Is Strategy and Does It Matter?* London: Thomson Business Press.

Wikipedia (nd) Craigslist {online} http://en.wikipedia.org/wiki/Craigslist (accessed 18 June 2007).

Wilford, J. N. (2002) *The Mapmakers*, London: Pimlico.

Williams, F. (2000) 'Dublin: now fair and worldly', *New York Times*, 12 October.

Williamson, O. (1975/1983) *Markets and Hierarchies: Analysis and antitrust implications*, New York: Free Press.

Wills, G. I. (2003). 'Forty lives in the bebop business: mental health in a group of eminent jazz musicians', *British Journal of Psychiatry* 183, pp. 255–9.

Winner, E. (1997) *Gifted Children: Myths and realities*, New York, Basic Books.

Witelson, S. F., Kigal, D. L. and Harvey, T. (1999). 'The exceptional brain of Albert Einstein', *The Lancet* 353, p. 2149.

Wolfe, R. A. (1994) 'Organizational innovation: review and critique and suggested research directions', *Journal of Management Studies* **31**(3), pp. 405–31.

Woodward, J. (1965) *Industrial Organization: Theory and practice*, 2nd edn, Oxford: Oxford University Press.

Xie, A. (2007) 'Pouring cold water on global prosperity?', *South China Morning Post*, 17 March, p. A13.

Yu, R. (1998) 'Telescope maker seeks to expand its small universe', *Orange County Business Journal*, 4 May.

INDEX